Voices From the Language Classroom

CAMBRIDGE LANGUAGE TEACHING LIBRARY

A series covering central issues in language teaching and learning, by authors who have expert knowledge in their field.

In this series:

Voices From the Language Classroom

Qualitative research in second language education

Edited by

Kathleen M. Bailey and David Nunan

CAMBRIDGE
UNIVERSITY PRESS

Published by the Press Syndicate of the University of Cambridge
The Pitt Building, Trumpington Street, Cambridge CB2 1RP
40 West 20th Street, New York, NY 10011–4211, USA
10 Stamford Road, Oakleigh, Melbourne 3166, Australia

© Cambridge University Press 1996

First published 1996

Printed in the United States of America

Library of Congress Cataloging-in-Publication Data

Voices from the language classroom : qualitative research in second
language education / edited by Kathleen M. Bailey, David Nunan.
p.   cm. – (Cambridge language teaching library)
Includes bibliographical references and index.
ISBN 0–521–55127–7. – ISBN 0–521–55904–9 (pbk.)
1. Language and languages – Study and teaching.   I. Bailey,
Kathleen M.   II. Nunan, David.   III. Series.
P51.V65   1996
418'.007 – dc20   95–9959
                                                                    CIP

A catalog record for this book is available from the British Library

ISBN 0–521–55127–7   Hardback
ISBN 0–521–55904–9   Paperback

To Les,
who softened my voice by listening quietly.
– Kathi

To my co-editor and pal,
whose idea it was in the first place.
– David

Contents

Contents

Contributors

Ralph D. Adendorff, University of Natal, South Africa
Kathleen M. Bailey, Monterey Institute of International Studies, California
David Block, ESADE Idiomas, Barcelona
Cherry Campbell, Monterey Institute of International Studies, California
Martha Clark Cummings, Monterey Institute of International Studies, California
Patricia A. Duff, University of British Columbia
Donald Freeman, School for International Training, Vermont
Ian Harrison, Kanda Institute of Foreign Languages, Tokyo, Japan
Mick Hilleson, United World College of South East Asia, Singapore
John Hyland, Belmont High School, Los Angeles, California
Lia D. Kamhi-Stein, California State University, Los Angeles
Anne Katz, ARC Associates, Oakland, California
Denise E. Murray, San Jose State University, California
David Nunan, University of Hong Kong
Sabrina Peck, California State University, Northridge
Fauzia Shamim, University of Karachi, Pakistan
Peter A. Shaw, Monterey Institute of International Studies, California
Marguerite Ann Snow, California State University, Los Angeles
Peter Sturman, Chiba University, Japan
Amy B. M. Tsui, University of Hong Kong
Leo van Lier, Monterey Institute of International Studies, California
Janet Harclerode Yu, Santa Monica College, California

Preface

This is a collection of international stories that had its beginnings as a volume at a language teacher education conference in Hong Kong in April of 1991. Somewhere in the swirl of presentations and panels, while we are discussing our shared interest in research on teachers' decision making, Kathi says to David, "Hey, I've got this idea for a book." David replies, "Great! Let's talk about it in Singapore."

We next meet at a conference at the Regional Language Centre about classroom research. David says, "So, Bailey, what's this idea about a book?" All Kathi has is a title, a kernel, the inception of an idea – something about "Voices." It will be a book about learning and teaching languages, not as these processes are depicted in methodology texts and position papers, but as they are experienced and understood by language learners and teachers. At this conference Kathi meets Mick Hilleson for the first time, and he tells her about his research with secondary school students in Singapore. A good omen: Through a serendipitous conversation a possible chapter has emerged.

Kathi and David brainstorm about other possible contributors, thematic units, a focus, a timeline. No previously published papers. Multiple data sets to permit triangulation. Papers that provide a platform for teachers' and learners' perceptions. We divide up the work and meet again in three months in Los Angeles. We sketch out our philosophy and contact potential contributors – people whose work we respect and who have had experience working in the tradition of naturalistic inquiry. Some are too busy but suggest colleagues or graduate students whose research would be appropriate. The idea gains momentum. David hacks away furiously at his laptop, churning out letters and abstracts urging our authors to send us descriptions of their papers.

Vancouver, February 1992: The TESOL Convention. We meet again, juggling our calendars to find time to talk and think and court the publishers. (It is a strange idea after all. Will anyone be interested?) We go our separate ways, convinced that this project is worth doing, but wondering how it will get done.

Then the stories begin to emerge. The manuscripts arrive. Some are from colleagues or former students. Others are from distant friends whom we have not yet met. Some are based on the authors' master's theses, doctoral dissertations, or qualifying papers. Some are more polished than others, some more compelling, but each is powerful. They provide a forum for voices that have much to say about apparently mundane issues (classroom seating arrangements, registration procedures, lesson plans). But as we read the voices of teachers and students quoted in these chapters, we see that these concerns are not mundane at all when viewed from the participants' perspective. We are enmeshed, captured by the demanding narratives. We undertake to stimulate the global economy through long-distance telephone calls, faxes, photocopying, and massive express mailings.

São Paolo, July 1992: Another conference. David has finished his plenary. Kathi, who is sick and worried about her own plenary, is fidgeting and sniffling during Donald Freeman's presentation. About the third time Donald says, "You have to know the story to tell the story," Kathi regains consciousness through an antihistamine fog and realizes (unbeknownst to the speaker himself) that she is listening to one of the recurrent themes of the book. She accosts Donald after his talk and asks if he has promised the paper to anyone else. He is amused but cautious.

David and Kathi keep working at a distance. When we do meet at the California TESOL conference, we spend an afternoon at Kathi's office, trying to frame the contents for the book, shuffling and reshuffling the chapters. But we are stuck, unable to find easily divisible units in what has become a curiously textured web: There are too many connections. At the end of the conference, when Denise Murray quotes students' essays and poems during her plenary about diversity, we realize that hers must be the final chapter, the exclamation point, the "Amen!"

Atlanta, April 1993: The TESOL Convention again. (Has a whole year slipped by?) The pressure is really on now. We have some terrific papers by language teachers, learners, and researchers from around the globe. We send the manuscript to Cambridge University Press. They are definitely interested, but input from the reviewers sends us back to the drawing board and the chapters back to the authors: rethink, revise, rewrite.

Baltimore, March 1994: The TESOL Convention again. (Has *another* whole year slipped by?) David leads a colloquium based on the collection. Some of our authors meet one another (and us) for the first time. The word processing, faxing, and photocopying continue endlessly.

Washington, D.C., October 1994: We have to cut 250 pages from the manuscript. All the authors revise their papers *again*. Kathi eliminates adjectives and adverbs, trying desperately to delete lines of text, thereby deleting half-filled pages.

Monterey, December 1994: It's raining and raining. Kathi is printing out page after page, correcting punctuation and misplaced headings. (Please, *please* don't let the power go out or the computer go down.)

David faxes from Hong Kong, "Calm down, smile, stick the manuscript in the mail and convene a meeting of the Parched Throat Society."

Then suddenly – it's done. Two quiet reams of paper, waiting to be mailed. We are tempted to revel in metaphors about "harmonious voices in a chorus" to describe the resulting book. But we know a more appropriate audio-image is the clamor spilling from the open door of a room full of language learners, engaged in the purposeful cacophony of group work. There is much to be learned by listening to these voices from the language classroom.

Kathleen M. Bailey
David Nunan

Acknowledgments

Every author and editor feels that chapters in books ought to have some mechanism, beyond the printed page, for dealing with acknowledgments: something like that incredible moment of triumph in a motion picture theater when the theme music comes up and the credits roll across the screen, and every person even remotely connected with the film is acknowledged. But we are left with the print medium, in these acknowledgments, to thank the people behind the scenes – those whose work has helped these voices to be heard:

At the Monterey Institute of International Studies, Mary Davis, Julie Loreno, and Bea Williams, who photocopied, express mailed, and faxed enough pages to lay a path from Monterey to Sydney and on to Hong Kong; Sheryl Black and Christy MacAnally, whose flying fingers generated the correspondence to authors and publishers; and Robert Gard, President of the Monterey Institute, who provided a grant for clerical support that helped us finish.

At Macquarie University in Sydney, Mark Gregory and Ken Willing, whose combined computer wizardry turned multiple diskettes and a bizarre international assortment of word processing programs into a single relatively workable system.

At Cambridge University Press in the U.K., Colin Hayes, who was excited about the project from the very beginning; and in New York, Mary Vaughn, who encouraged us and helped us synthesize provocative input from the reviewers; and the reviewers themselves, who commented in helpful detail on various iterations of the manuscript.

Jennifer Tuman, our first incredible assistant editor, whose keen eye for detail, word processing skills, and knowledge of the field generated the cleanest final draft we have ever seen; and Aileen Gum, our second incredible assistant editor (can there be two such creatures?), whose initiative, calm reliability, and writer's ear saw us through the final revision stages. Finally, Diane Malamut came into our lives just in time to help with the tedious task of indexing.

And, of course, we thank the authors for their contributions, and in particular, their willingness to develop, revise, and trim the stories. We hope the resulting collection will inform, amuse, and inspire language teachers, potential language teachers, language students, and other interested readers around the world.

Introduction

The purpose of this introduction is to provide a context and rationale for the chapters in this volume. In what follows, we set out the terrain to be covered, and provide you, the reader, with a map to some of the substantive and methodological issues which you will encounter on your journey through the book.

Voices From the Language Classroom is written for teachers, teachers in preparation, teacher educators, and researchers involved in second or foreign language education. A number of studies will be of interest to second language acquisition researchers and students as well. We hope that the book is also useful for the nonlanguage specialist contemplating a career in second language education, since the volume elucidates several of the challenges confronting language educators around the world.

In addition to illuminating issues relating to the teaching and learning of languages, *Voices From the Language Classroom* can be used as an illustrative manual for those wishing to carry out interpretive research in their own teaching or learning situations. The studies reported here were conducted in the tradition of naturalistic inquiry (see Allwright and Bailey 1991: 41–42; Lincoln and Guba 1985). Although this tradition is just as important as experimental research in language education and applied linguistics, studies utilizing qualitative data gathered in naturally occurring settings have seldom been published as collections in our field. So along with presenting the findings of these studies, this book is intended to serve as a "sampler" for people interested in learning more about qualitative research in the naturalistic inquiry tradition. In hopes of furthering that learning process, we have included a set of "Questions and Tasks," at the end of each major section of the book, which readers may address individually or in study groups.

Naturalistic inquiry is a research paradigm in which naturally occurring events are studied. Investigations are conducted without the control over variables or the intentional intervention (the "treatment") found in laboratory experiments. In other words, the studies reported here are *empirical* but not *experimental* – and for this, we make no apologies. In a key text on naturalistic inquiry, Lincoln and Guba contrast this approach with the positivist (experimental) paradigm. Their five axioms of naturalistic inquiry are paraphrased as follows:

1

1. Realities are multiple, constructed, and holistic.
2. The knower and the known are interactive and inseparable.
3. Only time-bound and context-bound hypotheses are possible (in contrast to the positivist desire for time-free and context-free generalizations).
4. It is impossible to distinguish causes from effects since "all entities are in a state of mutual simultaneous shaping."
5. Inquiry is value-bound (in contrast to the experimentalist notion that legitimate inquiry must be value free, which is, in itself, a value statement).

(See Lincoln and Guba [1985: 36–38] in particular for an excellent summary of this juxtaposition. See also Allwright and Bailey [1991: 40–45] for a comparison of experimental research, naturalistic inquiry, and action research.)

As suggested by Lincoln and Guba's third point, the studies in this book clearly indicate the importance of context in understanding behavior. The role of context finds expression in a key tenet of ethnographic research, that of the naturalistic-ecological hypothesis:

The naturalistic-ecological perspective has, as its central tenet, the belief that the context in which the behavior occurs has a significant influence on that behavior. . . . [I]f we want to find out about behavior, we need to investigate it in the natural contexts in which it occurs, rather than in the experimental laboratory. Arguments in favor of field research as opposed to laboratory research are supported by studies of particular phenomena which come up with different findings according to whether the research is conducted in a laboratory or in the field. (Nunan 1992: 53–54)

All these chapters illustrate the context-bound characteristic of naturalistic inquiry. That is, the data were collected in naturally occurring contexts, rather than in experimental classrooms that were artificially created to enhance the researchers' control over variables.

Despite the differences of perspective, the chapters in this book share a number of other concerns. First, each is grounded in data, most of which are qualitative in nature. Qualitative data consist of records of phenomena which deal with the qualities or characteristics of those phenomena, rather than with measurements, frequencies, scores, or ratings. In recent years qualitative research methods have been adopted by education from anthropology and sociology, and several methodological texts have appeared (see, e.g., Marshall and Rossman 1989; and Van Maanen, Dabbs, and Faulkner 1982).

It is important to note that global references to "qualitative research" and "qualitative data" can be more productively examined if we separate concerns of *data collection* and *data analysis*. Allwright and Bailey have argued (1991: 65–68) that all four of the following combinations are possible:

1. Data collected quantitatively can be analyzed quantitatively (as is common in statistical studies).
2. Quantitatively collected data can be analyzed qualitatively.
3. Qualitatively collected data can be analyzed quantitatively.
4. Data can be qualitatively collected and qualitatively analyzed.

The contributors to this book utilize all four combinations, but it is the last which is most prevalent in these studies.

In addition, as far as possible, we requested that each chapter be based on multiple data sets, to permit data triangulation. *Triangulation*, a term borrowed from land surveying, refers to the idea that at least two perspectives are needed to obtain an accurate picture of any phenomenon (Denzin 1970: 472; van Lier 1988). Throughout these chapters, a rich array of data can be found, including lesson transcripts, observer's fieldnotes, research narratives, teachers' and learners' journals, stimulated recall protocols, interview data, and lesson plans.

Following Lincoln and Guba's point that "the knower and the known are interactive and inseparable" (1985: 37), we were careful to ensure that these studies developed the emic perspective (i.e., the viewpoints of the participants), as well as the researchers' etic perspective. As explained by Watson-Gegeo (1988: 579):

the emic or culturally specific framework used by the members of a society/
culture for interpreting and assigning meaning to experiences differs in
various ways from the researcher's ontological or interpretive framework (an
etic framework).

Although there is certainly variation in the chapters as to the centrality of the participants' voices, the authors have consistently brought out students' and teachers' viewpoints – either as the phenomena under investigation, or as part of the analytic procedures, or both.

Finally, each chapter is an original paper which has not been previously published. Some are by scholars whose work is well known in language classroom research, while others are by scholars who are not yet widely published in this field. All these authors write candidly about the research process, including discussions of the research problems they faced.

As editors, we tried to ensure that each chapter would mesh with the others to provide a broad picture of language teaching and learning. Indeed, it became a challenge to subcategorize the chapters within the volume as a whole because the collection of papers were interrelated on many methodological and thematic levels. For this reason, the introduction to each section includes both substantive summaries and methodological commentary on the chapters it contains. In what follows here, we will, therefore, comment only briefly on each chapter in terms of its place within the volume's overall structure.

The five sections of the book are ordered in such a way that we work from the inside and move outward. That is, we start with studies that involve classroom teachers, their actions and ideas, as the central focus. We then branch outward a bit to consider classroom dynamics and the interaction among teachers and learners. The third section looks at the classroom and beyond, as the authors consider some of the noninstructional issues which influence students' learning. In the fourth section, which discusses curricular issues, the view is broadened even further to encompass programmatic concerns. In the fifth section, wide-scale sociopolitical issues influence the interpretation of the data.

Each chapter will be briefly capsulized below to give you a sense of both the structure and the content of the book. In the introductions to the five main sections, you will find more detailed comments about both the substantive findings and the methodological issues presented.

Teaching as doing, thinking, and interpreting

The book opens with four chapters in the first section, which is entitled "Teaching as Doing, Thinking, and Interpreting." These chapters focus on the value-added nature of listening to teachers' voices in understanding language teaching and learning. The thematic focus on the teacher does not, of course, mean that the students' voices are ignored; the distinction between this section and the next is one of principal focus, not one of exclusivity of concern.

In the first chapter, Kathi Bailey explores etic and emic interpretations of teachers' on-line decision making. Bailey argues that while lesson planning is an important professional skill, language teachers must also know how and when to depart from the lesson plan, to make the best use of class time and to create learning opportunities.

In a companion piece to Bailey's, David Nunan uses several sources of data collected in Australia (lesson transcripts, observation notes, and stimulated recall statements) to provide insights into the dynamics of classroom interaction which would not necessarily have emerged if a single data source had been used. Nunan concludes in Chapter 2 that language classrooms represent cultures with their own norms of interaction, in which the notion of the "lesson" may not be salient to the participants on the inside of the action. His study reinforces Freeman's claim (this volume) that to tell the story one needs to know the story, and Katz's notion (this volume) of classrooms as socially constructed entities.

In Chapter 3, Anne Katz herself uses the notion of teaching "style" (in counterpoint to "methods") as a way of understanding instruction. By presenting portraits of four different composition classrooms, Katz demonstrates how "knowledge is socially organized, formed, and shaped by the participants in the exchange and by the context in which the exchange takes place." She builds a convincing case that it is teachers' interpretation of their classroom roles that is significant, not some externally defined method. Katz employs the powerful literary device of the metaphor, which enables her to create unifying themes from disparate data. By utilizing metaphor as an "estrangement device," Katz demonstrates that methodological labels (e.g., "process writing") tell us little about what teachers and learners actually do to create a climate in which teaching and learning occur.

The last chapter in this section is entitled "Redefining the Relationship Between Research and What Teachers Know." Donald Freeman identifies the gulf between practitioners and researchers and argues that it is crucial for two key questions – what teaching is and what people must know in order to teach – to be placed at the center of the second language classroom research agenda. In order to answer these questions, teachers' voices must be heard, and to be able to hear their voices, the field will have to expand its concept of research and its norms for research reporting.

Classroom dynamics and interaction

The chapters in the second section, entitled "Classroom Dynamics and Interaction," highlight the different perceptions of students and teachers in the instructional process.

The contribution from Fauzia Shamim is valuable because it presents one of the "hard realities" of language classes in developing countries – class size. The study looks at some of the direct consequences of large classes for language learning, in this case, in Pakistan. Shamim found that where students are located in a classroom (toward the front or the back) has a major influence on the learners' perceptions of themselves as learners, on the teachers' perceptions of them, and on their chances of succeeding in class.

In Chapter 6 Amy Tsui addresses a serious concern in most foreign language classrooms, that of encouraging students to speak in the target language. In places such as Hong Kong, where this study took place, the problem has an intercultural as well as a pedagogical dimension: Student-student interaction is simply not typical of the culture of most classrooms. Tsui first identifies teachers' perceptions of factors leading to student reticence (including low proficiency, fear of derision, teachers' intolerance of silence, uneven allocation of turns, and incomprehensible input). She then relates her data to the issue of anxiety, before outlining some of the strategies which the teachers in her study utilized to encourage students to speak in class.

David Block's chapter considers instructional events from different viewpoints, examining the way teachers and learners interpret classroom action and interaction. Methodologically, this study, like others in the volume, utilizes a range of data collection techniques including teacher and learner oral diaries, classroom observation, and researcher notes. Of particular significance is Block's observation that while learners tended to agree on what constituted an activity and how many activities occurred during class time, there were differences, in some instances major ones, between the various informants' views on pedagogical objectives, content, and procedures.

The classroom and beyond

In the third section of the book, we move beyond the classroom as we listen to learners' and teachers' voices. In each chapter, we see the importance of the learners' outside concerns (beyond those related solely to instruction) and their impact on language learning and use.

Cherry Campbell's chapter, "Socializing With the Teachers and Prior Language Learning Experience," contributes to an emerging tradition in language learning research, namely, diary studies. Campbell documents her learning of Spanish in Mexico, focusing on language acquired in interaction outside of the classroom. Data for the study came from journal entries and letters written during a two-month stay in Cuernavaca. The study reinforces the critical importance of social and affective factors in language acquisition, a point which has emerged in other diary studies. Another major theme, as the title indicates, is the perceived effect of Campbell's prior language learning experiences on her acquisition of Spanish. The chapter concludes with a discussion of the implications of the study for language teachers.

Martha Clark Cummings presents a case study of twenty "repeater" students in a writing class in New York City. For many of these learners, Cummings' class is their last chance, as one more failure would require them to withdraw from school. Cummings' narration allows the students to tell their own stories and to articulate their own hopes and fears. The resulting chapter is a powerful illustration of Freeman's message (this volume) about teachers' knowledge. The difference is that it is largely the students' stories which are being told, with the teacher's reflections adding a sometimes poignant narrator's voice.

Anxiety, which emerges as a factor in several chapters, takes center stage in the study by Mick Hilleson. Working within the context of an English-medium school in Singapore, Hilleson encouraged a group of sixteen-year-old students to evaluate their own reactions to the learning situation. The data were collected through a range of methods including diaries, interviews, and observations. By linking the data from his own students with the relevant literature, Hilleson is able to illuminate important issues of anxiety which can affect the language learning and performance of non-native speakers.

Sabrina Peck also investigates learners' attitudes and emotions, as documented in their diaries, but in a very different context. She worked as the administrator in a Spanish as a second language program designed for social workers in the Hispanic community of Los Angeles. Some of the students were themselves Latino, though others were not. Through the social workers' journal entries, Peck documents their awareness of developing cultural sensitivity.

Curricular issues

In Section IV we broaden the focus of the book to consider curricular concerns that influence language learning and teaching. What these chapters have in common is their diverse viewpoints on curriculum, materials, activities, registration, and assessment.

Ian Harrison's chapter investigates whether learners' classroom language behavior changed as a result of a large-scale curriculum renewal project in the Sultanate of Oman. The data for the study include lesson transcripts, inspectors' reports, interviews with inspectors, and reports from teachers' meetings. This chapter reinforces the view that in order to make sense of the complexities of the curriculum in action, one needs to triangulate data from a number of sources.

In Chapter 13 Ann Snow, John Hyland, Lia Kamhi-Stein, and Janet Harclerode Yu describe a project to improve teaching and learning in junior high school classrooms in the Mexican-American community of East Los Angeles. Through interviews conducted in English and Spanish, the study focuses on the students' reactions to the instructional processes in the curricular innovation. The researchers also elicited data on the strategies the learners themselves found to be successful in coping with the academic demands of school. Students expressed a significant preference for classes where more innovative procedures were used and for experiential learning activities, such as projects and experiments. Methodologically, the researchers found that the interview, as a research technique, enabled them to engage in an "instructional conversation" with the students in a way which revealed the learners' perceptions of effective teaching and learning.

The chapter by Peter Shaw examines the role of the ethnographer as a curriculum change agent. The data for this study came from an evaluation of the foreign language component in a professionally oriented graduate school. Research methods employed by Shaw included ethnographic observation of selected classes, student and teacher diaries, debriefing interviews, and tapes and transcripts. A major procedural dilemma which Shaw examines is the fact that he was knowledgeable about the field under investigation (i.e., language curriculum and pedagogy) and that he was also a colleague of those implementing the innovation, and therefore, a stakeholder in the curriculum development enterprise.

Peter Sturman investigates an important topic which has not often been addressed: learners' initial impressions of a language program, based on their first contacts with the teachers and administrative staff in the registration and placement procedures. Sturman analyzes qualitative and quantitative data derived from questionnaires administered at two schools in Japan. The resulting statistical and interpretive account reveals the importance of learners' early contacts with a program.

Sociopolitical perspectives

The last four chapters foray into political aspects of language education. The geographical contexts of these studies are tremendously varied: van Lier deals with the politics of being a "foreign expert" in a bilingual education project high in the Peruvian Andes, Adendorff explores the code-switching behavior of teachers in a KwaZulu boarding school in South Africa, Duff looks at dual-language school classrooms in Hungary, and Murray deals with multicultural classrooms in the United States.

In his report on a Spanish/Quechua bilingual education program in Peru, Leo van Lier documents the language use of children and teachers. In this eloquently argued piece, van Lier presents a vivid picture of an attempted educational innovation "in action." His chapter underscores the value of focused ethnographies. For most readers, the power of van Lier's account will underline the value of "portrayal" as a method and "understanding" as a goal of educational research.

In the next chapter, Ralph Adendorff explores the sociocultural context in which teachers switch between Zulu and English in their interactions with students. He uses data collected in various classrooms to explore the significance of switches between English and Zulu. The implications for language teacher education in South Africa are also discussed.

Patricia Duff conducts a vivid comparative analysis of two very different settings in Hungarian secondary schools: a traditional monolingual school, in which the dominant pedagogical strategy is that of recitation, and a dual language school, in which the instruction occurs mainly in English. The focus of Duff's study is the socialization of discourse competence in these two different instructional environments.

The research evaluates the impact of the massive changes wrought within the educational system with the end of Soviet domination in Hungary. Duff uses her data to explain issues of educational and linguistic reform in a rapidly changing political environment.

The closing chapter comes from Denise Murray, who illustrates her theme of diversity by drawing on many different studies, which she weaves together using the metaphor of the tapestry. Her concern is to go beyond acknowledging ethnolinguistic diversity and to show that diversity is a valuable resource that can enrich the classroom. Murray is not myopic when it comes to the challenges posed by such diversity, and she readily admits that these challenges "threaten to unravel the whole cloth." However, the chapter leaves the reader with a positive message, largely because Murray showcases the voices of the students themselves.

Conclusion

As we said in the preface, in planning this volume, we invited a number of language educators and researchers to interpret the voices heard in classrooms throughout the world. Our intent was to produce a collection of articles written by authors schooled in the traditions of naturalistic inquiry. Our hope was to bring together a series of rich descriptive and interpretive accounts, documenting the concerns of teachers and students as they teach, learn, and use languages. As editors, we believe that the colleagues who accepted our invitation have met and even exceeded the challenge we set. Of course, it remains for you, the reader, to pass final judgment on the success of our efforts.

This book was born partly out of frustration as we sought in vain for appropriate qualitative studies as models for our own students, and partly out of respect for and fascination with teaching and learning. For our part, we believe that this international collection represents a unique contribution to the field. We hope you will agree.

References

Allwright, D., and K. M. Bailey. 1991. *Focus on the Language Classroom: An Introduction to Classroom Research for Language Teachers.* Cambridge: Cambridge University Press.

Denzin, N. K. (ed.). 1970. *Sociological Methods: A Source Book.* Chicago: Aldine.

Freeman, D. (Chapter 4, this volume). Redefining the relationship between research and what teachers know.

Katz, A. (Chapter 3, this volume). Teaching style: A way to understand instruction in language classrooms.

9

Kathleen M. Bailey and David Nunan

van Lier, L. 1988. *The Classroom and the Language Learner: Ethnography and Second Language Classroom Research*. London: Longman.

Lincoln, Y., and E. Guba. 1985. *Naturalistic Inquiry*. Newbury Park, CA: Sage.

Marshall, C., and G. Rossman. 1989. *Designing Qualitative Research*. Newbury Park, CA: Sage.

Nunan, D. 1992. *Research Methods in Language Learning*. New York: Cambridge University Press.

Van Maanen, J., J. Dabbs, and R. Faulkner. 1982. *Varieties of Qualitative Research*. Beverly Hills, CA: Sage.

Watson-Gegeo, K. A. 1988. Ethnography in ESL: Defining the essentials. *TESOL Quarterly, 22,* 4, 575–592.

I Teaching as doing, thinking, and interpreting

In this section we focus on teachers. It is predominantly their voices we hear in these chapters, although the stories are told from the vantage point of the researchers who worked with these teachers. All of the authors in this section investigate what teachers do and what they think about their work. We hear teachers as they plan, as they enact and revise their lesson plans, and as they puzzle over possible ways to improve their teaching.

Substantive issues

One repeated theme arising in all the chapters in this section is the topic of teachers' cognition. The first two chapters, by Kathi Bailey and David Nunan, respectively, focus on language teachers' on-line decision making, a subset of teacher cognition. Although several studies on this issue exist in the general education literature (see Clark and Peterson [1986] for an excellent review), there are far fewer in the language teaching literature. Bailey and Nunan have both focused on this latter context, where the teacher is often faced with complex cultural issues, as well as with the additional decision of which language to use in the classroom and how to pitch the input to the learners.

The third chapter, by Anne Katz, investigates four different approaches to teaching college writing classes for non-native speakers of English. Through extensive interviews with teachers and observations of their classes, Katz derives vivid descriptions of four different teaching styles. These descriptions include the teachers' views of what is important in teaching writing, as well as an analysis of the teachers' behaviors as they enact these views in the day-to-day activities of composition classrooms. Although the teachers vary widely on a number of factors, we are left with convincing portraits of four professionals working effectively, teaching the same course within the same program differently. Through Katz's transcripts and fieldnotes, we hear these teachers explain their own views and their value systems.

Freeman's chapter supports the methodological rationale of several authors in this volume (most notably Martha Clark Cummings). He argues not only for the value of teacher research, but for fundamental changes in how the results of such research are presented. In an article entitled "Educative Research, Voice, and School Change," Gitlin (1990: 444) states that "educational research is still a process that, for the most part, silences those studied, ignores their personal knowledge, and strengthens the assumption that researchers are *the* producers of knowledge." It is this position that Freeman (this volume) challenges in his chapter:

To achieve a discipline of teaching . . . the knowledge that teachers articulate through the process of disciplined inquiry must become public. It cannot dissipate in the recesses of private conversations, staff rooms, or even schools. The interpretations which teachers develop through research need to enter the wider community, to compete with other disciplines as ways of understanding education, and of shaping public policy and debate.

Freeman cites several examples of what teachers know and how they articulate that knowledge. In doing so, he adds to a growing body of literature on teacher research in general education (see, e.g., Schulz and Yinger 1984; Strickland 1988). Relatively little has been written, however, about teacher research in the context of language education. (For exceptions, see Allwright and Bailey 1991; Burton and Mickan 1993; and Nunan 1990.)

Methodological issues

The four chapters in this section are examples of classroom research (Allwright 1983; Allwright and Bailey 1991; Bailey 1985; Chaudron 1988; Gaies 1983; Long 1980): The data were collected (primarily) in classrooms, investigating teaching and learning processes in formal instructional settings. The authors use video or audio recordings of lessons or observational fieldnotes, as part of the data base. These chapters also make extensive use of the observers' fieldnotes and transcripts, both of classes and of follow-up interviews with the teachers. A central research device here is *stimulated recall*, in which the researchers prompt the teachers' interpretation of events by focussing their attention on data collected in their own classrooms.

These four chapters are also characterized by an interplay of *etic* and *emic* interpretations (Pike 1964; Watson-Gegeo 1988: 579) of the qualitative data collected by the authors. To some extent the authors utilize etic (external) frameworks to begin their investigations of teachers' thought processes and actions. But each chapter also documents the emic (internal) perspectives of the teachers themselves, as they discuss the principles and philosophies that led to their decisions as to how to plan lessons, how to teach their classes, when and how to depart from their lesson plans, and how they viewed those lessons in retrospect.

In an exhaustive review of the first language research on teachers' thought processes, Clark and Peterson (1986) summarize the puzzle which provides the methodological rationale for these chapters:

> Teacher planning reduces but does not eliminate uncertainty about teacher-student interaction! Classroom teaching is a complex social process that regularly includes interruptions, surprises and digressions. To understand fully the operation of teacher planning, researchers must look beyond the empty classroom and study the ways in which plans shape teacher and student behavior and are communicated, changed, reconstructed, or abandoned in the interactive teaching environment. (p. 268)

In this section, though the settings vary widely, we hear teachers' voices discussing the dynamic tension between planning and acting as they reflect on lessons they had taught. In Katz's analyses of four teachers' styles, we hear the teachers' ideas about how they can best enact their roles. In Bailey's and Nunan's data, we hear teachers explain numerous microdecisions made during the course of lessons. Freeman's analysis of various teachers' ideas about their teaching provides convincing evidence of the rationality behind their actions. In all four chapters, teachers describe their views of effective teaching – reflecting their original planning, choices, and retrospective interpretation of events. In reporting their findings, the authors draw on their own experiences, both as teachers and as researchers, reflecting Freeman's claim (this volume) that "you have to know the story in order to tell the story."

References

Allwright, R. L. 1983. Classroom-centered research on language teaching and learning: A brief historical overview. *TESOL Quarterly*, 17, 191 – 204.

Allwright, D., and K. M. Bailey. 1991. *Focus on the Language Classroom: An Introduction to Classroom Research for Language Teachers*. Cambridge: Cambridge University Press.

Bailey, K. M. 1985. Classroom-centered research on language teaching and learning. In M. Celce-Murcia (ed.), *Beyond Basics: Issues and Research in TESOL*. Rowley, MA: Newbury House.

Burton, J., and P. Mickan. 1993. Teachers' classroom research: Rhetoric and reality. In J. Edge and K. Richards (eds.), *Teachers Develop Teachers Research: Papers on Classroom Research and Teacher Development*. Oxford: Heinemann.

Chaudron, C. 1988. *Second Language Classrooms: Research on Teaching and Learning*. New York: Cambridge University Press.

Clark, C. M., and P. L. Peterson. (1986). Teachers' thought processes. In M. Wittrock (ed.), *Handbook of Research on Teaching*, 3rd ed. New York: Macmillan Publishing Co.

Freeman, D. (Chapter 4, this volume). Redefining the relationship between research and what teachers know.

Gaies, S. J. 1983. The investigation of language classroom processes. *TESOL Quarterly*, 17, 4, 205–217.

Gitlin, A. D. 1990. Educative research, voice, and school change. *Harvard Educational Review, 60,* 4, 443–466.

Long, M. H. 1980. Inside the "black box": Methodological issues in research on language teaching and learning. *Language Learning,* 30, 1–42. Reprinted in H. W. Seliger and M. H. Long (eds.), 1983, *Classroom Oriented Research in Second Language Acquisition.* Rowley, MA: Newbury House.

Nunan, D. 1990. The teacher as researcher. In C. Brumfit and R. Mitchell (eds.), *Research in the Language Classroom.* ELT Documents #133. London: Modern English Publications and the British Council.

Pike, K. L. 1964. *Language in Relation to a Unified Theory of Structures of Human Behavior.* The Hague: Mouton.

Schultz, J., and R. Yinger. 1984. Developing inquiry skills in teachers. *Teacher Education Quarterly, 11,* 3, 101–114.

Strickland, D. 1988. The teacher as researcher: Toward the extended professional. *Language Arts, 65,* 8, 755–764.

Watson-Gegeo, K. A. 1988. Ethnography in ESL: Defining the essentials. *TESOL Quarterly, 22,* 4, 575–592.

1 The best laid plans: teachers' in-class decisions to depart from their lesson plans

Kathleen M. Bailey

En casa de herrero, cuchillo de palo.

This chapter begins with my own voice as a language learner and then carries me over the bridge of a professional puzzle, through the research literature and into the role of a classroom researcher, listening to language teachers' voices. The issue I wish to examine is the decision making of experienced teachers – those myriad points in our daily lives as professionals when we must make an on-line judgment as to what is best for our students, whether to stay with the lesson plan, safely on firm ground, or to head out into the uncharted waters of spontaneous discourse.

The beginning of the story: a learner's question

The story began for me when I was a student in an intermediate Spanish class. One day, while we were rolling our double *R*s by repeating words like *ferrocarril* and *herrero*, I remembered a Latin American proverb: *En casa de herrero, cuchillo de palo.* Although I muttered this proverb to myself, the teacher overheard me and asked me to explain it to the class. A rough translation is "In the ironmonger's house, there are knives of wood." The actual meaning is that one's professional skills are not necessarily put to use in solving one's own problems. After I explained this idea to my classmates (in Spanish), they generated several examples – the crazy psychiatrist, the dentist whose children have rotten teeth, the shoemaker whose children have no shoes, the linguist who is a poor communicator, and so on. We continued to chat about this paradoxical phenomenon for about five minutes, all in Spanish.

When the lesson was over, I realized that the teacher had spontaneously allotted 10 percent of the fifty-minute lesson to this unexpected

Earlier versions of this chapter were presented at various language teaching conferences. Thanks are due to Ally Joye, Christy MacAnally, Lance Savage, Jennifer Tuman, Doug Mandler, and Aileen Gum for help with the word processing of fieldnotes, transcripts, and the scrawly multiple drafts of the text. And I was both informed and humbled by Leo van Lier's comments, and by the editorial advice of David "Scissorhands" Nunan.

15

topic, which I had unintentionally suggested. Because *I* accidentally nominated the topic, I *know* the instructor had not planned on this excursion from her pronunciation lesson. Later it occurred to me that this responsiveness was one of the things that we most appreciated about our teacher, so I began to watch for examples of such flexibility in my own teaching and in that of other teachers I observed.

The story continues: an unexpected ending

A second example comes from two elementary school English classes in Milan, Italy. Two teachers jointly planned the lesson and then taught it in turns to two different groups. While the first teacher taught the lesson, the children were seated in a semicircle and the second teacher served as a peer observer.

The teachers had created a woodland scene with paper hills, a bush, a lake, a river crossed by a bridge, and a tree. They had also brought to class numerous stuffed animals, including a tiger and a monkey. In the story, the tiger lived in the hills and the monkey sat under the tree. The other animals traveled back and forth between the two. In the first version of the lesson, the monkey was eating a banana, drinking a cup of water, and beating the ground with a stick. Each of the children spoke for the stuffed animal which he or she was holding. Each animal in turn asked, "Monkey, monkey, what are you doing?" And the monkey replied, "I am eating a banana and drinking some water, and if the tiger comes I will kill him!" (He beat the floor fiercely with his stick as he made this bold claim.) One by one, the animals came to visit the monkey and heard his boast. And then the animals went, one by one, to warn the tiger that the monkey wanted to kill him. The tiger repeatedly said, "Don't worry. I'm strong. Go home and have a rest." One day the tiger finally got annoyed with the monkey's bragging threats. He climbed down the hills, jumped over the bush, swam across the lake, walked across the bridge, and went to the monkey. "Monkey, monkey," said the tiger, "What are you doing?" And the monkey replied, "I'm eating a banana, and drinking some water, and sometimes I say stupid things." The children (and the observers) laughed and clapped at this humorous resolution to the story. Then the children said good-bye and the next group of students entered the room and the story began again, with the first teacher taking the peer observer's role.

This time, however, when the second teacher reached the climax of the story and the tiger was about to approach the flippant monkey, the following interaction took place. ("T" represents the teacher and "Ss" the students; glosses are given in brackets.)

T: But the monkey has – eh? — an enemy? Who is the enemy?

Ss: Tiger. The tiger.

T: The tiger. And he wants to kill the tiger. Good. [She pauses dramatically.] But one day, one day [slowed speech, dramatically drawn out] one day, the tiger gets – "Grrr!" – [making a growling sound with a fierce, angry face and fingers extended like exposed claws].

Ss: Strong! Strong!

T: Yes, the tiger is strong, but he's also [she pauses] – "Grrr!" [making the same growling noise and fierce facial expressions]. [The children murmur but no one says *angry*.] Angry? Angry? [The children murmur.] Is the tiger angry?

Ss: No. No.

T: Don't you think the tiger wants to go to the monkey?

Ss: No. [The children shake their heads.]

T: No? Never? Never? [The children shake their heads again.]

T: Do you think the tiger wants to go to the monkey? [The children continue to shake their heads]. No. Never. [She pauses, her voice taking on what I interpret as a slightly resigned tone.] It's all right. So we leave the monkey and the, the tiger in the hills and the monkey under the tree. So never, we never have war. Ma guerra [spoken in Italian]. Right? Never war? Always peace. Good. Good. Thank you very much to everybody.

At that point the class was over. The children thanked their bemused teacher in a chorus of voices and left the room, never having heard the intended punch line to the story. The teachers and I laughed, amazed at this group's unpredicted reaction.

With these sorts of examples in mind, I turned to the research literature, curious about what systematically collected data might be available regarding my puzzle. I hoped that Donald Freeman's comment (this volume) would apply to my endeavors: "When this notion of 'inquiry-motivated-by-curiosity' is applied to teaching, it can become tremendously useful. It can help the world-at-large recognize that, in the full complexity of teaching, things rarely go as planned and no two lessons are ever the same" (as the story of the tiger and the monkey clearly shows).

Literature review: researchers' voices

It is traditional in conducting an empirical study to review the relevant research literature. Three sorts of information seemed pertinent: the professional information on lesson planning, research on teachers' decision making, and classroom research describing surprising events in language lessons.

Kathleen M. Bailey

Lesson planning

Preparation for preservice teachers often includes advice and experience with lesson planning. Richards and Crookes (1988), in a survey of masters degree programs in TESOL, reported that developing lesson planning skills was ranked sixth out of the eight most important practicum objectives by the respondents to their questionnaire. Yet teachers may depart from their plans for a variety of reasons. Such departures can trigger interactions which range from well-executed, spontaneous learning opportunities to fuzzy, floundering digressions. The notion of plans that have gone astray is reminiscent of the often misquoted lines by Robert Burns (1785):

> The best laid schemes o' mice and men gang aft a-gley;
> An' lea'e us nought but grief and pain for promis'd joy.

A lesson plan is like a road map which describes where the teacher hopes to go in a lesson, presumably taking the students along. In this chapter, a lesson is defined as some time-bound unit of instruction, often structured around thematic units (e.g., vocabulary items, grammar points, functions, and literary selections). Lesson plans are shaped, at least in part, by factors other than those controlled by the teacher. These include the content and sequencing of information in the textbook and administrative time units (such as the frequency and duration of class periods). But most important for this study, the quality and quantity of students' participation also influence the lesson's realization, perhaps especially in a learner-centered curriculum.

Traditionally, a lesson is seen as a unit of a syllabus for a course, which is itself viewed as a component of a program's curriculum. Lessons are intended to help students accomplish the objectives of the course and the program. However, in summarizing research on teacher cognition, Freeman (this volume) states,

[T]eachers did not naturally think about planning in the organized formats which they had been taught to use in their professional training. Further, when they did plan lessons according to these formats, they often did not teach them according to plan. Teachers were much more likely to visualize lessons as clusters or sequences of activity; they would blend content with activity, and they would generally focus on their particular students. In other words, teachers tended to plan lessons as ways of doing things for given groups of students rather than to meet particular objectives.

Certainly lesson planning is a day-to-day professional responsibility. But being a professional also entails making the most of the unexpected.

Allwright and Bailey (1991: 25) note that a lesson is actually co-produced by the teacher and the learners:

It is likely that every teacher has had the experience of having something unexpected occur during a lesson. Whether it leads to derailment of the lesson or a contribution to learning is often largely a matter of how the teacher reacts to the unexpected, and the extent to which the co-production is encouraged or stifled.

Research on teachers' decision making

Much of the research on teachers' decision making comes from general education. Peterson and Clark (1978) investigated junior high school teachers' reports of their own cognitive processes as they were teaching. Videotaped lessons were used in the *stimulated recall procedure*, in which the teachers viewed and discussed the videos. Peterson and Clark identified four possible "paths" through a lesson. Path 1 was "business as usual." In this case everything proceeds well and there is no need for teachers to change their plans or behavior. In path 2, teachers see problems but have no alternatives, so they continue with their plans in spite of evidence that they are not working, a situation which may represent powerlessness or surprise for teachers. In path 3 (the least common in Peterson and Clark's data), teachers perceived problems, had alternatives available, but stuck with their plans or previous behavior. Path 4 was the second most frequent and increased with experience. In this case, teachers perceived problems, had alternatives available, and chose to change their behavior. The choice of path 3 had a negative correlation with student achievement and attitudes. Path 1 was associated with the learning of facts, and path 4 was associated with students' learning of higher order ideas. Peterson and Clark's analysis suggests that when teachers have options for altering lessons, students' learning is enhanced.

Leinhardt and Greeno (1986) also describe teaching as "a complex cognitive skill" which "requires the construction of plans and the making of rapid on-line decisions" (p. 75). They note that "skilled teachers have a large repertoire of activities that they perform fluently" (p. 76). Leinhardt and Greeno were concerned with the dynamic tension between preactive decisions and interactive decisions: "The conscious planning activity of teachers reflects only a small fraction of the planfulness that actually characterizes skilled teaching" (ibid).

Westerman (1991) conducted research (in a general education setting) which yielded one model representing expert teachers' decision making and one representing novice teachers' decision making. Compared to novices, expert teachers were more aware of the students in the preactive phases (before lessons) and monitored more often for student cues (behavior and/or learning) during the lesson (the interactive phase).[1]

In recent years, researchers have studied teachers' decision making in language lessons. Freeman (1989) describes teaching as a dynamic decision-making process. He notes that teachers are faced with both macrodecisions and microdecisions, but "the decision as a unit of teaching remains constant, even though its content is continually shifting" (p. 31).

Often teachers' in-class decisions have to do with what could be better. Politzer (1970) articulated a "Principle of Economics" based on his study of high school French classes, in which he examined effective teaching behaviors. Given that each activity consumes time, Politzer concluded that "the value of any [language teaching] technique depends, in part, on the relative value of other techniques that could have been used in place of the one actually selected by the teacher" (p. 41).

Woods (1989) also conducted research on second language teachers' decision making and proposed a model which incorporates two types of decisions. *Sequential decisions* occur when one decision follows another in a sequence but isn't part of the previous decision: In planning, a teacher may say, "After the quiz the students will prepare for their written assignment about the environment." *Hierarchical decisions* occur when decisions are carried out as a means of achieving a previous decision: "The students are investigating ecological issues in order to write about the environment. First they will review the vocabulary on the environment and then do the reading. Next they will answer the comprehension questions, and finally they will brainstorm about ecological problems in this geographic area." These examples depict *planning* decisions (preactive decisions in Westerman's model), but teachers' decisions made "on-line" in "real-time" are also sequentially or hierarchically related.

Johnson (1992) used stimulated recall to examine six preservice ESL teachers' interactive decision making. She examined frequency counts of student performance cues, teachers' instructional actions in response to those cues, teachers' interactive decisions, and their use of prior knowledge during instruction. Johnson concluded that the teachers in her cohort "rely on a limited number of instructional routines and are overwhelmingly concerned with inappropriate student responses and

---

1 The term *interactive decision making* may lead to some confusion. The phrase refers to decisions made in class, "on-line," in "real time." That is, these are decisions made *during* but not necessarily *through* interaction.

maintaining the flow of instructional activity" (p. 129). She suggested that preservice teachers must recognize the "routines and patterns which experienced ESL teachers rely on to lessen the number of conscious decisions necessary during instruction" (ibid.).

In Nunan's study (1992: 135) the primary research question was "What is the nature of the professional decisions made by teachers in planning and implementing their language programs?" Nunan observed nine Australian ESL teachers in the mid-range of experience. In the post-lesson debriefings, the teachers commented on where they had deviated from their plans. Thirty percent of their decisions involved management and class organization. Their language decisions most often involved vocabulary, followed by pronunciation and grammar. Nunan concludes,

While it is naive to assume that what gets planned will equate with what gets taught, and that what gets taught will equate with what gets learned, this does not mean that planning, including the formulation of objectives, should be removed from the equation. While the plans that teachers lay will be transformed, if not metamorphosed, in the act of teaching, such plans provide a framework and structure for the interactive decisions which the teacher must later make. They also provide a set of criteria against which such interactive decisions may be evaluated. (p. 161)

(This chapter and Chapter 2 in this volume were both guided by Nunan's work in this area.)

Malcolm (1991) also investigated language teachers' decision making when he observed one hundred classes of Aboriginal students in West Australian primary schools. Malcolm identified three macro tasks (the management of content, of participants, and of face) which teachers accomplished through the strategies he investigated. The paper begins with several "abrupt and verbalized changes of strategy" (p. 1), which reveal teachers' decisions to abandon their plans in the face of non-cooperation from the learners.

These studies of teachers' thought processes illustrate the complexity of interactive decision making in instructional settings. The literature on teacher cognition represents a largely etic (external) perspective on the topic, giving the researchers' analyses. But, as Larsen-Freeman (1990) has pointed out in her call for a theory of language teaching, "There is only scant research looking at what teachers believe – and yet this is what teachers act upon" (p. 266). In the tradition of research using journals and stimulated recall to access teachers' ideas, this chapter documents teachers' emic (internal) perspectives about their interactive decision making. It is here that those who "know the story" will tell the story.

Classroom research: surprising events

Transcripts from research on language classrooms are full of evidence of teachers' on-line decision making. One of the best known bits of such discourse is found in the transcript about Carlos's trousers, collected in a university EFL class in Mexico (Long 1980: 16). The transcript documents the teacher's reaction when a student named Carlos yawns audibly in class. The teacher responds to Carlos's yawn by calling on him to answer the display question, "All right, Carlos, do you wear trousers?" Carlos's response ("Alway [sic] . . . all my life") provokes laughter from the other students.[2] The lesson continues, including a curious "teacher-induced error" (see Allwright and Bailey 1991: 110–111), in which the teacher first models an incorrect word stress ("trou*sers*") and then corrects Carlos's repetition of the model ("*Trou*sers"). I have argued elsewhere (ibid.: 111–112) that this exchange may represent the teacher's attempt to reassert control after the unexpected developments in the classroom discourse.

Another example of in-class decision making comes from Allwright's (1980) study of adults studying ESL in Los Angeles. The vocabulary lesson feels like a tug-of-war, with a student, whose pseudonym is Igor, steering the lesson in one direction (a discussion of antipollution traffic measures taken in Moscow) while the teacher tries to deliver the vocabulary lesson she had planned using a reading which dealt with air pollution. Allwright realized that one reason why Igor got proportionally so many more turns than his classmates is that the teacher continually sought clarification of Igor's unexpected comments, thereby apparently delaying or even derailing her own plan for the lesson.

Perhaps the most dramatic published example of a teacher's departing from a lesson plan comes from a lower-intermediate ESL lesson on the present perfect auxiliary *have/has* (Allwright and Bailey 1991). The class was practicing questions and answers in the present perfect, when a student entered the room late, rather flustered because some things had been stolen from her husband's car. The teacher sympathetically used the student's experience as a topic, asking the others, "Have you

2 Rafael Gomez (personal communication) has suggested that Carlos may have been engaging in humorous one-upsmanship common in Mexico – a kind of word play which involves double meanings. Carlos may have associated the teacher's question, "Do you wear trousers?" with the Spanish expression, "tener pantalones" (literally "to have trousers/pants," but meaning "to be daring"). So his response ("Alway [sic] . . . all my life") and the resulting laughter potentially take on an additional cultural meaning, which the teacher may not have shared. However, this interpretation is speculative because I did not personally speak to the teacher in this case. In all other instances reported in this chapter, I was either present in the classroom and collected the data myself, or (as in the case of the data from Allwright [1980]) I discussed the data with the teacher shortly after the lesson.

ever had anything stolen?" In the ensuing discussion about theft, one student asked the teacher, "What about you?" As it turned out, the teacher had been robbed four times in the previous year, triggering the students' expression of concern for their (young, single, female) teacher. The teacher admitted that she did not feel very safe in her apartment, especially since the police had recently arrested a Peeping Tom (a voyeur) there. The learners were fascinated by this term, which the teacher explained, although one student confused *peeping* with *pee-pee*, a slang expression which she had heard her children use. Another student asked about the origin of the term *Peeping Tom*, and then suggested *Peeping John* would be better.

By this point, the grammatical focus of the lesson had dissolved. The discussion topic had apparently become "strange things that happen in Los Angeles." Finally the teacher asked the students if they knew the term *flasher* (exhibitionist). One learner asked if it was the same as *streaker*. As the discussion became more colloquial, the teacher asked, "You ever seen a flasher? You ever seen one?" In using the slang term *flasher*, the teacher used a familiar feature of casual spoken English: She deleted the auxiliary *have*: "(Have) you ever seen . . . ?" In this moment of exuberant conversation, the teacher herself had completely abandoned the very point of the original lesson plan (ibid.: 56).

Allwright (personal communication) has noted that departures from the lesson plan are sometimes beyond the teacher's power: Something just happens that the teacher cannot control before a decision must be made. A dramatic example comes from a diary study entry (Bailey 1980: 60–61) about a heated discussion following a test the students felt was unfair. The teacher was clearly not expecting this extremely tense discussion, which took up over half the class period. In the journal entry about the unfair French test, we have a classic example of what Hammersley and Atkinson (1983) have called "natural experiments" (pp. 31–32) – occurrences which are noticeable because unexpected events "reveal what happens when the limiting factors that normally constrain a particular element of social life are breached."

All these examples are familiar cases from language classroom research that document situations in which teachers dealt with the unexpected. Sometimes the result feels authoritarian (as in the example of Carlos's trousers) or lighthearted ("You ever seen a flasher?"). And sometimes teachers must deal with outright hostility (as in the reactions to the French test). Yet in none of these cases do we have the teachers' explanations for the on-the-spot decisions they made. It was my intent, in conducting this study, to try to unravel the mysterious processes that influence teachers' decision making. The resulting discourse can be amusing or perplexing, or even enlightening, but it is often not what the teacher laid out in the lesson plan.

Kathleen M. Bailey

Current explorations: the emerging story

The preceding examples fascinated me, whether they came from my own experience as a learner, from observing language classes, or from published research. This information led me to ask: *Why* do teachers decide to depart from their lesson plans? In particular, what principles guide teachers' decision making?

The cohort and the setting

In this exploration I gathered data in the classes of six experienced teachers working in the Intensive ESL Program, which I directed, at the Monterey Institute of International Studies (MIIS). At the time I collected these data, the program consisted of courses in the four skills, grammar, and TOEFL preparation. In addition, about 40 percent of the students' time was spent in "content courses." (See Shaw, this volume, for a discussion of content-based instruction.) The following data are derived from lessons taught to the same group of students in these courses.

These are relatively small classes, with five to ten students in each. The learners represent many first languages, although most are Asian. They have varied reasons for studying English (to enter community colleges, to enter MIIS or another university, for social or professional reasons, etc.). Throughout this chapter I use pseudonyms in referring to the students; the teachers chose to use their real names.

In this particular cohort, the teachers and students were familiar with me as an administrator, substitute teacher, and classroom visitor. The six teachers I observed were all female. They had all taught ESL at MIIS for at least three prior eight-week sessions, and some had taught there for many years. For this reason, I had several end-of-session students' evaluations of the teachers, which I used as independent confirmation that they were skilled as well as experienced. Thus the interview and classroom data discussed here are from experienced teachers who hold masters degrees. They may not be typical of other language teachers: The small and highly interactive classes, the teachers' preparation, and the use of a teacher-controlled syllabus and flexible materials all may have influenced their decision making.

Data collection

In gathering information from the teachers, I requested appointments for classroom observations,[3] and the teachers chose whether or not they

---

3 I am grateful to the many teachers and students around the world who have graciously allowed me to observe their classes. In particular, my thanks go to the faculty members

wished to participate in the actual study. Once an observation was scheduled, I requested a copy of the regular lesson plan. Conducting the observation involved making an audio cassette recording and taking observational fieldnotes. The running fieldnotes were subsequently developed into prose descriptions of the classes I had observed.

The follow-up interviews were also audio-recorded. They included questions about the typicality of the lesson plan, what had preceded and would follow this lesson, the teacher's perceptions of the lesson, how well the lesson "fit" in the time available, and whether the teacher was aware of any departures from the plan. When the teacher identified an unexpected event recorded in the fieldnotes, or when there was an apparent discrepancy between the lesson plan and the actual lesson, I asked the teacher to explain how and why she had decided to proceed, using the stimulated recall procedure.

Finally I asked the teachers to articulate the principles which had guided their decisions, as if they were explaining them to a novice teacher. At the end of the interview I explained the focus of my study and invited further comments. At that point several teachers offered interesting examples and insights from previous lessons. I later transcribed selected parts of the lessons and the interviews. My main interest was in documenting the factors which guided these experienced teachers' interactive decision making – and particularly the criteria by which they decided to depart from their plans.

Conversations with ESL teachers: principles guiding interactive decision making

This section of the chapter reports on the teachers' reflections about why they chose to depart from their lesson plans, if they had. While my interpretations were certainly influenced by the research on teachers' decision making, which provided etic frameworks for analysis, this section develops an emic interpretation of the events, derived from the teachers' remarks in our post-lesson interviews. Because I am interested in the teachers' operative knowledge, I have organized their ideas in terms of several principles which guided their decision making.

In the sections that follow, I will represent the teachers' ideas in their own words, indicating where I have extrapolated from their comments.[4] As Freeman (this volume) has noted, "In this process of teachers' artic-

of the Intensive ESL Program at the MIIS, who shared with me their lesson plans, their time, and their insights.

4 In the interest of space I have deleted from the transcripts many of the interviewer's discourse maintenance moves (the times I said "Uh-huh" or "Yeah" as "I'm-with-you" feedback to the speaker). The teachers' comments are quoted as they occurred.

ulating, in their own voices, their understandings of what they know lies the start of a redefinition of the relationship of teaching and research."

Serve the common good

In these data, two of the teachers, Leila and Pam, explicitly talked about the situation where a student poses a question or has a problem that the teacher perceives to be an issue for other learners as well. In these cases, the teachers were willing to depart from their lesson plans because they thought that dealing with the individual's issue would benefit the group.

One example arose at the end of a writing lesson, when Leila read aloud a lengthy thesis statement for the students to use in their homework assignment. A student named Evelina asked if the thesis sentence was a run-on sentence, since she had been working on correcting run-on sentences in her own writing. Leila said no and gave a brief explanation. Evelina pursued her concerns about run-on sentences for five minutes as Leila interacted with her. This episode occurred near the end of the class, and the fieldnotes state that Leila glanced at her watch twice during this period. In our discussion I asked Leila (L) about her willingness to deal with Evelina's grammar issue, given that the lesson had been about thesis statements and that they were running out of time.

K: Were you tempted at any point to say, "I'll talk to you after class"?
L: No.
K: No. Because –
L: [She thinks.] I don't – it just didn't seem appropriate. You know, it's something that she obviously wanted to be answered right there and then. If it were something that she alone was working on, then I'd say, "Okay, see me after class and we'll talk about it." I think this was something that maybe all of them could have benefitted from.
K: Mmhm. Okay. So there's a sort of "public good" thing. You weren't feeling rushed at that time?
L: Not really [she pauses], but I came back to what I'd started about the two parts [of the thesis statement]. 'Cause otherwise I think I would have gotten topic sentences that didn't relate to either part of the thesis statement.

From Leila's comments and our subsequent discussion, I inferred that one principle teachers used to decide when to depart from their lesson plans may be summarized as "serve the common good."

The following transcript is from the post-lesson conference with Pam, who taught the TOEFL Preparation class. The class met once a week for only two hours. Pam's comments clearly reveal the dynamic tension teachers feel in making on-line decisions which influence the time available to cover their lesson plans. Her remarks also illustrate the "serve the common good" principle.

K: Okay, at 12:29, almost 12:30, you told the students you'd go over the four item types which are common on the TOEFL. How were you feeling about your timing at that point?

P: Well, I realized that we had gotten way behind what I had hoped for. But that's often the case when I do plan. . . . I often plan much more than I end up being able to handle. I often find that I don't do everything that I have planned in my lesson plan. I kind of let the moment dictate what we end up doing. I sort of use my own judgment as to how much I want to get done and how much I wanna push.

K: Yeah, and it looks like you're using factors in the classroom that enable you to select from the lesson plan menu that you've given yourself.

P: Right.

K: What are those factors?

P: It depends on how much I feel is really important to do before we have the next class, whether it's preparation for homework, or for the next class. If we really need to get that stuff done, then I'll push harder, and tell people, "Well, let's do that next week." And that we're gonna deal with that next week, not today, or whatever. But if I think someone has brought up a good topic that can benefit other people, then I'll let it go, lots of times, and see what happens.

Thus in classes where the teacher judges that several students have a problem (whether linguistic, factual, or cultural) related to one student's question, the teacher may invoke the principle of "serve the common good." The widespread nature of the problem, or perhaps the students' observable interest in the issue, justifies spending more time than the teacher had originally planned.

Teach to the moment

I talked with Joyce after observing her advanced speaking and listening class. Joyce's students listened to or read the news daily and started class with a discussion of current events. In reviewing the lesson plan, I asked Joyce if it was typical. In the following interview transcript, she (J) comments on her plan and then describes the class of the previous day.

J: In general it's typical – it depends on the kind of class. Like for this class, uh, in general I put down an outline for myself so I know what I'm gonna do. But I don't actually write down what I'm gonna do, because I tend *not* to stay with it.

K: Explain.

J: Um, for example, the day before this class, my student teacher and I had planned on doing something, and it was kinda sketchy because we hadn't had real good communication, and we walked in and the Primaries [the national primary elections] had been the day before. And we started talking about the Primaries, and it got to "What is the electoral process?" and we dropped the whole lesson plan, and explained the electoral voting system.

K: Why?

J: Because they [the students] wanted to know. Because they asked. And, in general, um, in, because of what we were gonna do was an info. gap activity, which is all very well and good, but this was *true* information exchange. They really wanted, they wanted to know.

Joyce's comments illustrate the idea that "lessons don't exist" – that teaching and learning transcend temporal lesson boundaries, and this fluidity is reflected in the discourse (Nunan, this volume). In this class Joyce *completely* abandoned a lesson plan to discuss the electoral college system when students asked about it just prior to the national elections. Her decision exemplifies the notion of a "window of opportunity." The unplanned alternative to the lesson plan was judged desirable because of its timeliness. Peter Shaw (personal communication) has noted that in elementary education, this idea is referred to as "teaching to the moment."

Further the lesson

The following excerpt comes from the post-lesson conference in a content course on the environment. Naomi, the teacher, had divided the students into two groups to brainstorm about local conservation measures for air pollution and water conservation. Then all the group members were to collaborate in writing their ideas on the blackboard. Naomi told one student, Evelina, to start writing for her group. Our post-observation conference begins with my orienting comment about Naomi's directive to the class. (Maki is the least proficient member of this group and of the class.)

K: Uhm, at 10:22 you told Evelina to write on the board. [Reading aloud from the fieldnotes] "Fatima, Evelina, and Maki [the members of one group], negotiate who will write which items on the board. Naomi wants each student to do some of the writing. As Evelina and Priscilla [a student from the other group] write on their respective blackboards, Maki explains about busses being left running for two hours in Shinjuku [a part of Tokyo] while tourists look around. He and Junichi [a member of the other group] discuss this in English. . . . Maki starts to write on the blackboard, but then he and Fatima unload the task (in a friendly way – they were smiling) onto Evelina." And you said it was okay if she wrote the whole thing for them. Why did you change your mind?

N: Well, because I noticed that Evelina was reading her list to Maki, and Maki was [she pauses] writing a word and then going, "What?", writing a word and going, "What?", and I just thought it would take too much time and [she pauses] it looked like she wanted to write it anyway, so . . . [her voice trails off and the sentence is left unfinished].

Here Naomi decided to override her preactive managerial decision, which she had announced publicly to the class: She decided that having one fairly proficient student write the group's list would be more efficient than her original strategy for involving all the group members. Thus the procedural change in the plan was a means of promoting the substance and the progress of the lesson.

Accommodate students' learning styles

Some teachers departed from their lesson plans in order to accommodate their students' learning style preferences. An example comes from a writing course that Penny taught for lower intermediate learners. The students brainstormed about topics in two groups and then explained their group's chosen sequence for organizing the essay. At one point, when the students were having trouble with the prepositions *in*, *on*, and *at*, Penny drew three concentric circles (like a bull's-eye on a target) on the board and gave a brief explanation of when to use each preposition. The students copied the drawing and the writing lesson continued, almost as if the small grammar lesson had been a brief side trip.

Later, when I asked about this episode, Penny (P) explained that she had taught this level many times and was very comfortable with explaining grammar points. She described her decision to use this recycled strategy – a technique from her "bag of tricks" which inserted the mini-lesson on the grammar point into the writing lesson. She was aware that the grammar issue was a departure from her lesson plan, and even referred to it as "getting sidetracked." Yet she was also able to get back to her original plan and to articulate her choice to digress, explaining that the students' learning styles factor into her decision making.

29

P: Uhm [she pauses], it was a narrative that they were doing and it had a lot of prepositions in it. . . . They were born *in* this country, *on* this day, *at* this place. And it was just [she pauses] messy. And I had devised my own little mini-lesson on how to present these prepositions of time and place, as a target [she pauses] with the largest circle being the *in*, the next circle *on*, and the most precise the *at*. And so I just stopped what we were doing. . . . So I did the bull's eye and would write it around the circle. So *in* is a place, a country, a state, a town. *On* is a street or a corner. *At* is the address. Then the time, the month, the year. . . . And I have to visualize and *they*, those who are visual learners, *really* latched on to it!

K: When you say you had done a little mini-lesson with your bull's eye model . . . had you prepared *that* for that day, or was it something you'd done in the past and you'd pull it up?

P: I've had it. I just had it in my mind.

K: Okay. So, when you went into class, did you know you were gonna do that –

P: No.

K: Or you decided to do it in class?

P: I decided to – I had no idea I was going to do that . . . When you think about it, it's the same level year after year. It's always the same level. They have predictable problems. So I have my little grab bag of activities that I know might come up. I just, you *know* that. I didn't prepare for, for it for *that* lesson. Uhm, *I* was looking for something else. I wanted to work on pretty much on the thesis statement. That's what I had in my mind to do that day. But they couldn't get beyond that. They were very frustrated with the surface level problem, and I think that's appropriate, to stop when they wanna stop . . .

K: Yeah. Did you get any reactions from them?

P: Yeah, they love that, that kind of stuff. They love grammary, pencilly, writey-down things. [We both laugh.]

Here we may interpret Penny's decision to focus briefly on the prepositions *in*, *on*, and *at* as a hierarchical decision (in Wood's [1989] model) used to promote a superordinate task (the writing of personal narratives). The teacher utilized the visual model of the target as an aid in explaining the relative specificity of *in*, *on*, and *at*, partly for the benefit of the visual learners (". . . and *they*, those who are visual learners, *really* latched onto it!").

Another example of a teacher making decisions on the basis of her understanding of a student's learning style comes from a lower-intermediate grammar class taught by Elizabeth on Monday morning.

It begins with Elizabeth (E) reminding the students about their assignment to give a presentation about their countries. One student, Eriko (S), was apparently not prepared.

E: Part of your homework for Friday, which we're gonna do today, is to tell us a little bit about your countries. 'Member we talked about articles? Megumi and Naoyo already did it, but we need to hear from Geraldo and Eriko and Fatima. [To Eriko] You don't want to do it? (Did) you bring pictures? Remember I asked you to bring pictures of your country?

S: Uh-huh [affirmative intonation].

E: And you were gonna talk about places and articles and you were gonna describe your country.

S: Uh-hm [affirmative intonation].

E: Are you ready?

Ss: [Laughter]

S: [Nervous laughter] No, no.

E: No, you want to do it another day? Want to do it on Wednesday?

S: Okay.

In the post-observation conference, I asked Elizabeth about this interaction.

K: Okay, what happened with Eriko?

E: I think she forgot to bring her pictures.

K: Ah-hah.

E: And she needs a lot of modeling. And uh, she wasn't there on Friday to see the other models.

K: Uh-huh.

E: This way, today she saw the models. And I'm sure she forgot to bring pictures. So Wednesday, I'll have her go.

Here Elizabeth's decision to postpone Eriko's report is based partially on her feeling that Eriko "needs a lot of modeling," just as Penny's mini-lesson was motivated, in part, by the students' preference for "grammary, pencilly, writey-down things." These teachers' perceptions of their students' learning styles are factors in their interactive decision making.

Promote students' involvement

Elizabeth's lesson plan says "1 min. speeches about their homes – tape record." At 10:14, Elizabeth called on Fatima, who showed pictures of Turkey as she spoke. My fieldnotes say:

31

Fatima explains that you can swim in the south and ski in the north in the same season. She smiles and looks proud of her country. . . . At 10:21, Elizabeth takes some papers from her table as Fatima continues talking. (OC [observer's comment]: Does this mean that Elizabeth wants to move on to the next part of the lesson?) Elizabeth looks down at the papers on her lap briefly. Then she invites questions. . . . [Questions follow from the group.] At 10:27 Elizabeth says, "Great! Thank you! It's a beautiful country."

In our conference, I asked Elizabeth about her decision to continue a one-minute activity for thirteen minutes:

K: At 10:21 you took some papers from your table as Fatima continued talking. And my question to you was, does this mean that, uh, Elizabeth wants to move on to the next part of the lesson?

E: *Yes* [said quickly and emphatically].

K: And again you looked down at the papers on your lap briefly.

E: Uh-huh.

K: Tell me what was going on there in your mind.

E: Uhm [she pauses], I was interested in what she was saying, and [attenuated] I thought her pictures were great and she obviously felt *so good* [said emphatically] about her country and how beautiful it is, and even her homework that she'd done was very detailed and stuff and I didn't want to verbally cut her off. I just wanted to try and send a very subtle message that time, time – we had to . . . [she pauses and her voice trails off].

K: Did she get the message?

E: Yeah, I think she did.

K: Okay. Uh, at 10:27 you said, "Great! Thank you! It's a beautiful country." Uhm, this was after you, you – it's interesting because you had the papers on your lap, but then you invited questions. . . . Now, when, let's see [I look through the fieldnotes], so you told her at 10:14 [Elizabeth laughs an amused laugh of realization] it was her turn.

E: [She laughs] Uh-huh.

K: At 10:27 you ended her turn.

E: Yep.

K: And I noticed that your, your lesson plans says "one-minute speeches about their homes."

E: Uh-huh.

K: So if my subtraction serves me right, this was a thirteen-minute speech.

E: Yep.

K: Was that okay?

E: [In-breath] It was. On Friday, uh, when Megumi and Naoyo did it, they each took about ten minutes. It was a little long, but it was okay.

K: Mmhm. What did that do to your lesson plan?

E: Cut off the communicative activity at the end.

K: Mmhm. Interesting. Uhm, you've just explained the particulars to me, but if there were a principle behind the decision that you made, to let her [Fatima] continue, what would that abstraction be? How would you articulate that principle?

E: [She pauses] For letting her continue?

K: Uh-huh.

E: Uhm [she pauses], hmmm. [She pauses] Uh, the, the principle would be that she was very involved in the activity, very engaged in it, and that that is as valuable as my little communication activity at the end of the class. And that when someone is that engaged, uhm, [she pauses] and her classmates seemed interested, when someone's that engaged, you be flexible with time. And you let it go.

Here Elizabeth has unknowingly echoed Joyce's statement: "[W]hat we were gonna do was an info. gap activity, which is all very well and good, but this was *true* information exchange."

In the preceding example we see a decision-making principle which arises often. To promote the students' involvement, teachers create the time to do so by eliminating some portions of their own lesson plans. This is an illustration of teachers using Politzer's (1970: 41) "principle of economics" – the idea that since classroom time is so limited, the value of any activity is partially determined by the offsetting value of the activities the teacher could choose to do instead.

Sometimes the teacher's desire to promote students' involvement and reward relevant contributions creates a sense of tension for the teacher: How far should one allow the students to determine the topics and the amount of time spent on each? The following excerpt comes from a conversation with Eve, following an observation of her content course on advertising. The students had been examining persuasive devices used in print-medium advertising, including *shock value*, which grabs the readers' attention and causes them to remember the product names. Shock value was illustrated by an ad with a photograph of a person with AIDS (Acquired Immune Deficiency Syndrome). One of the students, Evelina, felt that the ad was immoral (because it capitalized on one person's misfortune) and that such ads should be censored. Eve utilized Evelina's contribution, although she was concerned about getting into the topic of censorship, given the time constraints on her lesson. In our post-observation interview I asked Eve (E) to summarize the point she had hoped to make. She explained that she wanted the students to see that the company also had freedom of speech.

E: But, I mean, that was sticky. I didn't – I could see where that was going just because of what she said, and so I had to address it, but

33

I didn't want to go into that because that could just be hours and hours and hours.

K: Uhm, so that [censorship] was a thought that she [Evelina] brought up that wasn't in your lesson plan for the day.

E: Right.

K: Okay. And you decided to deal with it because –

E: Because she brought it up, and because it's directly related, and I think it's a serious issue, and one that probably the others had been thinking about 'cause we, I guess we mentioned it a little bit on Monday. Uhm, but I didn't want to go into it thoroughly – I, I didn't really know how to handle that actually, because it just, I mean that could be a whole lesson.

In this instance Eve's lesson plan had included the notations "student opinions" and "discuss ethics in advertising (ongoing)." She did want to elicit the students' opinions, and Evelina's comments were relevant, in terms of both topic and task. Even though Eve saw the issue of censorship as too big to cover at that time, she did not wish to stifle Evelina's contribution, so she spent some time on the topic that the student had raised.

Distribute the wealth

In the following post-observation conference, Penny and I are discussing Fatima (again, a pseudonym), whom several teachers had identified as creating problems. It seemed that Fatima appeared to be very bored and impatient when her less verbal (though no less proficient) classmates tried to speak English. In the writing lesson I observed, Fatima tried to take another student's turn. At that point Penny used a brief, gentle, but clear hand signal to stop Fatima from interrupting the other student. I asked Penny (who had previously been my student) about this issue:

K: What happens when you're working with Fatima, when you're working with a class, and Fatima pops up? What happens in your mind?

P: Mmhm. Well, Fatima was my student at [another school]. Uhm, so I am pretty comfortable with that kind of a student. *I* was that kind of a student, popping up, as you recall. [We both laugh.]

K: But I don't remember you ever stealing turns.

P: No, not so much, but, uh, but wanting, just thinking what we ha– what we have to say is just *so* germane to the [she laughs] what's going on at that moment. So I can relate. I can relate to her, her place in the class. . . . Uhm, she paid her money, but they paid their money too. And I try to be sensitive to my students as, really, consumers, and she doesn't get more than her money's worth, at the expense of the other students.

Here Penny attributes her skill at dealing with a problem student to her empathy: ". . . I am pretty comfortable with that kind of student. *I was that kind of student, popping up, as you recall.*" We saw other examples of this empathy when Penny referred to the visual learners in her class and said, "I have to visualize," and, "I can relate to her." I asked Penny to reconstruct her decision to prevent Fatima from stealing another student's turn:

K: What, what led you to the decision to say [with a gesture], "No, Fatima, you've had enough."
P: Mmhm. I think it's just the idea of turns. You know, it's like the maître d' in the restaurant. You give a waitress a table and then you give a waitress in another section a table. And you just don't fill up one section. There's just – a sense that "You said a nice point, that was a really nice point" and if there are five facts that I already know are gonna belong, and she's said one or two, then there are seven people in the class.

Another example of the "distribute the wealth" principle is found in Eve's content class on advertising. Two students got into a discussion in which the other members of the class did not actively participate. There came a point at which Eve pulled them back into the discourse of the larger group. In the post-observation conference I asked about her reasoning.

K: Well, when you're in that situation, and you're making that decision, whether to pull it back to the lesson plan or let it go, what makes you decide? What do you think you use – [I pause]
E: [She begins to laugh] The look on everybody's faces [laughing], everybody else who's not involved. Like it was clearly Fatima and Junichi discussing this, and, uhm, Evelina and Priscilla were kind of like "Okay, okay, okay" [said with a slightly exasperated "let's-get-on-with-it" tone of voice]. So . . . if everyone or the majority is not actively engaged and . . . it's not benefiting or interesting for them, then I want to pull it back. If everybody's into it, then I go for it.
K: Mmhm. And "into it" means – [I pause].
E: Excited, uhm, obviously interested, by facial expressions and participating in the conversation, and, okay, "Can I say something? Can I say something?" [indicating students bidding for turns]. And it was clearly just something between Junichi and Fatima, so, so that's why it was kinda weird, but uh, we got back on topic so it was okay.

In these data, the teachers operated with this "distribute the wealth" principle to keep the more verbal learners from dominating classroom interaction, as well as to encourage the less outgoing students to participate more often.

There are probably numerous other reasons, or principles, underlying language teachers' on-line decision making, but the data from this study consistently offered these. The reasons given by these teachers are congruent with the current philosophy of learner-centered teaching, which invites (or perhaps even demands) "co-produced outcomes" (Allwright and Bailey 1991). Furthermore, as Westerman (1991) has pointed out, skilled teachers have reasons for what they do and can articulate those reasons.

Implications: back to Robert Burns

Kaplan (1963) states that "scientists and philosophers use a Logic – they have a cognitive style which is more or less logical and some of them also formulate it explicitly" (p. 8). The former (the day-to-day practice of logical decision making) is what Kaplan calls "logic in use"; the latter (the codified rules by which science is conducted) is "reconstructed logic." As a profession, language teaching entails a great deal of logic in use, which is not fully articulated or described: For the most part, we lack a reconstructed logic. In using the term *reconstructed logic*, I am not referring to prescriptions and guidelines about how we *ought* to plan lessons. Instead, I am referring to the articulation, the reconstruction and re-creation, of the logic which experienced teachers use in their daily practice of the profession.[5] In these data, we see some co-produced outcomes of the post-observation interviews where these teachers articulate, often for the first time, the operative principles that drive their in-class decisions – thereby reconstructing their *logic in use*.

The lessons I observed in conducting this study, like the published literature on language classroom research, are full of moments when the teachers arrived at what van Lier (personal communication) has called the "change-relevant moment." That is, teachers reach a point when they must decide either to continue with the planned sequence of events or to digress from the plan.

When faced with the unexpected, teachers can stick (more or less rigidly) to the lesson plan (paths 2 and 3 in Peterson and Clark's [1978]

---

5 Leo van Lier (personal communication) has suggested that such discussions with teachers could lead to preliminary construction of retrospective logic, rather than the verbal *re*construction or re-creation of logic that had been in use during the lesson. This point leads to the curious notion that what we have, in my discussions with teachers, could be etically triggered emic analyses – or emically prompted etic analyses.

data), as did the less experienced teacher described by Nunan (this volume). Or, with options available, teachers can diverge from the lesson plan (Peterson and Clark's path 4). Such divergences can be conscious controlled choices, or they can be uncontrolled and outside of the teacher's conscious awareness. As Shavelson has pointed out (1973: 18), "Any teaching act is the result of a decision, whether conscious or unconscious, that the teacher makes after the complex cognitive processing of available information." He further states that "the basic teaching skill is decision making" (ibid.; see also Freeman 1989: 31).

Once the teacher decides to depart from the lesson plan, the sequence of events may involve teaching strategies that have not been used previously. The teacher may have heard or read about these options, or seen them demonstrated. Or the teacher could take a risk and attempt a completely new, spontaneously generated idea. In the case of experienced teachers, the decision to depart from the plan is often smoothed by the ability to reach into the mental "bag of tricks" and pull out a previously used idea – thereby recycling a strategy judged to be successful in the past. (This process is illustrated in Penny's use of the target image to illustrate the prepositions *in*, *on*, and *at*.) The use of such strategies or routines allows the teacher to depart from the plan but minimizes the risk of doing so. This is one important part of what it means to be an "experienced" teacher: to have a mental lexicon of teaching strategies which can be called up as needed – skillfully, quickly, and with confidence (Leinhardt and Greeno's "large repertoire of activities" [1986: 76]).

It is my hope that the principles articulated here by experienced and effective ESL teachers will help new teachers as they try to navigate uncharted waters. Preservice teachers can learn by discussing these issues with one another and with more experienced cooperating teachers after their own lessons, or by examining videotapes or transcripts of lessons taught by other teachers. As Johnson (1992) points out, "Utilizing stimulus recall data from experienced ESL teachers may be one way of providing opportunities for preservice ESL teachers to trace the instructional decisions of experienced ESL teachers" (p. 129).

Inservice teachers can also reflect on their own lessons (perhaps with feedback from a peer or a journal) and discover their own strategies and actions in order to decide what has been successful. As professionals, we need first to discover and understand our practice, and second, to increase our professionalism through sharing our insights and understanding.

To achieve a discipline of teaching . . . the knowledge that teachers articulate through the process of disciplined inquiry must become public. It cannot dissipate in the recesses of private conversations, staff rooms, or even schools. The interpretations which teachers develop through research need to enter the wider community, to compete with other disciplines as ways of understanding education and of shaping public policy and debate. (Freeman, this volume)

Coming to understand our own practice is what is meant by "exploratory teaching" (Allwright and Bailey 1991).

Conclusion

The teachers described here were able to explain their reasons for their interactive decisions. In our discussions and in my thinking, the following labels arose for their decision-making principles: (1) serve the common good, (2) teach to the moment, (3) further the lesson, (4) accommodate students' learning styles, (5) promote students' involvement, and (6) distribute the wealth. I do not mean to suggest that these are the only principles which teachers use to make interactive decisions. They are simply the ideas that arose in this data set: These teachers probably rely on additional criteria for making decisions as the situation demands. And other teachers, working with different curricular and social pressures, probably use different criteria for in-class decision making.

In this chapter, I have attempted to make explicit some of the things that experienced teachers know – to begin to reconstruct their logic in use about departing from their lesson plans. Yet I have tried to do so by listening to the teachers' voices. Gitlin (1990) states that "educational research is still a process that for the most part silences those studied, ignores their personal knowledge, and strengthens the assumption that researchers are *the* producers of knowledge" (p. 444). In the approach I have taken here, the researcher's job is not to "produce" the knowledge that teachers have. Rather, it is first to get those who know the story to tell it, and then to retell the collected stories myself, but in the role of narrator, rather than creator.

I began this chapter with the well known lines about "the best laid schemes" (Burns 1785). I believe these teachers' stories point to the fact that our best-laid plans (or schemes, to give the poet his due) often go astray; but in realizing lesson plans, part of a skilled teacher's logic in use involves managing such departures to maximize teaching and learning opportunities.

The chapter also began with the proverb about knives of wood in the ironmonger's house. I sometimes think that we teachers are like the shoemakers' barefoot children: As a field we are concerned about our professional stature, yet we seldom examine our own practice and publicly address what it means to be professional. Clearly, a part of being a professional teacher entails "planfulness" (Leinhardt and Greeno 1986), and the awareness that decision making is a dynamic process, constantly at play before, during, and after lessons. It is my hope that this chapter has combined emic and etic perspectives in retelling some of the knowledge that teachers have (to paraphrase Freeman [this volume]) in order to "achieve a discipline of teaching."

References

Allwright, D., and K. M. Bailey. 1991. *Focus on the Language Classroom: An Introduction to Classroom Research for Language Teachers*. Cambridge: Cambridge University Press.

Allwright, R. L. 1980. Turns, topics and tasks: Patterns of participation in language learning and teaching. In D. Larsen-Freeman (ed.), *Discourse Analysis in Second Language Research*. Rowley, MA: Newbury House.

Bailey, K. M. 1980. An introspective analysis of an individual's language learning experience. In R. C. Scarcella and S. D. Krashen (eds.), *Research in Second Language Acquisition: Selected Papers of the Los Angeles Second Language Research Forum*. Rowley, MA: Newbury House.

Burns, R. 1785. To a mouse (Stanza 7). In *The Collected Works of Robert Burns*. Boston: Little Brown.

Freeman, D. 1989. Teacher training, development, and decision making: A model of teaching and related strategies for language teacher education. *TESOL Quarterly, 23*, 1, 27–45.

(Chapter 4, this volume). Redefining the relationship between research and what teachers know.

Gitlin, A. D. 1990. Educative research, voice, and school change. *Harvard Educational Review, 60*, 4, 443–466.

Hammersley, M., and P. Atkinson. 1983. *Ethnography: Principles in Practice*. London: Tavistock Publications.

Johnson, K. 1992. The instructional decisions of pre-service ESL teachers: New directions for teacher preparation programs. In J. Flowerdew, M. Brock, and S. Hsia (eds.), *Perspectives on Second Language Teacher Education*. Hong Kong: City Polytechnic of Hong Kong.

Kaplan, A. 1963. *The Conduct of Inquiry: Methodology for Behavioral Science*. New York: Harper & Row.

Larsen-Freeman, D. 1990. On the need for a theory of language teaching. In J. Alatis (ed.), *Linguistics, Language Teaching and Language Acquisition: The Interdependence of Theory, Practice and Research*. Washington, DC: Georgetown University Press.

Leinhardt, G., and J. G. Greeno. 1986. The cognitive skill of teaching. *Journal of Educational Psychology, 78*, 2, 75–95.

Long, M. H. 1980. Inside the "black box": Methodological issues in research on language teaching and learning. *Language Learning, 30*, 1, 1–42.

Malcolm, I. G. 1991. "All right then, if you don't want to do that . . .": Strategy and counter-strategy in classroom discourse management. *Guidelines: A Periodical for Classroom Language Teachers, 13*, 2, 1–17.

Nunan, D. 1992. The teacher as decision-maker. In J. Flowerdew, M. Brock, and S. Hsia (eds.), *Perspectives on Second Language Teacher Education*. Hong Kong: City Polytechnic of Hong Kong.

(Chapter 2, this volume). Hidden voices: Insiders' perspectives on classroom interaction.

Peterson, P. L., and C. M. Clark. 1978. Teachers' reports of their cognitive processes. *American Educational Research Journal, 15,* 4, 555–565.

Politzer, R. L. 1970. Some reflections on "good" and "bad" language teaching behaviors. *Language Learning, 20,* 1, 31–43.

Richards, J. C., and G. Crookes. 1988. The practicum in TESOL. *TESOL Quarterly, 22,* 1, 9–27.

Shavelson, R. J. 1973. *The Basic Teaching Skill: Decision Making*. R&D Memorandum No. 104, Stanford, CA: Stanford University, School of Education, Center for Research and Development in Teaching.

Shaw, P. (Chapter 14, this volume). Voices for improved learning: The ethnographer as co-agent of pedagogic change.

Westerman, D. 1991. Expert and novice teacher decision making. *Journal of Teacher Education, 42,* 4, 292–305.

Woods, D. 1989. Studying ESL teachers' decision-making: Rationale, methodological issues and initial results. *Carleton Papers in Applied Language Studies, 6,* 107–123.

2 Hidden voices: insiders' perspectives on classroom interaction

David Nunan

> As I explore my teaching by describing –
> recording, transcribing, and coding
> communications – rather than by seeking
> prescriptions and judgments from others,
> patterns are broken both consciously and
> unconsciously. I have sought alternatives
> in teaching and found them. After I found
> that I have alternatives, I felt freer and
> securer about deciding on activities for
> the students. Throughout the internship, I
> have learned how to see teaching more
> clearly and differently. In other words, I
> realized how much more I can do . . .
> (Gebhard and Ueda-Montonaga
> 1992: 190)

In an eloquently argued case for the evolution of a nexus between class-room research and teacher education, Wright (1992), describes a situation familiar to almost anyone who has ever walked through a school while a lesson is in progress.

Imagine we walk down the corridor of a school and hear much noise coming from a classroom. We might at first assume that it is the result of the teacher having lost control of the class (or some other plausible explanation). On arrival and entrance to the classroom, we find the students engaged in an activity which involves animated discussion, in groups, with the teacher participating as a monitor in the activity. (p. 194)

In this anecdote, Wright provides a warning against drawing conclusions about behavior without knowing the context in which the behavior occurs. He wryly concludes that "we can only know what the noise is about by referring directly to the context in which the noise occurs" (ibid.).

It seems to me that a great deal of research in our field is conducted

I should like to acknowledge and thank the teachers who took part in this study, and also David Cervi, who assisted in transcribing some of the interactions on which it is based.

41

in contexts where classroom noise either is unheard or is considered irrelevant and therefore removed from the equation before the numbers are added up and their significance determined. This lack of contact with the reality of the classroom has driven a wedge between researcher and practitioner which threatens to become a gulf unless steps are taken to bridge it. In this chapter, I would like to make a modest contribution toward closing the gap between theory and practice, and between researcher and teacher. I shall try to do this by giving teachers an opportunity to have their voices heard, and their perspectives and interpretations presented.

The study

In this section, I shall describe the subjects and context of the investigation and the research question. I shall then set out some of the data and provide my own descriptive and interpretive account of those data. Because ethnographic investigations of this type are data rich, my account must necessarily be selective.

The cohort

The participants in this study were nine ESL teachers who were teaching in Australia and were also undertaking some form of professional qualification. They varied greatly in their professional backgrounds and length of experience. Three had been practicing for less than one year. The others ranged in experience from one to fifteen years.

The research question

The question which provided my point of departure was relatively easy to pose: In what ways are the processes of classroom instruction illuminated by the voices of the teachers? Finding answers in the data described herein was less straightforward. Moreover, as I analyzed these data, other questions and issues emerged, and I had to struggle to retain the original focus while admitting emerging insights into the analysis.

The research procedure

The data for the investigation were gathered through a four-stage procedure.

1. *Before the lesson.* Before the lesson began, I obtained background information on the teacher and took a copy of the teacher's lesson

plan. (The teachers were asked to provide a detailed lesson plan, as well as biographical data in advance of the lesson.)

2. *During teaching.* The lesson was observed and recorded, and notes were taken to assist in the transcription process. Particular note was taken of those points at which the teacher deviated from the lesson plan.

3. *After the lesson.* Immediately after the class, I talked about the lesson with the teachers, asking them to focus on those points at which they had deviated from their plan.

4. *Follow-up.* The lesson was transcribed and a copy was sent to the teacher to annotate. The transcripts, annotations, and post-lesson protocols were then analyzed using a range of qualitative data analysis procedures. (For a description of such procedures, see Nunan 1992.)

In attempting to gain insights into the question I had posed, I revisited the transcripts, my observational notes, and the teachers' post-lesson protocols and annotations many times. As I aligned the different sources of data related to critical classroom incidents, adding successive layers of interpretation, the incidents themselves were transformed, as we shall see.

Data analysis

This section discusses some of the themes which emerged from the data. Given the quantity of data and constraints of space, I have been selective in the choice of issues and amount of data provided. However, I hope that enough supporting data are provided to sustain my case.

Getting the action going

In the ebb and flow of any given lesson, there are several critical moments. The first few minutes seem particularly important in creating the appropriate tone of the lesson, and the atmosphere which is established at the beginning of the class often persists for the duration of the lesson.

The value added by the teacher's voice is illustrated by the following incident. I had noted the beginning of one lesson in the following field-note record.

The students wander into the class in twos and threes. As they begin to settle down, the teacher makes several of them change places. Students seem lethargic after lunch. Teacher then introduces and revises vocabulary. This goes on for over ten minutes, and the students begin to seem rather restive. I wonder why she's going on so long.

In this observation there is an implicit criticism of the pacing of the lesson. In the post-lesson debriefing, when asked for a commentary on this part of the lesson, the teacher reported:

. . . in the initial eliciting, I found it quite difficult to elicit the clothes – you know, "What am I wearing? What's he/she wearing?" I got a bit [annoyed] at that point because we did it last week, you see. It just makes you realize. We did it as a warm-up activity a week ago, and it had just gone totally out of their heads. So that was another thing I'd not anticipated. I thought they'd just tell me – and they didn't.

The teacher's voice here reveals several things. First, it dramatizes the fact that lessons are not discrete entities that come neatly prepackaged. As a course evolves over days, weeks, and months, a culture emerges through the interaction of personalities and events. Without an understanding of that culture, many of the events which occur in a particular lesson will be meaningless to the outside observer. One of the unfortunate realities of much classroom research is that it is carried out on individual lessons (and often on relatively short segments of individual lessons). This denies the researcher access to data which would render many seemingly odd or irrelevant interactions meaningful. Second it shows that particular classroom events only take on meaning within the context of the course. In order to understand classroom events and the interpretations of those events by teachers and learners, we need to step outside the artificial temporal framework of "the lesson." (I shall return to this point later.) The third observation which we can make here relates to the teacher's theory of learning, and the assumption that the work which had been previously undertaken would be sufficient to ensure that learning had taken place. Throughout the data, there is evidence that everything that is said and done in the lesson, and all comments on the lesson, are underpinned by beliefs (often implicit) about the nature of language, learning, and teaching.

Particularly notable was the fact that very few lessons began with the teacher's explicitly laying out the objectives for the students. The exception was the following.

T: Okay now, the approach we're gonna take here – there will be some traditional grammar in this, but what I'm going to try to give you is some analytical skills. Of how to analyze your own writing. Skills that you can take away from here and use them. Okay? It's not just grammar we're looking at. It's . . . we're looking at how do I make myself understood to somebody else? Right? And how can I work on this on my own all of the time? Now some of you gave me some examples of writing in the beginning and I've looked at that to see exactly what kind of writing is it that you want to do and that you have to do. Okay. And we've . . . we've called this course scientific writing and the type of writing you do is what we call [writes on board] "report writing."

In fact, this was the only lesson in the entire data base in which the teacher laid out the pedagogic terrain to be covered with more than an off-hand comment. How can we account for this apparent failure to address a basic pedagogical imperative? That is, how can we account for the fact that only one teacher bothered to explain to the students what it was they were supposed to be learning? I believe it demonstrates that the notion of a "lesson" is not particularly salient for the teachers who took part in the study. Boundaries which appear tangible in a timetable dissolve against the emerging culture of the classroom. There is evidence in the data, both in the lesson transcripts and the reports of the teachers themselves, that more salient than the "lesson" are the analytical units of "task," which is smaller than "lesson," and "course" which is larger. This is explicit in the following opening gambit and commentary.

T: Remember last week when we were talking about our businesses that we were role playing and we went to the ideas centre and we had Lee to discuss our proposals for expanding into developing countries, and what I felt was that it would be a good idea to read about something which was a successful expansion into a developing country.

On reviewing the lesson transcript, the teacher made the unprompted comment that she "wanted to make a special effort to make a connection with previous lessons."

In several cases, the teachers launch directly into the "meat" of the lesson. For example, in one lesson, the teacher entered the room, turned her back on the class, and wrote on the board: "A woman's place is in the home." She then turned to the class and said:

T: Any comments about that sentence: "A woman's place is in the home"?
S: Half correct.
T: Half correct? Why d'you say that Henry?
S: Em, woman's place not just at home. She should be go out and go work.
T: Yeah? What about the man?
S: Man is the same, I think.

The teacher justified this rather abrupt beginning to the lesson by stating, "I didn't feel the need to use any other warmer than the initial stimulus for the functional target language, as I know these students well."

In this section, I have presented some of the data relating to lesson openings. These data illustrate a number of emerging issues which reappear later in the study. First, "lesson" is not a particularly salient label for those involved in the teaching/learning process. Second, in order to understand classroom behavior, we need to study that behavior in the context in which it occurs – that is, in classrooms constituted for the purposes of teaching and learning, not in those which are established to provide cannon fodder for researchers. Third, in order to understand what is going on, we need to set the interpretations of the researcher against insights provided by the other actors in the educational drama.

Maintaining control over the flow of events

In reflecting on the lessons, teachers paid a great deal of attention to classroom management, particularly in maintaining control over the flow of events. In a previous study, I noted that this tendency to focus on classroom management rather than pedagogy was something that distinguished less experienced teachers from more experienced ones. (However, I would also reiterate that the concept of "experience," while familiar to most of us, defies definition, interacting as it does with other critical variables such as professional development opportunities and intensity, as well as length of service.)

The close attention to managing and controlling lesson "flow" is illustrated in the following extract. In her lesson plan, the teacher had indicated that she intended to run a pair work activity in which students observed each other and then sat back-to-back and described what the other was wearing. This is a fairly standard way of practicing present continuous tense, a difficult tense to practice in any meaningful way because we rarely describe what we are doing in face-to-face interactions. However, during the course of the lesson, this activity simply did not happen. I remarked on this in my observation notes with a query. In the post-lesson debriefing, the teacher reported, "I dropped the activity . . . [because] . . . it probably would've gone on a bit too long, and as it was, I was short for time anyway, so I made a decision to drop that." Later in the lesson, in response to a question about the selection of partners in pair work and whether she let students self-select, the same teacher reported, "Oh, I get them to mix around. I like to change the pairs quite a lot. That's why its good to get them in two groups and then split them up for a different part of the listening."

Another major departure from the lesson plan occurred as students were working in small groups sequencing a transcript of a listening text which had been cut up. The following extract and my fieldnotes illustrate what happened:

[Students get in three groups on the floor.]
T: I'll give you five minutes to do this, five minutes.
T: [About sixty second later, T says] Two minutes.
[She rewinds her tape.]
T: Come on, this group's nearly finished. One minute. One minute left.
T: Okay, we'll listen to the conversation now. Okay, so as you're listening to the conversation, can you check your sequence?
[The students listen to the interview and rearrange their strips of paper.]
T: Finished? Perfect. What does – this mean? [She writes on the board "Erm".] (Erm) Erm. Is that a word?
S: No.
T: Erm. Why, why've got that there? Why? Why erm?
S: We have some little bit time. . . .
T: It's because we're listening to it. Listening to what's written down, so don't worry, don't think oh what does erm mean? It's just erm. And how do they say "yes." Do they say "yes"?
S: Yeah (Yeah) – Australian accent.
T: Australian accent do you think? (Yeah yeah) Anything accent.

As I observed this interaction I noted:

Teacher is really hustling the students. Several groups appear to be struggling. She then calls attention to a minor filler on the tape. What's the point? Won't it simply confuse the students?

In the debriefing, the teacher provided the following explanation.

[W]hen they were doing the sequencing on the floor, they were taking quite a lot of time to do that and two groups hadn't finished, and I looked at my watch and I said hurry up, one minute left, and played the tape while they were still halfway through sequencing it. And then I only actually played the tape once, I didn't play it through again, but they'd got the right order by this stage. I just made the decision on the spot to tell them what 'erm' and 'yeah' were, 'cause one of them said, 'Erm' what's 'erm'?

Here is yet another illustration that something which made little sense to an outside observer made perfect sense to those on the inside of the action. I believe this opacity to an outsider of many things that happen in the classroom reinforces the need for classroom stories to be told from the inside. In another classroom, the following interaction took place.

T: You know when you're agreeing, like Shigeru did to me before. And it's nice to say, "Mmm, and it's good to relax," and then Jill said, she started to tell Patricia something now, and what does she say, Chong Dok?

S: Well, you see . . .

T: [T takes over] . . . it's like this. When you're starting to tell a story sometimes, you start, you say, "Well, you see, it's like this." And that means you're starting to tell what it was like. Like Shigeru, he was really telling me a story about why he was late. He could have said "Well, you see, Jill, it's like this. The train missed me this morning." Okay, and then Patricia says, "I've said my increase has been remarkable" and Patricia says – Shigeru?

S: Yes, I saw that, but you must be careful.

T: Yes, that's right. And then Jill says . . . Yami?

S: Yes, I know.

It is almost impossible to convey interpersonal and affective aspects of the classroom in lesson transcripts. In the preceding extracts, the teacher and students weave the interaction together effortlessly, as though it had been rehearsed. While the interaction is largely meaningless to the outsider, the students find it amusing and make their contributions on cue. As it turned out, the obscure references were to an in-joke shared only by the class. Here is another example of Freeman's (this volume) dictum that to tell the story one must know the story.

In explaining why the previous interaction happened when it did, the teacher reported that:

The students generally welcome both humor and personalizing of material to them. A little humor always helps to maintain interest and motivation. In this part of the lesson, we were using a little story that had evolved during the course.

In addition to illuminating the complexity of the classrooms, the transcripts and teachers' commentaries provide fascinating insights into teachers' styles. The teacher quoted in the following extract was relatively inexperienced and felt that she could not abandon her predetermined course of action, even though the students were evidently experiencing difficulty with it and the flow of classroom events was obviously affected.

I began to realize the students were finding the activity quite complex and hard, but it was too late to change it or abandon it, as they did need introducing to the vocabulary before starting to read the article. I ended up having to bring the pairs together.

From the data, it seemed that the more experienced teachers were much more comfortable with monitoring the class and modifying their lesson in the light of ongoing feedback. Here is a typical comment:

The warmer was beginning to take longer than I wanted to by this stage. I was beginning to wonder whether to pursue it for longer to involve all students in this stage or to move on. I feel less confident of timing at this level than at higher levels.

Another teacher said, "I realized that as the tape quality was poor I would have to distribute the written language from the tape sooner than expected."

The images and metaphors used by the teachers are also revealing. The data are shot through with references to pace, flow, tempo, and movement. One teacher noted, "Time was running out. I had to keep the pace moving along."

In another classroom, the teacher drew an activity to a rather abrupt halt, despite the fact that it seemed to be going well. The teacher accounted for this abrupt change of pace in terms of classroom management by saying, "The time limit prevailed again and I had to draw a halt. This activity was going well. Maybe if I'd anticipated my timings better I could have given students longer to work on this role play, which they got quite a lot out of."

In this section I have provided additional data on the importance of the insider's voice in helping to understand the life in language classrooms. In procedural terms, a great deal of classroom interaction is aimed at maintaining the flow of classroom interaction. In research terms, once again, we see that it is difficult to interpret the interactions without additional insights from those on the inside.

The instructional process

One striking point to emerge from the data was the relative paucity of what might be called direct instruction, in which the teacher explicitly instructs the learners. This might seem odd, given the fact that the layperson probably sees the "bringing of good news" as the central function of instructors. In addition, a great deal of the explicit instruction which occurred came about as the teachers responded to the immediate needs of the students. The majority of these impromptu explanations concerned vocabulary which students found difficult.

T: ... "collateral" actually means sort of security on somebody who is taking out a loan. If I was a very wealthy person – I'm rich and you want a loan – you are poor – I could be your collateral – you would take out the loan and I would have the security for the loan. I would say to the bank "Yami will pay back the money and if she doesn't, I will give the bank the money." Collateral, security, another person arranges to be –

49

S: Another person guarantee for you to borrow money from the bank?
T: Yes, that's right.

Direct evidence from students that they had "got it" was particularly important for most teachers, and when it occurred, the teacher's decision to engage in direct instruction was vindicated. For instance, in reviewing this piece of interaction, the teacher reported, "I was pleased this explanation was clear to the students. I think I'm gradually improving in explaining, defining, and giving instructions for them."

On some occasions the explanations were prompted by a direct request from a student. In many instances, however, the explanations were prompted by the teacher's intuitive perception of the students' needs. For example, in one lesson the teacher was working with an authentic tape in which an interviewer asked a series of questions about the interviewees' life-styles. Rather than using complete question forms, the interviewer signaled the questions through intonation: "Drink?" rather than "Do you drink?" This gave rise to the following interaction.

T: What question does the interviewer ask? The interviewer? What question does the interviewer ask? What's the question in here?
S: You smoke?
T: You smoke? You smoke? That's not a proper question is it really? Proper question is do you smoke? So he says "you smoke?" We know it's a question because . . . why? You smoke? . . .
S: The tone.
T: The tone . . . the . . . the . . . what did we call it before? You smoke? What do we call this?
S: Intonation.
T: Intonation. You know by his intonation – it's a question.

When I observed the lesson, I was puzzled by this interaction. Why "deauthenticate" a piece of authentic interaction by saying that the interviewer was not asking "proper" questions? At the end of the lesson, I asked the teacher about this.

T: . . . And also the on-the-spot decision of like when it said "drink?"
DN: So you hadn't actually planned to teach that?
T: No, I hadn't. I mean, really, that would be an excellent thing to do in a follow-up lesson – you know, focus on questions.
DN: In fact, what you're asking them to do in their work is focus on the full question forms, and yet in the tape they're using a . . .
T: . . . Wasn't, yeah. So, I suppose it's recognizing one question form by the intonation, then being able to transfer it into the proper question "Do you drink?" rather than "Drink?" I mean, that would be good to spend a lot more time on at another point. But

it seemed like it was good to bring up there. Just to transfer the information.

Here is another example of classroom interaction which makes little sense within the immediate context of the lesson in which it occurs, but which can be justified within the broader context of the course and the teacher's overall goals and objectives. I asked whether the principal objectives of the lesson – listening to authentic texts for key information – might have been subverted by the secondary aim of introducing and practicing question forms. The teacher, however, was quite comfortable with this.

DN: I'm wondering if it's too heavy a load to have the twin aims, the listening for key information aim and also the focus on questions aims – whether it's better to separate those out and look at the questions in a separate lesson?

T: What, the question forms. . . . Well when I first looked at the material, I thought it was quite a straightforward listening, so therefore if I give them a split listening, it'll make it more challenging for them. I took the decision to do that and I don't regret that. I mean, question forms are always difficult things to do, they're always difficult to slot in unless you do a whole lesson on question forms so to throw them in now and again like that is quite valid – so to give the both focuses I thought was fine.

She was able to vindicate this stance by pointing out that:

I did anticipate that they would have a lot of problems with question forming, and their intonation and their spelling and things just need huge amounts of work on. But as regards the activities, I didn't feel they were beyond their capabilities at all. I think they achieved quite a lot. I mean initially looking at it you think, "Oh God, there's so much there." But they did actually succeed in filling the whole thing out.

Not all direct instruction was concerned with pronunciation, grammar, and vocabulary. Several teachers provided input on language skills and learning strategies, such as the following:

Remember how we've been talking about the importance of looking at the heading and the pictures and some of the big writing to guess what the article's about? So what sort of idea could you get from just, not reading the small writing but just looking at the pictures and seeing the heading?

Another teacher took a similar perspective, focusing on strategies for dealing with unknown vocabulary.

[B]efore we start to read the article I'd like to help you with some vocabulary, and I've got a special activity that will help you to guess and learn the vocabulary that you need to know in order to do the article, to understand the article.

Despite the range and diversity of contexts which gave rise to them, and regardless of the skills of the teachers and proficiency levels of the learners, these pieces of discourse all illustrate the central theme of this piece: that the universe in which a particular discourse is constructed is a collaborative achievement of the actors who inhabit that universe.

Discussion

In this section, I shall draw out some of the substantive and methodological issues which emerged during the course of the study.

On the substance of the study

As I struggled with the wide variety of teachers, learners, course types, and contexts contributing data to this study, and as I ran and reran the data through the filter of my own prejudices and experiences, an important insight began to emerge. Despite the variety of teaching styles, learner types, and course objectives, at a certain level of abstraction, all of these classes have one thing in common: They all illuminate an experiential view of the educational process. This experiential view is contrasted with traditional education by Kohonen (1992) in a key position paper on experiential language learning. The traditional view of knowledge is seen as objective and factual and separated from the knower, while the experiential view sees knowledge as tentative, subjective, and intimately tied to the knower. Kohonen also contrasts the problem-solving approach of traditional pedagogy with the problem-posing approach of experiential learning. While traditional education is teacher-directed, with a focus on the acquisition of knowledge, the experiential approach values the contributions which learners make to the learning process. It is active and dynamic and focuses on the development of skills rather than on the acquisition of factual knowledge.

This constructive and interpretative concept of education is reflected in the extracts presented here. They show that both teachers and learners are actively involved in the construction and interpretation of their worlds. In addition, the interpretations of the teachers are central to the understanding of these worlds. The logical next step to pursue is to involve learners themselves in the interpretation of the pedagogic worlds they inhabit. In Kohonen's words, the experiential model offers potential for a learning atmosphere of shared partnership, a common purpose and a joint management of learning. Class behavior is owned by the whole group, of which the teacher is but one member. As the rules of conduct are agreed upon jointly, all share the responsibility for decisions and discipline. (ibid.: 31)

In retrospect, the image which endures in my own mind is one of teachers and learners collaboratively constructing and inhabiting their own worlds. In this co-construction, the "official" curriculum, which resides within the mandated documents, lesson plans, commercial textbooks, and bureaucratic directives to teachers and learners, is transformed, sometimes radically, in the experiential and ongoing interactions between the active participants in the classroom drama. In this drama, I am an outsider, a shadowy figure inhabiting a world which is neither connected to the ongoing drama, nor entirely divorced from it. As such, I have a voice, but it is only a partial one. It is a voice which needs to be complemented by the other, oftentimes, hidden voices of the classroom, if anything like a three-dimensional picture of what drives the learning process is to emerge.

On methodological issues in language teaching research

The procedure used in this study was designed to give a voice to the teachers whose work was being investigated. At the conclusion of the lesson, teachers were provided with an opportunity to comment on what had happened, what unexpected events had arisen during the course of instruction, and what they felt had been the outcomes of the class. When the lessons had been transcribed, the teachers were provided with transcripts and given a further opportunity to comment on the lesson.

All of the teachers who took part in the study talked about the data collection procedure itself. Most also pointed out that the objective record of the lesson revealed many things which had not been apparent to them during the ongoing pedagogic action. The following examples illuminate their concerns:

Rather a wordy explanation now that I see it in black and white.

Maybe I should have got on to the vocabulary activity earlier instead of spending so much time talking in rather vague terms about the article first.

Quite a complicated explanation. Maybe a demonstration would have been simpler.

I ask a lot of questions without waiting for students to answer them.

I find difficulty in controlling the level of my language when talking *about* the target structure or function at this level.

53

In retrospect, maybe it would have been better to have them do something oral here and delay the writing.

In retrospect I realize it would have been more useful to get students to summarize by feeding back to the class, rather than concluding the lesson with a lengthy monologue.

It is clear from these comments that collaborative research not only provides insights into what happens as teachers and learners work together, but also acts as a device through which teachers can reflect upon their work and grow professionally as a result of that reflection. In this way theory, research, and practice are bound together and become mutually reinforcing.

In the preface to my book on research methods (Nunan 1992: xi–xiii), I suggested that two alternative conceptions of the nature of research provide a point of tension within the book. The first view is that external truths exist "out there" somewhere. According to this view, the function of research is to uncover these truths. The second view is that truth is a negotiable commodity contingent upon the historical context within which phenomena are observed and interpreted.

This study adheres unashamedly to the second conception of research just outlined. I would like to argue that qualitative and interpretive studies of teaching and learning, such as this, provide an alternative view of language classrooms to those accounts which emerge from the psycho-statistical research paradigm. In the field of general education, Stenhouse (1983) was able to argue that by the end of the 1970s, the illuminative tradition "now seems to have got off the ground both in research and evaluation. It no longer needs to fight to establish itself as an alternative to the 'psycho-statistical' paradigm worthy of consideration" (p. 1).

Things are rather different in the field of second language education. Recently I reviewed fifty widely reported pieces of classroom-oriented research. Of the fifty, I found that only fifteen were carried out in classrooms which were constituted for language teaching purposes. A further seven collected data from mixed environments. The majority of the studies ($n = 28$) are based on data collected outside the classroom in laboratory ($n = 20$), simulated ($n = 6$), and naturalistic ($n = 2$) environments. I concluded from this study that future researchers would benefit from the informed incorporation of five key points into their designs and the execution of their studies.

1. The implementation of more contextualized research – that is, classroom-based, as opposed to classroom-oriented, research.
2. An extension of the theoretical bases of research agendas.
3. An extension of the range of research tools, techniques, and meth-

ods, adopting and adapting these where appropriate from content classroom research.

4. A reevaluation of the distinction between process-oriented and product-oriented research.
5. A more active role for classroom practitioners in applied research.

(Nunan 1991: 249–274)

I believe that the study described here goes some way toward incorporating at least some of these points into its design.

Conclusion

In this chapter I have presented, through the discourse of teachers and learners, an insider's view of language instruction. It is now time to return to the point where I began and the question around which this entire enterprise revolves: In what ways are the processes of classroom instruction illuminated by the voices of the teachers? I hope I have ably demonstrated through the discourse of the classroom that to understand what is going on in language classrooms the voices of the teachers (and ultimately of the learners as well) must be heard. Classroom research, therefore, must become a collaborative enterprise between researcher, teacher, and learner. In the words of another contributor to this volume:

Questions of what teaching is and what people know in order to teach are absolutely central; to avoid them is folly for everyone concerned with education. When these questions are ignored, the immediate, daily, and intimate knowledge of teachers and learners is belittled because it is overlooked and trivialized. . . . The findings of researchers and others concerned with understanding education ought to be viewed with legitimate skepticism if these people do not seriously entertain this central issue of what teaching is and of what people know in order to do it. (Freeman, this volume)

References

Freeman, D. (Chapter 4, this volume). Redefining the relationship between research and what teachers know.

Gebhard, J., and A. Ueda-Motonaga. 1992. The power of observation. In D. Nunan (ed.), *Collaborative Language Learning and Teaching*. Cambridge: Cambridge University Press.

Kohonen, V. 1992. Experiential language learning: Second language learning as cooperative learner education. In D. Nunan (ed.), *Collaborative Language Learning and Teaching*. Cambridge: Cambridge University Press.

Nunan, D. 1991. Methodological issues in classroom research. *Studies in Second Language Acquisition, 13*, 2, 249–274.

1992. *Research Methods in Language Learning.* New York: Cambridge University Press.

Stenhouse, L. 1983. The problems of standards in illuminative research. In L. Bartlett, S. Kemmis, and G. Gillard (eds.), *Perspectives on Case Study.* Geelong, Australia: Deakin University Press.

Wright, T. 1992. L2 classroom research and L2 teacher education: Towards a collaborative approach. In J. Flowerdew, M. Brock, and S. Hsia (eds.), *Perspectives on Second Language Teacher Education.* Hong Kong: City Polytechnic of Hong Kong.

3 Teaching style: a way to understand instruction in language classrooms

Anne Katz

> Most discovery, ultimately, is a process
> of explaining the known.
> > (Tannen 1984: 38)

The professional journals of those who teach writing to both native and non-native users of English have expounded the efficacy of a variety of instructional techniques. In recent years, for example, teachers have been encouraged to teach about the writing process, conduct writing conferences with their students, and focus on meaning rather than form in responding to student papers. As with most educational innovations, these calls for change focus primarily on describing the innovations and their apparent benefits with little mention of how these innovations might be implemented within an existing educational context. This chapter takes a closer look at how teachers implement many of these same innovations in writing classes. It describes the interaction between teachers and university students as students are engaged in learning how to improve their writing skills in a second language.

Traditional descriptions of classroom teaching within the second language field have used such constructs as "approach," "method," and "technique" to define specific features of different methodologies that have come in and out of language teaching fashion (Anthony 1963). Richards and Rodgers (1982) provide a well-known example of such a classification scheme. They analyze method in terms of "approach," "design," and "procedure." Approach designates both a method's theory of the nature of language and its theory of the nature of language learning. Design includes a definition of linguistic content, specifications for the selection and organization of that content, and a specification of the role of learners, teachers, and materials. Procedure encompasses the techniques utilized in the classroom. It is at the level of technique, the authors theorize, that "differences in approach and design are likely to manifest themselves" in terms of "different types of activities and exercise in materials and in the classroom and in different uses for particular exercise types" (p. 163), thus illustrating similarities and differences between methods.

The goal of Richards and Rodgers' typology was to provide information to help practitioners determine which method to adopt in the classroom. Although such classification schemes are of value for comparing different language teaching philosophies and theoretical premises that form the basis for different methodologies, they suffer from two major flaws that make them inappropriate for understanding what really occurs in classrooms.

First, such typologies provide programmatic descriptions of what *ought* to be found in classrooms. These descriptions are generated by an analysis of methodological statements (e.g., Richards and Rodgers' [1986] comparison of Total Physical Response and Community Language Learning). Whether or not teachers exhibit any, some, or all of these behaviors cannot be ascertained a priori from such analyses. In addition, these typologies assume that the teacher acts as a cipher, an instrument who will apply "techniques" in some uniform and unobtrusive way. However, the data collected in this study show that teaching style – encompassing teacher beliefs, goals, interpretations of syllabi, and knowledge of content material – affects the way techniques and procedures are applied in the classroom, even when the teachers sampled have all been designated "good" teachers.

Allwright (1983), in his historical review of classroom-centered research on language teaching, points out that the focus of researchers on differences at the technique level reflected a response to the general inability of research to discover more macro-level differences that affected language learning outcomes. Yet he argues that even "small-scale research at the level of technique" failed to provide evidence to differentiate the effectiveness of different methods in order to support prescriptions for teacher training.

In order to find ways to describe classroom differences, Allwright charts the retreat from prescription to description and from a focus on technique to a focus on classroom processes. Within a process framework, the language lesson has been viewed as *"a socially constructed event,* as something that is the product of the interactive work of all the people present"* (ibid.: 196). Analyses grounded in this perspective are based on what participants in the classroom *do* to create the instructional context. A major factor contributing to this context is the teacher's style, defined as the manner in which the teacher interprets his or her role within the context of the classroom, for the teacher occupies a pivotal role in creating the culture of the classroom. As Michaels (1985: 79) observes in her study of the impact of microcomputers on student writing, "[O]ne must first understand the classroom itself as a complex learning environment in which the teacher is a key determinant of social organization and students' access to knowledge." The main premise for both Michaels' work and the present study holds that knowledge is socially organized, formed and shaped by the participants in the exchange and by the context in which the exchange takes place. One way to look at four different classrooms, then, is to analyze how teachers create these learning environments.

Setting

This study was set at a large, urban state university in the United States, which serves a large and diverse student population (26,000 students at the time of the study). All the undergraduate students, like students at other U.S. campuses, must fulfill written English requirements in order to graduate. Native speakers of English can fulfill these requirements by taking a freshman English class and a sophomore English class, and by passing, when they are juniors, an English proficiency essay test. Non-native speakers of English have another option; they may enroll in ESL courses to meet the written English requirements. There are four courses in the sequence of ESL courses. Students are placed into classes by scores on an ESL placement test. Progression through the sequence of classes in order to satisfy the written English requirements depends on "satisfactory performance" in each class along the way.

The largest number of ESL students (about 40 percent) is enrolled in English 310 classes, the course in the sequence that may substitute for the required sophomore English class. These classes also serve as the first formal introduction to the basic tenets of longer discourse, writing ranging in length from several paragraphs to entire essays. These assignments are designed to prepare students for the academic writing required in their university content classes. The focus, then, is on academic preparation, helping students to write discourse such as answers to essay questions and summaries of expository texts. Both the number of students enrolled at this level and its status as the first writing class in the sequence of courses offered influenced my decision to observe and analyze classes at this level.

Students

On the average, there are twenty-five students enrolled in each ESL composition class at this university. A survey conducted by the ESL section of the English department found that ESL students came from a wide variety of backgrounds. Forty-three different native languages were represented, ranging from Amharic to Yoruba. The distribution of students within these languages, however, presents a different picture. Five languages represent about 70 percent of the students. The largest concentration of students (37 percent) reported Chinese as their native language. The next largest group (12 percent) were speakers of Indonesian. Arabic speakers were 8 percent, and Spanish and Farsi speakers were each 6 percent. An analysis of the visa status of students reported in the survey shows that 13 percent were U.S. citizens, 50 percent were permanent residents, and only 37 percent had a foreign student visa or some other visa.

Teachers

From among the English 310 teachers, four (three women and one man) were selected on the basis of three criteria: (a) interest in participating in the study, (b) recognized excellence of teaching, and (c) teaching style. Ratings of excellent performance were based on student evaluations and staff observations. In the discussion that follows, these teachers are referred to as Meg, Sara, Ron, and Karen (pseudonyms).

Teaching style was determined in two ways. Initially, teachers were categorized on the basis of evaluations made by the course coordinator at the university. She observes all of the teachers regularly and, thus, has made informal, holistic judgments about teaching style among the instructors. After I began classroom observations, audio-taping of conference interaction, and teacher interviews, teaching style was defined more closely in terms of specific behaviors.

Data for analysis

The teacher portraits illustrating teaching style are based on data from the following sources:

1. Two audio-recorded, formal interviews with each teacher, one at the beginning of the semester and one at the end.
2. My journal notes collected informally over the course of the semester.
3. Classroom observations over the course of the semester (two weeks at the beginning of the semester, one in the middle, and one at the end), averaging eleven hours per teacher.

The classroom observations were documented via extensive fieldnotes and audio recordings, which were later transcribed. The teachers also provided copies of all the material they distributed throughout the semester. While the data base does not include teachers' responses to the analyses, such data would be useful to include in future research in this area. Owing to space limitations, excerpts from the data used in the following analyses have been shortened. To examine longer excerpts, see Katz (1988).

Teaching style

In this study, teaching style serves as the point of comparison among the four teachers. Ideally, points of comparison should be clearly defined in order to permit systematic analysis of the data. Teaching style, however, is a slippery construct. Defining it is akin to explaining either the "art" or "science" of teaching itself. Do we perceive teaching style as the result or the cause of classroom behaviors? Is it primarily connected to teacher beliefs or to teacher actions? In this chapter, to capture the complexity of the construct, the definition of teaching style encompasses both behavior and beliefs.

All teachers engage in similar activities – for example, transmitting information, beginning and ending classes, asking questions, answering them, telling stories, and assigning work. A particular teaching style emerges as that set of behaviors is arranged into varying patterns, creating distinctive learning environments for students. Teaching style may be seen as similar to Hymes' (1977) description of speech style. Rather than defining style as a separate linguistic unit, Hymes points out that style "is more a configuration than a level" (p. 168). Specific styles result from proportion and frequency of occurrence, as well as the presence or absence of contrasting units. In a similar manner, then, the "configuration" of teacher behaviors contributes to a particular teaching style.

To compare the four teachers in this study, I've chosen a set of teacher activities as well as illustrative segments of teacher talk about what they do. Tables 1 and 2 present a set of common classroom events across teachers. By examining these tables, we can discover the similarities and differences across teachers as they engage in shaping their writing classrooms. The portraits that follow combine an analysis of these behaviors with excerpts from teacher interviews as we talked about their goals and beliefs about writing and teaching, discussing specific aspects of what occurred in their classrooms.

The key argument in this chapter is that the manner in which teachers interpret their roles within the context of the classroom affects the way methods, techniques, and procedures are applied in those classrooms. Thus, rather than focusing the talk about these classrooms in terms of methods, approaches, or techniques, or in terms of good versus bad teaching devices, I will describe each classroom in terms of teaching style.

Since teaching style is a construct not easily operationalized, I have chosen to use metaphor as my research tool, as a lens to focus on each classroom. Miles and Huberman (1984) suggest that metaphor offers the researcher two important qualities: (a) Metaphor can reduce data by taking a number of particulars and making a generalization; and (b) it also can create a pattern, pulling together separate bits of information. Through these two qualities, metaphor acts as a heuristic for capturing the essence of each teacher's style.

While the advantages of the metaphor's pattern-making characteristic

TABLE I CLASSROOM EVENTS: SETTING THE SCENE

	Class openings	*Late policy*	*Taking roll*	*Teacher's use of space*	*Quizzes*
Meg	Takes roll, closes door; no latecomers may enter	No late arrivals; includes "tardiness policy" in course description	Takes roll at beginning of class by calling students' names	Moves throughout the room	No
Sara	Asks "How are you?/How was your weekend?"	Lenient	Takes roll by passing around sign-in sheet	Moves throughout the room	No
Ron	First two weeks: starts with class business – roll call, passing papers, review of previous class; later: song assignment by individual students	Ten-minute leeway; after that, no late arrivals	Takes roll at beginning of class by calling students' names	Stands in front and moves throughout the room	No
Karen	Starts with class business – giving assignment, returning papers, talking about homework	Lenient	Takes roll from collected homework; strict policy – drops grade one-third for 3+ absences	Stands mostly in front of the room	Yes

for researchers are self-evident, using metaphors also carries the danger of shaping perceptions rather than clarifying them. I would argue that this study avoids this pitfall for several reasons: (a) The metaphors emerged over the course of time (the semester of observation), only becoming fully developed at the end of this period of data collection and analysis; (b) as well, the decision to use metaphor as a research tool was made well after data collection was underway as a means of

TABLE 2 CLASSROOM DISCOURSE: MOVING THE ACTION ALONG

	Dominant structure of talk in classes	Turn selection	Use of narratives	Use of rhetorical questions
Meg	Question-answer sequences	Addresses questions to class and specific students; makes sure all students are involved	Very few; emerge late in semester / Stories about self / To provoke laughter; provide brief example to illustrate teaching point	Rarely uses them since questions are usually answered by the class or individual students
Sara	Lecture / Group work	Addresses questions primarily to the class; avoids "embarrassing" students	Very few; found in beginning; fewer later on / Stories about self/family / To establish camaraderie; provide brief example to illustrate teaching point	Found interspersed within lectures to the class
Ron	Song assignment / Lecture / Question-answer sequences	Addresses questions to a variety of individual students and to the class	Frequent / Stories about self/others / To present information; provide context; provide extended example to illustrate teaching point, establish camaraderie	Rarely uses them since questions are usually answered by the class or individual students
Karen	Lecture	Addresses questions to the class	Very few / Stories about self / To provide brief example to illustrate teaching point	Found frequently in lectures to the class

dealing with the nature of the data uncovered; (c) the metaphors evolved not only from observing teacher activities but also from listening to teachers' own voices as they talked about their role in the writing classroom. Thus, while the teachers did not consciously nominate specific metaphors to characterize their teaching styles, their talk about the issues involved in teaching varied in patterned ways consonant with the behaviors observed in the classroom and with the metaphors chosen to illuminate those activities.

The following sections present portraits of the four teachers, using the metaphors of the choreographer, the earth mother, the entertainer, and the professor to characterize each teaching style. The format of each section is similar. I begin by defining the metaphor, as it emerged from the talk of each teacher, and then present what happened in the classroom.

Meg: the choreographer

According to the American Heritage dictionary, a choreographer is "one who creates, arranges, or directs dances for stage performances" (Morris 1976: 238). The focal point of this metaphor is control at a distance: The choreographer acts as both source and arranger of the material others will work with.

Certainly these two characteristics are evident in Meg's classroom. In fact, she herself supplies the metaphor in the first formal interview of the semester. In explaining why she stresses class attendance, she states, "I just like them [the students] to be in class 'cause my classes are really tight and they're usually *orchestrated* or *choreographed* in a way, for a purpose, and so if they miss, they'll be sure not to do very well on the writing assignment." The theme of direction, of carefully structuring and arranging instruction, returns again and again throughout Meg's interviews as she discusses the skills she is trying to teach, the topics she assigns, the activities she schedules, and the question-answer sequences she designs for involving students in generating the content of the class.

Responding to questions on the structure of the course and the sequence of topics she chose, Meg explained that paper topics were tied to the skills she was trying to teach: "I tried to think of topics and ones that I've used that lent themselves to teaching those skills, and ones that interest the student." Her course, then, was planned so that skills were recycled over the semester.

Those things [were] reiterated for each assignment and how in this particular assignment would you do, would you "show." What kind of transition device or what kinds of cohesive devices could you use to make it easier for your reader to follow your opinions and to realize that you're presenting support here or that you're presenting a new idea or that you are going to present a contrasting idea here.

Meg also explained that she carefully designed her class activities to lead students to developing their writing skills.

I understand now more the different writing tasks that they're supposed to be able to accomplish by the end of the semester in 310. I understand more what's going to be a problem . . . inherent in the task itself now after teaching the course for a while, so I try to prep them for that a lot better and to try to build activities that will help them go through those learning steps so that it's not "Do the assignment and then remedy it with several new revisions or several new drafts afterwards."

One of the more remarkable characteristics of Meg's classroom is her use of apparently carefully crafted sequences of questions and answers. Within these sequences, Meg elicits from and transmits to students the material for each lesson. When asked how she sets up these sequences and chooses students, she answered:

So certain students I know had a little bit more highly developed, you know, sort of introspective, or senses or introspection and analytical powers. And inductive stuff, too. So I know that I could ask them maybe a more abstract, a little more difficult question. And other students I would really try to create a lot more, or facilitate more, in my wording of my questions so that they had something more tangible, that's more visual image or something like that, that they could latch on to . . .

This attention to the structuring of tasks carries over to the development of teaching materials. For example, to help students prepare their writing assignments, Meg designed checklists for students to use in looking over their papers. These sheets acted as graphic representations of what she was looking for in each paper. Meg assumes that the information in the assigned writing textbook is not always accessible to her students. So rather than use that text, Meg distributes materials from her own "book," several sheets (copied on a duplicator) at each session. Table 3 provides a comparative look at teacher-made materials utilized across the semester. Meg has the most (thirty-six) of the four teachers compared. Echoing her argument for why students should attend class, Meg feels that her teacher-based materials are important for students, enabling them to complete the tasks she sets up for them.

Meg's explanations of what she does in class may not seem remarkably different from what any "good" teacher plans to do in a language classroom. It is not, however, the mere presence of these characteristics in her talk that promotes the metaphor of "choreographer." Rather, it is suggested through the frequency with which the attending images of

TABLE 3   TEACHER HANDOUTS

	Total	Course intro- duction	Essay assign- ment	Text examples	Check- lists	Sen- tence level	Rheto- rical level	Quizzes
Meg	36	3		7	5	9	12	
Sara	28	2	1	3	2	6	14	
Ron	29	2	2	24				
Karen	18	3	1	5	3	2	2	2

structuring and arranging appear in her discussion of her instructional aims.

If we look at what goes on in the classroom, we can see how the metaphor actually plays out. In the first weeks of class, as both teacher and students are assessing each other, Meg clearly lays the ground rules for behavior in her classroom. She has a firm policy about absences and lateness and so takes roll at the beginning of class. Once finished, she closes the door and no more students may enter the classroom.

Students are asked to sit in the same place each time so she can re-member where they are and so learn their names more quickly. When she collects the first sets of writing assignments, she rejects a few that have not been prepared according to one of her specifications – they aren't stapled. She informs those erring students where they can find a stapler and reminds them they can put the papers in her mailbox with-out any penalty as long as they do so by a certain hour in the after-noon.

As she goes through extensive question-answer sequences, she calls on individual students, at times using the roll book, at times relying on nonverbal cues (e.g., a nod of her head). The pacing seems quick relative to the other teachers; she talks rapidly, and the discussion moves to all parts of the room as she selects students to participate in the lesson.

Meg's class meets twice a week for one hour and fifteen minutes. The blocking of classroom interaction varies over the course of each session. Table 4 shows the distribution of class time in terms of interactional groupings: teacher to class; small, student-run groups; and individual work. The distribution shows movement among these three kinds of classroom interaction. This variation in kinds of interactional groupings in the classroom provides evidence of the careful structuring of activities described by Meg in the interviews as a strategy for, as she put it, "prepping them [the students] for an assignment."

Again, while all teachers plan varied activities, it is the degree of structuring that conjures up the metaphor used in this portrait. This

TABLE 4   INTERACTIONAL GROUPINGS

	Meg	Sara	Ron	Karen
TC	*79.1	*64.0	*65.3	*79.7
Ind	11.4	2.2	6.0	6.5
Grp	9.5	*28.7	9.0	13.8
Ss		5.1	3.3	
SC			*16.4	

Figures indicate percent of class time. An asterisk indicates the dominant interactional grouping(s).

  TC: teacher-to-class interaction
  Ind: individual work (freewriting, exercises)
  Grp: group interaction
  Ss: student-to-class interaction in which students assume brief control of the class (introductions, name games)
  SC: student-to-class interaction in which one student takes charge of the class for an extended period of time

degree will become more apparent in the activity described herein and as other teachers in this study are described.

As a primary example of the degree of structuring involved in Meg's planning of instruction, let's look at the question-answer sequences that constitute the major activity during teacher-class interaction. As Table 4 shows, teacher-class interaction takes up an average of 79 percent of class time. Teacher-class interaction may assume many forms: It may consist of the teacher's lecturing to students who, presumably, take in and process the information they receive; students may respond as a class or individually, spontaneously or at the behest of the teacher. In the case of Meg's classroom, a majority of the teacher-class interaction consists of extended question-answer sequences involving, over the class period, all of the students.

This extensive use of questions to elicit the major points of Meg's daily lesson increases apparent student involvement in the structuring of the class since student talk, in the form of answers, helps to create the content of the lesson. Yet this strategy also allows the teacher to retain control over both the content and the direction of talk. It is the teacher who chooses the topic for these instructional "conversations" and, as Phillips (1972: 377) observes, "it is the teacher who determines whether she talks to one or to all, receives responses individually or in chorus, and voluntarily or without choice."

The following dialogue occurs in the middle of the semester. Students have returned to a teacher-class format after spending twenty-five minutes in groups discussing a handout filled with questions about two essays written by students from a previous semester, which they were to have read. Each essay addresses the same topic – how someone else's use of stereotypes affected that student. In groups, then, students have been analyzing each paper and comparing them, guided by the discussion questions on the handout. The return to a teacher-class format is designed to allow students to "share" the fruits of their labors in groups. The teacher has started the exchange by asking the class in general if there was anything in particular anybody liked about the first essay they were to discuss. The class is quiet but attentive, carefully watching as Meg moves around the room. A student answers that there were a lot of details.

T: Anybody else in the room, is there anything else you liked about the paper except for the fact that it had a lot of details?
S1: The title.
T: You liked the title? Okay [some laughter in class] why did you like the title?
S1: It is short and it impress the reader.
T: Okay. It got your interest. It was short. Okay. I agree. It's a pretty clever title. I mean, when I saw that title, "No, I'm Not a Buddhist," um, it got my attention.

After a discussion of the essay's pluses and minuses, the teacher begins to focus the students' attention on particular bits of information conveyed in the essay.

T: So, how did this stereotype affect her, [S1]? How does this stereotype that her friends all have that, uh, a vegetarian must be a Buddhist or a Taoist, how does that affect her life? Where does she first tell us how it affects her?
S1: Um, there's a xxx=[1]
T: =Why don't you read, where is that sentence located where she tells us?
S1: [Reading] "Because of these stereotypes, I am bothered by people with religious curiosity, and I am looked at and treated differently by my Chinese friends."
T: Okay. Good. And so it's at the bottom, it's at the end of the first

1 The following transcription conventions are used:
= stands for latching (i.e., cases when there is no pause and no overlap between turns)
/ /   / /   stands for overlap
/   /   is used when one speaker interrupts the turn of another speaker without taking a turn, generally back-channel cues

paragraph where she tells us the specific effects of the stereotype on her."

Meg continues to elicit information about the essay in a series of questions that Heath (1978) has termed *topic focusers*, ways of getting others (in this case, students) to direct attention to a topic of immediate concern to the questioner (here, Meg). The following are additional examples from Meg's lesson:

"How does it (the topic sentence of paragraph three) relate to paragraph two?"
"How does she tie this paragraph back to paragraph two?"
"That word *besides*, what kind of relationship is it showing?"
"Did any of you have a chance to summarize the conclusion?"
"What was the purpose of that conclusion?"

These questions ask for information designated by the teacher as of immediate concern to her agenda for the lesson.

The following dialogue is an excerpt from the next class. The formal opening routines are over; students have done a brief, focused free-writing on the characteristics of weak essays. Meg has moved into the central block of teacher-class interaction, which constitutes the day's lesson on essay structure, still drawing on the previous class's discussion of the essays about stereotypes. She is at the board, noting down students' responses into a grid of information for them to record in their notebooks.

T: Come on. What makes a paper interesting?
S1: Examples.
T: Examples. Okay. [T writes *examples* on the board.] Examples. Anything else?
S2: Comparisons.
T: Okay. Comparisons. All right, if it's appropriate, okay. Comparisons. [T writes *comparisons* on the board.]
S3: Fluency [spoken very softly].
T: Mmm?
S3: Fluency.
T: Fluency, okay. What do you mean by that?
S3: Well, uh, transitions xxx.
T: Okay, uh, uh, transitions, okay, yeah. Remember the Chinese vegetarian one, "No, I'm not a Buddhist"? Very choppy, difficult to read? Transitions, joining of ideas. Any last minute things people want to add to the list here?
S4: Cohesiveness.
T: Okay, good, cohesiveness. Want to repeat what that is [S4]?
S4: I think, just sticking to the topic. Cohesiveness xxxx

Meg continues with this question-answer strategy, eliciting additional features of text that help to make essays interesting, organized, and effective. She then bridges into a brief discussion of the purpose of writing itself. Here Meg is essentially retrieving information she has already disseminated in earlier classes. Her questioning, then, serves a dual purpose. First, it gets the students to take an active role in constructing the lesson by providing the content of the lesson. Second, as Meg noted in our second interview, she can recycle topics previously introduced in different rhetorical contexts, thus reinforcing the skills she wishes to teach. Both goals, however, are achieved by Meg's careful structuring of the questions.

The following dialogue takes place about a half hour later.

T: Once again, somebody, just to make sure everybody knows what a stereotype is, uh, let's see, oh, [S1], what is a stereotype?

S1: It's a, it's a cloud, actually/

T: /a cloud?/

S: It's a cloud that's affecting you indirectly. It's an image.

T: It's an image, it's an image? Okay. An image. Another word for an image is, what? If you have an image of someone?

S2: An idea?

T: Could be an idea, a picture. Okay. Now, if somebody didn't know what a stereotype was, I don't know that they'd really know from this definition, exactly. Okay. What else about a stereotype? It's an image or an idea about what?

S3: About a particular group.

T: A particular group, okay. It's not only negative, but I think they tend to be more negative than positive. But they're not always. Okay. Uh, so it's, an idea, a general idea that people have about a group. Okay. Um, they do see it as harmful because it's saying that everybody in that group is that way. Okay. Or that there are certain ways, you know, we see people, or we expect them to be a particular way just 'cause they're a member of a certain group.

S4: [Asks a question that is unclear]

T: Traditions? Um, well, sometimes people get, where do stereotypes come from?

S5: Cultural.

T: Often, culture. What else? How do we get stereotypes? Those of you who are recently come over here, I'm sure you probably had some ideas about what [the city] would be like, or what Americans would be like? Okay. Where did you get those ideas?

S6: People.

T: People, how else?

S7: News.

T: The news, how else?

S8:   Movies.

T: Movies, right, the media. TV movies, you know, don't always give
      the clearest picture of what, you know, life is like in the U.S. Or
      what Americans are like. All right, so they're ideas that we have
      based on limited knowledge, you know, as fallen out information
      usually. Is there truth to stereotypes?

S9:   No

S10: Some.

T: Sometimes. Sometimes there is a little bit, but, uh, they usually
      begin, you know, we make a general idea about people to struc-
      ture our perceptions. But where they become to be harmful is if
      we say "everybody is that way" and we are not open minded.

In this excerpt, Meg's questions are after new information, the definition of the term *stereotype*, which is a key concept in the essay students have just been assigned. Her questions ask them to supply bits of
information about the concept of stereotype that she then expands upon
during her conversational turn.

Like other teachers, Meg utilizes a variety of strategies to assist her
students in learning the content of her class: She employs class opening
routines to focus students' attention on the day's business, she creates
materials to guide them in learning course content, and she engages
them in carefully crafted question-and-answer sequences to ensure their
participation in classroom activities. Meg, however, employs these strategies in a pattern that reflects her own style of teaching. She essentially
directs what students learn, creating the material they study and
arranging it in what she has determined to be appropriate forms for
consumption. It is through this careful structuring that Meg "choreo-
graphs" each day's lesson in her semester's syllabus.

Sara: the earth mother

While the term *earth mother* isn't found in the American Heritage
dictionary, its prominence, particularly during the late 1960s and
1970s, has made it a familiar image in U.S. culture. The term conjures
up a picture of a nurturing female,[2] attuned to the primacy of human
relationships, using human relationships as a haven in stressful times.
In a classroom setting, the image emphasizes the role of affect in mediating the intellectual activities making up the business at hand. The
tool for ensuring successful relationships is communication among participants.

---

2 *Earth mother* is a nonsexist, nonpejorative term in popular usage.

71

In her second, end-of-the-semester interview, Sara evokes this earth mother metaphor with her focus on the importance of personal contact in mediating instruction. (In referring to conferencing, Sara [S] is describing a meeting between the teacher and a student to discuss the student's writing.) In the following transcript, "I" is the interviewer.

I: Do you think the students had a sense of responsibility about their writing? You know, something else that you talked about in the first interview?

S: Yes, and that has been more reinforced than anything this semester for me. I found that people who I've missed conferencing until late in the semester, I'm so sorry that I saw them late. Because I realized that they needed a little "Hi," you know, "I'm you're English teacher," you know. And I had three or four students who I saw at the end of the semester who I realized that if I had seen early in the semester would have done better work.

I: That kind of personal contact would have reinforced that sense of responsibility?

S: Absolutely, absolutely. I really believe that. And I do believe, I do believe that it works, I really do. I think that they suddenly are not anonymous in your class. You know where they come from, and exchange stories a little bit. Sometimes it's hard. I don't have too many Thailand stories, you know. [Laughter] But, and you connect with them and then there's this, maybe it's deceitful in a way, you know, it's sort of using the personal contact. But if it works, who cares? If it gets them to write and to like it and to improve, I guess, that is what's important.

Here Sara is explaining her strategy of using the personal relationships built up during conference as the basis for helping students acquire the writing skills she is teaching. Her claim that personal contact mediates the learning about writing belies the ostensive formal academic focus of a university writing class.

This theme of the primacy of personal relationships returns again and again in her talk. For example, in evaluating one of her students, she states, "But he's a good student. He's a good, participating student. He was right there with me and responsive and interested, I think, and he did fine." It is apparent also in her disappointment about the class's seeming inability to respond to her. After talking about her eagerness to look at the class evaluations and her firm belief that many of the students, as individuals, liked the class, she went on:

But as a group it just didn't happen for me . . . And I just don't feel it worked for them either. That is one of the major reasons that I was breaking them into groups so much. Because I would stand there and I would ask a

TABLE 5   INTERACTION GROUPINGS OVER THE COURSE OF THE
SEMESTER (PERCENT OF CLASS TIME)

		Early in semester		*Mid-semester*		*End of semester*
Meg	TC	77.50%	TC	77.5%	TC	84.0%
	Ind	15.75%	Ind	17.0%	Ind	8.5%
	Grp	6.75%	Grp	5.5%	Grp	7.5%
Sara	TC	68.3%	TC	59.3%	TC	56.0%
	Ind	3.7%				
	Grp	19.3%	Grp	40.7%	Grp	44.0%
	Ss	8.7%				
Ron	TC	83.0%	TC	43.50%	TC	56.0%
	Ind	3.0%	Ind	7.00%	Ind	12.0%
	Grp	3.0%	Grp	22.75%		
	Ss	7.0%				
	SC	4.0%	SC	26.75%	SC	32.0%
Karen	TC	90.9%	TC	60.0%	TC	68.5%
	Ind	2.0%	Ind	15.0%	Ind	12.5%
	Grp	8.0%	Grp	25.0%	Grp	11.5%
					Ind to	
					Grp	7.5%

TC: teacher-to-class interaction
Ind: individual work (freewriting, exercises)
Grp: group interaction
Ss: student-to-class interaction in which all or most students par-
     ticipate for a few minutes at a time (introductions, name games)
SC: student-to-class interaction in which one student takes charge
     of the class for an extended period of time

question and dead silence. And then I would tease them about it and then
there would still be dead silence. Usually that will loosen up a group enough,
you know. But it was one thing after another, one ploy after another to get
them going, and interested, and involved and it just didn't seem to happen.

A look at the distribution of class time according to interactional
groupings, as shown in Table 4, confirms Sara's assertion that group
work was an important component of class time. Overall, teacher-to-
class interaction comprised 64 percent of class time (as compared, for
example, to Meg's 79 percent). More interesting, the pattern of interaction seemed to change over the course of the semester. Table 5 high-

lights this pattern by condensing the twelve classes observed into three groups that reflect the three observation periods of classroom data collection: Group one consists of a cluster of seven classes at the beginning of the semester; group two is composed of three classes near the middle of the semester; and group three is made up of the last two classes observed at the end of the semester. As the table shows, teacher-to-class interaction declined from 68.3 percent to 56 percent of class time as Sara incorporated increased amounts of group and individual work into her syllabus.

Sara makes her "active participant" agenda clear to the students when, for example, she sets them up for group work in which they are to brainstorm for ideas as a pre-writing activity. In explaining how to work through the class assignment, she admonishes them to "help each other," to "share the idea(s)" so that each student contributes and receives help in these group information exchanges. Again, the assumption operating here seems to be that communication will lead to understanding.

Sara's choice of classroom activities also reflects an emphasis on personal contact central to her earth mother image. Sara begins the semester's business with a classroom exercise that allows her to make contact with each student. She writes a general statement on the board, "My mother is nice." Then, going around the room, she calls on each student to tell her and the class what is nice about his or her mother. As each student answers, Sara repeats and expands the answer. At the same time, she asks the student's name. As she goes around the room, calling on students, she adds general but evaluative comments such as "I'm hearing a lot of different ideas in this. We're hearing a lot of good things." The back-and-forth sequence of student comment and teacher response allows Sara to engage in personal communication with every student in the class. During this highly interactive part of the lesson, the students and the teacher laugh; occasionally, students even interpose comments of their own about what another student has said.

At the end, Sara talks about her own mother and then gets to the academic "point" of the lesson: What do students think about *nice* as an effective descriptor? Sara elicits other "empty" words from the students, such as *terrible, beautiful,* and *good,* writing each on the board. By the end of the lesson, she has made verbal contact with each student, exchanged personal information, and led this melange of communication activity to a lesson on choosing specific language.

As demonstrated before, Sara emphasizes communication among class members as well as between class members and herself. Besides having them do a great deal of work in pairs and in groups, she encourages students to exchange phone numbers so that they can develop class networks for relaying and sharing information. Working in a small classroom, crowded by rows of seats, she occasionally rearranges the chairs into one big circle so that learners can face one another. She tells the students that such a seating arrangement will facilitate communication.

The structure of the day's lesson also reflects an emphasis on facilitating interaction. Like all of the teachers, Sara takes roll, but she does not use roll call as an opener for the day's business. Instead, she sends around a sign-in sheet that students initial. Her class openings are fairly informal, with an emphasis on setting a friendly tone. When she arrives in the classroom, she chats briefly with students near the front or those waiting to have a word with her. When it's time to begin, she signals the opening of business with the formula, "How are you?" The prominence of this formula became apparent by its absence at the start of one class. In the second week of observation, Sara inadvertently omitted this opener, beginning instead with "What I'd like to do today . . ." Stopping herself in mid-phrase, she repaired the sequence, continuing with "How are you today?"

Her late policy, unlike Meg's, is lenient. She explained that she'd rather see students come late than not at all. Sara is convinced that in-class time is important, whatever quantity of it students are present for. She sees her task as trying to make it as painless as possible.

One of Sara's tools for easing students into her lessons is humor. In her classes, more than in any of the other three teachers' classes, laughter plays a prominent role in setting the mood. In fieldnotes taken on the first day of classroom observation, I reflected, "She invites laughter – not at students, but at some personal anecdote or an extension of meaning, a turn of phrase to what students have said."

Her humor assumes several forms. Her own ready laugh evokes from students easy laughter and grins in response. This laughter, along with comments, jokes, and asides, often punctuates her discourse with students. She may also use visual effects to elicit a response. For example, after reading a paragraph quickly to the class and then asking, "What do you think?" she pantomimed a yawn and the process of falling asleep as she waited for some volunteer to come forward with a response. The students laughed, relieving the tension set up by the teacher's initial question to the class.

Sara rarely calls on students in class, relying instead on volunteers to answer questions she addresses to the class as a whole. This is her strategy to avoid embarrassing students. She doesn't want students to feel uncomfortable by having to perform when they might not be up to the task set by the question. Sara conveys a sense of the "class as community" in her use of first person plural pronouns in discussing agendas for the class. For example, rather than announcing a completed plan for the final exam, Sara included the students in deciding on the date for the exam while she gave them the assignment for their last essay. Many of Sara's questions are designed to focus the class's attention on their level of participation or understanding. Her repertoire includes rhetorical response markers such as "OK?" "Right?" and "You with me?" without sufficient pause in her monologues for students to respond.

Sara feels another major task is to encourage students to share responsibility for what happens in the class. As she explained in the interview excerpt quoted earlier, this sense of responsibility is connected to the personal contact Sara encourages. She believes that when students have a one-to-one relationship with a teacher "who connects with them as a person," they develop a sense of responsibility about their work. Such a connection "makes them take it [students' writing] more seriously" because they begin to feel they really can become better writers.

Sara also recognizes that the degree of student preparation for her class affects what she does in class. For example, at the beginning of observation 10, Sara asks, "Did you do the freewriting? [Pause] Honestly." Some students reply that they have, and the number seems to be sufficient for Sara to proceed with her plan to break the class into small groups for an additional pre-writing activity utilizing the homework. At the end of class, she returns to the importance of preparation.

Depending on how well prepared you were for today's class, it probably was more or less interesting to you and more or less helpful for you. Because I think the more prepared you are for a class like this, the more helpful the group work is, and the more involved you are. I think it was fun today.

The last, but perhaps most pervasive, method for encouraging student participation is through her emphasis on group work, designed to encourage students to actively engage in working out the ideas for assignments and to exchange feedback on how effectively members of the class have performed assigned tasks. As shown in Table 5, group work increased proportionately over the course of the semester. The content of teacher-to-class interaction also seemed to change over the same period. At the beginning of the semester, Sara used the teacher-to-class interaction for the exposition of main lesson points. In these classes, teacher-to-class interaction introduced the point of the day's lesson, such as the need for specific details or the use of cohesive ties. As in Meg's classes, the pair work involved students working through exercises designed to allow them to practice the material being taught.

While teacher exposition of information during teacher-to-class interaction clearly continues throughout the semester, later classes seem to show a shift toward greater student involvement in constructing lessons. In these classes, teacher-to-class interaction is often used to guide the student interaction in groups so that larger and larger chunks of work are accomplished in group exercises as the teacher circulates around the room.

The interaction in the ninth class observed (during the middle period of observation) illuminates this shift. After the usual informal exchanges marking the beginning of class, Sara quickly guides the students into groups for a brainstorming activity. She outlines only what is needed for this first part of the day's activities. After eleven minutes of group work, she calls to the groups, "Let me tell you the next step." After a few minutes of exposition, she turns to the board to illustrate the next step and to provide additional specific examples of the assigned task. This period of teacher-to-class interaction lasts for nine minutes. Students then return to their groups for fifteen minutes to work on the new task. Sara moves from group to group, checking on students' progress, answering questions, helping them devise procedures to do the assigned activity. In the next five minutes of teacher-to-class interaction (which occurs near the very end of the class period), Sara gives the class the next step in the lesson, referring to the homework assignment she's written on the board. In the last five minutes of class, students return to their groups to continue to work together on the assignment.

In this class, Sara's role is fashioned more along the lines of a facilitator, providing information and procedures to guide students through the assigned material, for the most part, on their own. As already noted, Sara's language reflects a focus on checking student comprehension of the procedures she has just outlined. She encourages students to rely on themselves and each other for generating the material of the day's lesson, so that from this group interchange they develop a greater understanding of the processes needed to develop writing assignments from initial stages of general ideas to later stages of coherent, specific prose.

This pattern of teaching activities, teacher language, and participant structures that emerges over the course of a semester illustrates how Sara approaches and interprets her teaching tasks, making choices that differ not necessarily in kind but in degree from those of Meg. The result of these choices is a teaching style that creates a different environment for learning. Sara's role in the classroom, as earthmother, is to provide a nurturing ambiance in which her students' development can take place.

Ron: the entertainer

In an interview, Ron said, "[T]he last thing I did in 310 was tell a story." I asked what story he had told. Here is his response.

I was telling them about the relationship between [the] teacher and writing, and I said that a teacher can't really show you how to write, but I can show

how you can learn from your own writing. And that that's what you have to do, now that the course is over. You have to continue learning about writing, but now, it's up to you. So I told the story, an Indian story, from India, of a wise man who was so smart, he knew everything. And people would line up on Sundays in front of his hut and they would ask him for advice and they would ask him if they would have children or if they would have a husband. And to each question he would know the answer. And then there were these two boys in the village who were punks [young toughs]. And they wanted to trick the old man and humiliate him in front of everyone. So they got a chicken and they said, let's do this. Let's put it behind our back, like this. And we'll go to the wise man and say, "Is this a live chicken or a dead one?" And if he says the chicken is alive, we'll wring its neck and give it to him. And if he says it's dead, we throw the chicken in his face. So the day comes, Sunday, and there's a long line of people, and the boys finally come up to the old man and he looks at them very carefully. And they say, "Wise man, is this chicken behind our back alive or dead?" And he says, "The answer is in your hands." Now by telling a story like that, I can make a point better than if I stood in front of them and said, from now on you have to learn from your own writing. From now on it's in your hands. The story makes it memorable.

Turning to the dictionary again, we find that to entertain is "to hold the attention of; amuse." It is fair to argue that all teachers strive to hold the attention of their students so that they can teach them. To "hold the attention" of his students so that the main points of his lessons were, indeed, memorable, Ron used a variety of strategies that demonstrated a flair for dramatic action more consonant with the popular image of an entertainer.

One major component of this dramatic action is his skill as a successful raconteur. The stories entertain as well as inform his students. As Ron tells these stories, his face is serious – a "straight" delivery that seems to underscore the earnestness and the importance of what he's telling his students. He repeats key phrases and nods his head, lips pressed together, as he emphasizes a key point.

While all of the teachers in this study used anecdotes at some point, only Ron used narratives extensively, in terms of frequency, length, and function. Like others, he told anecdotes about himself. In the first class observed, he described a Chinese New Year dinner he had attended the night before. The point he shared with the class was that he had felt like a foreigner at that dinner, if only for that night, so he could empathize with their feelings of strangeness to U.S. culture.

Unlike the other teachers, however, Ron told short stories about other people as well. In that same first class, he gave a short history of an essay used for a class model leading to an assignment. He talked about the student who had written the essay, his life in New York, and the people he met there who figured prominently in the essay. In telling this story, Ron provided a context for the writing, illustrating vividly the impact of a real world on the creation of text.

Unlike the other teachers, Ron also told extended narratives, such as the one introducing this section of the chapter. These stories served to present key lesson points that might otherwise be addressed with more conventional teacher exposition. This function of Ron's stories contrasts with the ways Meg and Sara use anecdotes in their classrooms. For them, short narratives are the "extras" in a lesson plan, useful either for additional illustration to long exposition about grammatical or rhetorical lesson points, or for establishing rapport with their students. For Ron, his stories carry a greater functional load: They often *are* the main lesson point, with short bits of exposition serving to show how the story relates to the day's lesson.

Ron's interest in text units as a teaching device is apparent in Table 3. If we look at an analysis of Ron's materials, we can see that twenty-four out of twenty-nine of the handouts he used throughout the semester were samples of text. He used these pieces to explain and illustrate the content of the course, as well as to capture students' interest in the material.

Ron's narratives illustrate one aspect of his flair for incorporating drama into the classroom, an aspect, of necessity, that required thought and planning. However, some of the drama characteristic of this classroom derived from the impulsive nature of several of Ron's actions.

Classroom teachers exist in an institutional context. Here that context consists of, at the least, a section, a department, and a school. At the time of this study, Ron had been at this university for several years; thus he could be considered knowledgeable about the institutional context. At the end of the second month of the semester, he decided to reduce weekly class meetings from three to two, and to require student conferences with each student every other week. When the ESL coordinator heard about Ron's restructuring, she was aghast. While Ron "got away" with this independent restructuring move, unprecedented at this university, neither he nor others have repeated it.

In this instance, drama derives from both the radical nature of restructuring class time and the impulsiveness of the act. This impulsiveness seems characteristic of a nature that revels in the unexpected, the unplanned. For example, when asked if he had a set format for his conferences, Ron replied, "Well, if it were the same every time, it would be so boring I couldn't do it!" It is the unexpected nature of his conferences that appeals to Ron, that sets conferences apart from classes. He goes on to explain:

That's the kick about conferences. Every single one is different from the one before it. That's what makes them so different from classes. One class on

Monday in 310 and one class on Wednesday in 310 and one class on Friday. You know there's going to be a ballpark response to those. My response to those classes, the way I teach them, is going to be about the same.

This is not to say that Ron's classes always followed the same, pre-planned format that one might imagine. Owing to a sudden illness, Ron missed four classes in a row. Returning to the class, he decided to stage a "name game" in which the students sat in a circle and each succeeding student had to introduce all of the previous students in the circle. This activity, certainly not related to any writing lesson, took twenty minutes of the fifty-minute class period. In a post-class interview, Ron explained why he had decided to initiate this activity.

In this class, in this 310, I felt that I had, there was a moment where I was about to cease to be a person. In fact, when I walked into that classroom on Wednesday, I felt that they didn't even recognize me . . . So I felt, wow, I have really receded. I am not, you know, a presence any more. I don't have that authority bit, the authority you need. You've got to have that at least. I felt, God, I'm even in danger of losing that. So I had to go to the most personable level I could find. The only thing I could do at the moment was, memorizing everybody else's names.

This awareness of his audience's reactions reinforces the image of Ron as an entertainer. As well, because Ron feels that for writing to be real, there has to be a sense of exchange between real people, the "personable" is important in his writing classes. Sensing the danger of losing the "personable," then, he chose to restructure the day's activities in order to return to some level of personal interaction.

Perhaps the single activity most illustrative of Ron's flair for the dramatic is the song assignment. While it incorporates writing activities used by other teachers, such as revision, conferences, and freewriting, the structure is uniquely Ron's. It asks students to select a song they like and then write about it. However, that's not quite all they need to do.

The sequence, including preparation and presentation, went as follows. Students would select a song, write out the lyrics, and compose a short essay. Before presenting their work to the class, each student would have a conference with Ron to go over his or her work. The lyrics and the essay were typed and duplicated by each student, and, on the day of their "performance," distributed to classmates. Each day's "performer" assumed control of the class for this activity, moving from a row seat to stand at the front of the room. Each played a cassette tape of the song and then read the essay. In an activity echoing Ron's emphasis on the importance of the personal between reader and writer, the members of the class, including Ron, would then write a response to what they'd just heard, turning over their responses to the student "performer." Ron did not collect this writing, nor did he read it. The responses were written solely for the student presenter.

The day's song assignment took over as the conventionalized beginning of Ron's class and consumed, on the average, fourteen minutes of the fifty-minute period, or about 28 percent of the class time. Interactional groupings for the semester of observed classes can be found in Table 4. When these classes are grouped by the three data collection periods, as in Table 5, it becomes evident that the song assignment sequences comprised a large block of class time once they became daily fixtures of the class routine. By incorporating the song assignment into the daily routine of the class, Ron guaranteed a large dose of dramatic flair for each class session. It is this very flair for the dramatic, characteristic of so much of the semester's classes, that creates an image of Ron as the entertainer.

Karen: the "professor"

One way to look at university classrooms is as a stage for two major roles, those of student and of teacher. So far in this chapter I have argued that the individual teaching style of those observed in this study has colored the characterization of the teacher role to such an extent that metaphors, such as "choreographer," "entertainer," and "earth-mother," capture the sense of what was going on in those respective classroom dramas more fully than the use of terms such as *teacher* or *method*. It is somewhat ironic, then, that for the last teacher portrait I will need to fall back on more traditional notions of teaching for the image evoked by Karen's classroom.

Since all of us occupy classroom space for a significant portion of our lives, we each possess a folk notion of what a professor is. Professors stand in front of classes, delivering lectures on the content under study. They are concerned about this content, be it a history lesson, problems in calculus, or a reading exercise. Of all of the teachers in this study, Karen comes closest to matching this folk image of the professor.

In her first interview, Karen talked about the format of her writing conferences. She preferred to skip the "How do you feel?" type of question for opening the conference, explaining, "That's my personality. And so I just get down to business right away." Given this focus on getting directly to the point, she liked student-initiated conferences since "we get right to work."

This emphasis for getting to the point as directly and as efficiently as possible is found, as well, in her plans for the classroom. In discussing the place of teacher talk in the classroom, Karen pointed out,

I don't want to talk the whole hour myself or just go over things, you know. This is the right answer, and this is the right one. There's a certain amount of information either about writing or about the topic that I want to get across though. Sometimes it seems most efficient in a fifty-minute class just to talk.

And talk she did. Looking at Table 4, we can see that for Karen, teacher-to-class interaction consumed nearly 80 percent of the semester's classes. This high percentage of teacher-to-class interaction just barely surpasses Meg's total of 79.1 percent, leading to the suspicion that Meg and Karen conduct similar classrooms. Yet these classrooms actually differ dramatically in terms of how each teacher plays out her lessons during these frames of teacher-to-class interaction.

Most of Meg's periods of teacher-to-class interaction consisted of extensive and carefully shaped question-and-answer sequences, designed to deliver the content of each day's lesson. Karen, on the other hand, utilized her teacher-to-class interaction quite differently. Like the professor of folk knowledge, she delivered the lesson content by means of extensive lectures. So, for example, at the beginning of the semester, Karen carefully outlined what was involved in learning a second language, using chalkboard graphics to explicate her text. Topics as diverse as relative clauses, the form of bibliographies, and the differences between fact and opinion were all treated in this same manner.

To ensure that students carefully heeded what she said in her lectures, she gave them quizzes on the lecture material during the first month or so of classes. These were short essay exams, with questions like, "What three things *don't* you include in a conclusion?" As revealed in Table 1, Karen was the only teacher in the cohort to give quizzes.

Like Meg, Karen attempted to structure her writing assignments so that students were "well on their way" when they left her class to work on their own. Her objective was to ensure that students "don't get too off base" when they write. She felt that when learners got too far off the target of what they were supposed to do, they became discouraged about their writing ability. Her job, then, was to try to prevent these detours by carefully constructing the sequence of activities, preparing students for each writing assignment. Unlike Meg, she performed this job primarily by explaining, summarizing, and describing rather than by engaging students in questions and answers.

The question forms that did appear, embedded in her lecture discourse, were usually rhetorical questions (i.e., questions ostensibly addressed to the class, but for which she had allotted no response time). Instead, Karen immediately answered them herself. The following excerpt illustrates this strategy. It is taken from a class that occurred in the middle of the semester. Karen has just finished her class opening sequence of collecting rewrites and assigning the homework exercises for the next class. (When she refers to *loop writing*, she is describing a freewriting exercise in which students return to previously introduced topics and develop them further.)

T: All right, uh, today's work is going to concern a reading which I'm going to give to you. I'll give you all a copy but I don't want you to read it yet. It's from a book that was written for Chinese who are going to come and study in the United States. And it's not an ESL book or anything. But it just has a couple of pages that I thought were worth working on because paragraphs are not simple paragraphs and I want you to look closely at them. In fact, we're going to go backwards from what you usually do. If you write a complex essay, and after you brainstorm, after you loop write, or after you do anything to get your ideas out and get this group of ideas, and then you have to do something with them. You have to organize them, right? How do you organize your ideas? You all have a step for organizing ideas? Or do you just skip that part? You just get your idea and write it down in the order that it comes?

S: [Volunteering the answer] Rescramble it.

T: Rescramble, replace? One method for doing that in a more organized way is to do what? [unintelligible] foundation for an outline. You all have a copy of this outline format, did you bring it? Get it out. If you don't have it, I'll give you another one. [She pauses as students search their notebooks for the handout.] Have you ever used an outline before?

Ss: [A few students answer "yes."]

T: In a lot of composition classes you're required to use outlines every time. [She pauses as students continue their searching and then redistributes the handout to students unable to find it.] Okay. So we're on the last step before we're ready to sit down and write the paper. Now, I personally don't use outlines every time I write. In fact, I have a strong dislike for outlines for shorter papers, but many people rely on them for everything they write and in that way they can have more organized writing. Have you found that sometimes you write an outline and your paper doesn't fit the outline? Has that every happened to anybody? You write an outline because the teacher says you have to? But then when you start writing, your paper goes in a different direction. I think what happens is that . . . [The teacher continues the discussion of writing outlines.]

As the excerpt shows, when Karen did pause sufficiently for a response from the class, only a few students attempted to answer. Part of this limited participation may have stemmed from the fact that Karen stationed herself primarily in the front of the room, either near the chalkboard or in front of to the side of her table. As a result, most of the students who did occasionally participate came from the rim of students sitting in the rows closest to her. It was this body of students whom she tended to call on during those occasions when student responses were required. Infrequently, someone from outside this inner circle would participate, generally as a volunteer. But those in the rear of the classroom could usually count on remaining anonymous observers. (See Shamim [this volume] for a discussion of action zones in classrooms.)

Part of the limited participation also may be explained by Karen's feelings about calling on students, with which this questioning behavior is congruent. As Karen explained in the final interview, while she might, once in a while, call on specific students, she relies most often on students who volunteer to answer.

To support the clarity of her lectures, Karen at times seemed to lapse into "simplified" speech, forms consistent with descriptions of "foreigner talk" (Ellis 1985). She rarely used contractions, and she typically articulated distinctly and at a slowed rate. Occasionally, simple primerlike phrases slipped into her text, for example, "Errors are our friends" and "Through our mistakes we learn."

When asked about possible speech modification, Karen pointed out that "students need time to think" even if this slowing down of the pace may seem boring for some students. This comment harkens back to the image of the professor, the intellectual focused intently on the content of the course. Karen directs her attention to what she sees as essential in any writing course – the ideas conveyed by the writing. It is this focus on ideas that provides the center for her approach to teaching writing. As she explains in the end-of-semester interview, "I figure my function as a teacher of composition is to help them see how to verbalize a thought."

One technique to help students work with ideas in their writing is the use of journals. Karen is the only one of the four teachers who required a journal that students turned in on a regular basis. Over the semester, students wrote eight journal entries. These were ungraded pieces of writing. Karen determined whether entries would receive credit based on length alone: Each entry had to be two and one half to three pages long. Her comments were restricted to content and rhetorical structure. Her purpose in getting students to keep journals was to provide an opportunity for them to produce ungraded writing. More frequently, journal topics were designed to lead students to explore topics later given, in more complex forms, as formal writing assignments. Through such exploration, went her assumption, students would develop their ideas about particular topics. Again, ideas and their development provided the focus for this assignment.

Karen brings up the importance of ideas in her discussion of how conferences helped students with their writing.

Often their writing comes easier if they've had a chance to express what they have to say orally. So you give them that idea – at least they have one chance to talk to someone who cares about their ideas . . . in a sort of intellectual way discuss ideas and maybe they can take that experience and use it as a technique to develop ideas in the future in their writing.

For the most part, it seems to be this focus on ideas that generates the necessary enthusiasm that allows Karen to continue to teach writing. Rather than emphasizing structure and grammar, she remarks, later in the same interview, "I'm more excited about having ideas and then saying them well and try to give my students that sort of enthusiasm."

Karen's perspective on what counts in writing certainly differs from, for example, Sara's. For Sara, the important matter of a writing class, the development of writing skills, can only be accomplished through the mediating influence of personal contact. For Karen, what counts can be defined along more traditional lines. What counts is the very essence of what Karen thinks writing is all about: the ideas represented in the text. This focus on content, accompanied by classroom interaction consisting primarily of formal lectures and attendant rhetorical questions, create an equally traditional image – that of the professor.

Discussion

In this chapter, I have used metaphors about individual teaching styles as lenses to understand how each teacher employs the "tools" of teaching in unique ways within each classroom. Such tools include the materials students are given, the topics they write on, and the ways in which teachers block out the time of each class into a variety of interactional groupings, as well as the rules teachers employ to organize and manage the classroom.

There are two purposes to this analysis: (a) on a general level, to make sense of the complexity involved in understanding the teacher's role in creating the classroom context; and (b) to provide descriptions of the teaching styles of the teachers in this study, which will lead to a fuller understanding of how teachers use specific instructional techniques as part of their instructional plan.

As I argued at the beginning of this chapter, if we want to understand the dynamics of classrooms, if we want to have a very real sense of the climate of instruction, we cannot depend solely on traditional descriptions, such as approach, design, or procedure. Methodological labels, such as the "process" approach currently popular in writing instruction, offer few insights into what teachers actually *do* as they apply the precepts of a curricular innovation to the planning of a class syllabus or the designing of a day's lesson.

In the case of the teachers I worked with, there were many features in common. All four classes were sections of the same kind of class. The teachers had been directed to follow a common departmental syllabus. The classes were composed of similar student populations. Three of the four teachers (all except Meg) used the same writing text, and all of the teachers used the same reader. Many of them shared materials and writing topics. All espoused the same goals (to make students better writers rather than better users of grammar) and the same approach (to teach writing as a process, with a focus on meaning rather than form).

With all of these similarities, however, the reality of each classroom looked quite different. By analyzing teaching style, by looking at *how* teachers did the "same" things, I could make sense of those differences.

References

Allwright, D. 1983. Classroom-centered research on language teaching and learning: A brief historical overview. *TESOL Quarterly, 17,* 2, 191–204.

Anthony, E. M. 1963. Approach, method, and technique. *English Language Teaching, 17,* 63–67.

Ellis, R. 1985. *Understanding Second Language Acquisition.* Oxford: Oxford University Press.

Heath, S. B. 1978. Outline guide for the ethnographic study of Literacy and Oral Language From School to Communities. University of Pennsylvania, Graduate School of Education.

Hymes, D. H. 1977. Qualitative/quantitative research methodologies in education: A linguistic perspective. *Anthropology and Education Quarterly,* 8, 165–176.

Katz, A. 1988. Responding to Student Writers: The Writing Conferences of Second Language Learners. Unpublished doctoral dissertation, Stanford University.

Michaels, S. A. 1985. Classroom processes and the learning of text editing commands. *Quarterly Newsletter of the Laboratory of Comparative Human Cognition, 7,* 3, 70–79.

Miles, M. B., and M. Huberman. 1984. *Qualitative Data Analysis: A Sourcebook of New Methods.* Beverly Hills, CA: Sage.

Morris, W. (ed.). 1976. *The American Heritage Dictionary of the English Language.* Boston: Houghton Mifflin Co.

Phillips, S. U. 1972. Participant structures and communicative competence: Warm Springs children in community and classroom. In C. B. Cazden, V. P. John, and D. Hymes (eds.), *Functions of Language in the Classroom.* New York: Teachers College Press.

Richards, J. C., and T. S. Rodgers. 1982. Method: Approach, design and procedure. *TESOL Quarterly, 16,* 2, 153–168.

1986. *Approaches and Methods in Language Teaching: A Description and Analysis.* New York: Cambridge University Press.

Shamim, F. (Chapter 5, this volume). In or out of the action zone: Location as a feature of interaction in large ESL classes in Pakistan.

Tannen, D. 1984. *Conversational Style: Analyzing Talk Among Friends.* Norwood, NJ: Ablex.

4 Redefining the relationship between research and what teachers know

Donald Freeman

> Research is not primarily a process of
> proving something, but a process of
> discovery and learning. This view of
> research . . . allows classroom teachers
> to take seriously the ordinary business of
> their lives as teachers.
>   (Cindy Ray, Pioneer Valley Regional
>   High School, Greenfield, Mass.)

I have often heard a conversation between teacher and researcher that runs something as follows. After hearing a researcher talk about findings, the teacher may say: "That's interesting . . . but what does it mean for me in my classroom? How does it relate to the learners I'm teaching? What am I supposed to *do* about it in my situation?" Or, after hearing a teacher talk about an aspect of teaching, the researcher may respond: "That's all well and good, but where is the evidence? On what basis can you say that? How do you *know* it's true?" So an awkward silence has grown up between teacher and researcher; in it has flourished a gulf between what teachers know about practice through doing it and what research can say about teaching and learning.

The awkward silence among doing, knowing, and telling

In a benchmark article entitled "The Impact of the Language Sciences on Second Language Education," Stern, Wesche, and Harley (1978) offer a classic outline of the distinction.

Two commonly held views of the relationship between research and teaching are roughly as follows: First, theoreticians and researchers formulate theories, develop concepts, and carry out "pure" research within certain disciplines.

I am grateful to have had the opportunity to present some of these ideas at the 1992 Wisconsin TESOL Conference, the 1992 Braz-TESOL Convention, and the October 1992 Southeast Regional TESOL Conference. My thanks to participants at those meetings for conversations which have sharpened my thinking. This work was supported in part by a grant from the Spencer Foundation.

The findings of these studies are applied in education and lead to an improvement in classroom performance. . . . Second, an educational need, demand, or deficiency is discovered . . . [which] stimulates research and theory related to [it]. The findings are applied and the need is met, the demand fulfilled, or the deficiency remedied. (p. 397)

The authors observe that neither of these views actually play out in practice, which gives rise to a basic realization:

Educational practice has not necessarily been visibly improved in spite of . . . a high level of research activity. Questions then begin to be asked. Has the wrong research been funded? Have researchers done a bad job? Should there be less emphasis on research? Has there been a defect in communication between the theoretician-researcher and the practitioner? . . . Is the practitioner at fault by failing to adopt what research can offer? Are there other influences at work that override the effects of the research? *Is the conception of the relationships between research and practice at fault?* (ibid.: 398; emphasis added)

While these are all reasonable questions, the last one seems to me to be the most central. Over the years, the dominant conception of the relationship between research and classroom practice has been one of implied transmission. There has been an entrenched, hierarchical, and unidirectional assumption that interpretations developed and explanations posited through research can – and should – influence in some way what teachers understand, and therefore what they do, in their classroom practice. Yet, as we know, this does not happen, which revives the basic question: What is the relationship between research and teaching?

"You have to know the story in order to tell the story"

Like many involved in both classroom teaching and research, I have wrestled with this question. The interaction of two experiences recently served to catalyze my own thinking. The first led me to rethink the question itself; the second evolved into a response of sorts. Together their interaction helped to frame a view of teachers' knowledge of classroom practice and how research can express that knowledge.

First, the question. At a meeting at which teachers were discussing the research they were doing in their classrooms, I was struck repeatedly by the clear authority with which they spoke. Their questions had the uniquely grounded quality of the practitioner's point of view; their evolving answers reflected the texture of their classrooms and followed the contours of their teaching (see, for example, Gallas 1991). The work they were reporting illuminated the complexities of learning and teaching in the best sense, which gave rise to my question: Why label these inquiries "research"? Why not simply recognize them as part of good teaching, teaching which tries to understand learners and their learning?

Later, the shape of an answer appeared. It came serendipitously, as such things often do, when I was making dinner for my family. In the midst of the usual "second-shift" chaos of homework and table setting, the radio played an interview with a jazz singer named Barbara Lee. The interviewer asked Ms. Lee about Cole Porter, a repertoire which Lee does with particular clarity. How, the interviewer wondered, did Lee manage to sing such familiar songs so simply and yet with such new-found power and directness. Lee responded, "You have to know the story in order to tell the story."

Thus the question and the answer were joined. Why is classroom inquiry not simply good teaching? What is gained by calling it "research"? It seems that when teachers undertake such activity, the notion of what research is, what it examines, how it is done, and how it is talked about, all change. Lee's comment, "You have to know the story in order to tell the story," crystallizes the nature of these changes. In this chapter, I want to examine first what it means to *know the story* of teaching and learning and, second, *how the story* in its single or multiple forms *is told* by teachers, researchers, and others concerned with understanding education. So I will map out a series of relationships between knowing the story of teaching – who knows it and how it is known – and how that story is told.

There is a central dilemma embedded in this relationship. Teachers and learners know the story of the classroom well, but they usually do not know how to tell it because they are not often called upon to do so, nor do they usually have opportunities. Researchers, curriculum developers, and policymakers, on the other hand, are very skilled at telling certain things about classrooms; however, they often miss the central stories that are there. This divergence can lead to different perspectives on what teaching is and what is important within it. Thus it can become grounds for the "intimate divorce" between research and teaching.

To bridge that gap and to fully understand teaching, we must take an approach which puts the person who does the work at the center. We need to ask: What do teachers know in order to do what they do? This question lies at the intersection of how teachers are prepared, how professional licensure is promoted, how research is conducted, how classroom materials are developed, and how meaningful educational policy is generated. The deceptive simplicity of the question masks the difficulty of unraveling, researching, and fully understanding it. What teachers know, and how that knowledge finds its way into their practice, must become a vital concern of those who want to understand and to influence education. This refocusing, however, will shift the nature of research in fundamental ways. It is these changes in how we view teaching and research which are captured in Barbara Lee's phrase, "You have to know the story in order to tell the story."

"Knowing the story": three views of teaching

The next section describes three views of teaching: the behavioral view, the cognitive view, and the interpretivist view (Freeman 1991). Each is illustrated with a painting. Although fine art is not commonly used in papers in our field, each painting here typifies a *stance* toward the world that an artist (and possibly *researcher*) may take.

Teaching as doing: the behavioral view

When we ask what teachers know in order to teach, we are crossing a great divide. In the world in general, and in schools in particular, teaching is generally seen as doing things – as behaviors and actions which lead, we hope, to other people's learning. At best teaching is seen as instructional (Rosenholtz 1989). But very often in the current state of education, especially in the United States, it is seen as largely custodial. Teaching is doing, and "doing" means taking care of learners (Freedman, Jackson, and Boles 1983; Lightfoot 1983a). From a sociopolitical perspective, some have argued (Apple 1985; Liston and Zeichner 1990) that this behavioral view contributes directly to de-skilling since it breaks teaching down into routinized activities, which lead to intensification in teachers' work lives when their jobs become like the repetitive performance of routine tasks (Apple and Jungck 1990).

The major domain of educational inquiry which investigates this view of teaching-as-doing comes under the paradigm of process-product research (Dunkin and Biddle 1974; for a critique, see Shulman 1986). These are studies which try to relate what teachers do in lessons, the *processes* they use, with what students do, or ultimately what they learn, as *products* of these lessons. Within this view, the story of teaching lies in the generalized patterns of activity and behavior that are derived from what teachers and learners do in classrooms.

Assembled from generalizations, this story is often portrayed in fixed and stylized terms. Teaching becomes a still-life of behaviors (Figure 1) or a landscape of activities (Figure 2), detached from both the world in which it takes place and the person who does it. The hand of the person who is creating the image is disguised within the painting itself. To tell this story, research is concerned with linking actions to particular results or outcomes.

In order to examine processes and to assess their outcomes as products, researchers often create detached, stylized images of the messiness of teaching; they can then stand outside these images to examine what

Figure 1. *Woman With Chrysanthemums* by Edgar Degas, Metropolitan Museum of Art, New York/SuperStock.

is going on within them. The study of teaching becomes the examination of images of what is done in classrooms, of teachers' and students' behaviors and activity (Figure 3). However, these orderly relationships may lie more in the images themselves than in the world they are meant to capture.

In the field of language teaching, much classroom-based research adopts a general process-product view, which relates teacher behaviors to outcomes in student learning (Long 1980). In introducing his survey of such work, for example, Chaudron (1988) writes:

This book reviews classroom-based research and attempts to provide confirming or disconfirming evidence for claims about the influence of language instruction and classroom interaction on language learning. This is achieved by comparing studies that describe *teachers' and learners' behaviors in classrooms* and synthesizing them into generalizations about the processes that take place in second language classrooms. (p. xv; emphasis added)

Studies of wait time, which examine how long teachers wait after asking a question before calling on a student to reply, provide a good example of this type of research. Researchers have tried to establish

Figure 2. *The Wheatfield* by Jacob Isaakszoon van Ruisdael, Musee des Beaux-Arts, Lille (Giraudon/Bridgeman Art Library).

connections between the length of the wait time and the type and accuracy of student answers. The findings are generally that when the wait time goes beyond the teacher's usual "gut" reaction time, students' answers improve in content and complexity (Rowe 1974; Tobin 1987).

However, the behavioral view of teaching adopted in process-product research tends to codify extremely complex processes. Teaching is simplified by not attending to the role that teachers and learners, as thinking people, play within it. To study wait time for example, one might ask: Why does the teacher choose to ask that particular question? Why does he or she call on that student? These questions probe the behavior of questioning within the context of teaching. In a review of wait-time research, Carlsen (1991: 157) points out:

Research on questioning has generally failed to recognize that classroom questions are not simply teacher behaviors but mutual constructions of teachers and students. The meaning of questions is dependent on their

93

Figure 3. High Museum of Art, Atlanta, Georgia (David Forbert/Super-Stock).

context in classroom discourse, the content of questions cannot be ignored, and questions may reflect and sustain status differences in the classroom.

As in this instance of investigating a common classroom phenomenon like questioning, when teaching is viewed as doing things, it can easily be divorced from the teacher who does them. Such compartmentalization allows for teaching to be explained in terms which are behavioral, impersonal, and beyond the contexts in which it occurs. Thus, teaching can be portrayed in the stylized findings of so many pictures on a wall.

When we ask the question, What do teachers know in order to teach?, we are recasting this view. It is no longer sufficient to speak of teaching simply as doing, to describe it in terms of teachers' and learners' behaviors in classrooms. The question pushes us to consider the cognitive dimension in what goes on in teaching and learning.

Teaching as thinking and doing: the cognitive view

When teaching is seen from a cognitive perspective, one which combines thought with action, our view is reframed in important ways. Now teaching can include the crucial cognitive and affective dimensions which accompany, and indeed shape, the behaviors and actions that teachers and learners undertake in classrooms. This view also opens up a new realm of inquiry. If teaching has a cognitive component, one

94

needs to ask, What is it that teachers know? How is that knowledge organized? How does it inform their actions?

Since the late 1970s these questions have motivated the domain of educational inquiry known as teacher-cognition research (Clark and Peterson 1986; Shavelson and Stern 1981). It is useful to hear how the first researchers in this area described the shift from a behavioral to a cognitive view of teaching. Introducing the proceedings of the second international conference on teacher thinking, Halkes and Olsen (1984: 1) wrote:

Looking from a teacher-thinking perspective at teaching and learning, one is not so much striving for the disclosure of *the* effective teacher, but for the explanation and understanding of teaching processes as they are. After all, it is the teacher's subjective school-related knowledge which determines for the most part what happens in the classroom; whether the teacher can articulate her/his knowledge or not. Instead of reducing the complexities of teaching-learning situations into a few manageable research variables, one tries to find out how teachers cope with these complexities.

To understand how teachers "cope with the complexities" of their work, these researchers argue for a view that takes into account not only what teachers are doing but what they are thinking about as they do it. This means looking at teaching from a different perspective.

To know the story of the cognitive view of teaching, we have to know how teachers conceive of what they do. To tell this side of the story we have to place teachers' perceptions – their reasoning, beliefs, and intentions – at the center of any research account. This poses an image of teaching that shows both what is seen and how it is seen, an image that reveals both the view, and the limitations which frame it, on the canvas (Figure 4).

Recent research on lesson planning provides an example of this cognitive orientation to understanding teaching. When trainees are taught to plan lessons, they are usually introduced to the notion of objectives, of specifying the content they are teaching, and of blending that content with appropriate activities (Celce-Murcia and Gorman 1979; Gower and Walters 1983). Beginning teachers are taught to plan in this way in order to help organize what they will do in their lessons and to identify which actions will carry out their purposes most efficiently and effectively. This is all based on the assumption that experienced teachers plan from objectives to activities and that doing so makes their lessons more effective.

In the late 1970s, however, when teacher-cognition research began to probe the actual processes that teachers use in their planning, interesting findings emerged. In twenty-two different studies using a variety of methods (summarized in Clark and Peterson 1986: 260 – 268), re-

Figure 4. *La Condition Humaine* by René Magritte (© C. Herscovici, Brussels/Artists Rights Society [ARS], New York) "I placed in front of a window, seen from inside a room, a painting representing exactly that part of the landscape which was hidden from view by the painting . . . Which is how we see the world: we see it as being outside ourselves even though it is only a mental representation of it that we experience inside ourselves."

searchers examined how teachers actually planned lessons in order to expose the complex interaction between the planning and the execution. Working largely within a decision-making framework, this research investigated the relationship between what teachers had thought about ahead of time for the lesson, referred to as their *pre-active* decisions, and what they were thinking about as they taught it, referred to as their *interactive* decisions (Calderhead 1981; see Johnson [1992], Nunan [1992], and Woods [1989] for examples in language teaching).

Although perhaps surprising to many, these findings converge on teachers' daily experience of planning and are thus quite familiar to those who work in classrooms. Researchers found that teachers did not naturally think about planning in the organized formats which they had been taught to use. Further, when they did plan lessons according to these formats, they often did not teach them according to plan. Teachers were more likely to visualize lessons as clusters or sequences of activity; they would blend content with activity and would generally focus on their particular students. In other words, teachers tended to plan lessons as ways of doing things for given groups of students rather than to meet particular objectives (Clark and Peterson 1986: 260–268).

These findings are captured in the words of one experienced teacher, Barbara Fujiwara, who describes her own planning process (Graves, 1996). Writing about how she planned a listening comprehension course for university students in Japan, Fujiwara offers wonderful insight into the cognitive side of her work.

Although I do try to articulate objectives, my method of planning still begins with activities and visions of the class. It's only when I look at these visions that I can begin to analyze why I am doing what [I'm doing]. I also need to be in dialogue with students, so it's hard for me to formulate things in the abstract without some kind of student input. . . . So my planning process is based on layers and layers of assumptions, experiences, and knowledge. I have to dig down deep to find out why I make the decisions I do.

Studying how teacher planning actually works raises some subtle but important problems with the cognitive view of teaching. As Fujiwara points out, teaching is not simply an activity that bridges thought and action; it is usually intricately rooted in a particular context. This may be why, when asked about aspects of their work, experienced teachers will often preface their responses with the disclaimer, "It depends. . . . "

At an annual teaching convention a few years ago, I ran into a colleague in the halls. An experienced teacher, she mentioned a session she had just seen which she found interesting. The presenter had participants rate various common techniques by whether they would use them in teaching and then whether they would like to learn from them as students. The intent was to illustrate the parallels and discontinuities between what teachers do and what they prefer as learners. My colleague found the exercise extremely frustrating: "How can I respond in that sort of exercise as a teacher when so much of which technique I use depends. It depends on so many things."

If one adopts a behavioral view of teaching, these "It depends" responses are viewed as reflections of the imprecise nature of what teachers know. Within that perspective, the highest forms of knowledge are abstract, acontextual generalizations, such as grammatical knowledge or methodological procedures. The highly personal and contextual "It depends" understandings that teachers bring to their work are difficult to integrate into such abstract knowledge.

When teaching is seen as cognitive activity, these "It depends" statements offer evidence of the individual and subjective nature of what teachers think about in their instructional work. However, this cognitive perspective makes measuring such knowledge according to prescribed general criteria very difficult and messy. Hence it creates problems for groups that are creating professional standards for teachers (NBPTS 1989). To account for these "It depends" understandings on which classroom practice is based, we need a view of teaching that is founded in the daily operation of thinking and activity in context, a view of teaching I have referred to as "knowing what to do."

Teaching as knowing what to do: the interpretivist view

Teachers are constantly involved in interpreting their worlds: They interpret their subject matter, their classroom context, and the people in it. These interpretations are central to their thinking and their actions. Classrooms and students are not just settings for implementing ideas; they are frameworks of interpretation that teachers use for knowing: knowing when and how to act and react, what information to present or explain and how, when to respond or correct individual students, how to assess and reformulate what they have just taught, and so on (Berliner 1988; Carter and Doyle 1987; Doyle 1977).

In this interpretivist view, the "It depends" statements that teachers make sum up quite handily what teaching is. They offer evidence of the highly complex, interpretative knowledge that teachers use to do their work. A case in point is a fact that all teachers learn very early in their careers that teaching and learning have a deeply seasonal rhythm. In North American classrooms, September is different from December, especially just before the holidays, which is different from March, which is different from early June. Similarly on a daily basis, 8:30 A.M. is different from just before lunch, which is different from 2:45 P.M., which is different from an after-work class at 7:00 in the evening. Although this seasonality is generally trivialized as common sense, it is integral to how teachers plan, how they conduct lessons, and how they manage groups of learners.

Such seasonal knowledge arose in a study which I did on how students and teachers came to understand content in a second language classroom. My colleague in the study, Maggie Brown Cassidy, is a high school French teacher. On this particular afternoon, she was talking to a student who had been disruptive in the class that had just taken place during the last period of the day. Cassidy's comments displayed seasonal knowledge as an interpretation of the boy's actions when she asked him, "What class do you have before this?" Before he could respond, Cassidy answered her own question, saying: "That's right, you guys have gym. Well, no wonder your energy's all over the place" (Freeman 1992: 61).

In this view, knowing the story involves understanding how teachers interpret their worlds. It is difficult to conceive of telling this story without having the teacher centrally reflected in it, providing the organizing voice. Research that views teaching in this way encourages teachers' perspectives and voices because it depends on their understandings to achieve its validity. Such research provides a mirror that reflects the teacher centrally in the account, just as Velazquez did in painting himself into *Las Meninas* (Figure 5).

Knowing the story of teaching involves more than is usually considered. Knowing how to teach does not simply entail behavioral knowledge of how to do particular things in the classroom; it involves a cognitive dimension that links thought with activity, centering on the context-embedded, interpretive process of knowing what to do. This contextual know-how is learned over time; its interpretations shape truly effective classroom practice. Knowing the story of teaching includes all of these elements. For this reason, telling the story is more complicated than simply reporting on how things are done in classrooms, or even providing the reasoning – theoretical, personal, or otherwise – for those ways of acting. If teaching involves the continual interplay of interpretation and environment, then its story is complex and subtle, and it is quite complicated to tell, which raises the place of research.

"Knowing how to tell the story": the place of research

In this section, I consider teachers' knowledge as stories and then define research. I argue that, in essence, research involves seeking viable interpretations. I then address questions of genre and understanding in

Figure 5. *Las Meninas* by Diego Velazquez, Prado, Madrid, Spain (Al-ilnari/Art Resource, NY).

teacher-research. Finally, I return to the theme of the chapter: research and what teachers know. The five paintings introduced earlier become the framing metaphor for my conclusions.

Teachers' knowledge as stories

To refer to what teachers know in order to teach as "stories" is not to trivialize it. In fact, much recent work in education has focused on what Bruner (1986) calls "narrative ways of knowing" (see also Carter 1993). To characterize teaching as stories – stories of knowing what to do – calls attention to two important lines of argument. The first is a feminist critique that teachers, who are predominantly women in most educational settings, may well have unique ways of knowing (Belenky, Clincy, Goldberger and Tarule 1986; Gilligan 1982). Images, metaphors, and visual and narratively related ways of organizing understandings – often discredited in the world at large as intuitive, subjective, or common-sensical – may well provide the vital substance of what teachers know and how they think. The second point raises issues inherent in telling such stories. It may not be that what teachers know is subjective or unsystematic, but that researchers, who generally import their methods and their notions of truth and validity from the natural sciences, have overlooked such knowledge because they are using an incomplete means of examination (Mishler 1990).

The notion of teachers' stories is useful and powerful in considering what teachers know and how their knowledge develops over time (Clandinin 1986; Clandinin and Connelly 1987). Elbaz (1983, 1992), a researcher involved in narrative studies of teachers' ways of knowing, makes the following observation about teachers' stories.

Initially, a "story" seems to be a personal matter: There is concern for the individual narrative of a teacher and what the teacher herself, and what [others], as privileged eavesdroppers, might learn from it. In the course of engaging with stories, however, we are beginning to discover that the process is a social one: The story may be told for personal reasons but it has an impact on its audience which reverberates out in many directions at once. (1992: 423)

Stories have plots; they unfold in ways that are surprising and sometimes defy normal logic, yet they are deeply coherent. Stories are also, as Elbaz points out, social; they engage others in a web of understanding. Both points are relevant when we refer to what teachers know as their stories. Teachers' knowledge and understandings develop through time with an internal, lived coherence (Freeman 1994). This knowledge is also built on interpersonal relationships; it is individually constructed within a network of social experience. Like nurses, child-care workers, and others involved in caring professions, teachers are primarily concerned with the worlds of others (Cummings, this volume; Noddings 1984; Ruddick 1989). Thus it makes sense that their knowledge should be primarily social and interactive, that "it *should* depend" on the context and those who are in it.

Research as seeking viable interpretations

When we accept that teaching is complex and highly contextual, and at the same time deeply coherent and dependent on relationships and the worlds of others, the question becomes, to paraphrase singer Barbara Lee, How then can its story best be told? What is the place of research in the telling of teaching?

I define research as a basic process of developing and rendering viable interpretations for things in the world. On a human level, this is a normal and natural preoccupation, as we can see with young children who constantly ask "why": "Why do leaves change color in the fall?" "Why is it hot in the summer and cold in the winter?" "Why do Cheerios float?" It seems part of our humanity to naturally seek out reasons for the phenomena we encounter. The curiosity that motivates inquiry is universal and leads to myriad interpretations about our worlds. Given this natural human process of inquiry we may well ask, How are the interpretations developed or uncovered by research different? What makes them somehow "better" than the usual forms of interpretation which answer our curiosity about the world? To put the question in another way: What gives power to the interpretations of research? Why are they privileged over common sense?

Lee Shulman (1988), a prominent educational researcher, has argued that the essential difference lies in the fact that research adheres to method.

To assert that something has method is to claim that there is an order, a regularity, obscure though it may be, which underlies apparent disorder thus rendering it meaningful. Method is the attribute which distinguishes *research* activity from mere observation and speculation. (p. 3; emphasis added)

Drawing on Cronbach and Suppes (1969), Shulman defines research as a process of "disciplined inquiry." He asserts that "[w]hat is important about disciplined inquiry is that its data, arguments, and reasoning be capable of withstanding scrutiny" (1988: 5). Thus both the findings and the methods, the interpretations and the ways in which they have been arrived at, must be open to examination, questioning, and critique.

Like any inquiry, the research process begins with curiosity about something in the world: questions, or "local puzzles" (Allwright and Bailey 1991: 198), or as one teacher put it in reporting on her research, simply "feeling uncomfortable about something in the classroom" (Williams 1992). When this notion of inquiry motivated by curiosity is applied to teaching, it can become tremendously useful. It can help the world at large recognize that in the full complexity of teaching, things rarely go as planned and no two lessons are ever the same.

When teachers themselves begin to inquire into this complexity of teaching, they make a useful distinction between themselves and their practice. They grant themselves permission as well as space to talk about what is happening in their classrooms and what is causing them to be curious about their teaching. Often such curiosity is motivated by what departs from intention, by what may not be working as the teacher had planned or foreseen. Thus when teachers inquire into teaching, they take risks and become open and vulnerable to examining and chronicling the messy complexities of classroom practice.

To recognize and label these inquiries as research is crucially important because it places them within an acknowledged framework that gives them value and prestige. "Research" is a label which lets teachers be – and talk publicly about being – vulnerable to the variability of their craft while continuing to be professional about it. Admitting vulnerability can weaken teachers' sense of authority over what they do, or it can strengthen it. Although everyone may recognize that there is wide variability inherent in teaching, talking about it is usually seen as counterprofessional. When this questioning of practice takes place within a framework labeled "research," understanding the complexity of teaching can become a public and legitimate part of being a teacher.

Inquiry is, in Shulman's formulation, half of the research process; "being disciplined" is the other half. The term *disciplined* refers to both the process of looking – how phenomena are examined – and the traditions and bases from which that looking is done. Shulman (1988: 16) writes:

Educational research methods are . . . disciplined in that they follow sets of rules and principles for pursuing investigations. They are also disciplined in another sense. They have emerged from underlying social or natural science disciplines which have well-developed canons of discovery and verification for making and testing truth claims in their fields.

Clearly issues of research methodology enter in at this point. There are often legitimate debates about whether "rules and principles for pursuing investigations" have been properly followed – in other words, whether the research was carried out in a disciplined manner. More important than the orthodoxy of methodology, however, is the basic fact of making public how an inquiry has been conducted. Is the way of looking appropriate to what one is trying to find out? Does the means of research suit the intended ends?

This process of making public how a piece of research has been done exposes two critical and intertwined aspects of the authority of teacher-researchers. One is their stance; the other is their vulnerability. It is often difficult to understand certain phenomena that are central to classroom life without participating in them. The teacher's stance as a researcher is unique in this regard, offering the access and insight of a participant observer, one who can both watch and intervene, who can listen and interact. Developmental psychologist Michael Cole introduces the work of teacher-researcher Vivian Paley with that point:

The preschool teacher is in a unique position to resolve some of the very
issues left unresolved by others who study children and their development.
. . . She can combine the observational/intervention strategy favored by the
ethnologist with the participant-observation methods of the anthropologist.
Present from the time children first enter the classroom until they graduate to
their next educational institution, she is in a perfect position to trace their
development across long stretches of time and a broad range of specific
contexts. (Paley 1986a: ix–x)

Although the uniqueness of the teacher's stance within the research
process is clear, the vulnerability of authority is perhaps more difficult
to decipher. When operating as researchers, teachers can be open about
the gaps, lapses, and changes of course that occur in their daily work
because these become sources of study. Paley (1986b: 124) describes
this process in her teaching:

The act of teaching became a daily search for the child's point of view
accompanied by the sometimes unwelcome disclosure of my hidden attitudes.
The search was what mattered – only later did someone tell me it was
research – and it provided an open-ended script from which to observe,
interpret, and integrate the living drama of the classroom.

Thus the vulnerability of the teacher-researcher can be transformed into
a strength which provides the opening for inquiry. In contrast, the same
type of vulnerability by the researcher can lead to disputed findings. For
researchers, lapses in practice may become errors of method which, in
turn, can become threats to the validity of their work. For teachers,
lapses in practice can offer windows through which to glimpse what is
going on in their teaching.

I believe the label of "research" can serve to strengthen what teachers
do in several important ways. By adopting a research stance of disciplined inquiry in their work, teachers can provide themselves with the
space to be curious and vulnerable to what is happening in their classrooms. The term *research* also creates a public framework and means
for seeking and sharing interpretations of teaching and learning. Moreover it can encourage fuller, public conversations about those interpretations, thus creating entry for teachers into discussions of policy and
disciplinary knowledge.

This is the second sense of "discipline" in Shulman's (1988: 5) definition:

Disciplined inquiry not only refers to the order, regular, and principled
nature of the investigation, it also refers to the disciplines themselves which
serve as the sources for the principles of regularity or the canons of evidence
employed by the investigator.

Psychology, sociology, anthropology, linguistics, history, and philosophy are disciplines that serve as foundations for researching education. But they also point to the fundamental problem: Education is not itself a discipline. It is, as Shulman points out, "a locus containing phenomena, events, institutions, problems, persons, and processes which themselves constitute the raw material for inquiries of many kinds" (ibid.).

If teachers are to be heard when they undertake inquiries into teaching and learning, they must either enter into existing disciplinary conversations or create new conversations of their own. There are advantages and disadvantages to both paths. Existing disciplines offer established frameworks by which procedures and results can be judged as meaningful; each discipline has its own recognizable, comfortable place in the world. Creating a new discipline of teaching – which is distinct from, but part of, the field of education – is a major challenge. Doing so assumes that teaching is itself a way of knowing the particular world of the classroom and what happens within it. Teaching is knowing what to do under particular and unique circumstances; to borrow from Paley (1986b), it is "a daily search for the learners' point of view" (p. 124). Within this new discipline of teaching, teachers are best positioned to inquire into this way of knowing and to voice their findings.

Teacher research: questions of genre and understanding[1]

To achieve a discipline of teaching, however, the knowledge that teachers articulate through the process of disciplined inquiry must become public. It cannot dissipate in the recesses of private conversations, staff rooms, or schools. The interpretations that teachers develop through research need to enter the wider community, to compete with other disciplines as ways of understanding education and of shaping public policy and debate. To do so we must consider: In what voice are the findings of teacher research best told? What forms or genre should these understandings take?

There is a voice in which research is usually told; it often comes to mind when we think of academic writing for example. Built around certain rhetorical devices, the genre has a certain power and status attached to it (Brodkey 1987). Social scientist Howard Becker (1986) points out, for example, that the passive voice in which research accounts are generally written masks the author and creates a detached sense of objectivity and truth to the findings. The genre also has a particular history. Although we may tend to think of it as timeless and,

1 My thanks to Ann Phillips of the Brookline Teacher-Research Group for helping to clarify this notion of genre.

therefore, perhaps, true, the voice in which research is told has itself evolved from stories of natural observation to arguments for or against particular theoretically derived positions. As Charles Bazerman (1988), a teacher and historian of writing, has noted in studying the early proceedings of the Royal Academy of Sciences:

Those reported events identified as experiments change in character over the period from 1665–1800. The definition of experiment moves from any made or done thing, to an intentional investigation, to a test of a theory, to finally a proof of, or evidence for, a claim. The early definitions seemed to include any disturbance or manipulation of nature, not necessarily focused on demonstration of any preexisting belief, nor even with the intention of discovery. With time, experiments are represented as more clearly investigative, corroborative, and argumentative. (pp. 65–66)

Given that the scientific genre is not absolute, it is certainly worth questioning whether this form, with its restricted structure and dependence on passive, abstract, detached language, can adequately and usefully express the raw immediacy of "how teachers cope with the complexities" of classroom practice (Halkes and Olsen 1984: 1) and how they conduct this "daily search for the learners' point of view" (Paley 1986b: 124).

Does the prevailing language and genre of research truly serve teachers in articulating what they know about teaching? Or does it distort the telling of stories of teaching and learning from their classrooms? Would it be more useful and appropriate to develop and strengthen the personal ways of expressing what teachers learn through this process of disciplined inquiry in teaching? Indeed, it is ironic to talk about including teachers' voices in discussions of teaching and learning when those voices must be rendered in specialized forms in order to be heard or considered legitimate contributions.[2]

Questions of form and genre are not abstractions; they go to the heart of how teachers' understandings enter the wider public arena in which knowledge is legitimated and policy is formed. For too long teaching has been treated as something which certain people do and others research, license, and legislate. Thus teachers are constantly having what they know defined for them by others. In this process, definitions quickly become injunctions, and what teachers actually know is confused with arguments over what they should know. So the subtle and

2 The work of Paley (1979; 1981; 1986b) and of Ashton-Warner (1965) are two notable counter examples to this point. Kidder (1989) and Freedman (1990) are cases of outsiders writing about teachers and their work in a genre afforded them as journalists. In working with portraiture, Lightfoot (1983b) has experimented with genre to present research findings about effective schools; Cambone (1990) has written in a similar way about teaching children with special needs.

vital qualities of what teachers understand are forced into neat categories for purposes of curriculum development, licensure, teacher education, and so on.

This process does not help to improve teaching or the work lives of teachers. The complexity of teaching cannot be cleaned up simply by pretending it is not there; order cannot be forced on to it by writing and talking in a detached voice about its messiness. Teacher research, broadly construed, offers a very important antidote to the perspectives of non-teachers on what teaching is or what it should be. However, teacher research need not mean that teachers must assume researchers' ways of thinking, talking, framing questions, or seeking answers. Teacher research should refer to the process by which teachers seek interpretations and give voice to what they know by virtue of their experience, combined with close and disciplined examination of their practice. In this way, a discipline of teaching is developed.

Such work may result in research findings in the typical sense. It may also result in stories, narratives, anecdotes, or conversations. As atypical of standard research genres as these may seem, they have the potential to render what teachers know in ways that are useful, acceptable, and valid for the knowers: teachers, those learning to teach, and those who seek to better understand teaching and learning (Maxwell 1992). Some will argue against the validity of such accounts, primarily because they are based in narrative, which they may consider a subjective form. The crucial issue, however, may center on the notion of validity itself, as Mishler (1990) has argued in proposing the test of trustworthiness by which to assess such accounts.

The essential criterion for such judgments is the degree to which we can rely on the concepts, methods, and inferences, of a study, or a tradition of inquiry, as the basis of our own theorizing and empirical research. If our overall assessment of a study's trustworthiness is high enough for us to act on it, we are granting the findings a sufficient degree of validity to invest our own time and energy. (p. 419)

In this view, validity is linked to action rather than to the creation of a canon of what are sometimes termed *objectively truthful findings*. Assessments of validity are based on what one does about what one knows, and this is particularly true in teaching where interpretations must connect to action (Lee Shulman and Shirley Brice Heath 1993; personal communication). Judgments of validity continue to reflect the discipline of the particular inquiry, the trustworthiness of what has been understood, how it has been studied, and by whom. In the case of teaching as a discipline, however, these judgments are measured against activity, and as assessments they can become part of the continuing

fabric of teaching, thus propelling teachers and others into further conversations and recursive examinations.[3] So teaching can become a way
of knowing the world of the classroom, what is going on within it, and
how it relates to and reflects the worlds of the school and the community.

For example, the following piece of research explores a daily classroom incident through a different genre. Ann Carlson (1992: 8; reprinted by permission of the author), the teacher-author, writes about
a pull-out ESL lesson in which a third-grader arrives in tears over
something that has happened in his homeroom.

The Card Game

I shuffle the game cards again as
the small brown face
across the table crumples,
shameful tears sliding down his chin.

More shuffling, more
tears. I wait, calculating the time
I have for this
latest international
crisis.

What happened?, I ask,
Cards slap the table.
He stares as from a dream.

I know he has no English
words for one more Anglo face today.

We are both shuffling now.

I trade another five minutes
for a smile,
a familiar joke.
There is so little time.

I can't fix it for him or
any of them but
I can shuffle the cards.

I have no gifts for this
child but a smile,
a joke, a language
that will never speak to his heart.
Such gifts!

---

3 This is, in fact, an alternative perspective on the so-called action research cycle (Kemmis and McTaggart 1982; Nunan 1991).

Carlson's account is a disciplined examination of her experience of the incident, expressed in her own voice. It exposes the complexity of knowing what to do in one instance in the classroom, and how the wider world is refracted through that instance. The poem is, as Jordan (1989: 935) calls it, "a package of situated knowledge"; its validity lies in our ability to immediately recognize – or not – its trustworthiness. In this process of teachers articulating, in their own voices, their understandings of what they know lies the start of a redefinition of the relationship of teaching and research.

Research and what teachers know

I have argued that teaching is a complex, messy business of knowing what to do in the classroom. Given what it is, I believe the stories of teaching can best be told in ways that involve those who teach in the telling. In the words of singer Barbara Lee, "You *do* need to know the story in order to tell it." However, to capture the full complexity of classroom teaching and learning through research, several norms must change.

The process that we call research must become more open and accessible to teachers. For too long research has remained alienated from the lives of those in classrooms, perhaps on purpose. This distance has helped to accord status and privilege to certain ways of understanding what teaching is and expressing those understandings in the communities of policy, curriculum development, and administration. To see research as a basic process of curiosity pursued with a certain self-discipline begins to make it accessible. Research can also become more achievable within the very real demands on time and energy that shape teachers' daily professional lives.

To make the results of this process public, I believe new genres are needed. The usual forms of telling associated with research are impoverished. They are restricted as well as restricting. Current ways of articulating research are not readily available to teachers or learners who are unprepared to alter their voices and what they have to say in order to fit within the confines of the genre. When teachers adapt to the researcher stance without challenging it, they can allow the genre of research to subtly alter their concerns and insights. It is crucial to recognize this fact and to break out of these restricted forms in order to understand what teaching is and what teachers know in order to do it.

Clearly various ways of seeking and expressing interpretations will endure in the educational research process. The phrase "knowing the story in order to tell it" captures a series of relationships between teaching and research that frame the continuum of that variety. Some aspects of teaching can most easily be seen as pictures on the wall (Figure 6a and b), viewed, and analyzed from the outside (Figure 6c). It is important, however, not to overlook the fact that these interpretations have been arrived at in a particular way. These findings are paintings that do not show the artist; they are stories that do not reveal the teller. They draw our attention to the representation, but not to the process by which it was done or the person who did it.

To tell this aspect of the story, it is crucial to bring teachers' thinking about teaching into the accounts of the act itself (Figure 6d). Such research begins to illuminate how researchers do what they do because it explicates the thinking that shapes their actions. By showing the way in which the artist has framed what he or she sees, we can recognize the strengths and limits of the account. Although such research does show teaching in its fuller complexity, it still does not truly address the role of the teller. What the story is and how it is told depend on the teller.

Research that reveals the identity of the teller (Figure 6e) is critical in both a political and an epistemological sense. When the teller is fully and centrally reflected in the story – as is Velazquez, who painted himself reflected in the mirror at the center of *Las Meninas* – we have a new picture. If the teller of the story of teaching is the teacher, we can be permitted access to invaluable insights. Although we need to acknowledge the strengths and the shortcomings that such access provides, we must also recognize its basic legitimacy.

Questions of what teaching is and of what people know in order to teach are absolutely central; to avoid them is folly for everyone concerned with education. When these questions are ignored, the immediate, daily, intimate knowledge of teachers and learners is belittled because it is overlooked and trivialized. Likewise, the work of policy-makers and curriculum developers is jeopardized because their proposals are not based on a solid foundation. And the findings of researchers and others concerned with understanding education ought to be viewed with skepticism if these people do not seriously entertain the central issue of what teaching is and of what people know in order to do it.

To redefine the relationship between teaching and research, these questions must become central concerns. We must recognize that teaching has the potential to be a way of knowing what is going on with learners in particular lessons or, to paraphrase teacher-researcher Vivian Paley, to be "a daily search for the learner's point of view." As Paley (1986a) observes of her work:

The classroom has all the elements of theater, and the observant, self-examining teacher will not need a drama critic to uncover character, plot,

(a)

(b)

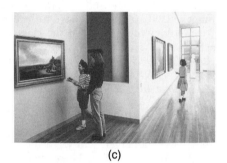

(c)

(d)

(e)

Figure 6.

and meaning. We are, all of us, the actors trying to find the meaning of the scenes in which we find ourselves. (p. 131)

When pursued in a disciplined manner, teaching itself becomes a form of research. It is a matter of balancing and assembling different points of view, each of which knows – or can know – aspects of the story of teaching and learning. This insight will entail recognizing diverse ways of telling those stories so that more voices can be heard.

References

Allwright, R., and K. M. Bailey. 1991. *Focus on the Language Classroom: An Introduction to Classroom Research for Language Teachers*. Cambridge: Cambridge University Press.

Apple, M. 1985. *Education and Power*. New York: Routledge.

Apple, M., and S. Jungck. 1990. You don't have to be a teacher to teach this unit: Teaching, technology and gender in the classroom. *American Educational Research Journal*, 27, 227–254.

Ashton-Warner, S. 1965. *Teacher*. New York: Simon and Schuster.

Bazerman, C. 1988. *Shaping Written Knowledge: The Genre and Activity of the Experimental Article in Science*. Madison: University of Wisconsin Press.

Becker, H. 1986. *Writing for Social Scientists*. Chicago: University of Chicago Press.

Belenky, M., B., Clincy, N. Goldberger, and J. Tarule. 1986. *Women's Ways of Knowing: The Development of Self, Voice, and Mind*. New York: Basic Books.

Berliner, D. 1988. *The Development of Expertise in Pedagogy*. Washington, DC: American Association of Colleges for Teacher Education.

Brodkey, L. 1987. *Academic Writing as Social Practice*. Philadelphia: Temple University Press.

Bruner, J. 1986. *Actual Minds, Possible Worlds*. Cambridge, MA: Harvard University Press.

Calderhead, J. 1981. A psychological approach to research on teachers' classroom decision-making. *British Educational Research Journal*, 7, 51–57.

Cambone, J. 1990. Tipping the balance. *Harvard Educational Review*, 60, 217–236.

Carlsen, W. 1991. Questioning in classrooms: A sociolinguistic perspective. *Review of Educational Research*, 61, 157–178.

Carlson, A. 1992. The card game. *TESOL Journal*, 2, 8.

Carter, K. 1993. The place of story in the study of teaching and teacher education. *Educational Researcher*, 22, 5–12, 18.

Carter K., and W. Doyle. 1987. Teachers' knowledge structures and comprehension processes. In J. Calderhead (ed.), *Exploring Teachers' Thinking*. London: Cassell Publications.

Celce-Murcia, M., and T. Gorman. 1979. Preparing lesson plans. In M. Celce-Murcia and L. McIntosh (eds.), *Teaching English as a Second or Foreign Language*. Rowley, MA: Newbury House.

Chaudron, C. 1988. *Second Language Classrooms: Research on Teaching and Learning.* New York: Cambridge University Press.

Clandinin, D. J. 1986. *Classroom Practice: Teacher Images in Action.* London: Falmer Press.

Clandinin, D. J., and M. Connelly. 1987. Teachers' personal knowledge: What counts as "personal" in studies of the personal. *Journal of Curriculum Studies, 19*, 487–500.

Clark, C., and P. Peterson. 1986. Teachers' thought processes. In M. Wittrock (ed.). *Handbook of Research on Teaching* (3d ed.). New York: Macmillan.

Cronbach, L. J., and P. Suppes. (eds.). 1969. *Research for Tomorrow's Schools: Disciplined Inquiry for Education.* New York: Macmillan.

Cummings, M. C. (Chapter 9, this volume). Sardo revisited: Voice, faith, and multiple repeaters.

Doyle, W. 1977. Learning the classroom environment: An ecological analysis. *Journal of Teacher Education, 28,* 51–55.

Dunkin, M., and B. Biddle. 1974. *The Study of Teaching.* New York: Holt, Rinehart, and Winston.

Elbaz, F. 1983. *Teacher Thinking: A Study of Practical Knowledge.* New York: Nichols Publishing.

1992. Hope, attentiveness, and caring for difference: The moral voice in teaching. *Teaching and Teacher Education, 8,* 421–432.

Freedman, S. 1990. *Small Victories: The Real World of a Teacher, Her Students, and Their High School.* New York: HarperCollins.

Freedman, S., J. Jackson and K. Boles. 1983. Teaching: An imperiled "profession." In L. Shulman and G. Sykes (eds.), *Handbook of Teaching and Policy.* New York: Longman.

Freeman, D. 1991. Three views of teachers' knowledge. *IATEFL Teacher Development Newsletter,* December, 1–4.

1992. Collaboration: Constructing shared understandings in a second language classroom. In D. Nunan (ed.), *Collaborative Language Learning and Teaching.* Cambridge: Cambridge University Press.

1994. Knowing into doing: Teacher education and the problem of transfer. In D. C. S. Li, D. Mahoney, and J. C. Richards (eds.), *Exploring second language teacher development.* Hong Kong: City Polytechnic of Hong Kong.

Gallas, K. 1991. Arts as epistemology: Enabling children to know what they know. *Harvard Educational Review, 61,* 40–50.

Gilligan, C. 1982. *In a Different Voice: Psychological Theory and Women's Development.* Cambridge, MA: Harvard University Press.

Gower, R., and S. Walters. 1983. *Teaching Practice Handbook.* London: Heineman.

Graves, K. (1996). *Teachers as Course Developers.* New York: Cambridge University Press.

Halkes, R., and J. Olsen. 1984. *Teacher Thinking: A New Perspective on Persisting Problems in Education.* Lisse, Netherlands: Swets and Zeitlinger.

Johnson, K. 1992. Learning to teach: Instructional actions and decisions of preservice ESL teachers. *TESOL Quarterly, 26,* 3, 507–536.

Jordan, B. 1989. Cosmopolitical obstetrics: Some insights from the training of traditional midwives. *Social Science and Medicine, 28,* 925–944.

Kemmis, S., and R. McTaggart. (eds.). 1982. *Action Research Planner*. Geelong, Australia: Deakin University.

Kidder, T. 1989. *Among Schoolchildren*. Boston: Houghton Mifflin.

Lightfoot, S. L. 1983a. The lives of teachers. In L. Shulman and G. Sykes (eds.), *Handbook of Teaching and Policy*. New York: Longman.

1983b. *The Good High School: Portraits in Character and Culture*. New York: Basic Books.

Liston, D., and K. Zeichner. 1990. *Teacher Education and the Social Conditions of Schooling*. New York: Routledge.

Long, M. 1980. Inside the "black box": Methodological issues in research on language teaching and learning. *Language Learning, 30*, 1, 1–42.

Maxwell, J. 1992. Understanding and validity in qualitative research. *Harvard Educational Review, 62*, 279–300.

Mishler, E. 1990. Validation in inquiry-guided research: The role of exemplars in narrative studies. *Harvard Educational Review, 60*, 415–442.

National Board for Professional Teaching Standards [NBPTS]. 1989. *Toward High and Rigorous Standards for the Teaching Profession*. Washington, DC: NBPTS.

Noddings, N. 1984. *Caring*. Berkeley: University of California Press.

Nunan, D. 1991. *Understanding Second Language Classrooms*. Englewood Cliffs, NJ: Prentice Hall International.

1992. The teacher as decision-maker. In J. Flowerdew, M. Brock, and S. Hsia (eds.), *Perspectives on Second Language Teacher Education*. Hong Kong: City Polytechnic of Hong Kong.

Paley, V. 1979. *White Teacher*. Cambridge, MA: Harvard University Press.

1981. *Wally's Stories: Conversation in Kindergarten*. Cambridge, MA: Harvard University Press.

1986a. *Mollie is Three: Growing Up in School*. Chicago: University of Chicago Press.

1986b. On listening to what children say. *Harvard Educational Review, 56*, 122–131.

Rosenholtz, S. 1989. *Teachers' Workplace: The Social Organization of Schools*. New York: Longman.

Rowe, M. B. 1974. Wait-time and rewards as instructional variables, their influence on language, logic, and fate control: Part one – Wait-time. *Journal of Research in Science Teaching, 11*, 81–94.

Ruddick, S. 1989. *Maternal Thinking: Towards a Politics of Peace*. New York: Ballentine.

Shavelson, R., and P. Stern. 1981. Research on teachers' pedagogical thoughts, judgments, decisions, and behaviors. *Review of Educational Research, 51*, 455–498.

Shulman, L. 1986. Paradigms and research programs in the study of teaching. In M. Wittrock (ed.), *Handbook of Research on Teaching* (3d ed.). New York: Macmillan.

1988. The disciplines of inquiry in education: An overview. In R. Jager (ed.), *Complementary Methods for Research in Education*. Washington, DC: American Educational Research Association.

Stern, H. H., M. B. Wesche, and B. Harley. 1978. The impact of the language sciences on second language education. In P. Suppes (ed.), *Impact of Re-*

search on *Education: Some Case Studies.* Washington, DC: National Academy of Education.

Tobin, K. G. 1987. The role of wait-time in higher cognitive learning. *Review of Educational Research,* 57, 69–95.

Williams, K. 1992. Classroom Community and the Writing Process. Paper presented at the Conference on Teacher Research, sponsored by the Literacies Institute, May, Lexington, MA.

Woods, D. 1989. Studying ESL teachers' decision-making: Rationale, methodological issues, and initial results. *Carleton Papers in Applied Linguistics,* 6, 107–123.

Section I Questions and tasks

1. The title of this section, "Teaching as Doing, Thinking, and Interpreting," was taken from three views of teaching discussed in Chapter 4. How do these three views of teaching (doing, thinking, and interpreting) emerge in Chapters 1, 2, and 3?

2. If you have teaching experience, think of a time when some unexpected event occurred in a class you were teaching. What was the event? How did you handle it? What was the outcome? Have you ever departed from your lesson plan for any of the reasons described in Chapter 1? If so, what was the situation? Are there other "principles" by which teachers decide to depart from their lesson plans? Try to state these additional principles and give an example of each.

3. In Chapter 2, Nunan explores the difference between his interpretations of classroom events (as the outside observer) and those of the teachers involved. Arrange to observe a class and talk with a teacher afterwards. What, if any, differences emerge between your viewpoint and the teacher's? What accounts for these differences (e.g., experience, knowledge about the students and the course)? What types of training might help teachers and observers engage in more effective classroom observations and post-lesson discussions?

4. Nunan (Chapter 2) reports the retrospections of a relatively new teacher who said she realized "the students were finding the activity quite complex and hard, but it was too late to change it or abandon it." What might this teacher learn by talking to or observing the experienced teachers in Chapter 1? What advice would you give this teacher?

5. Chapter 3 gives descriptions of four teachers with different teaching styles: the choreographer, the earthmother, the entertainer, and the professor. As a student of composition, which, if any, of these teachers would you prefer? Why? As a teacher, what ground rules would you want to lay out before engaging in a similar explanation of your teaching with a researcher or fellow teacher?

6. If you have teaching experience, consider which (if any) of Katz's metaphors (Chapter 3) describes your teaching style. What would be an apt characterization of your teaching style? If you are just beginning to teach, what sort of style would you like to develop?

7. The teaching described in the Chapters, 1, 2, and 3 all occurred in environments where the learners were exposed to English as a second (rather than a foreign) language. In your experience, do similar experiences occur in foreign language classes? In much larger classes?

8. Summarize Freeman's position (Chapter 4) in fewer than thirty words. Then compare your summary to those of your colleagues. Do you agree with Freeman? Do they? Why or why not?

9. Imagine yourself in the role of a language learner. What ideas in these first four chapters struck you as interesting? Could you relate to the experience of the learners described? If so, how? If not, why not?

10. Imagine yourself in the role of a language teacher. If Freeman (Chapter 4) is right – if "you have to know the story to tell the story" – then what story about teaching and learning can *you* tell? Write or tell your story to a sympathetic group of classmates or colleagues. What are their responses? What is your reaction to the experience of telling the story?

11. Imagine yourself in the role of a researcher. (*a*) Which of the procedures and data sets described in Chapters 1–4 seem to be the most useful to you? Which would you prefer not to use? (*b*) If many people were to agree with and be influenced by Freeman's position, how would his ideas change research as it is currently known? How would these ideas influence research reporting in books and scholarly journals?

12. If you could talk with these four researchers in this section (Bailey, Nunan, Katz, and Freeman), what questions would you like to ask them?

II *Classroom dynamics and interaction*

This section contains studies carried out in three very different geographical and pedagogical contexts (in Pakistan, Hong Kong, and Spain). Despite the varied sites in which the studies were conducted, they share a number of characteristics. All the language learners are working in situations where English is a foreign (rather than a second) language. (Although this point may be arguable in the social and economic context of Hong Kong, it is a given in English classes there, as Tsui's data will demonstrate.) The most important feature these chapters have in common, and the reason why they have been brought together in this section, is that they are all concerned with classroom dynamics and its effect on the quality of interaction.

Substantive issues

The major focus of concern for Fauzia Shamim in Chapter 5 is that of class size, a serious issue in the educational systems of many developing countries like Pakistan. Shamim sets out some of the direct consequences of large classes for language learning. She has found that the physical location – where students actually sit in a classroom – has a powerful influence on the quality of the learners' educational experience and even on their chances of success. In her chapter, Shamim raises questions about the limitations of importing into large classes instructional management techniques which have evolved within the culture of small or medium-sized classes.

Amy Tsui's chapter (on English teachers' action research projects in Hong Kong) explores a specific problem as it is perceived by the teachers: getting reticent students to talk in their language classes. Like Shamim, Tsui is concerned with the realities imposed by the cultural contexts in which she works in Hong Kong, and the challenges posed by this context for teachers who wish to utilize techniques from other traditions and educational contexts. Tsui investigates a major challenge in many, if not most, foreign language classrooms – that of getting students to interact orally in the target language. For students of English in Hong Kong, doing so involves many risks. Chapter 6 begins with a discussion of factors that teachers perceive as contributing to student reticence, perceptions gathered as the teachers conducted action research projects on issues that concerned them. Tsui then sets out some of the strategies which the teachers in her study utilized to encourage students to speak. The strength of Tsui's chapter is that it utilizes data collected and analyses conducted by the teachers themselves, and it presents the resulting insights the teachers gained. One of the unanticipated findings is that several teachers have discovered how their own discomfort with silence influenced the interaction patterns in class. Tsui also relates the teachers' explanations of *why* learners don't talk to a substantial body of research literature on language classroom anxiety.

The setting for David Block's study (Chapter 7) contrasts with those of Shamim and Tsui; it takes place in a specialist language school in Barcelona, Spain. This chapter provides a window on the classroom by examining the same events from different points of view. Its key thematic concerns are learner autonomy and the resulting gap between the way teachers and learners interpret classroom interaction. By bringing together data from different sources, Block interprets and reinterprets classroom events from different perspectives. He examines closely the interaction between "Ann," a teacher, and "Alex," a student whose point of view contrasts with hers. This heuristic strategy enables Block to demonstrate the disparities in informants' views on pedagogical objectives, content, and procedures.

Substantively, these three chapters share a common concern, which has to do with the cultural appropriacy of importing pedagogical techniques devised in one culture into another culture. In each case, we see that such borrowing causes problems and creates challenges for both teachers and students. Although these challenges are not insurmountable, they do require the techniques themselves to be transformed. This, as far as we are concerned, is to the good. Given the particularities of individual cultural contexts, any pedagogical proposal, of whatever complexion, needs to be contested against the local reality. The two untenable propositions then, are that ideas should be imported uncritically from one context to the next and that ideas should be rejected outright on the grounds that "they would never work here."

Methodological issues

Chapters 5–7, like others in this volume, utilize a range of data collection techniques, including teacher and learner interviews, classroom observation, teacher and learner oral diaries, classroom observation, the researchers' fieldnotes, and teacher action research reports. Action research is a systematic approach to investigating one's own situation. It uses the iterative steps of planning, acting, observing, reflecting, and replanning to develop local understanding and bring about improvement.

Action research started in the United States in the mid 1940s as an approach to investigating social problems (see, for example, Lewin 1946). It has recently resurfaced as a viable alternative to both experimental research and naturalistic inquiry, particularly in the United Kingdom (Nixon 1981) and Australia (Carr and Kemmis 1986; Kemmis and McTaggart 1982; Nunan 1990). By definition, action research is participatory in nature: People study their own settings (Argyris, Putnam, and Smith 1985; Hustler, Cassidy, and Duff 1986). In Chapter 6 we see a group of English teachers from Hong Kong conducting action research projects to investigate their own attempts to get their students to talk more in class. Tsui's chapter documents how these teachers implemented their strategies for increasing students' verbal output, and then determined which strategies were successful and which were not.

The one technique which is shared across the three studies in this section is the combination of introspection and retrospection. That is why we have chosen to evaluate these ideas here. (The reflecting stage of action research includes both of these processes.) Introspection is "the process of observing and reflecting on one's thoughts, feelings, motives, reasoning processes, and mental states with a view to determining the ways in which these processes and states determine our behavior" (Nunan 1992: 115). Retrospection, on the other hand, is the process of collecting similar data after the event under investigation has taken place. The techniques of introspection and retrospection have been imported into applied linguistics from cognitive psychology, where they have aroused considerable controversy. There are indications that they have generated, and will continue to generate, a similar degree of controversy in applied linguistics (see, for example, Faerch and Kasper 1987). The major criticism has to do with the status of the introspective data. Does the verbalization process accurately reflect the cognitive operations giving rise to a particular action? In other words, to what extent can we believe what the informants have to say? Another criticism relates to the time lapse between the introspection and the event itself. Nisbett and Wilson (1977) argue that the technique should be treated with caution because the gap between the event and the reporting will lead to unreliable data.

Notwithstanding criticisms of introspective and retrospective data collection techniques, we believe that with reasonable care threats to internal and external validity can be averted. We are confident that Shamim, Tsui, and Block have taken due care. We also support the use of the technique itself, because it is a fact of life that the data could simply not have been collected in any other way.

Beyond introspection and retrospection as means of data collection, however, the authors in this section have utilized the participants' introspections and retrospections as part of the interpretive analyses. In each case, certain frustrations are heard: The students in Shamim's large classrooms plaintively explain to the observer what it's like to sit at the back; the teachers Tsui describes *want* their students to talk, yet some discover how they themselves inhibit student talk; and Ann (the teacher in Block's study) plans, thinks, teaches, rethinks with utter dedication, while Alex sees many of her activities as futile. In each of these three chapters, we hear the voices of teachers and students contributing not just to the puzzle pieces, but to clues about our emerging understanding of classroom dynamics.

References

Argyris, C., R. Putnam, and D. M. Smith. 1985. *Action Science: Concepts, Methods and Skills for Research and Intervention.* San Francisco: Jossey-Bass.

Carr, W., and S. Kemmis. 1986. *Becoming Critical: Education, Knowledge and Action Research.* London: The Falmer Press.

Faerch, C., and G. Kasper. (eds.). 1987. *Introspection in Second Language Research.* Clevedon/Avon: Multilingual Matters.

Hustler, D., T. Cassidy, and T. Duff. (eds.). 1986. *Action Research in Classrooms and Schools.* London: Allen and Unwin.

Kemmis, S., and R. McTaggart. 1982. *The Action Research Planner.* Victoria, Australia: Deakin University.

Lewin, K. 1946. Action research and minority problems. *Journal of Social Issues,* 2, 34–46.

Nisbett, R., and T. Wilson. 1977. Telling more than we can know: Verbal reports on mental processes. *Psychological Review,* 84, 231–259.

Nixon, J. (ed.). 1981. *A Teacher's Guide to Action Research.* London: Grant McIntyre.

Nunan, D. 1990. Action research in the language classroom. In J. C. Richards and D. Nunan (eds.), *Second Language Teacher Education.* New York: Cambridge University Press.

    1992. *Research Methods in Language Learning.* New York: Cambridge University Press.

5 In or out of the action zone: location as a feature of interaction in large ESL classes in Pakistan

Fauzia Shamim

> I told a boy he could leap fences
> and he soared over mountains
> I told a boy he was stupid
> and to his ignorance he was chained
> (Robertson and Steele 1969: 31)

Large ESL classes are a "hard reality"[1] in developing countries such as Pakistan, India, Sri Lanka, Indonesia, and Nigeria, where teachers everyday face classes which are sometimes composed of a 100 or even 200 students (see, for example, research by Coleman 1989a and 1989b; Gorrell and Dharmadasa, 1989; Naidu, et al. 1992; Okebukola and Jegede 1989; Sabandar 1989; Shamim 1991). Although teachers have identified large class sizes as one of their major problems, we do not know for certain how teachers and learners perceive teaching and learning of English in large classes, as they are, in "difficult educational circumstances" (cf. West 1960). This chapter is part of a preliminary attempt to arrive at some understanding of the lives of teachers and learners (cf. Allwright and Bailey 1991) in one such context – that is, large ESL classes in Pakistan.

Description of the setting

The research reported here was conducted over six months in six secondary schools in Karachi, the largest cosmopolitan city in Pakistan. A total of 232 classes were observed in classrooms of twenty-seven different teachers. Furthermore, twenty teachers and twenty-one groups of learners (each group comprising three to five students) from the same classes were interviewed. (The corpus was part of the data collected for

An earlier version of this paper was presented at the IATEFL Conference in Lille, France, October 1992.

1 Some preliminary work has been done on teachers', and to some extent learners', perceptions of large classes in a number of countries in Asia, Southeast Asia, and Africa, by members of the Lancaster-Leeds Language Learning in Large Classes Research Project (now INCLASS or International Network of Class Size Studies) – for example, Coleman 1989a, 1989b; Locastro 1989; and Sabander, 1989.

a larger study on teacher-learner behavior and classroom processes in large ESL classes in Pakistan.)

Government schools in large urban areas like Karachi are characterized by overcrowded classrooms which represent a range of class size from forty-five to one hundred students and more.[2] The medium of instruction in these schools is Urdu, which is the national language in Pakistan. (These Urdu medium schools are compared to private or English medium schools, where it is comparatively rare to find a class with fifty or more students.)

Until recently the teaching of English in all state secondary schools was a compulsory subject in the first year. Now, however, efforts are underway to introduce English from class I in primary school (five- to six-year-olds) as part of the government's commitment to provide equal opportunities to all sections of the population, but, more important, as a result of the country's growing realization that English is important for trade and commerce and other fields of modern life.

The classrooms in Pakistan are mainly teacher-fronted for a number of reasons. These include:

1. The teachers' lack of awareness and/or feelings of insecurity in using other types of classroom organization.
2. The effect of culture, whereby the teacher is traditionally seen as an authority figure and is given respect for his or her age and superior knowledge.
3. The view of teaching/learning that is prevalent in the community where teaching is viewed as transmission of knowledge.

Moreover, the classrooms are physically overcrowded, with limited space for teacher movement. The common pattern in the majority of classrooms is that of an active teacher and passive learners. In addition, the teaching-learning of English in school classes is characterized by teachers' low proficiency in the language, a set syllabus (and textbook) required to be completed for exam purposes, and limited time. (The academic year is usually shortened because school often serve as centers for school-leaving or other exams and political disturbances in the city.) The classrooms in government schools are built according to government specifications, with space for twenty dual desks to accommodate forty students. Often three students have to share a desk meant for two. Most of the classrooms have four rows of five or six dual desks. There are narrow pathways between the first and second rows and between

2 A hundred students seemed to be the cutoff point in secondary schools in Pakistan. It was found that when class size exceeded 100, the students were redistributed, usually by creating another section. If there were no extra classroom, classes were held for different groups in the corridor or outside, on a rotation basis, to accommodate the newly created section.

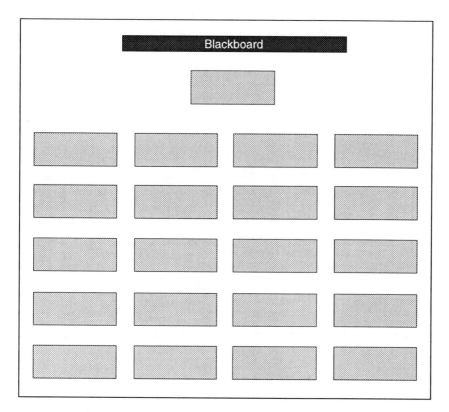

Figure 1. Layout of a typical classroom for forty students in secondary schools in Pakistan.

the third and fourth rows. With an increase in student numbers, more and more desks in the second and third rows are joined together to make extra space for additional desks or chairs, if they are available. Figure 1 shows the typical layout of school classes in Pakistan.

Teachers usually conduct their classes from the center of the front of the room. From this position they have easy access to the blackboard, which is almost always the only resource in the classroom other than the textbook. Thus, teachers directly face the middle two rows, but they can also "keep an eye on" students sitting in the two wings on the left- and right-hand side in the front two or three rows. It is not always possible, however, for teachers to "see" the students at the back of the classroom.

Thus the front of the classroom lies within the *surveillance zone* of the teacher. The back of the classroom is outside the teacher's *attention zone*. This seems to affect the behavior of the students in different locations – in the front or back – of the classroom.

Data from teachers and students

This chapter presents data from interviews with teachers and learners in large classrooms in Pakistan. Although the teacher-learner interviews were conducted in Urdu, all extracts from the interviews are given in translation except where noted. An effort has also been made, during translation, to keep to the spirit and idiom of the language used by the respondents. Thus English equivalents preferred locally in Pakistan have often been used in translation instead of equivalents in "standard" English (such as *less* instead of *fewer* and *copies* instead of *exercise books*.) The learner interviews were held in small groups of four to six students: S1, S2, and so on denote a change of speakers; however, S1 and S4 could be the same speaker (student) in a group. Pseudonyms are used both for teachers and learners.

In Pakistan teachers with the basic qualification for secondary school teaching (B. Ed.) are considered competent to teach English. Most of the teachers have a low proficiency in the language and teach English out of necessity rather than because they are inclined to do so. English language teaching is offered as an optional subject in the B.Ed. program, but it has an outdated syllabus. Furthermore, it is not a popular subject because trainees have low English proficiency.

The majority of secondary school teachers are female. For them the role of the teacher is often second to the social roles of wife, mother, and daughter-in-law. Teaching is seen mainly as a "comfortable" profession for women, a convenient means of supplementing the family income while leaving women ample time to fulfill their various domestic responsibilities. As teaching is a low-paid profession, male teachers often have a second job.

The students in secondary schools fall between the ages of eleven and sixteen. They are generally observed to have low motivation for studying. These students belong to different ethnic backgrounds, and English is often their third language. All students want to learn to speak English, but they see no obvious use for it in their present lives. Also, they have little exposure to the language outside of the classroom.

Reasons for learners' location in the classroom

The students perceive their location in the classroom with reference to the position of the teacher and the blackboard in the front of the classroom. Thus students in the first three rows consider themselves to be in the "front" of the class, while students in the fifth and sixth rows feel that they are at the "back" of the class. Students in the fourth row perceive their location variously as the middle or the back of the class-room.

The location of the learners in the classroom seems to be a result of one or more of the following factors. First, teachers try to impose or dictate location and succeed. The teachers in this study reported that class teachers assigned seats to the students, at the beginning of the school year, on the basis of height. However, they explained that "sub-ject teachers can change seats if they see that two friends talk a lot. Then we move one of them to sit somewhere else." Students reported that teachers often reallocated seats on the basis of student ability. As one student noted, "In the English class the teacher tells the weaker girls at the back to come to the front and sends some girls from the front rows to the back."

Second, teachers try to dictate location but are eventually defeated in their efforts to do so or are forced by the learners to reconsider their earlier decisions. The students in one class reported that the teacher had initially assigned the seats according to the students' height. However, very soon the students changed their seats, rearranging their locations according to personal preferences for different zones in the classroom. The teachers confirmed that "[i]n the beginning the teacher assigns seats but later they [the students] settle it themselves" because "[t]he teacher doesn't have a lot of control over this."

Third, teachers do not attempt to dictate location and the students decide for themselves. There seemed to be tough competition among the students for getting the front seats in the classroom. The students said that they used various strategies to get a place in the front:

S1: If you come regularly you can come early and grab the front seats.
S2: I grabbed my seat in the front row the very first day before other boys had come.

The unwritten rule in one classroom was that "whoever comes first in the morning and keeps his bag reserves the seat. Then no one can re-move the bag."[3] Although many students would like to sit in the front, not all are willing to make the extra effort involved in getting the front seats.

Location as a feature of interaction in large classes

As mentioned earlier, the classroom space is perceived by the teachers and students as divided into two distinct zones: the front and back of

---

3 Coleman (1991) also mentions coming early to class as one of the strategies used by learners in large classes.

the classroom. As the two major sources of input (i.e., the teacher and the blackboard) are situated up front, the front becomes the place where all the action takes place. This seems to be particularly true in large classes, where the teacher is (or is considered to be) the major and/or only resource available in the classroom.

It seems that the general pattern of teacher-student interaction and the degree of learner participation in classroom activities in large classes is linked significantly to the location of the students in the front or the back of the room. In fact, it was observed that only a few students in the front rows participated in the lesson in any way. This is evident in the following extract from my classroom observation notes describing a part of a reading lesson.

Mehnaz [the teacher] continues with the reading passage she had started yesterday. After making a few students read it out aloud – when she calls some students from the back of the class to the front in order to read, probably so that she can hear them better when they are closer to her – she begins to read out the passage phrase by phrase (in fact, word by word), which the students recite in chorus after her. Only the children in the first four rows are repeating, while the children in the last three rows are busy talking to each other quietly, or doing other things.

It was mostly the students in the front of the room who were selected by the teacher for reading the text aloud or answering the teacher's questions in class. In teacher-fronted large classes these were the only forms of in-class student participation. Further, the questions-answer exchange between teacher and students was often the only pattern of teacher-learner interaction. The only bit of discourse that was initiated by the students was to confirm whether they should copy something in their text copies or grammar copies. Sometimes they also plucked up enough courage to ask the teacher which page she was reading from (i.e., if they were unable follow it the first time it was announced at the beginning of the lesson).

In contrast to the students at the front, those at the back either did not volunteer or were unable to read aloud when nominated by the teacher to do so. This pattern is illustrated in the following notes from my research diary.

Two things were particularly noticeable in Sughra's class today. (1) Only eight to ten students (out of fifty-two students present in a class of eighty-five) from the first two rows volunteered to read by raising their hands. The teacher selected one of them and the student read reasonably well. The smooth rhythm of the lesson was disturbed when the teacher decided to call upon some students from the back to read [probably because of my presence in the class]. As they hesitated and stumbled in their reading, it cast a jarring note, breaking the earlier smooth rhythm of the lesson. The teacher began to feel annoyed and soon reverted to calling on the volunteers from the front rows only, and the class somehow regained balance and proceeded smoothly as before. (2) The students' help was enlisted by the teacher for the purposes of classroom management as well as her personal work.

It was also observed that the majority of teachers created within their large class a smaller class of students who sat in the front. They seemed happy to teach this "smaller" class of students and ignored the students at the back, as long as these students tacitly agreed not to disturb the class and at least copied down the answers from the blackboard. An extreme example of this phenomenon was observed in the class of one teacher who enjoyed the reputation of being a "good" teacher in her school. She had sixty-five students in her class. However, she was really teaching a class of only eight students – the monitors who sat in the first row. They answered all the questions and served as barometers for pacing the classroom activities. One day when she had given them dictation, it was obvious that she only considered the students in the front as worthy of her attention. The following observational notes capture the classroom events towards the end of the period.

The teacher tells the monitors in the first row to first check their own work. "Then you'll exchange papers and each monitor will check four papers very quickly," she announces. Hina, who is the class monitor, is told to read out each word. The teacher asks her to read slowly. As Hina reads out a word, the teacher repeats it and then stops a while to allow the eight monitors to find the word in the book and check its spelling. The pace of the class is set up by the monitors in the first row, and the teacher only waits for them to find the word and check it before moving on to the next word. The students at the back cannot keep pace and look very bewildered. When all the words have been checked the monitors walk back to collect the papers from their rows. A third student sharing a desk with Hina and Unaiza in the front row is told to move back so as to give the two monitors space to work. Some students at the back begin to do other work while the monitors are busy checking their papers.

Furthermore, the teachers directed different types of questions to students at the front and back of the classroom. More difficult questions were asked of students in the front rows, while students in the back were often told to repeat the same answers. It was also observed that the teachers asked questions from students in the back (a) to control mild forms of misbehavior, by publicly showing the students' incompetence, or (b) to bring them back to the "fold" when they were observed as not paying attention to what was being taught in the front. Thus it seemed that the students in the back were addressed basically for punitive or control purposes because neither the teacher nor the other students expected them to be able to read well or answer questions.

A few students in the back also commented on the difference in teachers' wait time for questions directed at students in the front and the back of the class; teachers waited longer for answers from students in the front. The students felt that this reflected a difference in teachers' expectations from learners in different locations in the classroom. It was not possible, however, to record this phenomenon in any systematic way.

During their interviews, the teachers did not report any difference in their interaction with students in different locations in the classroom. Nevertheless, as will be discussed herein, they had definite opinions about the kinds of students who sit in the front and back of the room, which seemed to influence their behavior toward the students.

Learner characteristics and patterns of classroom behavior

What kinds of students sit in the front and the back of the classroom, and why do they choose to sit there? In the present study, it was found that teachers and students can attribute certain character traits to students who sit in the front and the back. Further, specific patterns of behavior are associated with students who prefer different locations in the classroom.

The majority of students in this study perceived a link between different types of students and their location in the classroom. For example, the students in the front were considered to be industrious and hardworking, as illustrated in the following student comment.

The advantages of sitting in the front are for those who study regularly and complete their work on time. They get up early in the morning and go over their work so it's beneficial for them [to sit in the front]. If you don't study then there is no advantage.

Several students in the front claimed that they were accustomed to sitting in the front because, as one student commented, "She is my favorite teacher and I enjoy studying in her class. This is my fixed place. I'm not accustomed to sitting at the back. I've always sat in the front."

Another reason students preferred the front zone seemed to be their awareness of the teachers' negative view of the students who sat at the back of the room. Thus the students in the front did not want to be considered "dull" or "bad" by the teachers. One girl said, "I don't enjoy sitting at the back (because) the teacher thinks that girls at the back don't study." Another commented, "Girls at the back are considered dull. Teachers think they don't study – that they talk a lot and I couldn't tolerate that. Our Maths teacher says this frequently."

Students who sat in the front seemed to have more self-confidence. This could be due to their personality type, but it could also be a result of their location in the classroom, as two students who now sit in the front confessed:

S1: I used to sit at the back. I was afraid of sitting in the front. But now I'm not afraid any more.
S2: Earlier I was also afraid of sitting in the front.

The teachers also thought that students in the front were "usually clever," perhaps due to the learners' strong personality type, which may have helped them to get a seat in the front in the first place. One teacher made the following point in English:

The smart children are quite active and dominating in the class, so they take the seats in the front row. And the children who are weak are not weak in studies only but also in behavior. So they are suppressed.

The teachers felt that the students who sit in the front do so because they want recognition; consequently, they participate actively during the lesson.

Yes, girls at the back either don't pay attention or if while teaching I ask the meaning of a word we've met before – the girls in the front answer and girls at the back don't raise their hands.

In contrast, the students who sat in the back had a very negative view of what they perceived as "tricks" used by the students in the front for getting the teacher's attention. One student expressed the idea this way:

What really annoys me is that girls in the front write the translation of the lesson in their textbooks at home, so they can easily give the translation, etc., when told by the teacher to do so in class.

The teachers considered the students at the back to be "dull" and "lazy" compared to students in the front. (During the course of learner interviews, one student asked me pathetically, "Miss, you are also a teacher. What is your opinion about girls who sit at the back?") They further opined that the students who choose to sit in the back rows want to be outside the attention zone and hide from the teacher. (As seen earlier, the attention zone is limited to the front of the classroom in teacher-fronted large classes.) One teacher remarked:

Even some shorter girls sit at the back. For the teacher there is no difference, but the students in the back row are usually dull. They want to hide behind

131

but some students at the back also want to work. But mostly it is not true. They are lazy – that's why they sit at the back.

The teachers also believed that these students sat in the back because they wanted to keep their "weaknesses," such as their low ability level and bad handwriting, hidden from the teacher.

Thus for teachers the difference between the students in the front and the back seemed to be quite clear: The students in the front are clever; they have a strong personality type and work hard and participate actively in the lesson. In contrast, the students in the back are dull; they have weaker personality types and are generally not interested in their work.

Like their teachers, students in the front seemed to have a very negative image of the kind of learners who sit in the back. According to them:

1. The students in the back are careless, and they do not take interest in their studies.
   S1: At the back only those boys sit who like to make mischief.
   S2: Bad boys.
2. They have a lower ability level.
   S1: The boys at the back are not good in their studies.
   S2: They are all dull.
3. They lack the confidence to answer the teachers' questions or participate in classroom activities in any other way.
   S1: Girls at the back prefer to sit there because they are afraid.
   S2: They are afraid of answering the teacher's questions.
   S3: They want to hide from the teacher so that she doesn't ask them any questions.
4. They talk a lot.
   S1: They [students at the back] talk a lot and even disturb us [girls in the front].
   S2: That's what everyone says, that girls at the back talk a lot – and it's true really.
   S3: Tall girls sit at the back and they are always talking. In front there are shorter girls and they don't talk.
   (There was a general agreement among the students in the front that some students "fight to get a place at the back" because it is easier to talk to one another there.)
5. Students in the back do other work during the lesson.
   S1: They read storybooks. And they are always talking.
   S2: They do other work and Miss doesn't know about it.
   One student commented, "Whenever the teacher is teaching, girls at the back are doing their homework of other subjects or doing some other work though they have their books open in front of them."

6. They do not complete their work. A few students felt sympathetic toward the students who sit in the back rows. Consequently they tried to rationalize the apparent apathy and attitude of nonwork of these students.

S1: [They don't try] Because they have household work to do.

S2: No, Miss. They suffer from inferiority complex.

S3: Their home environment is such that they don't get an opportunity to study at home because they have to do household chores. But if they try, they can also work.

Thus the reasons for sitting in the back can be attributed to students' personality types and their home background. The back of the classroom soon becomes a haven for these students – a place to hide from the teacher, particularly when they have not completed their work. Several teachers pointed out this vicious circle of events. One said, "So some students don't work due to problems at home. Now when they haven't done their work they sit at the back trying to hide from the teacher for fear of being scolded."

The few students at the back who agreed to be interviewed[4] complained that they were obliged to sit there because of their height. They also claimed that the teachers' differential expectations of students in different locations in the classroom colored their attitude and behavior towards the students in the back.

S1: Even if a girl talks in the front the teacher is bound to suspect girls at the back.

S2: Miss, this is true. No matter how hard they try, girls at the back always have a bad reputation.

S3: Students both in the front and the back talk an equal amount but only girls at the back are blamed for talking.

It seems significant that both teachers and the students in the front have a low opinion of students in the back. As a result, they have few expectations for students in the back, which in turn affects their attitude and behavior toward these learners.

Conditions and opportunities for learning

The students who sit in the front of the classroom are generally perceived to be better than the students who sit in the back. But are stu-

---

4 The students who were identified by the teachers for learner interviews were invariably found to be among the brighter in the class who sat in the front rows. Although it was possible to ask for student volunteers the second time around (i.e., if more than one group of learners was interviewed from the same class), the students at the back were generally too shy and lacking in confidence to volunteer for the interview.

dents in the front inherently "good"? Are students in the back intrinsically "dull," or do they become dull by sitting in the back? To answer these questions we need to look more closely at the conditions and opportunities for learning available for students located in the front and the back of the classroom.

The front zone

The front of the classroom seemed to be the choice location. There was a general consensus among students about the advantages of sitting in the front, the most important being a "better" understanding of the lesson, perhaps owing to the students' close proximity to the teacher. Also, there is less distraction and noise in the front. One student said, "By sitting in the front you understand better and get more attention from the teacher." This feeling is also evident in the following comments.

S1: Miss, it is easier to understand [in the front].
S2: We understand more quickly. At the back students distract you by talking.

As a result, students in the front are able to complete their work on time.

As mentioned earlier, the front of the class also falls within the attention zone of the teacher. This helps the teacher keep track of what the students in the front are doing. The constant monitoring by the teacher also becomes a source of motivation for these students to work better. Several students also mentioned increased attention from the teacher, and the benefits associated with it, as one of the major advantages of sitting in the front.

S1: The boys in front sit quietly as they are under the teacher's eye.
S2: We like to sit in the front.
S3: It's easy to understand and the teacher asks you more questions.
S4: He asks what we have understood and we can answer all the questions.
S5: Sir also knows if the students in the front are understanding or not.

One girl said, "The teacher knows the names of girls in the front. If you sit at the back she doesn't even get to know your name."

According to the students, there are at least two further advantages of sitting in the front. The first is the ability to see the blackboard and hear the teacher. Second, there are more opportunities for participation in classroom activities.

The students in the front are also entrusted with certain privileged jobs such as that of a "checker." (A few teachers appointed some brighter students as "checkers" to assist them in checking the huge amount of written work in their large classes.) A group of students told me that one of their friends was a checker "because she is in the front."

As mentioned already, both the teachers and the students consider the students in the front to be better than the students in the back. The reasons for the better classroom performance of students located in the front zone can be summarized as follows:

1. Students in the front fall within the attention zone of the teacher; therefore the teacher can monitor their work more easily. This motivates students to work better.
2. Students in the front do not talk by virtue of being "under the direct gaze of the teacher." Hence they are able to concentrate on the lesson. As a result, they are able to understand the lesson which, in turn, enables them to complete their work.
3. The students in the front can see the blackboard and hear the teacher clearly.

Thus the environment in the front zone seems to be more conducive to learning, and the students in the front have more opportunities to participate in activities. It can be concluded, therefore, that the students in the front do not necessarily have a higher ability level, but they possess an initial motivation for learning in the classroom (and probably also a stronger personality) by virtue of their having chosen to sit in the front in the first place. This, along with the availability of the optimal conditions for learning in the front zone, including the general environment of work around them, motivates them further to work harder. As a result they become "good" students.

The back zone

In contrast to the front zone, the atmosphere in the back zone seems to be distracting and nonconducive to work. In fact, the conditions and opportunities for learning at the back of the room seem to be the mirror image of those found in the front.

Students who sit in the front reported that there was a lot of noise in the back. The students in the back also complained that they could not hear the teacher.[5]

I sit at the back while the teacher stands in front and teaches girls in the front only. We can't hear her at the back. She starts teaching immediately (as

5 Holliday (1991) mentions poor acoustics as one of the major problems in large university classes in Egypt. As a result of this and related problems, Holliday and his team developed a "distance learning" methodology for use in large classes.

she comes into the class). The girls in front take out their books quickly while we get late.

Indeed, during my observation of this class, despite my best effort, I was never able to hear the teacher's instructions directly from where I sat in the back. The teacher had a very soft voice and addressed her instructions to the students in the front of the class only. The instructional message was somehow transmitted to us at the back of the class, but it took a while to do so.

Horne (1970) draws attention to acoustic limitations in learning a foreign language, particularly English. He is of the opinion, rightly in my view, that "the student needs to hear the foreign language three to five times more distinctly than he hears his native language in order to understand it" (p. 145). A student in the front commented, "They [students at the back] can either not hear the teacher clearly or can't understand."

Furthermore, students in the back cannot see the blackboard clearly. This situation was observed in the majority of classes I visited, as illustrated in my observational notes:

The teacher gives "words/meanings" to the students by writing them on the blackboard. There is a great deal of activity in the classroom as the students take out their exercise books. Some students stand up to do so as they can't reach their bags easily due to limited space. (Mostly three students are sharing a dual desk meant for two students.) The teacher gives the meanings both in English and Urdu. Two students leave their seats to visit friends in other parts of the classroom. Some students have not taken out their exercise books until now and are still busy talking to their friends.

Five students leave their seats to go to the front of the classroom to copy from the blackboard; another ten students at the back stand up at their seats to see the blackboard clearly. The teacher continues to write more words and their meanings on the blackboard. The three students sitting in the row in front of me are busy talking to each other.

The teacher walks around the class to check if everyone is working [copying] or not. As she does so some students want to know which exercise book to write in ("Miss, rough or fair copy?"). Others want to know if they should write *Pacific English* [the name of their textbook] on the top of the page, as the heading, in their exercise books before copying the vocabulary list.

Three students move closer to the blackboard to see it more clearly. Now approximately sixteen students are standing at their seats. A few students walk around the classroom (not always the same students) or change their place; however, all of them are busy copying from the blackboard.

As can be seen in this example, whenever the teacher wrote something on the blackboard during a lesson, such as a vocabulary list, many students from the back either moved to the front of the room, stood up at their seats, or had to crane their necks forward in an effort to see the blackboard.

Because the teacher conducts the lesson from the front of the classroom, the students in the back find it difficult to pay attention. This is evident in the following comments by a teacher.

I think when students sit in the front they realize that the teacher is watching them. They do not get involved in mischief as compared to children sitting at the back of the class. Children at the back are away from the "direct gaze" of the teacher so they get involved in talking and mischief. Children in the front are likely to get caught more easily so they are more careful.

Students in the back cannot always understand the lesson owing to the physical distance between the teacher in the front and their location in the back of the classroom.[6] As a result they do not complete their work. Further, their "copies" tend not to be checked. This was observed by several students.

S1: [A student from the back] No matter how much they work, their copies are not checked because the teacher will only reach them after she's finished checking the copies of girls in the front, and if the entire class period is spent in checking copies of girls in the front then girls at the back are left.

S2: [A student from the front] No, this is not right. If you finish your work quickly your copies will also be checked earlier. Girls in the front complete their work on time so it's checked first while girls at the back don't do their work.

S3: [Another student from the front] The girls at the back only do their work in the Sindhi period[7] because the teacher is very strict.

It was revealed during the interviews that the students in school classes in Pakistan put a high premium on getting their work checked by the teacher. The fact that the copies of students in the back are not checked by the teacher could be very demotivating for them.

It has been established that in very large classes even the minimum conditions for learning, such as hearing the teacher and seeing the blackboard, are not available at the back of the room. Moreover, it seems that the difficult learning conditions at the back create an environment of nonwork, which can negatively influence the "good" students in that location. As one student commented,

6 This observation seems to be in agreement with Hall's concept of proxemics (1969, in Horne 1970), according to which the "close phase" of the physical distance between the teacher and the students is four to seven feet while the "far phase" is seven to twelve feet. Hall suggests that beyond twelve feet the teacher ceases to be a member of the group and becomes a lecturer with a more formal style.
7 A class period allocated for teaching Sindhi, a regional language of Pakistan.

It happens with us also. Sometimes if we sit at the back it's as if the devil takes hold of us. You are influenced by the environment around you. If everyone is talking you also want to join in.

Thus the nonavailability of some essential conditions for learning in the back zone can have a negative impact on both the classroom performance and the motivation level of the students in that location in the classroom.

Now to return to the two questions posed earlier: Are students in the front inherently "good"? Are students in the back intrinsically "dull," or do they become dull because of their location? It seems from this discussion that (a) all the "action" takes place in the front zone in large classes in Pakistan, as this is where the teacher and the blackboard are located, and (b) the students' behavior and performance are influenced significantly by their various locations in the classroom.

The students who are already highly motivated (or have a strong personality) choose to sit in the front. Further, the students in the front, by virtue of their being in the action zone, get increased opportunities for learning in the classroom. As a result, their classroom performance is better than that of students who are seated in the back, and their level of motivation is higher. In contrast, the students in the back have an initial low motivation, as well as limited opportunities for learning. The extra effort required, for example, in seeing the blackboard clearly and getting attention from the teacher results in their losing interest in the lesson. Consequently, the students in the back are unable to understand the lesson or participate in classroom activities; therefore, they are perceived as "dull" by the teacher and other students. This leads to a further decrease in their motivation level.

The effect of location on different types of students in large classes could perhaps be explained better by borrowing an analogy from the field of economics: In large classes, the rich (better students) who occupy the choice locations in the classroom become richer while the poor (weaker students) become poorer.

In or out of the action zone

It seems that for the majority of students, sitting in the back of the classroom can be very demoralizing. In fact, unless they are already very highly motivated, it results in students' losing interest in their work. However, both the teachers and the students believe that the students in the back would improve in their studies if they moved to the front of the room. Indeed two students described how their classroom behavior and, therefore, their overall performance had changed considerably as a result of their changing location in the classroom.

S1: I used to sit at the back and didn't take much interest in my studies. But Miss advised me to sit in the front and to take interest in my work. So now I sit in the front and I've improved considerably. At the back I was mostly busy in talking. The teacher told me, "You can do well," and that I should try and develop my hidden talent. So she told me to sit in the front and it has made a lot of difference. First I didn't study at all but since I've been sitting in the front I get a lot of attention from the teacher and I can also understand the lesson.

S2: All girls at the back are not dull. I also used to sit at the back but as I said earlier girls at the back are either very good or very weak. But you can work hard while sitting at the back also.

S3: Miss, I have moved from the back of the class to the front. I didn't study at the back but since I've moved to the front I've started studying.

These comments indicate that sitting in the back rows does not have an adverse effect on those few students who are highly motivated. However, these "good" students also try to move to the front or the action zone as soon as they can manage to do so.

The students who are out of the action zone must make a great deal of effort to gain entry into the action zone. A student who had been "graduated" from the back to the front recalled her experience.

When I came to the arts group I was so confused because all my friends were in the science group. And I got a place right at the back of the class, so that's where I began to sit. Then I tried to work from there only. Miss, girls at the back talk a lot. But I tried to study in that only. Whenever the teacher asked a question I used to raise my hand very prominently.

Furthermore, it seems that by trying to participate in classroom activities (e.g., answering teachers' questions), students in the back have to put themselves in a position of greater risk than students in the front because neither the teacher nor their classmates expects them to answer correctly. Hence they are interrupted and generally not given an opportunity or encouragement to self-correct.[8] In fact, the teacher and other students look down upon the efforts made by students in the back to participate in classroom activities. This is evident in the following student comment.

Actually when a girl from the back begins to answer, before she gets a chance to complete the answer, a girl from the front gives the answer. So

8 That these behaviors are used by teachers to communicate their expectations to the students has also been noted by other researchers (for details, see Good and Brophy 1987: 128–129).

what the girl at the back was saying is cut short. The teacher considers girls in the front better so when they answer the teacher listens to them carefully. In this way girls at the back suffer.

Another problem is peer pressure. One learner noted, "Students laugh when girls at the back make a mistake because they think they are dull." Another pointed out, "If girls at the back try to work, their friends ridicule them and say: Oh! so today she's also become studious!" It seems that only a few students who sit in the back have the necessary willpower and determination to move into the action zone in the face of all the odds, including pressure from their peers. But once they are successful in gaining the membership to the front zone, they automatically gain access to other privileges, such as increased attention from the teacher. Although a few students manage to move from the back to the front of the classroom, it was found in this study that the location of the students generally remains stable during the course of an academic year.

The teachers, like these students, seemed to be aware of the differential effects, both beneficial and harmful, of different locations in the classroom. Yet, they often exhibited an ambivalence in their attitude toward the effect of location in large classes. For example, the teachers agreed that the location of the students (i.e., where they are in relation to the action zone) has an important influence on their classroom performance and learning in general, but they did not like to admit (probably due to the teacher's traditional role as an authority figure) that they could not keep an eye on all the students. The following observation by a teacher reflects this ambivalence quite clearly.

It is possible that they [students] become smart by sitting in the front. We tried to move them around but found that when you make them sit in the front they improve, whereas children at the back – I don't think they are inherently bad – but children in the front sit so close to the teacher that they automatically begin to study. They develop interest while a child at the back thinks, though it's not true, that he is out of the teacher's "range." Teachers can see all the children but they think they can hide from the teacher and therefore pay less attention. That is why they begin to lose interest, thinking that they can get away and the teacher will not see them.

It is significant that the teachers felt obliged to change the location of the students, particularly at the time of the annual inspection. Several teachers explained their rationale:

The teacher assigns the seats and at the time of inspection these intelligent children [in the front] are made to sit at the back and children from the back are moved to the front because the inspectors sit at the back.

... especially at the time of inspection we have to do this – put the bright children in different corners of the room so that we get an answer from every part of the classroom – otherwise the inspection team gets a bad impression.

A few teachers made a conscious effort to improve the situation. Several teachers tried to keep the students in the back on-task by using strategies such as calling upon them during the lesson to pay attention, asking questions in between the lessons, and allocating turns randomly to students at various locations in the classroom. One teacher said that she tried to solve the problem of students' inattention at the back by changing the location of the learners regularly. A few other teachers also suggested that the optimal conditions for learning could be provided to all students, at least for some time during the school year, by moving the learners on a regular basis in the classroom.

Sometimes the teachers also tried to extend their attention zone by walking to the back of the classroom. However, walking around to monitor the students' work, or even going to the back of an over-crowded classroom, was almost an impossible feat for many teachers, particularly in very large classes.

One teacher used a unique method for extending her attention zone to the back of the class by assigning the task of monitoring the class, while she was teaching from the front, to a student monitor. This strategy was observed to have the desired effect of keeping the students in the back quiet and apparently on-task. The nature of this procedure, as well as its effects, were also reported by the students in that class.

S1: In our English class one student stands at the back because students at the back talk and make a noise. So either Naseem or Imran are assigned this duty.[9]
S2: They check if all the students are looking at their books. If anyone is talking they make him stand up. This is the only period in which there is no noise and the students work. Otherwise in all other classes something or the other is happening.

Thus a few teachers have tried to bring the students in the back into the action zone by using various strategies. These include asking students questions; moving learners forward into the action zone, while continuing to teach from the front of the classroom; and extending their attention zone to include the students at the back of the class by occasionally moving around the classroom themselves.

9 The job of monitor was entrusted to these two students on the basis of their general reputation as "tough" boys in the class rather than their academic abilities.

Summary and conclusion

In Pakistani schools, the teacher is virtually always in the front of the classroom in large school classes. The students perceive the classroom space as well as their location in the classroom vis-à-vis the position of the teacher and the blackboard in front. Thus the classroom seems to be divided into two zones, the front and the back. At the beginning of a year, teachers assign students their seats in the front or the back according to their height. However, the students often rearrange their location later for personal reasons, and sometimes the students are allowed to choose their own location at the beginning of the year. Further, students are attributed with certain behavior patterns and character traits, by teachers and their classmates, based on their classroom location. In fact, a close link is perceived between different types of students and their choice of location in the front or back zone of the classroom.

The front is the place where all the action seems to take place. The learners in the front are able to see the blackboard and hear the teacher clearly; consequently, they are able to understand the lessons better. Because students in the front are in close proximity to the teacher, the teacher finds it easier to monitor their work and generally to "keep an eye on" them. This close monitoring by the teacher motivates the students to work harder. As a result, the students in the front participate more actively in classroom activities and are usually perceived as "smarter" than students in the back. Furthermore, the learning conditions in the back are less than optimal. The students there have difficulty seeing the blackboard and hearing the teacher. Consequently, they do not pay attention during the lesson and cannot answer questions in class. They are out of the "teacher's range," so they feel free to indulge in nonproductive activities, such as talking, or do other work while the teacher is teaching in the front. Because their location in the classroom does not help students in the back understand or learn the teaching points, they are considered dull and begin to lose self-confidence. The back of the class then becomes a place of refuge – a place to hide from the teacher. The back zone seems to have its own culture and rules for classroom behavior, which members find difficult to break. However, students with a higher level of motivation sometimes manage to move out of the back zone by dint of sheer hard work and individual effort.

Generally, teachers think that learners who are weak or lazy prefer to sit in the back so that they can "hide" from the teacher. Learners, on the other hand, feel they are "doomed" if they have to sit in the back, so they lose interest and the motivation to work. What is interesting, however, is that both the students and teachers are aware of the differential effects of different locations in the classroom. In fact, a few teachers even use some strategies to bring the students in the back into the action zone or to extend their attention zone into the back of the class. Despite these efforts, a distinct difference can be observed in the nature and pattern of interaction between the teacher and learners situated at different locations in the classroom.

The aim of this chapter has been to direct attention to two points in particular: First, the stereotyping of the students according to their various locations in the front or the back of the classroom, and consequently the teachers' and other students' expectations of these students, seems to have a significant effect on their behavior and achievement. Second, secondary school learners in Pakistan seem to work better when they are "under the direct gaze" of the teacher. In other words, their interest and motivation to work increases in direct proportion to the amount of attention (supervision) they receive from the teacher. However, in large classes, close monitoring by the teacher is not only difficult, owing to inadequate space for the teacher to walk around the classroom, but it can also be very taxing for the teacher who teaches at least three to four large classes a day.[10]

The findings of this study underline the need for the teachers to monitor, very consciously, the quality and quantity of their interaction with students located in the front and back zones of their classrooms. Furthermore, it seems imperative that teacher educators take into account both the location of the learners and their perception of classroom space vis-à-vis the teacher, as well as the sociocultural background of both the teachers and the learners, before recommending "solutions" to help teachers extend the action zone without eroding their status or authority in the classroom.

References

Allwright, D., and K. M. Bailey. 1991. *Focus on the Language Classroom: An Introduction to Classroom Research for Language Teachers.* Cambridge: Cambridge University Press.
Coleman, H. 1989a. *Large Classes in Nigeria.* Project report no. 6. Leeds: Lancaster-Leeds Language Learning in Large Classes Research Project.

10 One suggestion given by most teacher educators for handling large classes is to devolve responsibility in the classroom by using different instructional and classroom management techniques, such as pair and group work (Nolasco and Arthur 1988). In fact, these techniques aim to train the learners to be independent of the teacher and to take responsibility for their own learning. However, as mentioned earlier, the learners in most school classes in Pakistan seem to work better when the source of control is external and imposed rather than internal and voluntary. Thus it becomes very difficult for the teachers to use group work effectively in these large classes.

143

1989b. *How Large are Large Classes?* Project report no. 4. Leeds: Lancaster-Leeds Language Learning in Large Classes Research Project.

1991. Learners' Strategies in Tertiary-Level Large Classes. Paper presented at the Specialist conference on Current Research in Large Classes, Karachi, Pakistan.

Good, T. L., and J. E. Brophy. 1987. *Looking in Classrooms* (4th ed.). New York: Harper and Row.

Gorrell, J., and K. H. Dharmadasa. 1989. Sources of school stress for teachers in Sri Lanka. *Compare, 5*, 2, 115–125.

Hall, E. T. 1969. *The Hidden Dimension.* London: Bodley Head.

Holliday, A. 1991. Large University Classes in Egypt: The Application of a "Distance Learning" Methodology. Paper presented at the IATEFL conference, Exeter, U.K.

Horne, K. M. 1970. Optimum class size for intensive language instruction. *Modern Language Journal, 54,* 189–195.

Locastro, V. 1989. *Large Size Classes: The Situation in Japan.* Project report no. 5. Leeds: Lancaster-Leeds Language Learning in Large Classes Research Project.

Naidu, B., K. Neeraja, E. Ramani, J. Shivakumar and A. Viswanatha. 1992. Researching heterogeneity: An account of teacher initiated research into large classes. *ELT Journal, 46,* 3, 252–263.

Nolasco, R., and L. Arthur. 1988. *Large Classes.* London: Macmillan.

Okebukola, P. A., and O. J. Jegede. 1989. Determinants of occupational stress among teachers in Nigeria. *Educational Studies, 15,* 1, 23–36.

Robertson, D., and M. Steele. 1969. *The Halls of Yearning: An Indictment of Formal Education, a Manifesto of Student Liberation.* California: Andrew Printing Company. p. 31.

Sabander, J. 1989. *Language Learning in Large Classes in Indonesia.* Project report no. 9. Leeds: Lancaster-Leeds Language Learning in Large Classes Research Project.

Shamim, F. 1991. Defining Large Classes in Pakistan. Paper presented at the Specialist conference on Current Research in Large Classes, September, Karachi, Pakistan.

West, M. 1960. *Teaching English in Difficult Circumstances.* London: Longman.

6 Reticence and anxiety in second language learning

Amy B. M. Tsui

Interviewer: What stops you from speaking up?
ESL student: 'Cos my classmates also not speak up
. . . they affect me very much. . . .
Sometimes I really frighten . . . I am
afraid my classmate will laugh . . . I think
my English level is not good, so I am
shy to talk English . . . I hate English very
much because I think English is quite
difficult to learn . . . Educational system is
stressful . . . because many people if fail
in English . . . they effect (sic, affect) their
life.
Interviewer: Are you worried about failing in English?
ESL student: Very . . . very much.

Getting students to respond in the classroom is a problem that most ESL teachers face (Beebe 1983; see also Katz, this volume; Lucas 1984; White and Lightbown 1984). In a study of student responses to teacher questions, White and Lightbown (1984: 229) found that out of an average of 200 questions asked in a fifty-minute lesson 41 percent received no response. The problem of getting students to respond is particularly acute with Asians students, who are generally considered to be more reserved and reticent than their Western counterparts (see, for example, Chaudron 1988; Lucas 1984; and Sato 1982). Tsui (1985: 17–19) studied two ESL classrooms and found that in both teacher talk took up more than 80 percent of the total talk and that there were no instances in which the students initiated a question. In one classroom, no student volunteered to answer the teacher's question. In the same classroom, the teacher repeated a question eight times and still failed to get a response from the students. Wu (1991: 13) analyzed four ESL lessons in Hong Kong secondary schools, and his observations are very similar to

I would like to thank Arthur McNeill for his helpful suggestions. I am also grateful to Elizabeth Walker for allowing me to use the chapter opening quote from her research on language learning anxiety of secondary school students in Hong Kong.

Tsui's (1985): No student took the initiative to seek clarification or check confirmation from the teacher, and there was not a single learner question.

Although one should avoid making the sweeping generalization that talking equals learning (see Allwright 1980), and forcing students to participate when they are not ready (see Allwright and Bailey 1991: 144), one cannot deny that participation is very important in language learning. When students produce the language that they are studying, they are testing out the hypotheses which they have formed about the language. When they respond to the teacher's or other students' questions, raise queries, and give comments, they are actively involved in the negotiation of comprehensible input and the formulation of comprehensible output (Swain 1985), which are essential to language acquisition. From a pedagogical point of view, contributions from students, as pointed out by Katz (this volume), help to create the content of the lesson.

In the present study, ESL teachers working in secondary schools in Hong Kong were asked to reflect on their own teaching and identify a specific problem that might form the basis for classroom action research. Over 70 percent of a group of thirty-eight teachers identified getting more student oral response as one of their major problems. The following excerpts from their reports illustrate their perception of the problem.

During English lessons, there was a general lack of response to questions asked. Students were eager to learn and yet they seemed unable to bring themselves to participate actively in class.

Students had little involvement throughout the whole lesson. Thus they found no interest in it. They were passive and dared not speak out. For most of the time, they just uttered single word answers like "Yes" or "No."

[T]he pupils were very passive and quiet. Even when they were called on to ask questions and comment, they kept silent.

They were generally shy and unwilling to speak in English. . . . Some tried but gave up at last.

Students are too passive in my class. They seldom answer my questions voluntarily. What I can do is just assign one or two of them to give me response or reaction. Worst of all, most of them simply sit there doing nothing but listening or sometimes daydreaming.

These observations were echoed by Wu (1991: 15).

[The] students are reluctant to volunteer to answer questions. General solicits almost invariably fail to elicit any verbal responses. The data reveal that students in general have a habit of waiting to be called upon before answering. Of all the questions asked in four lessons, only one answer is volunteered.

The aim of this chapter, then, is to examine teachers' perceptions of the factors that contribute to student reticence, and to document these teachers' attempts to address the problem. The success and failure of these attempts, as reported by the teachers themselves, will be discussed in light of the research on language learning anxiety. Unfortunately, it was beyond the scope of the present study to investigate the learners' viewpoint beyond what is recorded in the transcripts. (For a discussion of students' ideas about their reticence, see Hilleson, this volume.)

Data collection

The present study is based on the classroom action research project reports of thirty-eight ESL teachers who were practicing teachers enrolled in the Postgraduate Certificate in Education program at the University of Hong Kong. This is a two-year, part-time in-service teacher education program for secondary school teachers. The teachers were predominantly Chinese, with teaching experience ranging from two to thirty years. Except for two teachers, all of them teach in secondary schools.

Secondary schools in Hong Kong go from Secondary One (grade 7) to Five (grade 11). After Secondary Five, there are two years of pre-university study, referred to as Secondary Six and Seven. The average class size is thirty-five to forty students. Most classrooms are very formal. Students have to stand up to greet the teacher at the beginning and the end of the lesson, and they have to raise their hands and wait for the teacher to call upon them to speak. They also have to stand up when speaking.

English is the medium of instruction for English lessons in most schools. The schools are divided into five bands according to the academic ability of the students. Band One is the best and Band Five is the poorest. The English proficiency of students varies a great deal, ranging from near-native competence for some upper secondary students in some Band One schools, to serious problems in expressing themselves for those in Band Five schools. The schools in the present study consist of all bands.

In their classroom action research projects, the teachers videotaped or audio-recorded their own lessons and reviewed the tapes to identify one specific problem that they had in teaching. They then designed a list of strategies to overcome the problem and carried out these plans for four weeks. While they were trying out the strategies, they kept a diary of what went on in the lessons and their own reflections. At the end of the try-out period, they videotaped or audio-recorded another lesson and evaluated the effectiveness of their strategies. Then they wrote a report which described the problems identified, the implementation of the strategies, and an evaluation of the strategies. The report also included transcripts of lesson segments which illustrate the success or failure of the strategies.

Teachers' perceptions of student reticence

In the following section, I shall outline how teachers perceive the problem of student reticence and its contributing factors. Data from both teachers' reflections and their own classroom recordings will be quoted for illustration.

Students' low English proficiency

In their reports, most teachers attributed student reticence to low English proficiency. The following excerpts are from the reports of two teachers. The first one is a teacher of Secondary Five (grade 11), the other Secondary Six (grade 12).

[My] students' language proficiency is not good enough to express their ideas clearly in English during group discussion. In fact, the English standard of most of my students is very low.

I think the students' failure to respond to teachers' question was a result less from lack of knowledge but more of the insufficient English proficiency.

The next two examples from the teachers' classroom data support these observations. They are from a Secondary Five (grade 11) lesson in an English medium school. (Readers should recall that these teachers are non-native speakers of English, and that what they say or write is quoted verbatim.) Utterances which illustrate the points made are marked by arrows.

1. T: First of all let's find out what a debate is. Is there anyone who knows what a debate is?
   Ss: [No response]
   T: Joseph. Do you know what a debate is?
→ J: Um . . . Is it . . . sorry I don't know.
2. T: . . . But I would like to ask what are rhetorical questions for? Are they questions expecting answers? Brian, what do you think?
→ B: Ah. . . . I don't know.
   T: What about you Mickey?
   M: Sorry I don't know.

T: Is there anyone who knows what are rhetorical questions for?
Ss: [No response]

We can see from Joseph's response in (1) that he appears to hazard a guess at first, as indicated by "Is it . . . ," but then he decides not to take the risk and resorts to a declaration of ignorance. It is likely that he is either not sure of the answer or has difficulties in expressing himself. Similarly in (2), Brian, after some hesitation, resorts to "I don't know" as a safe way out. However, there are also examples from the same lesson in which students do know the answer and can express themselves, but do not take the initiative or provide an the answer when the teacher asks for volunteers, as in example (3).

3. T: And what does speaking for the motion means? Is there anyone who wants to answer this question?
   Ss: [No response]
   T: Okay. Natalie, when I say you are speaking for the motion, what do I mean?
→ N: Um . . . you mean I . . . I support the motion.
   T: Correct. Very good. Thank you for your attention.
4. T: . . . At the beginning of the speech you should address the chairman and the audience first, right? Jeanne, how do you address the Chairman and the audience at the beginning of the a debate speech?
   J: Mr. Chairman, ladies and gentleman.
   T: Yes, good.
→   And what do you usually do in the first paragraph of your debate speech? Any volunteers?
→ Ss: [No response]
   T: No? Okay, Lily can you answer this question?
→ L: Is it define the motion clearly?
   T: Yes, very good.

Examples (3) and (4) show that students are able to answer the questions when they are nominated by the teacher. This observation suggests that language proficiency is not the only factor that contributes to student reticence. In fact, example (1) already suggests that Joseph could have made a guess, if he were not afraid of making mistakes. In other words, students' level of self-confidence and their willingness to take risks are important factors that affect their readiness to respond.

Students' fear of mistakes and derision

The second reason commonly mentioned in teachers' reports is students' lack of confidence and fear of making mistakes and being laughed at.

149

The following are excerpts from teachers' reports (emphases in these excerpts are mine).

They are unwilling to speak in English for *fear that they may make silly mistakes in front of the brighter students.*

[T]here are reasons why the students don't respond to my question. It may be that they don't know the answer to the question, or they know the answer but they don't want to give [the] answer because it is so simple or complicated that *they are afraid to be laughed at. . . .*

I asked students questions about the story. But for the first few times, most of the students remained very quiet when I asked them questions. I asked them individually. I wondered whether they prepared their lessons or not. Actually, most of them did but *they were too shy to give me an answer even [though] they knew the answers. Also, they were afraid of losing face in front of their classmates if they gave me a wrong answer.*

One of the teachers conducted a survey of a Secondary Two (grade 8) class of forty students by asking them to fill out a questionnaire. Eighty-eight percent of the students said that they have no incentive to speak in English. When they were asked to state the reasons, 82 percent of those respondants said that they do not have confidence, 46.3 percent said they do not know how or what to say, and 36.5 percent said that it is because their classmates do not speak in English either.

The students' lack of confidence is also reflected in their unwillingness to speak up in class. They either take private turns instead of offering the answer to the whole class (see Allwright and Bailey 1991: 127), or when called upon by the teacher to answer a question, they speak in a very soft voice, which is barely audible to the teacher and not at all audible to the whole class. This can be seen from the following example taken from a recording of a Secondary Three (grade 9) lesson.

5. [The teacher is going through the terms for different kinds of drugs.]
    T: And tell your partner in Chinese, okay? Marijuana. Okay, you've got that in Chinese, Henry? Tell your classmates loudly.
→ S: Dai-ma [Cantonese translation of *marijuana*]
    T: Louder!
→ S: No. [meaning he does not want to say it louder] . . .
    T: Scars. Have you got scars anywhere? If you . . . if you h . . . ?
→ S: Hurt [saying it softly]
    T: Loudly.
    S: Hurt.
    T: Hurt yourself, then you got a scar.
       . . .

T: "Offered," that means, can you give me another word for "offered"? Another word? [Looking round the classroom and spotted William who whispered the word to himself.] Good. William. Louder.

S: Give.

T: Given, not give, because it is passive voice. . . . My second question is "Do you know that in Hong Kong, drugs are divided into two groups mainly?" Have you ever heard of that? The first one is . . . Yes! [looking at one of the students uttering a word in Cantonese] Yes! You've got that in Cantonese. Can you say that loudly? What is it?

S: Yuen sing [Cantonese translation of *soft* in "soft drugs"]

The scenario in (5) is a familiar one in Hong Kong schools. In a fifteen-minute segment of this lesson, the teacher directed twenty questions to the students, out of which ten were responded to by students whispering the answer. If the teacher had not noticed these private turns and then gotten students to repeat the answer loudly, student reticence would have been even more prominent.

Students' fear of making mistakes and being negatively evaluated can be teacher-induced. Teachers with unrealistic expectations tend to inhibit students' participation. This can be seen in these excerpts from teachers' reports:

Though my attitude might be gentle and encouraging, *I was expecting some correct answers most of the time.* Given the [sensitive] nature of class, *they would feel the strain and were less willing to contribute unless they felt they have got the 'right answer'.*

Most of the students said that they understood my questions but they did not know how to answer them or how to express their opinion. *They emphasized that they were afraid that their answers could not satisfy me.*

In example (5), we have an instance of an appropriate answer of "give" as another word for "offered," and yet the answer is rejected by the teacher because it is not in the correct form. As the teacher in the first excerpt immediately above points out, teachers' unreasonable expectations inhibit student participation because students will remain silent rather than risk not measuring up to the teacher's expectation.

Teachers' intolerance of silence

A third reason many teachers identify is intolerance of silence in the classroom. Many teachers report that they themselves dislike or are afraid of silence and that they feel very uneasy or impatient when they fail to get a response from students. Therefore, when a response is not forthcoming, teachers do one of the following: allocate the turn to another student, provide the answer themselves, or repeat or modify the question. The following piece of classroom data illustrates the problem.

6. [The teacher is discussing the effects of being addicted to drugs.]
    T: . . . Don't just look at the books. Just think from your general knowledge. Can you think?
→   Timmy, can you hurry up? What are you doing?
→   Okay, Ryan? Hurry up. Think. Can you all write down? What are the effects? Write down. What did you say just now? [Looking at one of the students.] Die. What else? Pardon? Louder please. Priscilla, can you say it louder? Louder, louder.
    S: Skinny. [Then silence for a while.]
    T: Anything else? Affects, how does it affect you and your –
    Ss: Family.
    T: Family. Good. [Looking at one of the students.] Can you try to think more?
→   Quickly, quickly. Anything else? If you always take drugs, what happens to you? What happens to you? [Teacher gives a hint by putting her hand in her pocket.]
    Ss: No money.
    T: Yes, waste money. Good. Any more? Think.
→   Quickly.

In this excerpt the teacher not only gives little or no wait time, she also puts a great deal of pressure on students to come up with an answer. The effect of pushing students to answer questions literally within seconds is well captured by one teacher who wrote, "[T]his would frighten the students, stop them thinking and suppress their wish to answer questions."

    This phenomenon of a very short wait time after questions is prevalent in classrooms. Rowe (1969), in examining a large number of elementary school L1 science classes in the United States, found that the average wait time was only one second. White and Lightbown (1984) analyzed seven transcripts of fifty-minute ESL lessons from grades 8, 9, and 10 in a French school in Montreal. They report that the average wait time in these transcripts was 2.1 seconds (p. 229). The reasons that White and Lightbown give (ibid.: 236) are first that teachers need to cover the syllabus in a specified period of time, and second that teachers are afraid that a longer wait time will slow down the pace and lead to boredom and disruption in the classroom. These reasons are shared by ESL teachers in Hong Kong, as can be seen from a report from one of our teachers.

I do not pause that much because *I am afraid that students chat during lessons, they become noisy.* Besides, I have the idea that pausing is equal to silence. . . . Furthermore, time is precious, too precious.

However, there are other more deep-rooted reasons which have to do with teacher beliefs about effective teaching. This can be seen from the following excerpts from teachers' reports.

[T]o me, silence is a result of teacher's inertia, when silence occurs, it means [the] teacher is not making the lesson productive enough for students to learn.

[S]ilence gives me the sense of failure because in my hidden vision success means being quick and highly efficient. . . . *I speak a lot because deep down I believe that teaching, effective teaching, is imparting knowledge all the time. . . . Consequently, I hiddenly feel that I would not do my duty and would be a failure unless I spoke a lot.*

The teachers in the present study have the misconception that an effective teacher should be able to solicit immediate responses from students and that a responsible teacher should be talking all the time. The converse relationship between teacher talk and student talk is well expressed by one teacher who wrote, "When there is more teacher talk, there will be less student participation, resulting in long silences in the classroom that will prompt the teacher to talk even more."

Uneven allocation of turns

Closely related to intolerance of silence is the uneven allocation of turns. In order to avoid not getting responses from students, teachers tend to ask brighter students from whom they are sure of getting an answer. (See Shamim, this volume, for a report of a parallel pattern in Pakistan.) This has been reported by these teachers as another reason for the lack of student response.

More often than not I thought that I tried to choose people at random but I suspected . . . that *I asked students I knew would be able to give an answer, thus many of the students were not given a fair chance.* . . . It was apparent to me after watching the first video and monitoring during my subsequent lessons that I unconsciously asked the same students questions. After further analysis, it also appeared that they were for the most part those who I knew would know the answer.

Some students do not want to give responses because they are often ignored by the teacher.

And reflecting on their classroom behaviour, the teachers felt that they tended to allocate turns to brighter students from whom they were sure of getting a correct answer in order to make themselves feel good about their own teaching, to avoid going over the teaching points again, and to avoid silence. The following excerpts illustrate this tendency.

As a teacher, I can identify that *I have a need to feel successful, a good way to have this reaffirmed is to ask those students who I know will give me the answer that I want – what better way to show "real" learning is taking place!* If I ask others I may run the risk of finding out that some students haven't understood what I have so painstakingly been teaching. That then means I have to re-evaluate my methods and the responsibility is back on me.

I often ask them [students who put up their hands] to answer questions because I want to save time. Normally they would not put up their hands if they do not know the answer. Then I do not need to explain the answer and *can cover more in the lesson.* . . . I am afraid of silence in class. Sometimes when I ask a student a question and he does not know the answer, he will just stand up and keep quiet. When I ask another student to help him, this student may also keep quiet because he does not know the answer as well. *But if I ask the one who puts up his hand, there will not be a moment of silence.*

The effect of allocating turns to brighter students is that, as one teacher points out, the weak and shy students feel neglected. The more they feel neglected, the less willing they are to contribute.

Incomprehensible input

Many teachers attribute the lack of response to students' not being able to understand teachers' instructions and questions. They report that their own questions are often vague and difficult to understand. For example, one teacher had a discussion with a class of forty about their difficulties in answering her questions. Five of the students said they did not understand her questions at all. She reported, "They only heard my voice. It was only a sound but meaningless." After analyzing the forty-five questions that she asked in one lesson, this teacher found that fifteen of them were very vague and incomprehensible. Another teacher noted:

After viewing myself asking questions, I realized that *what I thought were simple and clear questions were in fact quite difficult to understand.* Not only this but the questions were often *confusing and not specific enough.* . . . The result is that students who do not understand the question fall into two categories: either they ask for clarification and I try to rephrase the question or they remain silent.

This teacher was lucky because at least there were some students who would ask for clarification. Another teacher, however, was not so lucky. She reports,

I asked the students to prepare their story in advance before the class. It was a total disaster because only a few of them had done their work. Most of the students did not even read a line in the chapter. . . . I was pretty angry and I even wanted to punish the students. But later *I found that the students did not do their preparation work because they did not understand what they were supposed to do.*

What has been described here is in fact fairly typical in Hong Kong schools. Most students in Hong Kong will not ask the teacher even if they do not understand what the teacher is saying, especially if the students have to ask the question in English. When the students remain silent, the teacher has no way of knowing what the problem is. Hence, no remedial measures are taken. This leads to further incomprehension, resulting in further silence.

In this section five reasons were identified by the teachers in the present study as contributing to the lack of students' participation: (1) the students' low English proficiency; (2) their fear of making mistakes and being ridiculed by classmates; (3) the teachers' intolerance of silence, which leads to a very short wait time for students to think about the question and come up with an answer; (4) the unequal speaking opportunities afforded to each student by the teacher; and (5) the overly difficult teachers' language input. In the following section, we shall explore how these factors are related to language learning anxiety.

Language learning anxiety

To understand better how these five factors contribute to student reticence in ESL classrooms, we need to understand language learning not only as a process of acquiring linguistic rules or participating in communication activities, but as a process in which individual learners are constantly putting themselves in a vulnerable position of having their own self-concept undermined and subjecting themselves to negative evaluations. This process is stressful and likely to generate much anxiety in the learners. Guiora (1983: 8) describes second language learning as "a profoundly unsettling psychological proposition." Language classroom anxiety is a widespread phenomenon which Horwitz, Horwitz, and Cope (1986: 128) describe as "a distinct complex of self-perceptions, beliefs, feelings, and behaviours related to classroom language learning arising from the uniqueness of the language learning process." The uniqueness of language learning lies in the fact that learn-

155

ers are required to perform in a language that they are still trying to master. This requirement has effects on the learner's self-concept (see also Foss and Reitzel 1988: 439). As Horwitz et al. (1986: 128) point out, "any performance in the L2 is likely to challenge an individual's self-concept as a competent communicator and lead to reticence, self-consciousness, fear, or even panic." When communicating in a language in which they are not fluent, learners cannot help but feel that they are not fully representing their personality and their intelligence.

The uniqueness of language learning also lies in the fact that learners are much more vulnerable to criticism and negative evaluation than in other subjects because the chances of making mistakes in the language class are much greater. A learner may get the answer right in terms of content, but wrong in terms of form or pronunciation. Example (5), in which the teacher asked for the passive voice after the student provided the correct lexical item, is a case in point. And given the importance that many ESL teachers attach to correctness, the constant error correction students receive from the teacher can be seen by them as a form of mild public humiliation (see Allwright and Bailey 1991). Labov (1969) maintains that speaking in class is perceived by black students as "high-risk, low-gain" because they believe that anything they say may be held against them. Similarly, speaking in ESL classes is high-risk, low-gain (Beebe 1983: 43). This position is supported by Horwitz et al.'s (1986: 129) report that speaking in a language classroom is the most frequently cited cause of concern for anxious foreign language students who sought help at the Language Skills Center at the University of Texas.

Studies on language learning anxiety

The prevalence of language learning anxiety in ESL classrooms and how it affects speaking in class has been investigated by Horwitz et al. (1986). They developed a Foreign Language Classroom Anxiety Scale and administered their questionnaire to seventy-five university students. In general, those who scored high on the anxiety scale reported that they were afraid to speak in a foreign language. Nearly half of the respondents reported that they started to panic when they had to speak without preparation in language classes. Nearly one-third said that they were nervous and confused when speaking in their language classes. Nearly half rejected the statement that they felt confident in speaking in foreign language classes. About 10 percent reported that they were afraid of being laughed at by their peers and that they would skip classes, overstudy, or sit in the last row to avoid the humiliation or embarrassment of being called upon to speak.

Liu (1989) carried out a survey of secondary school students in the

People's Republic of China. A questionnaire closely modeled on the one developed by Horwitz et al. (1986) was administered to 512 students. The subjects either agreed or strongly agreed with a number of statements: that they find it embarrassing to raise their hands to answer questions in class; that they are very nervous when the teacher asks them a question which they have not prepared for; that they are afraid of making mistakes; that they feel very uneasy when they cannot express themselves; that their English is not as good as that of their fellow classmates; that they will repeat the answer to themselves first before offering it to the whole class.

Student reticence and language learning anxiety

From the preceding discussion, we can see that the factors identified by our teachers all contribute to language classroom anxiety. Students who have low English proficiency tend to be anxious. Liu's study (1989) found that the anxiety scores of students whose English had been rated as "poor" by their teacher were much higher than the scores of those whose English was rated as "good." However, this does not mean that students with high English proficiency have little or no anxiety. As Allwright and Bailey (1991) point out, some very competent learners are anxious because if they do not make mistakes, they will stand out from their peers and be resented. To avoid this, they deliberately make mistakes. Yet, by so doing, they may be criticized by the teacher. Some students, therefore, resolve the conflict by withdrawing from the interaction. (See Shamim, this volume, for a discussion of peer pressure in language classes.)

The anxiety generated by trying not to show that one is better than the rest is perhaps even more serious among Chinese students, whose culture emphasizes modesty. In a study of the sociocultural factors affecting students' classroom behavior, Wong (1984, cited in Wu 1991: 15) suggests the following "rules" governing the use of English among some Hong Kong secondary school students.

1. You should not demonstrate verbal success in English in front of your peers.
2. You should hesitate and show difficulty in arriving at an answer.
3. You should not answer the teacher voluntarily or enthusiastically in English.
4. You should not speak fluent English.

Indeed, it is a widespread phenomenon in Hong Kong schools that students who know the answer will not take the initiative and answer the question until they are asked by the teacher to do so. And as Wu (1991: 15) observes in his analysis of classroom data, "when students are called upon to respond, they may prefer to hesitate and give short answers where possible so that they do not give their peers the impression that they are showing off." In examples (3) and (4), the students' reluctance to volunteer an answer to the teacher's question could be owing to their lack of confidence. But it could also be because they are inhibited by this "maxim of modesty" in the classroom.

The second contributing factor (lack of confidence and fear of making mistakes, being criticized and ridiculed) is related to language learning anxiety (see also Price 1991: 105). Horwitz et al. (1986: 127) discuss three types of performance anxiety which are related to language learning anxiety: communication apprehension, test anxiety, and fear of negative evaluation. Students who lack confidence in themselves or in their English necessarily suffer from communication apprehension.

The special communication apprehension permeating foreign language learning derives from the personal knowledge that one will almost certainly have difficulty understanding others and making oneself understood. Possibly because of this knowledge, many otherwise talkative people are silent in a foreign language classroom. (ibid.: 127)

Students also suffer from test anxiety and fear of negative evaluation. Test anxiety stems from fear of failure, which is closely related to fear of negative evaluation. In ESL classrooms, students are constantly required to perform orally in front of the whole class, which is one form of testing. Their performance is continuously evaluated by the teacher, and by their peers as well. It is therefore understandable that diffident students will try to avoid subjecting themselves to evaluation by the teacher and their peers.

The third factor, the teachers' intolerance of silence, also creates a great deal of anxiety. This is because for students who are still learning the target language, it is often impossible to produce an immediate response to the teacher's question. They need time to process the question and formulate an answer. The language teacher who keeps repeating the same question or the name of the student when an immediate response is not forthcoming is inadvertently undermining the self-esteem of the student. Heyde-Parsons (1983) studied how students' interaction with their teacher affects their self-esteem and found that those whose self-esteem scores were quite low from the start had sharply lower scores if the teacher simply repeated the question in exact wording when they failed to respond. To the teacher, repetition of questions may be a means to fill silence. To the students, however, it may be interpreted as a reminder that they are incompetent. Similarly, teachers who turn to another student for a response or who answer the question themselves upon getting no immediate response may be damaging the student's self-esteem, especially if a teacher shows signs of impatience. The student is considered a failure, without even having the chance to try. It would be even more damaging if the teacher were to ask the student to remain standing until another student has given an answer and the first student has repeated that answer correctly. This student is penalized and publicly humiliated for being not as good as his or her peers. This behavior, sadly, is still found among teachers in Hong Kong. In fact, one teacher in the present study reports, "I was not encouraging enough when one of my students gave me a non-acceptable answer. I just stopped him and said, 'No.' Furthermore I even told him to stand until I got the correct answers from other students."

The fourth factor, the uneven allocation of turns, is seen by the teachers as depriving some students of the opportunity to practice the target language. While this is true, there is a more profound effect on students. As one teacher points out, those who are seldom allocated turns will feel ignored by the teacher. Teachers who allocate turns in favor of brighter students will undermine the self-esteem of the weaker students. Those who allocate turns in favor of weaker students are likely to create anxiety in them, since they may perceive the uneven turn allocation as "picking on them" or "putting them on the spot," especially if they are reprimanded for not being able to answer the question or for making mistakes. The uneven turn allocation is used by teachers out of expedience to avoid silence, to avoid going over old ground, and to give themselves the illusion that learning is taking place. Yet, such a strategy may be perceived by students as the teacher's rejection of them as worthy individuals.

Finally, incomprehensible input is another source of anxiety. Counselors at the Learning Skills Center at the University of Texas found that anxiety primarily revolves around speaking and listening. They found that many students had little or no idea of what the teacher was saying during longer utterances. One student even reported that when his teacher spoke in a foreign language, all he heard was a loud buzz (Horwitz et al., 1986: 126). In the Horwitz et al. survey, 35 percent of the students agreed with the statement, "It frightens me when I don't understand what the teacher is saying in the foreign language," and 20 percent agreed with the statement, "I get nervous when I don't understand every word the language teacher says." Likewise, in Liu's (1989) study, students strongly agreed with the statement, "I always try to catch every word when listening to English. If I fail to do so, I will feel anxious and this affects my comprehension of what follows." They also agreed with the statement, "Before and when listening to English, I am worried that I fail to understand."

Studies on language learning anxiety reveal that anxious students are desperately trying to avoid humiliation, embarrassment, and criticism, and to preserve their self-esteem. Teachers, therefore, must acknowledge this anxiety (see McCoy 1979: 185) and appreciate the extent to which students' behavior can be affected by it and the extent to which teachers' behavior can exacerbate it. Otherwise, whatever strategies the teacher adopts to overcome the problem are doomed to failure.

Successful and unsuccessful strategies

In this section, I shall discuss the strategies used by the teachers in the present study. The reported success or failure of these strategies will be discussed in light of whether they seemed to alleviate or exacerbate language classroom anxiety.

Lengthening wait time

Many teachers dealt with the intolerance of silence by reminding themselves that silence is not necessarily a bad thing. They tried to lengthen the wait time after a question to allow students to think about the question and to come up with an answer. Some teachers even timed themselves to make sure that enough wait time was given. However, there were several teachers who report that this strategy did not work for their students. The following are excerpts from two reports.

[I have] *consciously allowed frequent and longer pause – wait time* for the students to think about the question and construct their answers. *However, I was still not satisfied with the students' response.* I think they are too passive and not participating enough in class. Most of the time [after] the question was asked, especially for questions which required explanation or elaboration, there was often silence, even though they [the students] had already been given time to do the thinking and constructing their response.

I did *try to give longer waiting-time but only to find that most of them are just standing there, either shutting their mouth tightly or uttering some unrelated Cantonese answers.* Consequently, I had to rely on some brighter ones to give me the relevant answers.

Obviously, the problem cannot be dealt with simplistically by merely lengthening the wait time. In fact, insensitive lengthening of wait time can exacerbate the anxiety rather than alleviate it. One teacher reports that she might have discouraged a student from participating in class by giving her excessively long wait time and pushing her to produce an answer.

There was a student who readily and voluntarily told me one of the point[s] she got down in her list but she just could not think of any valid example. After about *two minutes silence* and after the question has been rephrased and example given, she still could not give me an answer. I then told her to take her time and that we should come back to her later.

160

This teacher later reflects that by waiting two minutes for the student to respond, and by insisting that she provide an answer later on, she was in fact embarrassing the student and discouraging her from volunteering in the future.

Now I thought *if I had not been so insistent, she could have enjoyed the lesson more* rather than struggling to give me an answer at the expense of a whole lesson. Moreover, *this act might discourage her from answering any question in the future.* Maybe I could have stopped at this moment and asked the whole class to work on this. . . . Then she would not have been so embarrassed with all the eyes fixed on her. In other words, *I should have let her go.*

Improving questioning technique

Some teachers dealt with incomprehensible input by modifying their questions. Some report success; others report that it only made minimal differences.

I asked them to anticipate what kind of information they think could be found in the article. There was no response. I then broke the question down into several questions. . . . In the process, most students either murmured to themselves or [were] nodding or shaking their heads to show agreement or disapproval. Very few actually put up their hands and gave answers.

Although the teacher feels that getting minimal responses is an improvement compared with no response, she still finds this situation unsatisfactory.

Some teachers report asking more referential questions (questions to which the teacher does not know the answer) and open-ended questions (questions which have more than one acceptable answer), but they failed to elicit more student responses. In fact, one teacher observed that questions which require long answers put students off. This is in line with Wu's (1991: 10–11) observation in analyzing four teachers' questions in four lessons. He found that a large number of display questions (questions which get students to display knowledge) and referential questions failed to solicit any verbal response (cf. Brock 1986; Long and Sato 1983; Nunan 1987). The percentages of open-ended and closed questions which failed to get any response are also high.

We can see that although questions which are vague and difficult do have adverse effects on getting students to respond, it does not mean that modifications of questions, even when they are good modifications, will necessarily lead to more student response. A teacher can have very good questioning techniques and yet fail to alleviate students' anxiety in answering questions.

An effective strategy that many of the teachers in this study used was to get students to write down their answers before offering them to the whole class. By doing so, the teacher gave students time to think about the question and to formulate their answers. There is less pressure on them to produce a spontaneous answer.

[I] have students write down their answers before [asking them to give] a verbal answer. [This] would help ease the fear and pressure the students have when a question was shot at them.

I also asked my students some questions. Instead of giving the answer immediately after each question, students were asked to write down the answers in the textbook. After that, I repeated the question again and students checked their answers. As a result they felt more confident when giving me their answers.

Accepting a variety of answers

Another strategy reported by the teachers is to let students know that there is not always a "right" answer and to accept a variety of answers. One teacher suggested, "Avoid giving them the impression that there is always a 'right answer' to every question. [Be] more flexible in accepting variations in students' answers." Another teacher also points out that it is important not to make students feel that they must come up with the right answer every time a question is asked. She gave her students three choices at the end of each question. They could answer the question, ask for more time, or ask for help. She found this to be very effective because she elicited more verbal responses from students.

This was a very effective way of introducing the idea to the students that they don't have to know the "right" answer. In fact, often they need to really think about the question or they need help in coming to the right answer.

Peer support and group work

Allowing students to check their answers with their peers before offering them to the whole class also encourages students to speak up. Our teachers reported that, having done so, students had more confidence in their answers because they had peer support. One said, "Usually students tend to be more confident to speak up if they have done some discussion with their peers." Another said,

Some not-so-confident pupils were more willing and more confident to give their ideas. It might be because the pupils gained more confidence after discussing with their classmates and they felt less [threatened] because those questions required no model answers and they allowed a variety of alternative answers.

Several teachers reported that students tended to be more willing to speak up after they had had group discussions. This is not only because group discussions give students a chance to rehearse their thoughts to each other in a low-risk, high-gain situation, but also because they feel that they have the support of their peers when they put the answers forward. One of our teachers reported,

> When pupils came to join the class discussion after their own group discussion, some of them were willing to speak up. It might be because they had grown accustomed to the atmosphere and they were more confident after discussing with their classmates. And *it might be also because they did not have a strong sense of losing face even if the ideas put forward were challenged.* What they put forward was the opinions of the whole group – the product of a corporate work, not their individual work.

In other words, support from peers is just as important as support from the teacher in creating an anxiety-free atmosphere.

Focus on content

Activities which focus students on content rather than form were also reported as effective. In this case, students were not under the threat of having their mistakes corrected.

> As I walked to different groups, I did hear English spoken among students themselves. It seems that they were more concerned how to beat the other groups on the next day than the mistakes they made in speaking English.

> There was active participation among all the groups and although students had to speak/answer questions in English, they did not hesitate to answer those questions which they knew well about. Nor did they look as shy as before. . . . Their main concern was to beat the other groups.

One teacher observed that when she introduced an element of competition in two classes, the group with lower English proficiency was actually more responsive.

> I have always had the impression that students of this class have a relatively lower standard of spoken English and less self-confidence in answering questions. However, they did show positive response and effort in the whole lesson. In fact, they felt quite excited during the group discussions. Maybe the word competition gave them the stimulus to try harder.

While competitiveness may generate "debilitating anxiety" (Bailey 1983: 69; Kleinmann 1977: 105; Scovel 1978: 139), competition in which students have the support of their peers can generate "facilitating anxiety" which "motivates the learner to 'fight' the new learning task" (Scovel 1978: 139; see also Kleinmann 1977: 105). In our teachers'

163

reports, students were apparently so keen to beat other groups that they were willing to try harder.

Establishing good relationships

Finally, establishing a good relationship with students is extremely important in creating a conducive learning atmosphere in the classroom. One way of achieving this is to involve students in discussions about their feelings concerning language learning. McCoy (1979: 187) has referred to such discussions as "cognitive restructuring," which involves getting students to discuss their feelings and rationalize their anxieties about language learning. This process creates trust between students and the teacher.

Several teachers have employed this strategy and have found it to be very effective. One teacher wrote in her report:

This [relationship] is achieved by talking to the students, letting them know that if students do not respond it is very difficult for the teacher to teach well because she does not know how students are taking in what she has taught. I also considered it imperative to let them know that when they participate in class, they are taking part in the formulation of knowledge as well as learning to communicate orally in English which is vital for their career. It seemed that the message was well taken.

Apart from talking to her students as a group, this teacher also talked to individual students at recess and lunch time. Upon noticing that one of the boys frowned and looked exasperated every time he was called on to give an answer, she held a private session with him. The session helped her to see that questioning at random can create great anxiety in highly apprehensive students and that it is much better to allow them to volunteer to participate (see also Daly 1991: 11). At the end of the session, the teacher and student reached a contractual agreement that she would not nominate him until he was ready, and in return he promised to try harder. Her intention was to let the student know that he had complete control over whether he would speak or not so that he could be more relaxed in class. After a week or two, this student began to volunteer to answer questions.

Sessions like this are effective because they enable the teacher and student to work together to deal with anxiety directly. If the teacher and the student were to "consider themselves as a partnership and view themselves as trying together to overcome the problem of anxiety, then neither would see the other as a source of difficulty, and both could work together to deal with the common problem" (Crookall and Oxford 1991: 144).

Concluding remarks

From the teachers' reports on their attempts to overcome the perceived problem of student reticence, we can see that the successful strategies minimize language learning anxiety and the unsuccessful ones exacerbate language learning anxiety. To overcome this anxiety, which can be debilitating, it is essential to create a low-anxiety classroom atmosphere. As one teacher points out,

Our aim should be that they [the students] feel as comfortable and fear-free as possible. When students are not afraid of saying they don't know, this takes away some of the fear and embarrassment they might suffer as a result of getting the wrong answer or admitting that they don't know the answer. When we allow students to have time to think, to check with each other or even to admit publicly that they don't know the answer, without fear, then *this goes a long way in creating a good learning atmosphere where even the most shy and hesitant students can participate more actively.*

Helping our students to overcome their anxiety takes time. It would be unrealistic to expect this to happen overnight. One teacher reports that her students participated actively when she introduced group activities and panel discussions. But on the next day, they reverted to their reticent selves. McCoy (1979: 187) observes that even though his students had been through cognitive restructuring, it took them a long time to overcome the fear of derision. It is important for teachers to remember that when students are unresponsive, it is possible that they are affected by language learning anxiety rather than simply being unmotivated or incompetent. And it is our obligation, as language teachers, to be as supportive as we can. Recognizing and addressing language learning anxiety not only helps students to be more responsive, but also makes language learning a much more enjoyable experience. As Horwitz et al. (1986: 132) point out,

[I]f we are to improve foreign language teaching at all levels of education, we must recognize, cope with, and eventually overcome, debilitating foreign language anxiety as a factor shaping students' experiences in foreign language learning.

References

Allwright, D., and K. M. Bailey. 1991. *Focus on the Language Classroom: An Introduction to Classroom Research for Language Teachers.* Cambridge: Cambridge University Press.

Allwright, R. 1980. Turns, topics and tasks: Patterns of participation in language learning and teaching. In D. Larsen-Freeman (ed.), *Discourse Analysis in Second Language Acquisition.* Rowley, MA: Newbury House.

Bailey, K. M. 1983. Competitiveness and anxiety in second language learning: Looking *at* and *through* diary studies. In H. Seliger and M. H. Long (eds.), *Classroom Oriented Research in Second Language Acquisition.* Rowley, MA: Newbury House.

Beebe, L. 1983. Risk-taking and the language learner. In H. Seliger and M. H. Long (eds.), *Classroom Oriented Research in Second Language Acquisition.* Rowley, MA: Newbury House.

Brock, C. 1986. The effects of referential questions on ESL classroom discourse. *TESOL Quarterly, 20,* 1, 47–59.

Chaudron, C. (1988). *Second Language Classrooms: Research on Teaching and Learning.* New York: Cambridge University Press.

Crookall, D., and R. Oxford. 1991. Dealing with anxiety: Some practical activities for language learners and teacher trainees. In E. Horwitz and D. Young (eds.), *Language Anxiety – From Theory and Research to Classroom Implications.* New York: Prentice Hall.

Daly, J. 1991. Understanding communication apprehension: An introduction to language educators. In E. Horwitz and D. Young (eds.), *Language Anxiety – From Theory and Research to Classroom Implications.* New York: Prentice Hall.

Foss, K., and A. Reitzel. 1988. A relational model for managing second language anxiety. *TESOL Quarterly, 22,* 3, 437–454.

Guiora, A. 1983. The dialectic of language acquisition. *Language Learning, 33,* 1, 3–12.

Heyde-Parsons, A. 1983. Self-esteem and the acquisition of French. In K. M. Bailey, M. H. Long, and S. Peck (eds.), *Studies in Second Language Acquisition: Series on Issues in Second Language Research.* Rowley, MA: Newbury House.

Hilleson, M. (Chapter 11, this volume). I want to talk to them, but I don't want them to hear: An introspective study of second language anxiety in an English-medium school.

Horwitz, E., M. Horwitz, and J. Cope. 1986. Foreign language classroom anxiety. *Modern Language Journal, 70,* 1, 125–132.

Katz, A. (Chapter 3, this volume). Teaching style: A way to understand instruction in language classrooms.

Kleinmann, H. 1977. Avoidance behaviour in adult second language acquisition. *Language Learning, 27,* 1, 93–107.

Labov, W. 1969. The logic of non-standard English. In *Georgetown Monographs on Languages and Linguistics,* 22. Excerpts in P. Giglioli (ed.). (1972). *Language and Social Context.* Washington, DC: Georgetown University Press.

Liu, Xue-Huei. 1989. A Survey and Analysis of English Language Learning Anxiety in Secondary School Students in the People's Republic of China. MA dissertation, East China Normal University, People's Republic of China.

Long, M., and C. Sato. 1983. Classroom foreigner talk discourse: Forms and functions of teachers' questions. In H. Seliger and M. H. Long (eds.), *Classroom Oriented Research in Second Language Acquisition.* Rowley, MA: Newbury House.

Lucas, J. 1984. Communication apprehension in the ESL classroom: Getting our students to talk. *Foreign Language Annals, 17,* 6, 593–598.

McCoy, I. 1979. Means to overcome the anxieties of second language learners. *Foreign Language Annals*, 12, 185–9.

Nunan, D. 1987. Communicative language teaching: Making it work. *ELT Journal, 41*, 2, 136–145.

Price, M. 1991. The subjective experience of foreign language anxiety: Interviews with highly anxious students. In E. Horwitz and D. Young (eds.), *Language Anxiety – From Theory and Research to to Classroom Implications*. New York: Prentice Hall.

Rowe, M. 1969. Science, silence and sanctions. *Science and Children, 6*, 6, 12–13.

Sato, C. 1982. Ethnic styles in classroom discourse. In M. Hines and W. Rutherford (eds.), *On TESOL '83*. Washington, DC: TESOL.

Scovel, T. 1978. The effect of affect on foreign language learning: A review of the anxiety research. *Language Learning, 28*, 1, 129–142.

Shamim, F. (Chapter 5, this volume). In or out of the action zone: Location as a feature of interaction in large ESL classes in Pakistan.

Swain, M. 1985. Communicative competence: Some roles of comprehensible input and comprehensible output in its development. In S. Gass and E. Varonis (eds.), *Input in Second Language Acquisition*. Rowley, MA: Newbury House.

Tsui, A. B. M. 1985. Analyzing input and interaction in second language classrooms. *RELC Journal, 16*, 1, 8–32.

White, J., and P. Lightbown. 1984. Asking and answering in ESL classes. *The Canadian Modern Language Review, 40*, 2, 228–244.

Wong, C. 1984. Socio-cultural Factors Counteract the Instructional Efforts of Teaching Through English in Hong Kong. Unpublished manuscript, English Department, University of Washington.

Wu, Kam-yin. 1991. Classroom Interaction and Teacher Questions Revisited. Unpublished manuscript, Department of Curriculum Studies, University of Hong Kong.

7 A window on the classroom: classroom events viewed from different angles

David Block

> Definition of triangulation (found in
> masses of data):
> English: "To each his/her own"
> Catalan: "Cadascú per on l'enfila"
> Spanish: "Cada loco con su tema"

The basic idea that a learner's thoughts are far out of the reach of even the most ingenious teacher or researcher is not new in applied linguistics. We might go back to Dakin (no doubt drawing on the ideas of Corder 1967), who spoke of the "in-built syllabus," stating that "though the teacher may control the experiences the learner is exposed to, it is the learner who selects what is learnt from them" (Dakin 1973: 16). Over a decade later, Allwright (1984) pointed out that learners' interpretations of teacher intentions and what lessons "are about" often differ greatly from what teachers have in mind. Three years later, Breen (1987) argued that "learners are capable of playing havoc with even the most carefully designed and much used task" (p. 23) and that teachers must take such autonomous behavior into account when planning classroom activities. Finally, we find the cognitive anthropologist, Kempton (1987) who, after studying North American physics students in action, came to the disparaging conclusion that "in the face of formal physics training . . . students simply reinterpret classroom material to fit their preexisting folk theory" (p. 223).

All of these examples in one form or another point not only to the autonomy of learner thought but also to the existence of a gap between the way teachers and learners "see" the classroom and all that occurs within it. In previous papers (Block 1990a; 1990b; 1992a), I have made the argument that this difference in viewpoint is an essential element in any attempt to make sense of classroom events. In this chapter, my aim is to examine the similarities and differences found in the accounts which learners and teachers give of day-to-day classroom events. In other words, do teachers and learners find the same or different classroom events to be salient? What similarities and differences do we find among the different learner accounts? What about the researcher's interpretations of what others say and do? Finally, is there a high degree of agreement among all parties involved?

168

It would be neither accurate nor fair to say that my investigation is unique in applied linguistics. Indeed, I can think of two recent studies which have dealt with individuals' perceptions of classroom events, one by Slimani (1987; 1989; 1992), and the other by Breen (1991), which I shall now summarize.

Research by Breen and Slimani

Breen compiled the accounts of 106 teachers who took part in a language teaching/learning experiment at Lancaster University, England, during the period 1984–1988. All participants were graduate students in the Linguistics Department, and all of them had at least three years' teaching experience. The participants took on the following roles: teacher, observer, and learner (two to five per class). After each lesson, all present were asked to write their answers to questions about the class. Breen summarized the data collected for sessions when informants were asked to identify "the specific techniques adopted by the teacher . . . to help . . . learners with the new language" (1991: 219). He found that there were differences not only among the various informant accounts, but also within the same account by the same informant.

However, one is left to wonder if learners with no teaching experience would demonstrate the same pattern when recalling classroom events. Indeed Breen himself poses the question:

At present, we can only guess whether or not some direct method of investigation in more everyday teaching situations – especially with less sophisticated learners – will reveal a similar picture. (ibid.: 229)

Here Breen echoes a concern expressed in Allwright and Bailey (1991), Bailey (1991), and Nunan (1992a), namely that published studies of learner diaries (e.g., Bailey 1983; Schmidt and Frota 1986; Schumann and Schumann 1977) have dealt primarily with the views of trained linguists and not "less sophisticated" learners. An exception to this rule is Slimani (1987, 1989, 1992), who gathered the impressions of "less sophisticated" learners in a more "everyday classroom situation."

Slimani was interested in learner reports on uptake, defined as "what learners claim to have learned at the end of a lesson" (1989: 223). She asked thirteen Algerian first-year university students to individually complete an "Uptake Recall Chart" at the conclusion of six lessons she had observed and tape-recorded. The Uptake Recall Chart was made up of a list of questions about grammar, lexis, spelling, pronunciation, and other factors related to language. Three hours after completing their charts, learners were asked to examine them and indicate which of the items entered they thought they had learned.

Having collected her data, Slimani examined the relationship between her transcriptions of classes and the learners' uptake charts. Among other things, she found that an item topicalized by a fellow learner had a better chance of being qualified as uptaken than an item topicalized by the teacher. This finding to some extent undermines ideas which the teacher might have of directly influencing learning (or, in any case, perceptions of learning), as it would appear that teacher-generated discourse is less memorable than learner-generated discourse. A second finding from the study was that the learner who topicalized an item was less likely to report that item as uptaken than his or her classmates. As Slimani (1989) points out, this finding is consistent with work by Allwright (1980) and Ellis (1984), which suggests that it is not necessarily the high-input generators who retain the most from a class, but the learners who attend to the high-input generators.

My study: comparisons with Breen and Slimani

The study which I have carried out is both similar to and different from the studies carried out by Breen and Slimani. With them I share an interest in what informants recall when asked about language classes they have attended. I am, therefore, interested in investigating perceptions of reality. However, my study differs from both of theirs in important ways.

First of all, unlike Breen I was able to carry out my study in a naturalistic language learning environment (in other words, the class under investigation was not formed with research in mind). As a result, I was able to find student informants who were not experienced teachers but experienced language learners. In addition, all participants in my study used their native language. This stands in contrast to Breen's study, where all informants had to give their accounts in English despite the fact that many were not native English speakers. My study differs from Slimani's in that I was able to capture not only the learners' points of view, but also the teacher's and, on the three occasions when I observed, my own. Thus, regarding my data gathering, I was able to triangulate. Finally, unlike both Breen and Slimani, I asked informants in my study to give their accounts orally as opposed to in written form. As was the case with Breen's informants, they were given general questions as a guide; however, the oral medium meant that they were free to vary the order, agglomerate questions, or even omit them.

This move to an oral diary is, I think, an important one, especially if we return to the literature on diary studies cited earlier. In surveys of such studies (e.g., Allwright and Bailey 1991; Nunan 1989, 1992a), I have seen no mention of any attempt to combine the ideas of retro-spection, where the norm is for an informant to say what he or she thinks has happened, with the concept of a log where accounts of events are given on a regular basis.[1]

Setting up the study

My main research partners were six M.B.A. candidates (all aged twenty-five to thirty-two) who were completing an obligatory English require-ment, and their teacher, an English instructor who was interested in classroom research and, above all, finding out more about what her students thought. I selected these individuals in the following fashion. First, in early April 1992 I asked the teacher, Ann, if she would be interested in participating in such a study. (Here and throughout this paper, informants have been assigned pseudonyms.) She said she would, and we decided that the month-long course she would soon begin would be ideal. I might mention here that in January 1992, the M.B.A. stu-dents involved in this study began a series of one-month courses which met daily for two and a half hours. In the first week of April, when they were completing their third such course, I met with these students to discuss the study and ask for volunteers. Six students, all male, im-mediately stepped forward and said that they would be interested in keeping a diary on a day-to-day basis. I shall refer to them as Alex, Jon, Jose, Juan, Quim, and Rick. The other seven students in the class did not volunteer to keep diaries, but they did agree to give accounts of the class on those days when I was to be present as observer. They will go by the following pseudonyms: Alicia, Ariadna, Marta, Paula, Jaime, and Josep.

Before the first class began, the seven diary keepers (six students and the teacher) were issued cassette recorders and blank cassettes. Their brief was to keep an oral diary, reporting on what they thought was going on in class on a day-to-day basis. To help them, I provided written instructions and questions which I hoped might orient rather than pre-determine their discourse. Learners were given a sheet with five ques-tions in their preferred language. (Five of the learner informants chose to speak in Spanish and one did so in Catalan. The teacher spoke in her native English.) The five questions were posed with the following introduction:

1 Of course we cannot ignore the problems inherent in gathering retroactive reports on events. I refer the interested reader to detailed analyses to be found in Ericcson and Simon (1984), Faerch and Kasper (1987), and Nunan (1992a).

Before beginning your account, please remember to say your name, the date, and the time of your intervention, and remember that you can comment on whatever event which you think might have anything to do with what happened in class. We are particularly interested in your point of view as regards the following items:

1. What were the activities which most stood out in today's class?
2. What do you think was the purpose of these activities?
3. What do you think you learned today?
4. What did the teacher do to help you learn? What did you do?
5. Were there other events in today's class which you think are worth mentioning?

Thank you for your cooperation.

The teacher was given a similar guide, but with questions about her intentions and her actions:

1. What were the activities which most stood out in today's class?
2. What was the purpose of these activities?
3. What do you think students learned today?
4. What did you do to help them learn? What did they do?
5. Were there other events in today's class which you think are worth mentioning?

Thank you for your cooperation.

On three occasions during the course I observed the entire class, writing down whatever I thought was noteworthy. In addition, I made cassette recordings with a portable cassette player. On the days I observed, Ann ended class fifteen minutes early, and I asked all students present to come with me to the language laboratory to record their impressions of the day's class on a cassette, following the brief just reproduced. Meanwhile, Ann was elsewhere giving her version of the day's events on her cassette recorder. I organized data collection in this manner because my chief aim was to triangulate – gathering as many points of view as possible. By the end of these days, I had my notes, Ann's comments, the comments of those students who were not keeping a diary, the comments of those students who were keeping a diary, as well as recordings of two of the three classes which I observed. (On one occasion there were problems with the recording.)

In the next two sections of this paper I shall describe how I began my analysis, first by examining diary accounts day by day and later by focusing on the first day that I was present as an observer. (All learner excerpts have been translated into English from the originals in Catalan and Spanish.) As I hope to demonstrate, this procedure proved somewhat enlightening. More important, however, it suggested to me a different, perhaps more fruitful, way of examining my data which I shall discuss in the final section when I contrast the views of one learner, Alex, with those of the teacher, Ann.

Beginning analysis

This section of the chapter reports on my initial analysis of the data. I begin by considering the first two days of class in particular, and then embark upon a more detailed analysis of events one week later.

The first day

On the first day of class I was able to obtain reports from only four of my seven primary informants because one (Alex) was absent and another (Jon) did not have a cassette recorder (a technical problem which lasted the first week until the informant actually told me). The third (Jose) produced a recording which was of such poor quality that it could not be transcribed.

As I went through the accounts, it seemed fairly clear that a proficiency test took up most of the time and was practically the only activity reported on by the informants. All informants defined the test's purpose as being a way to check everyone's level. The teacher, Ann, spent some time explaining how the group as a whole had decided that instead of taking a break in the middle of class, it would be better to do two and one quarter hours of class and finish early at 2:15 every day. Ironically enough, none of the student informants mentioned this decision, which as I was to find later, would have a negative effect on the evolution of the class. Indeed, the only comments informants made which did not have to do with the exam were about the teacher: Rick and Juan said that she was helpful and nice. Not particularly satisfied with my harvest for the first day, I read through the accounts for the second.

The second day

On the second day I was able to obtain a total of six diary entries, which meant that all my informants except one gave an account of the day's events. (As I stated already, Jon was not to begin reporting until the second week.) I began reading the entries thinking about the first question on the informants' briefs: What were the activities which most stood out in today's class? I decided to begin with Ann, who seemed to divide the class into the following five activities:

1. A spontaneous explanation of comparatives at the beginning of class.
2. A skimming activity. The text, from *Headway Upper Intermediate* (Soars and Soars 1987), was about the importance of English in the world. Students were to form questions about the text.
3. A spontaneous explanation of the English auxiliary system with the schematic representation on the blackboard.

173

4. A vocabulary exercise on parts of the body.
5. Two listening activities in the language laboratory. The first on numbers and the second on accents.

Table 1 provides a breakdown of whether these five events were at least mentioned by the student informants. This type of categorical breakdown does not tell us how much attention was given to each of these segments. It only tells us if informants bothered to mention certain classroom events. Ann, for example, talked extensively about her explanation of auxiliaries and gave details about the two listening activities. The other three segments of class, by contrast, were given a broad brush. Quim mentioned only two of the activities described by Ann and did so giving very few details. Alex, who reported three days later, on Saturday, might have had a harder time remembering because of the passing of time. Nevertheless, he was able to cite four out of five of the activities which Ann described. Jose gave what we might call a thorough report but did not give many details about the actual content of activities. Finally, Rick and Juan were also brief but managed to give some details about actual content.

Space does not permit a detailed analysis of informant responses to the remaining four questions in the diary guide (for this, see Block 1992b). For this reason I shall be brief here. Regarding the second question, about the purpose of activities, only two student informants, Rick and Alex, provided direct responses. Rick's responses were extremely brief and not particularly illuminating: The purpose of the listening activity was to "understand what they say" and the question formation activity was a "reminder." Alex, on the other hand, took the question as an opportunity to critique the question formation activity. (I shall have more to say about Alex in later sections.)

Responses to the third question, about what students learned, were somewhat more extensive. The three student informants who gave direct answers (Quim, Rick, and Jose) stated that the class had served as

TABLE 1   ACTIVITIES REPORTED ON APRIL 22

Reporter	Comparatives	Reading	Auxiliaries	Body parts	Listening
Ann (T)	X	X	X	X	X
Alex*	X		X		X
Jose		X	X	X	X
Juan		X		X	X
Rick			X		X
Quim		X	X		

*Account given three days after the lesson.

a review. For example, Quim said, "We could say that today I didn't really learn anything new. But I suppose we have to keep on practicing and that's all right."

Rick was the only informant to address the fourth question (What did the teacher do to help you to learn? What did you do?), but he limited himself to saying that the teacher had "asked for examples" and that he had "tried to provide examples."

A week later: a detailed analysis

Only somewhat satisfied with my data collection for days one and two of class, I decided that I might do better to move on to the first day of class which I observed, one week later. I was especially interested in seeing to what extent my data would be enriched by the addition of accounts from the students who were not keeping diaries on a day-to-day basis along with the fieldnotes which I, as the observer, would be taking.[2]

What was salient?

An examination of my fieldnotes shows that for me, the observer, there were essentially five activities: a conversation warm-up as students drifted into class (five minutes), a vocabulary review before watching a recorded news broadcast (twelve minutes), viewing and discussing of the news broadcast (eighteen minutes), a practice test (twenty minutes), and an extended activity about job advertisements (fifty-five minutes).[3]

Table 2 shows how many of these activities the teacher and the twelve students mentioned. As I stated with regard to Table 1, not much can be gleaned from merely ticking off whether or not something was mentioned in the various accounts. Just about all I can do is suggest that the general consensus was that there were three major activities on this particular day of class: the news/listening activity, the test, and the job ad activity. The omission of the practice test on the part of several informants might be owing to it's being identified as a test as opposed to an activity.

The fact that only two learners mentioned the vocabulary warm-up and eleven (including the teacher) did not is harder to explain. In this activity the teacher asked students to call out words from their news exercise sheet that they thought they already knew. Perhaps in the minds of the students present it was seen as merely an affix to the news

2 A fuller, more detailed account of this particular day of class can be found in Block (1994).

3 I should mention here that on the days when I was present the class ended a quarter of an hour early and hence lasted two hours.

TABLE 2   ACTIVITIES REPORTED ON APRIL 29, 1992

Reporter	Warm-up	Vocabulary	Listening	Test	Job ad
Observer	X	X	X	X	X
Ann (T)			X	X	X
Alex		X	X	X	X
Jon		X	X	X	X
Jose			X	X	X
Juan			X		X
Quim			X		X
Rick			X		X
Alicia			X	X	X
Ariadna			X	X	X
Marta			X	X	X
Paula			X	X	X
Jaime			X		X
Josep			X		X

exercise. However, even if this is the case, it is still remarkable that in all the accounts there is no mention of individual lexical items. This tendency to leap over details is especially curious in light of Slimani's research on topicalization and uptake. While Slimani (1989, 1992) suggests that students are more likely to report that they have learned language items (in this case, lexical items) nominated by other students than items nominated by the teacher, in my study it seems that not one informant named a single individual lexical item which had come up during this exercise.

One reason for this collective omission in the accounts might be that the individual items were considered words which the students already knew, so informants did not consider them important enough to mention. Indeed, Alex, echoing Quim's comment about the class on day two, seems to make this point:

First of all there were words that we already know. And we never get to see words that we don't know, which means that the only thing we do is review the words we already know.

In other words, perhaps the informants did not consider the items which came up during this part of the class as relevant to my question about what was "learned." Once again, Slimani offers a particularly illuminating comment which might apply to this situation: "[O]ne could add that after a few hours of teaching, second language instruction becomes very much remedial as structural features are presented and represented for a review" (1992: 210). We might easily substitute "lexical" for "structural" in this quotation.

Another reason why individual vocabulary items were not mentioned might have to do with the very way the questions in my study were posed. Unlike Slimani, I did not ask students to say what grammar, words and phrases, or spelling had come up during class; rather, I simply asked them about activities and what they thought they learned. It could well be that unless the researcher explicitly asks for grammar or lexical items, as Slimani did, informants will not enter into such detail.

Yet a third explanation of why informants in my study do not provide vocabulary items might be memory constraints. Elsewhere (Block 1990a) I have suggested that what students remember about their classes might be episodes as opposed to language items learned. Thus, a student might recall that a listening activity was done, but would not remember the content. (See Tulving [1983] for a thorough discussion of episodic and semantic memory.)

To summarize this section, close scrutiny of the learner accounts shows that there was some degree of uniformity as regards the identification of activities. I remind the reader that the same applied to the accounts of the second day, and add here that in subsequent examination of all the entries on a day to day basis, there were always two to five distinct activities identified. It would seem, then, that we can make the generalization that learners in this study tended to perceive the class as divided into two to five chunks. Whether this range of identifiable activities is owing to memory constraints or to a tendency on the part of the teacher to organize long activities is a question I could only answer if I were able to set up several parallel studies.

On the other hand, I am in a somewhat better position to explain why, as the observer, I tended to note episodes which did not appear in the informant accounts. Perhaps the most obvious factor is that while I did my reporting live and was hence able to capture more detail, informants gave their accounts immediately after the class and were thus dependent on their long-term memories under a certain time constraint. In this sense, my report was more akin to what Ericcson and Simon (1984, 1987) would call a *think aloud account*, whereas informants were giving what would be termed a *retrospective account*.

Another reason for differences between the researcher's and the informants' reports has to do with perspective. My perspective might be termed *etic*, in that I have described events using a metalanguage acquired from the study of teaching situations. The learners' perspective, on the other hand, might be termed *emic*, in that the metalanguage which they have employed in their accounts is grounded in the day-to-day experience of being language learners. Ann's perspective, as the teacher, represents something of a combination of the etic and the emic, in that while she is obviously familiar with the technical etic meta-

language used by applied linguists when discussing classroom procedures, everything she says in effect becomes emic because she is an
insider informant in this study. (For a thorough discussion of *etic* and
emic see Watson-Gegeo 1988.)

Despite these differences, it would be unfair to suggest that all informants' reports were limited in scope just because they only mentioned three to five class events. In the next three sections I shall deal
briefly with responses which we might take as answers to questions 2,
3, 4, and 5 in the diary guide.

The purpose of activities

The question which was addressed by all informants (students, teacher,
and myself) was the second one: What do you think was the purpose
of the activities? However, all informants approached it from different
angles and hence gave different types of responses. In the learner reports, responses were consistently mimetic with the name for the activity itself, as the following comment from Paula about the listening
activity illustrates: "[T]he word says it – get us used to listening to
spoken English."

The teacher, Ann, had a more developed idea about why she was
asking learners to do certain activities, as she demonstrated in detail
regarding the purposes of the job advertisements exercise:

Several things. One, reading an advertisement and understanding . . . the
vocabulary that's used . . . being able to synthesize the information. Once
they get into groups on Thursday . . . each person has a different
advertisement that they have to summarize and explain to the other students.
Hopefully, amongst all of them, they will get a more complete list of
vocabulary or terminology that they can use or is used in writing
advertisements. After that stage I plan. . . . to ask them about what they
consider important in an interview. And then I will show them the video on
interviewing . . . giving them a person in the interviewing process on which to
focus. And the good things, the negative things that person does in the
interview. So, for example, there will be four possibilities. The interviewer:
good things that the interviewer does, bad things the interviewer does, good
things the interviewee does and bad things the interviewee does. Each person
will have one of those four possibilities. . . . We'll see what kind of feedback
and how much information they can give back from the video.

This excerpt is particularly interesting in light of the fact that, as we
shall see later, not all present in the class were as clear about the direction of this long series of activities which were part of a general project
on job advertisements.

What do you think you learned today?

As I mentioned earlier, learners tended to give answers which were mimetic with the names of the activities. Thus, for example, a listening activity meant the improvement of listening skills, a speaking activity the improvement of speaking skills, and so on. Apart from skills, learners also mentioned one area of knowledge – vocabulary – quite often. However, as was noted in the previous section and as we shall see in the following excerpts, no details were provided.

Paula: Learn, uh . . . some new vocabulary, especially about business. In the last exercise, some vocabulary. And in the first one, the listening, as well. Above all, vocabulary.

Ariadna: What I learned most was a little vocabulary. Some comprehension, too. And trying to speak, to express myself well. With the test, the truth is that I don't think I learned much.

Jordi: What you learn listening to the BBC news is getting used to listening to it. There were also some words which – I think with this activity the most important thing is to learn new words.

Other informants were not sure if they had learned anything in particular:

Marta: What I learned today . . . I don't think it's noticeable from one day to the next.

Jaime: About what I learned, uh, not much. Today, not much. I suppose a little vocabulary.

Rick: Did I learn anything? Uh, average. A word or two, but you forget that easily.

Thus, learners either made general comments about having learned vocabulary (again, no items were mentioned) and how they had improved their speaking or listening skills, or stated that they had not really learned anything at all. On the one hand, these responses might raise suspicions about the reliability of learners' accounts of their classes. After all, they seem to be based on the highly suspect assumption or belief that if one does an activity which is qualified as a listening activity then one must be improving one's listening skills. While it might make intuitive sense that one improves one's listening by listening, there is certainly no evidence to be found in language classroom research that the relationship between doing and learning is automatic. However, if learners actually believe in such an automatic relationship, it is a factor worth taking note of as it provides us with some insight on how learners make sense of classrooms. Regarding comments to the effect that nothing was learned, I refer to the previous section where I mentioned Slimani's rather pessimistic suggestion that students at the intermediate level see very little language which is really new.

The roles of teachers and learners

In response to question 4 (What did the teacher do to help you learn? What did you do?), informants gave answers which attributed to the teacher a dual role of parent and enforcer. (See Block [1990b, 1992a] for a discussion of these roles, and Katz [this volume] for information on other roles teachers enact.) Thus, Ann was seen as a provider in that she "gave us a dictionary," "prepared the questions for the video, the test and the ads exercises," and "came around to help when we were working in groups." However, she was a provider with total control over what went on in class, an enforcer of sorts, as she "told us to look up words . . ." and "made us speak English," and in more liberal moments "gave us more time to finish the last activity about jobs" and "let us go outside the class to work in groups without the pressure of the teacher."

When discussing their own contribution in class most student informants attributed to themselves a willingness to participate:

Josep: [W]hat we do is pay attention and listen to the video. In the case of the job ads, pay attention to the text and underline the important expressions. . . .
Ariadna: As regards personal work, uh, try to get involved a little.

"Get involved," however, is a vague expression at best, and several informants admitted that when they went outside the classroom to the corridors to work on the job ads activity, they either finished as quickly as they could or did not get around to finishing at all. In both cases, there was certainly more L1 spoken than English, apparently because the teacher was not there to "control" students.

Alicia: [G]oing outside of class in groups, it's a little difficult to control us. So we can talk about anything, like we were talking about life in Sitges and life in Barcelona . . . and we were speaking in Spanish. Even though this was after doing the exercise. But it's difficult, going outside of class and all that, to control what we do and if we really speak in English.

The idea that students will not do anything unless a teacher is present to "make them" is certainly not new. However, I am certain that when Ann asked students to go outside the class and work on the ads activity in groups, she in no way had the idea of "control" in mind. More likely, she thought she was treating them as mature adults who were aware of their responsibility to speak English whenever possible. However, there was obviously a lack of communication between learners and teacher in this regard as the former saw the teacher's absence as a sign that they had to do little if any work related to their English class.

Other events

Several items which I reported as eventful were either mentioned by very few informants or, in some cases, not mentioned at all. For example, one informant noted that during the ads exercise people in her group had talked about "the people who had done interviews for the Olympics" (a popular topic at the time of the study, just three months before the 1992 Olympic Games were held in Barcelona). But no one said anything specifically about Rick (not even Rick himself!), who earlier had come late to class wearing a suit because he had gone for an Olympic Committee interview. I might ask if all present considered it too minute a detail to mention.

Other events which I noted but which were not mentioned by the informants included a problem Ann had with the VCR (she had forgotten to put the cassette in the machine) and a request from two students that Ann help them write a letter in English. In both cases, I thought that the individuals directly involved and affected would at least make mention of such events. However, nothing was said. Even my presence, which I thought might be the most salient nonpedagogical event of the day's class, was only mentioned by three individuals, Ann, Alex, and Jon. None of the three said I had altered the atmosphere of the class, suggesting that much talk about the negative effect of the observer's paradox might be exaggerated.

In all three cases, I might speculate that these events were not considered pedagogical and hence not worthy of mention. Nevertheless, examining all of the accounts across the study, there were occasions when more or less extracurricular events were mentioned. For example, from the accounts of the second week, I find one student, Alicia, talking about how she is sharing a house with a student from the United Kingdom.

Alicia: [P]ersonally, I can say that lately, for different reasons, I have been living in an English guy's house. And it's helping me a lot. I notice that I can understand more, that I can express myself better . . . I don't know. I'm happy with my English. We'll see what happens when I stop living with this English guy.

I have no answer to the question as to why some nonpedagogical events are more salient than others; this is obviously an area which will require further exploration.

Discussion of the detailed analysis

In the last two sections I have attempted to demonstrate that a linear analysis of the data collected shows a fair deal of uniformity and over-lap in what the different witnesses to classroom events report. However, I have not discussed a phenomenon which I could not truly grasp until I had read through accounts several times – that all of my informants had their particular quirks and individual styles. (Slimani [1992] also speaks of idiosyncrasies in her informants' responses.) Regarding reporting procedure, for example, I found that Rick had a tendency to read all of the questions in the diary guide while Alex never seemed to consult the sheet. Except for those days when I observed, all of the students tended to give their reports in the evening, at least six hours after class had ended while Ann tended to give hers immediately after the class had finished. Finally, regarding content, I discovered that all the informants had their own particular concerns. All of this diversity in reporting procedure, timing, and focus on content might leave us wondering about the generalizability of data collected in such open-ended, uncontrolled fashion. However, I would suggest that more con-trolled methods of data collection in this study would have impoverished the data to the point that it would have undermined the attempt to gain a window on the classroom from different angles. In other words, by leaving informants to their own devices, I was able to get more rather than less.

On this somewhat libertarian note we can move to the next section where I shall focus on the reactions of one student informant, Alex, and examine how Ann's diary entries parallel or diverge from what he re-ported about the class. A precedent of sorts in isolating two informants from a larger class is to be found in Allwright (1980), where the author justifies the detailed analysis of the classroom discourse of the teacher and one learner (from a class of ten or more): "This is the starting point for the case-study approach, where one learner stands out as of partic-ular interest" (Allwright 1980, cited in Allwright 1988: 178). While Allwright's reason for isolating the learner in his study was a "wholly disproportionate share of the identified turns" (ibid.), mine was the de-tailed analyses of classroom events which Alex provided on a day-to-day basis (which contrasted with the generally more superficial nature of most of the other informants' reports).

The gap: Ann and Alex

I hope to demonstrate to the reader that there was a very real gap between these two informants, a gap which perhaps need not have ex-isted. In discussing the gap between Alex's and Ann's perceptions of classroom events, I in no way mean to suggest that throughout the accounts I have collected during this study there was massive disagreement. Indeed, I made the point already that there was a high degree of agreement in what informants reported on a day-to-day basis. However, if we are to understand classroom culture better, we must examine not only harmony but conflict. Thus what follows will be the hard edge of the accounts I collected from Alex – in other words, those comments in which he questioned and criticized what was going on in class. I consider this approach somewhat of a departure from much research which has recently been done in teacher education where just about everything that is said about classes, teachers, and learners is positive (e.g., see articles in Day, Pope, and Denicolo 1990; Hargreaves and Fullan 1992; and Nunan 1992b). What I am interested in here are the concerns which Alex expressed during the study and which apparently were not addressed by Ann in class.[4]

Time utilization

One of Alex's chief concerns was the way that class time was utilized. Unless he considered an activity particularly informative, relevant, or challenging, he felt as though he was wasting his time. Thus, after only three days of class, he criticized overuse of the coursebook, *Headway*, because he considered its exercises to be "really mechanical." He gave the following report on a weekend because he hadn't been able to find the time to report on the days when he attended class.

... We did a few exercises from the book. Actually, so far we have been using the book too much because all of its exercises are usually too mechanical. If you understand a little grammar, if you do them ten times, in the end you know the mechanism, the trick. But doing them just to be doing them, it's actually so mechanical that in the end you don't even see the sentence.

On the same day, he did not value a listening activity where students had to distinguish accents because one could guess the accent by cues about geographical location.

Afterwards, we went to the laboratory where she played several tapes. The first one we had to distinguish where accents were from, which was impossible for us, except that they were talking about different cities and so you could more or less identify the city it was.

4 I might add here that Alex was by no means the only informant to show a critical attitude toward the class. Indeed, three other informants were equally negative in their comments on the teacher and the class.

A dictionary activity organized on the third day of class fared slightly better, although Alex still questioned its usefulness.

I suppose that it was a matter of discussing the meaning amongst ourselves and then looking for it in an English-English dictionary. I think the objective, although it was clear, I don't think you have to look in the dictionary when people have more or less done it.

Finally, Alex questioned the relevance of a discussion of natural disasters, which took place on the third day of class as well.

I suppose that people need to speak in English but bringing out such highly artificial subjects like these, people can't get into speaking in English because it's too artificial.

In her accounts, Ann spoke about all but one of these activities (the dictionary task), and in her words they did not seem as useless or as mundane as Alex had made them sound. Alex's comment about overuse of the coursebook was apparently in reference to one skimming activity on a text about languages in the world followed by a question writing activity (the answers are provided; students must form the questions). In this context, Alex's comment seems nothing short of exaggerated or at least premature. (He made it while talking about his first day in class.) According to Ann, the listening activity was not just a question of guessing accents as Alex suggested, but to understand "the information that was conveyed." Ann only briefly mentioned the vocabulary work with the dictionary and the discussion of natural disasters, suggesting that more would be done on the latter the following day.

It would seem that what we have here is a difference of point of view regarding purpose. The purpose of a skimming activity was to develop reading skills; however, Alex saw it as mechanical and too book-based. The listening activity was designed to develop listening skills in general; yet, Alex seemed to get hung up on whether learners were really expected to distinguish accents. The dictionary activity was no doubt skills-based and likely was simply to see whether or not students were familiar with using an English-English dictionary; however, Alex seemed to think the activity was useless. Finally, the natural disasters discussion was part of a larger packet of materials developed by a colleague which had been used successfully by several teachers in other courses. Alex and Ann agreed that this activity was an excuse to speak in English; however, they did not agree on the relative interest of the topic.

Practice tests

As the course progressed Alex turned his attention to two activities which were done fairly often in class, practice tests and vocabulary and grammar exercises. Four or five practice tests were administered during the class; vocabulary and grammar exercises were done just about every day. Well into the second week of classes, Alex said the following about practice tests.

And normally we don't study the grammar to use on these tests, which means that there are things which we never see, but nevertheless we are expected to work out on the tests. The tests have nothing to do with what we do in class. I'm not saying that the class is bad. What I'm saying is simply that these tests, unless they are corrected immediately, don't mean anything. Besides, I don't think a student should be evaluated for English he has never used.

On this same day, Ann expressed an almost identical opinion.

The idea of basing a program on discrete-point items, I'm not sure I agree with. After they did the test and they were doing another activity, one of the – a group of the students asked me about the test and asked me for my reaction. And I had to admit that things we're required to give – at least four out of five tests. It's my responsibility to give four out of five tests. I'll give them feedback on how they did. And we may talk about it in class if they're really interested. But . . . some items I find have no really, no correlation to any – to a person's degree of knowledge, what they can really do with the language. . . . And I told them I can either teach for the test or I can teach them things that will be more useful. And I have decided not to teach for the test or that would take up the whole class time and we wouldn't do anything else.

We might ask ourselves if Alex was in the group of students addressed by Ann when she admitted she was only administering the tests because she had to. Unfortunately, there is really no way of answering this question short of asking Alex or Ann (and this was not done), as the recording of that day's class provides us with no evidence one way or the other and my fieldnotes from that day show no mention of any such event. We can only conclude that if Alex *was* aware of Ann's views in this regard, he nevertheless chose to ignore them and continued to judge the class (and indirectly, Ann) for administering the tests, as indicated in this excerpt from a diary entry he made about a week later.

Actually these exams are proving to be really stupid because what we do in class has nothing to do with what is on the exams. All of which means that we are testing ourselves on concepts which we should have because we don't learn anything in class that we can use on the exam.

His criticisms peaked at the end of the course, when he made the following comment: "In any case, I still can't do this type of test. I still see them as stupid because they have nothing to do with the exit test and nothing to do with the English I know."

As stated in her diary, Ann was only administering these tests because they *did* have to do with the exit exam. We might ask why Alex had apparently been misled into thinking otherwise, taking into consideration that theoretically he could not have known what the exit exam looked like. (This was kept secret from M.B.A. students until the day of the exam.) In any case, the point here is that throughout the course he was not only aware of, but irritated by, the misfit between practice tests and class activities.

Vocabulary and grammar exercises

Alex was equally critical of vocabulary and grammar exercises, which were usually done as warm-up activities. From what I could gather from my own observations and informant reports, these activities might take as long as an hour to complete and go over, depending on how late students arrived and how quickly they managed to complete the exercises. Alex did not see the point. About halfway through the course he said, "I don't see the point of these exercises. Actually, if I go over what I have learned from these exercises, it can be narrowed down to very little."

When Ann spoke about these vocabulary exercises it was in a routine manner as something which was done at the beginning of class as a warm-up: "Yesterday in class we started with a vocabulary exercise as always." When this routine was not followed twelve days later, Ann commented wryly: "Today's class started out untypically. We did not do a grammar-vocabulary exercise at all."

When she did elaborate on these exercises, it was to criticize students' apparent inability to work things out for themselves or to make connections. For example, the same day that Alex was making his comment about the meaning and purpose of these exercises, Ann commented on what she saw as poor technique on the students' part.

Initially we did some vocabulary work from the Word Builder for them. I find that they don't take advantage of information that they already know or could find out very quickly. One of the things that I mentioned to them today was the idea of – especially when you have a limited amount of words for a fill-in-the-blank exercise – is read through the whole thing first, and fill in the things that sound most familiar because then that'll reduce the field of vocabulary that you have to deal with, that you have to juggle around and try to put in its place.

Four days later, Ann seemed to criticize students for not being able to make connections between what had been done and what was being done.

I think that they maybe noticed that a lot of – a lot – some of the vocabulary that we've been doing from the book, especially the exercises, the vocabulary keeps getting recycled and spiralled back and spiralled back. But, it seems like they have to be hit over the head before they accept it.

Nevertheless, examining Alex's comments, I do not get the impression that he was unaware of certain techniques he might adopt when doing these exercises. It seemed to be more the case that he did not see the point in doing the exercises in the first place. As he put it, "Above all, during these courses, we have *seen* phrasal verbs. Getting to use them and remember them at the same time has proven a little difficult."

Administration and procedure

When Alex criticized the content of the tests and the vocabulary exercises for their disconnection with language practiced in class, he also questioned the way they were administered. On the one hand, he complained that at times Ann would give the class an exercise to do and then leave them on their own while she went to get dictionaries or make photocopies. On the other hand, he spent quite a bit of time talking about the way exercises and tests were handled once students had completed them. In particular he was critical of doing any exercise or test which was not corrected immediately afterwards. The following two excerpts make this point well. The first comment was made after a class when this procedure was not followed.

Actually, what I find a little stupid is doing exercises and then not having the chance to correct them, because why am I going to do any exercise if I'm not going to know the mistakes I made afterwards.

The second was made after a class when the exam was corrected immediately.

After doing the exam, we corrected it and I really think that this is the most interesting part of the exam because you have put yourself to the test and after that you are correcting and realizing what your mistakes were.

Searching through Ann's diary entry for the class which Alex was referring to, I find no reference whatsoever to her having refused to correct exercises. What she did say about this activity was the following.

I mentioned to them that accepting the fact that they had other priorities before English, that periodically we would take time out of class in order for them to do what would traditionally be called homework.

I interpret her statement as meaning that the class had ended before everyone had finished the work. Indeed, this view is backed up by Jose

187

and Juan, who both seemed to recognize that Ann had intended to get students started on the exercises and thus put on them the onus to finish the work at home over the weekend. Jose went into great detail on this point.

And this took up most of the time since afterwards, I think there were thirty or thirty-five minutes left, and she took us to a very comfortable meeting room and there we did exercises she gave us. I think she must have thought it out in detail because there really wasn't enough time to finish the exercises in the time she had allotted and, uh, she suggested and asked us to finish them during the weekend and she said that since she knew we didn't really have any time she would have given us the morning to finish, but of course there wasn't enough time. In any case, I think that this measure was right on target because this way we feel morally obliged to do some work at home which is always beneficial. It's a way of telling us that she does her part but that we have to make a little effort, too, in order to get better faster.

Regarding the immediate correction of the exam two weeks into the course, Ann acknowledged that this had meant a change over the previous exam procedure, although she did not say why she had consciously decided to do things differently. She also did not mention in her account that on the same day she had returned the first tests to the class and gone over them as well and that once this was done, she asked that the students return them to her. This latter procedure did not sit well with Alex, who commented, "What surprised me about Ann was that she showed us the previous exam but she didn't want us to keep exams. She simply took them, showed them to us, and took them again. I don't know why." Apparently, Alex did not know that it is the program policy to never allow students to keep exams. The fear is that they could be copied and if they are used again (as they likely would be during an academic year), some students might be able to get advanced copies. Why this was not explained to students is beyond me. Of course it might have been explained, but Alex perhaps was not around to hear. In any case, his mention of this anomaly is the only one in all of the diary entries. I only mention such a small point as yet another example of a lack of communication between Alex and Ann in details about classroom procedure.

The long-term project

Perhaps the greatest communication gap vis-à-vis purpose can be found in the two parties' perceptions of a long string of activities which revolved around the theme of job interviews. From what I have been able to gather from my fieldnotes, learner and teacher diary entries, and the post-study interviews, Ann's plan was to take class participants through a well-planned step-by-step project, starting with an examination of job advertisements, and then carrying on to a selection of a job, presenting curriculum vitae (résumé), and finally to job interviews. From Ann's side of the classroom, what prolonged this thread which spanned three of the four weeks of class was inconsistent attendance: She did not want to do certain activities unless everyone was present because she knew that picking up the pieces the following day would be all the more time-consuming. The following diary excerpt from the ninth day of class makes this point quite well: "I decided not to continue with the interviewing project because there were four students missing. And we'll pick up on it again, hopefully on Monday."

From Alex's side of the classroom, this off-and-on approach to the same general theme of job advertisements seemed like nothing more than beating a dead horse. For example, five days later when the class returned to this thread after several days of doing other things, he commented:

After that, we did something in groups, an exercise we did last week. Today of course we had to remember because we hadn't dealt with it for a week, which was boring and the people didn't do it. . . . A task has a time limit regarding its relevance.

And two days later, he said the following.

I think that all exercises should be done quickly like we do with the video because you do a task like this, you do it again, you review it. . . . In the end you get tired. And this is what happened with the last task we did today because we did this task last week. And then we expanded on it the following week trying to do I don't know what. And today with all the things we had to do, on top of everything else, we have to do another exercise again and write an ad about this. In the end the task is too long.

Thus Alex was perfectly aware that the class was continuously returning to the same theme, job advertisements, but he did not really see the point. This is interesting given that other students in the class apparently did know that they were working on a long-term project, as Alicia's comment from May 14 indicates: "This has been a whole process in which we prepared ads, prepared our curriculums and stuff. And today it was the interviews."

Nevertheless, it seems that in Alex's mind, Ann had never made it clear to the class that all of the exercises about ads were leading to a final activity which he would ultimately find quite interesting. Indeed, it was only in the last days of the course when job interviews were filmed and then subsequently viewed and analyzed by the entire class

189

that Alex was able to see what all of the work had been for. On the day of the filming he said,

Actually, I should take back what I said about always doing the same exercise not being good, referring to the ad, reading the ad, writing it, drawing it, applying for it and everything else. . . . Today was interesting . . . we turned in our CVs, we wrote a letter to do the job interview. And today was really interesting but perhaps it would have been more beneficial if Ann had told us about the plan from the beginning, but doing it step by step, always working on the same thing is boring.

This point was made with even more force at the beginning of Alex's post-study interview, which took place over a week after the course had ended.

We never knew what the outcome was going to be. So we did exercises and exercises without ever knowing that we would end up doing this. Maybe if we'd been told from the beginning, it would have been more interesting.

What can we gather from this final example of the gap between Ann and Alex? As we previously observed, there is evidence that other students in the class knew that the ads exercises were part of a larger package leading to simulated job interviews. We might ask ourselves why Alex either did not know or chose to ignore this. There is also evidence from the data gathered that on other occasions Alex feigned ignorance when talking about classroom procedures he did not like. For example, throughout the study he constantly complained that he could not understand why the classes were held for two and a quarter hours without a break instead of two and half hours with a fifteen-minute break in the middle. The reason was very simple: On the first day of class, students voted in favor of this format so that they could finish fifteen minutes early. While Alex was not present on the first day of class, I discovered in our post-study interview that he did know that the decision had been taken.

I think not having a break was a mistake. . . . I didn't come the first day . . . it was an agreement already made. But you really noticed not having a break because it was two and half hours in a row and in the end tiring.

Why he went on to judge the teacher for a decision taken by the students in the class remains a mystery to me; nevertheless, his behavior in this case raises an interesting question about responsibility for what goes in classrooms. Clearly, a teacher can never be sure that he or she will not be held responsible for actions taken by groups of students in the class.

Discussion of the "gap"

The preceding is an account of just a small piece of the data I collected from Alex and Ann. What can be gleaned from this selection is that both informants tended to identify the same activities as salient; however, Alex seemed to be constantly in the dark about why he was doing these activities, which included stand-alone, independent grammar and vocabulary exercises, practice tests which were meant to prepare him for an exit exam, news exercises, and the individual tasks which made up the project on job advertisements and interviews. By contrast, as the organizer of all of these activities, Ann no doubt knew, albeit implicitly, why things were being done the way they were. She seemed to see the grammar/vocabulary warm-up activities as routine warm-ups (perhaps even reviews) and the news exercises as an opportunity for developing listening skills with a dose of open-ended conversation thrown in. The hated practice tests were, as we have seen, preparation for the exit exam and nothing else. Finally, the individual pieces of the long-term project on jobs were, from what I could gather from reports, perhaps the only example of connected activities. All other activities were reported on in such a way as to suggest that they stood alone.

What we have here in essence is a grading of activities. First, there are the throw-aways, activities which we might see as filling time. An exercise is done, it is gone over, the teacher trouble-shoots the problems which arise during its execution, and it is finished. It is a self-contained activity with a purpose which is mimetic with its name: a news-watching exercise is done in order to develop listening skills, a grammar activity is done in order to improve grammar skills, a vocabulary exercise is done in order to improve lexis, and so on. Second, there are exercises such as the practice tests which are done because of departmental dictates and which are goal-driven in that they refer to a product at the end of the course, the exit exam. Finally, there are activities which are clearly pieces of a larger puzzle. They are not stand-alone efforts, and they very clearly are goal-driven. This was the case with the string of activities dealing with the topic of jobs.

Unfortunately for Alex, all of the activities done in class were seen as a series of individual events which were never tied together to produce a coherent whole. He simply did not see the purpose of what he was asked to do in class on a day-to-day basis. One obvious lesson to be learned here is that it is important for teachers to continually discuss with learners why they are being asked to do certain activities. In absence of such communication, learners might be faced with no other alternative but to adopt a "survival orientation" (Breen 1987: 26). In this case, learners depend on "external criteria," in Breen's terms – doing activities because the teacher has asked them to, but investing no part of themselves in the process. The result here is that learners follow the teacher's lead but in no way identify with it. In order for learners to adopt what Breen has called an "achievement orientation" (which means that they see the purpose of participating in activities), they must at some point think about why they are doing the activities they are doing. The solution it would seem is for the teacher to make activity purposes clear to a class at all times.

Conclusion

Where does all of this leave us? Those interested in further research might consider any number of questions which this study has raised. I close this chapter with two suggestions.

First, those interested in teaching practice might take note of the idea that the analysis of pedagogical purpose is not solely the domain of teachers. Alex and the other informants in this study certainly provide us with ample evidence that learners are constantly attempting to make sense out of classroom instruction. As a consequence, it is incumbent upon teachers to make classroom activities seem sensible or coherent to learners. In the absence of this perceived coherence, learners will likely feel that they are wasting their time in class. Certainly, more research needs to be done into how teachers either succeed or fail in their attempts to make their lessons coherent to their students.

Second, regarding research methodology, one might further investigate the idea of individual differences in data provision among informants. Just as many authors have suggested that there are different types of language learners (e.g., Oxford 1990; Willing 1988), it might well be the case that there are also different types of informants. We might even ask ourselves if there is a correlation between the way an informant approaches data provision and the way he or she approaches language learning. For example, is an analytical informant such as Alex equally analytical in his choice of learning strategies? Finally, might a student, frustrated at the misfit between his or her individual learning style and the teacher's individual teaching style, react in an aggressive way by describing and evaluating the class in a negative manner, as Alex did?

References

Allwright, D. 1980. Turns, topics and tasks: Patterns of participation in language learning and teaching. In D. Larsen-Freeman (ed.), *Discourse Analysis in Second Language Research*. Rowley, MA: Newbury House (article reproduced in Allwright 1988).
     1984. Why don't learners learn what we teach? The interaction hypothesis.

In. D. M. Singleton and D. G. Little (eds.), *Language Learning in Formal and Informal Contexts*. Dublin: IRAAL.

1988. *Observation in the Language Classroom*. London: Longman.

Allwright, D., and K. M. Bailey. 1991. *Focus on the Language Classroom: An Introduction to Classroom Research for Language Teachers*. Cambridge: Cambridge University Press.

Bailey, K. M. 1983. Competitiveness and anxiety in adult language second language acquisition: Looking *at* and *through* diary studies. In H. Seliger and M. H. Long (eds.), *Classroom Oriented Research in Second Language Acquisition*. Rowley, MA: Newbury House.

1991. Diary studies of classroom language learning: The doubting game and the believing game. In E. Sadtono (ed.), *Language Acquisition and the Second/Foreign Language Classroom*. Singapore: SEAMEO Regional Language Centre, Anthology Series #28.

Block, D. 1990a. Seeking new bases for SLA research: Looking to cognitive science. *System, 18, 2,* 167–176.

1990b. Teacher and Student Metaphors for Language Learning. Talk given at the Novenes Jornades Pedagògiques d'Anglès. Published in R. Ribé (ed.). 1991. *Towards a New Decade: Novenes jornades pedagògiques d'Anglès*. Barcelona: ICE.

1992a. Metaphors we teach and learn by. *Prospect, 7, 3,* 42–55.

1992b. A Class Seen from Different Angles: An Exploratory Study. Upgrading paper for PhD candidacy, University of Lancaster.

1994. A day in the life of a class: Teacher/learner perceptions of task purpose in conflict. *System, 22, 4.*

Breen, M. 1987. Learner contributions to task design. In *Language Learning Tasks* (Lancaster Working Papers in English Language Education, Vol. 7). London: Prentice-Hall.

1991. Understanding the language teacher. In R. Phillipson, L. Kellerman, L. Selinker, M. Sharwood-Smith, and M. Swain (eds.), *Foreign/Second Language Pedagogy Research*. Clevedon: Multilingual Matters.

Corder, S. P. 1967. The significance of learners' errors. *International Review of Applied Linguistics, 4,* 161–169.

Dakin, J. 1973. *The Language Laboratory and Language Learning*. London: Longman.

Day, C., M. Pope, and P. Denicolo. (eds.). 1990. *Insight Into Teachers' Thinking and Practice*. London: Falmer Press.

Ellis, R. 1984. *Classroom Second Language Development*. Oxford: Pergamon.

Ericcson, K. A., and H. A. Simon. 1984. *Protocol Analysis*. Cambridge, MA: MIT Press.

(1987). Verbal reports on thinking. In C. Faerch and G. Kasper (eds.), *Introspection in Second Language Research*. Clevedon: Multilingual Matters.

Faerch, C., and G. Kasper. (eds.). 1987. *Introspection in Second Language Research*. Clevedon: Multilingual Matters.

Hargreaves, A., and M. Fullan. (eds.). 1992. *Understanding Teacher Development*. New York: Teachers College Press.

Katz, A. (Chapter 3, this volume). Teaching style: A way to understand instruction in language classrooms.

Kempton, W. 1987. Two theories of home heat control. In D. Holland and N.

Quinn (eds.), *Cultural Models in Language and Thought*. Cambridge: Cambridge University Press.

Nunan, D. 1989. *Understanding Language Classrooms*. London: Prentice Hall.

  1992a. *Research Methods in Language Learning*. New York: Cambridge University Press.

  (ed.). 1992b. *Collaborative Language Learning and Teaching*. Cambridge: Cambridge University Press.

Oxford, R. 1990. *Language Learning Strategies: What Every Teacher Should Know*. New York: Newbury House.

Schmidt, R. W., and N. G. Frota. 1986. Developing basic conversation ability in a second language: A case study of an adult learner of Portuguese. In R. R. Day (ed.), *Talking to Learn: Conversation in Second Language Acquisition*. Rowley, MA: Newbury House.

Schumann, F., and J. Schumann. 1977. Diary of a language learner: An introspective study of second language learning. In H. D. Brown, C. A. Yorio, and R. H. Crymes (eds.), *On TESOL '77: Teaching and Learning English as a Second Language: Trends in Research and Practice*. Washington, DC: TESOL.

Slimani, A. 1987. The Teaching/Learning Relationship: Learning Opportunities and the Problems of Uptake – An Algerian Case Study. Unpublished doctoral dissertation, University of Lancaster.

  1989. The role of topicalisation in classroom language learning. *System, 17*, 2, 223–234.

  1992. Evaluation of classroom interaction. In C. Alderson and A. Beretta (eds.), *Evaluating Second Language Education*. Cambridge: Cambridge University Press.

Soars, J., and L. Soars. 1987. *Headway* (Upper intermediate). Oxford: Oxford University Press.

Tulving, E. 1983. *Elements of Episodic Memory*. New York: Oxford University Press.

Watson-Gegeo, K. 1988. Ethnography in ESL: Defining the essentials. *TESOL Quarterly, 22*, 4, 575–592.

Willing, K. 1988. *Learning Styles in Adult Migrant Education*. Adelaide, Australia: National Curriculum Resource Centre.

Section II   Questions and tasks

1. The chapters in this section of the book all focus on some aspects of classroom interaction. If you could talk to these three authors, what questions would you like to ask them?

2. Have you ever been a student in or taught in a large language class, such as those observed by Shamim (Chapter 5)? What was the experience like? Did all the students have opportunities to speak? How were those opportunities created (group work, choral repetition, etc.)?

3. If you can observe a language class in session, keep a record of which students speak and which do not. Is there any discernible pattern related to students' seating? Ask the teacher to consider your data with you and explain his or her attitude toward and strategies for getting students to speak.

4. In Chapter 6 we see the results of several teachers' investigations into their students' participation patterns. The teachers came up with several possible reasons to explain students' reticence. Which of these reasons do you find most compelling? What other explanations have not been considered here? Give examples based on your own experience and/or background reading.

5. A key topic raised in Chapter 6 is anxiety, which is also a central issue in the chapter by Hilleson (Chapter 11). What might the teachers in Tsui's study learn from the students in Hilleson's, and vice versa? What advice would you give these teachers and learners?

6. Chapter 7 incorporates data from students' oral (tape-recorded) journals. In Chapter 8, Campbell said she made one tape-recorded diary entry but then abandoned the practice. What would be the advantages and disadvantages of tape-recording versus writing for making journal entries? Which would you prefer to do?

7. In Chapter 7 Block describes the difference in viewpoints between a teacher and several of her English students in Barcelona, Spain. He focuses on the differing view of the course which are held by the teacher and a student referred to as Alex. When you were a language student, did you understand the purpose behind the teacher's decisions? Why or why not? If you have teaching experience, think of a particular student who might not have understood (or agreed with) your rationale for the things you did in class. Give some examples of how you knew there were misunderstandings between you.

8. If you can observe a language class, try to follow Block's research strategy. First, identify the activity segments of the class as you watch. Afterwards, ask the teacher what activity segments were

used and why they were selected. With the teacher's permission, ask individual students to tell you what activity segments were used and what they thought was the purpose of each.

9. If you have studied language teaching methodology, you know that methods differ in terms of how much and when students are expected to speak in the target language. Should oral participation be encouraged, or even required, from the early stages of language learning? Explain your opinion. How do you think Shamim, Tsui, and Block would respond to this question?

10. Imagine yourself in the role of a language learner. What topic related to classroom interaction has puzzled you or even bothered you? How could you examine that issue from the learner's point of view?

11. Imagine yourself in the teacher's role. What is one aspect of classroom interaction that you would like to investigate? Think about the goal of potentially changing some facet of your own teaching. How could the procedures used by the teachers in Tsui's study (Chapter 6) be used or adapted to suit your purposes?

12. Imagine yourself in the role of a researcher. Which of these three studies would you like to continue? Why? What research procedures would you plan to use? Or think of a topic related to classroom interaction that you would like to investigate. Write three possible research questions related to that topic. Sketch out the research procedures you would use to answer them.

III   *The classroom and beyond*

This section consists of four papers which utilize entries in teachers' and language learners' journals as their primary source of data. Such investigations have been called diary studies, elsewhere in the second language acquisition research literature. What is a diary study? According to Bailey and Ochsner (1983: 189),

A diary study in second language learning, acquisition, or teaching is an account of a second language experience as recorded in a first-person journal. The diarist may be a language teacher or a language learner – but the central characteristic of the diary studies is that they are introspective: The diarist studies his own teaching or learning.

The diary studies are thus first-person case studies – a research genre defined by the data collection procedures (Bailey 1991). Proponents of this type of research say that the use of self-report data from personal journals allows us to tap into affective factors, language learning strategies, and the learners' own perceptions – facets of language learning and teaching experiences which are normally hidden or largely inaccessible to external observers.

Substantive issues

The first chapter in this section is an example of a traditional first-person diary study. The author, Cherry Campbell, was both the researcher and the language learner. In Chapter 8, Campbell analyzes her own experience studying Spanish in an intensive program in Mexico. In the process, she relates the trends in the data to her previous experience studying German in Germany. In both cases, Campbell's opportunities to socialize in the target language outside of class were perceived as more important than her in-class learning. Her journal entries allow us to see her experiences through the learner's eyes, to glimpse events and issues deemed important to her, which might have been missed in a nonintrospective analysis by an external observer.

Chapter 9 by Martha Clark Cummings tells a story of a particular class. It is based on entries in the journal Cummings kept as she taught a group of "repeaters" – students who had already failed their writing class at least once. The voices we hear are compelling; the themes of hope and frustration recycle and repossess these participants like their recurrent discussions of Sardo, the spirit who possessed the teenage girl in a story they had read. Cummings' sense of dialogue and her choice of descriptive details lead us, as readers, into the real-world pressures faced by adult ESL learners in an urban school system. Cummings' voice, as she recounts her experiences teaching these students, richly illustrates Freeman's (this volume) claim that "to tell the story you've got to know the story."

In recent years, in addition to analyzing their own journal data, researchers have also analyzed the diary entries of others. In Chapter 10, Sabrina Peck analyzes the diaries kept by adult learners of Spanish. Here the researcher was a participant observer, in the sense that she was the director of the Spanish program. The students in Peck's study were learning Spanish for professional purposes in their roles as social workers in Los Angeles, California, an ethnically diverse city with numerous social and economic problems. The social workers who kept these journals were both Hispanic and non-Hispanic. Their diary entries reflect initial cultural ambivalence, increasing cross-cultural awareness, and finally enhanced self-confidence and cross-cultural sensitivity. Peck was moved to synthesize several comments from these journals in order to tell the learners' stories.

Chapter 11, by Mick Hilleson, also analyzes diary data from second language learners – this time, secondary school students taking courses in English (their second language) in a boarding school in Singapore. Hilleson supplements the diary data with comments from interviews with some of the students. Using these data sets, he examines the students' ideas about their difficulty in speaking and the anxiety associated with studying in an English-medium school. Fortunately, the longitudinal nature of Hilleson's study allows us to see the students making progress (in both their English and their confidence) over time. Thus, Hilleson examines from the learners' point of view the same issue Tsui (this volume) discusses from the teacher's vantage point – the relationship between anxiety and reticence.

Methodological issues

The researcher-as-learner role, represented most clearly in Chapter 8, leads to what Matsumoto (1987) has called "introspective diary studies" (in that the data collection and the analysis are both introspective). Leo van Lier (personal communication) has suggested the term *direct analysis* instead. Published studies conducted in this tradition, a form of participant observation, include papers by Schmidt and Frota (1986), Schumann (1980), and Schumann and Schumann (1977).

In contrast, Peck and Hilleson both analyze data from several learners' diary entries in what Matsumoto (1987) has referred to as "non-introspective diary studies." We are, however, uncomfortable with this term since the learners' journal entries were introspective, even if the researchers' analyses were not. We prefer van Lier's term, *indirect analysis*. Other examples of this approach include Bailey (1983), Brown (1985), and Ellis (1989).

As is the case with any form of self-report data, diary studies have been criticized on many grounds. Seliger (1983) has argued convincingly that the mentalistic data (including diary entries) recorded by naïve reporters (i.e., nonlinguists, such as Hilleson's students) may not accurately report language learning processes. In contrast, the concern is often raised that when the researcher is, in fact, the language learner who made the diary entries (as in the direct analyses of Campbell's chapter), the experiences reported do not necessarily represent those of the "naive" learner who lacks the linguist's descriptive training and metalinguistic awareness.

Another of Seliger's concerns is that language learning involves both conscious and unconscious processes, but only those occurring within a learner's conscious awareness are available to be scrutinized (see, for example, Schmidt and Frota [1986] on the "notice the gap" principle). And of those, presumably only some unspecified subset will be discussed by the diarist. Furthermore, the calibre of the diary entries as data will be influenced by the learners' metalinguistic awareness and commitment to the diary process, as well as the time lapse between the event and the recording. Similar concerns have been raised by Fry (1988).

Proponents of the use of diary data have argued that these problems are offset by the potential value of the learners' introspections (Bailey 1991; Matsumoto 1987; Nunan 1989). We believe that these four chapters are valuable precisely because they give us access to the participants' voices. They often tell stories of discomfort, but moments of success – at times even triumph – emerge as well.

References

Bailey, K. M. 1983. Competitiveness and anxiety in adult second language learning: Looking *at* and *through* the diary studies. In H. W. Seliger and M. H. Long (eds.), *Classroom Oriented Research in Second Language Acquisition*. Rowley, MA: Newbury House.
1991. Diary studies of classroom language learning: The doubting game and the believing game. In E. Sadtono (ed.), *Language Acquisition and the Second/Foreign Language Classroom*. Singapore: RELC Anthology Series 28.
Bailey, K. M., and R. Ochsner. 1983. A methodological review of the diary studies: Windmill tilting or social science? In K. M. Bailey, M. H. Long,

and S. Peck (eds.), *Second Language Acquisition Studies.* Rowley, MA: Newbury House.

Brown, C. 1985. Requests for specific language input: Differences between older and younger adult language learners. In S. L. Gass and C. Madden (eds.), *Input in Second Language Acquisition.* Rowley, MA: Newbury House.

Ellis, R. 1989. Classroom learning styles and their effect on second language acquisition: A study of two learners. *System, 17,* 2, 249–262.

Freeman, D. (Chapter 4, this volume). Redefining the relationship between research and what teachers know.

Fry, J. 1988. Diary studies in classroom SLA research: Problems and prospects. *JALT Journal, 9,* 2, 158–167.

Matsumoto, K. 1987. Diary studies of second language acquisition: A critical overview. *JALT Journal, 9,* 1, 17–34.

Nunan, D. 1989. *Understanding Language Classrooms: A Guide for Teacher-initiated Action.* Englewood Cliffs, NJ: Prentice-Hall International.

Schmidt, R. W., and S. N. Frota. 1986. Developing basic conversational ability in second language: A case study of an adult learner of Portuguese. In R. R. Day (ed.), *Talking to Learn: Conversation in Second Language Acquisition.* Rowley, MA: Newbury House.

Schumann, F. E. 1980. Diary of a language learner: A further analysis. In R. Scarcella and S. Krashen (eds.), *Research in Second Language Acquisition: Selected Papers of the Los Angeles Second Language Research Forum.* Rowley, MA: Newbury House.

Schumann, F. E., and Schumann, J. H. 1977. Diary of a language learner: An introspective study of second language learning. In H. D. Brown, R. H. Crymes, and C. A. Yorio (eds.), *On TESOL '77: Teaching and Learning English as a Second Language: Trends in Research and Practice.* Washington, DC: TESOL.

Seliger, H. W. 1983. The language learner as linguist: Of metaphors and realities. *Applied Linguistics, 4,* 3, 179–191.

Tsui, A. (Chapter 6, this volume). Reticence and anxiety in second language learning.

8 Socializing with the teachers and prior language learning experience: a diary study

Cherry Campbell

> Many times at the bus station in
> Querétaro, where I often had to change
> for the bus to San Miguel and where I
> could get a good, quick lunch of avocado
> and coriander salad and tortillas, I just
> sat and looked at the destinations on the
> buses headed north. The names of
> border towns – Laredo, El Paso,
> Nogales, Tiajuana – made me think how
> close I was to home. In truth I couldn't
> have been farther away. Sometimes I
> thought I'd hop on a bus and stare out
> the window, and in a day or so, I'd be
> there. But I never did.
>
> (Morris 1988: 27)

Second language researchers have considered the effect of prior language experience on a linguistic level in many studies of transfer (Gass and Selinker 1983; Kellerman and Sharwood Smith 1986; Stockwell, Bowen, and Martin 1965). However, in terms of learning strategies, communication strategies, and other areas of psycho-and sociolinguistics, they have neglected the prior language learning experience of their subjects as well as ways in which that experience may determine the

My thanks go to the diarists for their commitment to working with this type of data; to Kathi Bailey, Leo van Lier, John Schumann, Roger Andersen, and Russ Campbell for their advice regarding previous versions of this chapter; and to Carolynn Schaut and Rona Nashiro for word processing help.

201

course of subjects' learning of new languages. This diary study shows how, in studying Spanish in Mexico, I situated myself so that I could acquire, via interaction outside the classroom by socializing with the teachers, a strategy which parallels my previous language-learning experience in Germany. Other diaries will be reviewed for similar evidence.

As is the case with all qualitative research, diary studies produce an enormous amount of data. Myriad factors that have influenced the learner's experience emerge from these journal data. Early second language journal researchers (Jones [1977] and Schumann and Schumann [1977], among others) attempted to categorize the cumulative evidence from their own data. More recently, in an attempt to begin comparison of available journal data, some researchers have shifted their focus to the major factors (rather than all or most of the influencing factors) found in their own data, later analyzing the journals of other learners and researchers, and looking for evidence of those same factors. An example of this more focused major-theme-comparison approach is Bailey's (1983) study, where she found that competitiveness and anxiety were important influences in her classroom language learning. She found similar evidence in ten other journals. Following this format, major findings from my journal will be compared to data from other language learning journals.

There are four major sections in this diary study: (1) setting and participants, (2) data collection, (3) findings, and (4) related studies. Once the research backdrop is discussed in the first two sections, the findings section presents my voice as a learner of Spanish through chronologically ordered excerpts from my language learning diary and an analysis of those excerpts. In the fourth section, voices of other diarists from related literature will be excerpted and analyzed thematically.

Setting and participants

In my intensive journal are my experiences as a beginning language learner in Mexico. I had never studied Spanish before going to Cuernavaca to spend two months at one of the many language institutes in that town. I traveled there alone and lived with a Mexican family, studied during the week, and did some traveling and sightseeing on weekends.

The school, with about a dozen teachers and twenty or twenty-five students, offered small classes of two or three students meeting with one teacher for four hours per day. Classes rotated weekly so that most students met with a new teacher each week. The classroom atmosphere was always friendly and occasionally lively. Much of the instructional work focused on syntactic and semantic forms, and some centered around communicative activities. After-class activities involving all the students complemented the instruction: singing folk songs, performing skits, playing recreational games, going on occasional out-of-town excursions, and so on. Sometimes students and teachers met in the evenings in downtown cafes.

Most of the students were Americans in their twenties, but there were also some Europeans and a couple of middle-aged students. The teachers were native Mexicans, mostly in their twenties, trained in language-teaching methods by the administrators of the institute. A close-knit group, the teachers were all siblings, in-laws, cousins, or very good friends who spent all of their free time together.

Having grown up in California, I was familiar with Hispanics and Mexican culture. Although I had felt drawn to the more distant European cultures and chose to study French and German in high school and college, I always knew at some point I would study Spanish. When I was in my late twenties, the opportunity arose for me to spend a couple of months in Mexico. I was showered by encouragement from family and envy from friends and colleagues, and this increased my motivation to go to Mexico and to learn the language well. My motivation for keeping the language-learning diary grew out of interest in a series of diary studies produced by researchers from my university (Bailey 1983; Jones 1977; and Schumann and Schumann, 1977).

Upon entering the language school in Cuernavaca, I worried that I would be treated differently than other students because of my background as a language teacher. In retrospect, it seems unlikely that this would have made any real difference in my experience. Nevertheless, at that time I disguised my identity, claiming that I was a composition instructor and a graduate student in creative writing. This gave me an excuse for spending large amounts of time writing in my journal.

Data collection

Before leaving for Mexico, I compiled a history of my previous language learning as well as information, albeit minimal and mostly incorrect, on Spanish vocabulary, phonology, and syntax that I had garnered while growing up in California. I also wrote about what I thought was important for me in learning languages, my motivation for learning Spanish, my choice of schools, and a few other impressions. All of this is included in my intensive journal.

The bulk of the data is composed of the daily journal entries, along with a few letters that I sent home to Los Angeles. On the average, my daily journal entries were three or four handwritten notebook pages long. I usually wrote once or twice each day, in the early morning or afternoon. Sometimes, usually on the weekends, I wrote more lengthy and frequent entries, up to sixteen pages per day. Also at times during the second of my two months there, I skipped days, and even failed to write for one two-week period. However, during the first month I wrote very regularly, and the journal entries are very complete. The entries were all made in handwritten form with one exception: once I tape-recorded a lengthy entry because so much had happened that I did not have time to write it all down. I was not comfortable taping and never did it again. The taped entry is transcribed and included in the journal. There are seventy-one separate entries in the journal, written on thirty-nine days during the two-month period. Five letters, or excerpts of letters, to my roommates in Los Angeles are also included because they provide some information not represented in the diary entries.

The journal entries and the letters reflect my thoughts, feelings, and experiences in class, in town, in my family living environment, in social situations with other American students and friends and with the Mexican teachers and friends from school. I tried to write about everything, especially what I thought was affecting my language learning. As it happened, I did not write very much about the classroom setting or my physical living environment.

In keeping with generally accepted diary study methodology (see Bailey 1983, 1991; Bailey and Ochsner 1983), I revised the original journal, producing an edited public journal usable by myself and others for research purposes. In editing the journal, which I undertook two years after the actual stay in Mexico, I tried to maintain my original stream-of-consciousness style and elaborated only when I felt the references would be very unclear to outside readers. Names were changed and very personal sections were deleted from the public version of the journal.

In the original diary entries, I frequently mixed Spanish words into my writing, as well as occasional German, French, and Swedish words. These instances of language mixing have been maintained in the edited version, and a translation occurs in brackets immediately following each instance. When there was an error in the spelling or syntax in these cases, I tried to indicate the correct form in parentheses within the brackets – for example, maistro [(maestro) teacher]. A few such glosses of my mixing occur in excerpts included in this chapter. The entire edited public journal is 225 typewritten pages and is, therefore, not included here.

Findings

Unfortunately I have no external measures, in terms of standardized tests, of my proficiency in either German or Spanish. Nor do I have data on how I acquired German (i.e., I have no specific documentation of the learning and communication strategies that I used during that prior experience). However, in an attempt to clarify the knowledge of German that I brought with me to the Spanish learning experience, as well as the knowledge of Spanish that I left Mexico with, I will provide an informal description of my skills in those languages.

My aural-oral German is very good. My comprehension is high in virtually all settings involving either formal or informal High German. (My comprehension of dialects is variable.) My speech is fluent in informal situations, although some grammatical problems occur. I have taken active part in formal discussions in German (e.g., in classes at the university there); however, I find formal conversation difficult now. Likewise, my informal writing in German is easy and fluent, excepting occasional grammar and spelling errors, but I doubt that my ability to write a formal academic paper remains. I find reading German newspapers or modern literature remains difficult, but possible. I have carried out second language research in the past several years using primary sources in German, and happily I can still do it.

Upon leaving Mexico, my comprehension of Spanish was good. I was able to understand most informal language that was spoken to me and was able to eavesdrop on conversations occurring around me. My spoken Spanish was simple and highly communicative, but not very eloquent. I could easily get my needs satisfied and even chat informally at great length, but I could not carry on serious or formal discussions for more than a few minutes. I did little reading and writing, other than reading simple modern short stories and writing a few brief paragraphs. My strengths in Spanish upon leaving Mexico were in the aural-oral skills. Two years later, I worked on my more formal speaking skills with a private tutor once a week for six weeks, and was able to discuss second language research, as well as my own research and academic plans, in order to pass an oral language exam for my doctoral program.

My prior experience

In my language learning history, written before my departure to Mexico, I speculated on a number of issues that were important to me as a language learner. This is one of those issues:

Having constant daily contact with a group of natives; people that I can talk with at length day after day; people that I can feel comfortable enough with to take risks and make mistakes and ask for corrections.

Here I refer to an immersion experience during college, when I lived in Göttingen, Germany, in a student dormitory and studied in a six-week German language course followed by content classes at the university. Other sections of my language learning history indicate my belief that the bulk of my acquisition took place in the social situations with this group of friends in *Haus 18* rather than in the language class or later during two semesters as a full-time university student. It was the group (made up of about twenty people) that provided me with a comfortable atmosphere for acquisition more than individuals from the group. I enjoyed the lively socializing with and the strong friendship of the group, and cultivated most of my German language in that situation. I considered this language learning episode successful, and it was with this prior experience that I arrived in Mexico.

From my review of the sheer numbers of relevant journal entries, socializing with the teachers emerges clearly as the most important influence on my language learning in Mexico, more important than my classroom study, associations with the family I lived with, or anything else. It will be shown that from the outset, knowing that I wanted to find a group of native-speaking friends, I chose to socialize with the teachers as a strategy which grew out of the prior language learning experience in Germany.

Throughout the remainder of this section, I will include excerpts which are representative of my entire journal. Also, I will describe concurrent phases of my acquisition of Spanish in terms of class instruction (input, not necessarily intake) and my participation (language use) in out-of-class interaction.

My out-of-class interaction in Mexico

From the beginning of my time in Mexico I was on the lookout for a group of Mexicans I would feel comfortable with and accepted by. In my first letter home to my roommates in Los Angeles, I reflected on a group of friends that I had met through an American friend living in Mexico City.

Week 1:   Also as I said, it was great at Jean's. One roommate is a photographer – very nice. And the other is a musician on tour for two months, so I can stay in his room when I go to Mexico City. She has a big group of musician friends and their friends. It's much like the Haus 18 group in Göttingen, but they're not students. I should try to visit as much as possible because it's clear I'm already accepted, and that's the perfect learning situation.

That group, however, turned out to be less than ideal since I was living and studying an hour and a half away in Cuernavaca.

The next close-knit group of friends that I came in contact with taught at the school in which I was enrolled. I joined frequent informally organized school social gatherings and tried to develop friendships with these teachers. But they were in an established set of companions and relatives, so at times it proved difficult trying to converse, let alone develop friendships. Sometimes my attempts were successful, sometimes not, even within the same setting during the same evening, as can be seen here during an evening with students and teachers in a downtown bar. All conversation between teachers and me took place in Spanish.

Week 2:   I sat down in a free place and realized that there were students at some tables and maistros [(maestros) teachers] at other tables. I didn't like that. Travis and Geri and I [American students] talked about going to the pyramids the next day, and when that was planned, I went across to sit with Manuel & Rosa and Mari & Gustavo [teachers]. I thought that this would work out well, that I'd be able to talk to them. No soap. There was no talk. I asked questions and was given short answers. They asked no questions. . . . I moved to talk to Enrique [another teacher], which wasn't too successful either, and then made my way back over to the student side and expressed my disappointment to Travis. Then all of a sudden I started talking to Vincente [(Vicente)] – a maistro [(maestro) teacher] who plays guitar for Tuesday folk songs, is a tad plump but has a nice face with big dimples. We talked about L.A., music, barriers between teachers and students and between students and the target culture, etc. It was great.

At this point in time I had been in Mexico two weeks, so my conversational ability in Spanish was still shaky. Classwork at that time revolved around brief questions and answers in simple present and past tense describing pictures and realia. Homework required memorizing lists of vocabulary generated in class. I disliked these assignments and complained in the journal that if the vocabulary items from these lists were not reinforced in my daily out-of-class usage, I didn't care to learn them. The preceding diary passage and others from this point in time show me using Spanish to ask and answer questions during informal social chat and, at times, discussing cross-cultural issues. The diary also documents a conversation at school breaktime, when the teacher coordinator complimented me on the accuracy of my speech, although I responded by complaining about speaking slowly and with difficulty. In other words, my conversational ability at this point in time was simple and labored, which may partially explain my difficulty conversing with the teachers.

But what I really think is that the difficulty I experienced was not so much in conversing, as in gaining access to the social group. Since the members of the group were teachers and I was their student, there existed a social power differential. Also there was an obvious solidarity within the group because of the close familial, professional, and social relations. Both the power differential and the group solidarity were working against my being easily accepted (Hudson 1980). Nevertheless, I made a conscious effort to access the social group because I knew that if I could become part of it, I would be able to acquire language while socializing with the members of the group, the teachers.

Let us consider my risk-taking behavior in this type of social situation. I was the only student that evening who crossed the room to initiate a conversation with the teachers. This may have constituted somewhat of a social risk. I felt the risk was worthwhile because of the potential gains in terms of my language learning. If I could become part of this group, I knew I would be able to learn Spanish more quickly and more easily because this was my experience when learning German. I may have been a high risk-taker in this setting, even though the diary indicates that I was a low risk-taker in other out-of-class situations (e.g., in daily interaction in stores, restaurants, bus stations, and so on). In these public situations, I acquired much more from eavesdropping, rather than participating in conversations. (Eavesdropping also proved to be a successful language learning strategy for John Schumann in Iran and Tunisia [Schumann and Schumann 1977].)

Besides going along to school social gatherings, I became interested in exchanging an hour of English tutoring with an hour of Spanish tutoring on a private basis with individual teachers.

Week 3: I see this tutoring exchange as a potential breakthrough for making Mexican friends. Mary Ellen said they often go for drinks afterwards at Pepe's and more teachers show up, etc. Also it will probably help my Spanish – of course, the extra hour of Spanish will, but maybe the teaching of English will too. I just hope my studying and my journal don't suffer. I don't mind if my visiting downtown suffers – I'd rather know I have extra time with Mexicans that get to know every corner of Cuernavaca.

I was interested in more than just developing friendships with the teachers in order to socialize; I also wanted acceptance and respect, which seemed possible through the tutoring. In this way the power differential would likely be lessened.

Week 3: Went to school at 5:00 this afternoon for tutoring. I was excited and a little anxious about it. I felt that this would be the start of a good "in" for me. This might help me get right in to the circle of teachers and be able to spend more time with them. I wanted to do well too. I wanted to teach well, so they would respect me.

Week 3: I felt like a much more whole person after the tutoring sessions than I have up until now. I was able to express myself so easily. . . . I also feel good because I feel like more than a student, or more than the average student here at the school. That's connected to my concern about what they think of me – whether they accept me.

I was attempting to become salient; I wanted to become especially notable compared to other students at school. Also note that the diary reflects an effect on my language development: "I was able to express myself so easily" in the Spanish tutoring session.

At this point in time I had been in Mexico nearly three weeks out of the planned two months. Classwork alternated between focus on structure (working through oral substitution drills, generating sentences using specified idioms and paragraphs using specified verb tenses) and free conversation (aimed at increasing our general fluency and clarifying questions we had about the society around us). The diary shows that I longed for class activities in which we could practice the structure while focusing on a context. I enjoyed the free conversation but wanted the instructor to nominate topics that would provide the context to logically elicit the structural forms we were studying. Also at this point, I was beginning to develop an awareness of suprasegmentals in language I heard outside of class. I occasionally heard Mexicans talking together using intonation that I initially thought indicated argument; however, I began to realize from the topic and the body language that, rather than arguing, these people were cajoling or teasing each other in a friendly way.

Besides tutoring, another way I sought saliency was through writing assignments for class. I did not begin having open-ended writing assignments until after studying one month, but once I was given such assignments, I tried to write inventively. This may have substantiated my feigned identity as a graduate student in creative writing, but according to what I wrote in the journal, I did this because I was hoping to make myself more noticeable.

Week 4: The other day I had an exercise in class, the content of which was about a man waiting in a park for a long time, finally leaving, and a woman coming out of a door laughing. For homework I was supposed to identify the woman and complete the story. I didn't want to write the obvious, so I came up with a James Bond thing about Hugh Hefner having been kidnapped. Luciana, my teacher this week, asked if I would copy it over and give it to her Monday. I asked why and she said she wanted to have it as an example because most students aren't very imaginative. Wow – exactly what I'm striving for: saliency, to be remembered, to be seen as out-of-the-ordinary.

The other night at Las Mañanitas [a restaurant where students and teachers met for drinks] Luciana asked if I had finished my fable (another homework assignment). I said yes, and that it was good. Jose asked if he could use if for the school newspaper. After Luciana read it the next day, she asked for it again for the newspaper. I copied it over and gave it to her yesterday. Again, just what I wanted.

The desire for saliency was probably based on the thought that if I were seen as a unique and interesting person, then this group of Mexican teachers would be open to friendship with me. It would be a means for me to enter the solidarity of the group. And given friendship with the group, I felt I might be able to learn better, an assumption based on my prior experience at having done so in Germany. I truly wanted to be a friend of the group and not simply a student at the school, a role that frustrated me and made me feel as though I could not express myself well in the language.

Week 4: One of the new teachers struck up a conversation with me. It was hard because he was practicing being "teacher." I'd be explaining something and he would encourage me to keep going each time I paused, by saying something like "si, que quieres decir?" [yes, what is it you want to say?]. It bugged me. . . . I was saying that since I don't live with my parents, when I have daily problems, I talk to friends or roommates about them. I don't usually go to my parents as a Mexican woman probably does. He kept asking what kinds of things I needed to talk to my parents about. I was saying that's not the point – examples aren't the point – the closeness to the family is what I was driving at. He kept asking the question with more and more hand motions. I didn't want to be treated like a student who couldn't express ideas. I didn't want to express what he was asking about, and he wasn't responding to my point. It happened a couple of different times.

This type of evidence occurs only occasionally in the journal, but it reflects the issue of power and solidarity again, showing my desire to be treated both as an equal in terms of social power as opposed to a subordinate student, and as a friend, one who could enjoy the group solidarity. It was in a social situation involving equality and friendship that I wanted to learn the language.

Halfway through my stay in Mexico, I began dating one of the teachers. Although my desire to become a friend of the group of Mexican teachers may have partially prompted my involvement with Vicente (nicknamed Tito), it was not the sole reason – there was a lot of emotional attraction to this friendly, observant musician and language teacher. Regardless of why it actually occurred, this dating certainly served as an entree by placing me in social situations with the group in which I would not otherwise have found myself, as in the following example where I was the only non-Mexican present.

Week 4: We took the bus to Pepe's. Some of the other maistros [(maestros) teachers] showed up. And I didn't know it, but it turned out to be a kind of family-school party. (Many of the teachers and administrators are related.) I was the only non-Mexican. It was difficult at times, in that I didn't know exactly what to do or say. But it was well worth it to see how they behave socially.

The amount of Spanish conversation that I was exposed to greatly increased once I began dating Vicente, and the social atmosphere was always light, easy, and therefore non-threatening. Because I felt comfortable with him, I asked for clarification when I needed it, which aided in the acquisition process.

Week 4:   Several times during the evening with Vicente I just couldn't believe that I was sitting there understanding the Spanish. A month ago I didn't understand a thing, and now I understand so much! I wasn't able to do all my talking just in Spanish. I would come up with an English phrase or word here and there. But he was speaking pretty normally, I think. I always told him when I didn't understand something, and then he would simplify or circumlocute.

After another evening, I remarked in the journal on the type of language, more informal than I had heard before, and on the playful mixing and switching.

Week 5:   There were plenty of positive aspects to the evening at the Piano Bar in terms of language learning. I heard a lot of slang and fillers that I haven't gotten anywhere else. Maybe I could pick some up if I had more of the input. I did have to talk a lot in Spanish, like to Alberto and Mari's brother. And with Tito I spoke Spanish and he often spoke English, but not all the time. I spoke English only when I had a difficult verb structure coming up – past modals, counterfactual conditionals, etc. I commented at one point on how I was speaking Spanish and he English, and he said it was fun. And it's true, it *was* fun. It wasn't at all a fight about what to speak. It was okay that we were speaking different languages. It was that I speak Spanish slowly and he English slowly.

Popular opinion holds that a good way to learn a language is to find a boyfriend or girlfriend who is a native speaker of the language. The documentation of my experience dating Tito (Vicente) supports this notion in three ways. First, I was able to participate in numerous social gatherings (parties, family gatherings, a wedding) to which I would not have otherwise been invited; at least no other non-Mexicans were invited. Second, I was comfortable enough with Tito, and he was patient enough for me to consistently elicit clarification about the language he and others were using. And finally, I was exposed to more language from more people speaking in various situations and registers, also apart from the group of teachers, than I would otherwise have been.

In class at this time, during my fifth week in Mexico, we were studying affective verbs, reported speech, and other complex verb structures using present and past tenses and progressive and perfective aspects. This instructor was clearly correcting our language far less often and less overtly than previous instructors had. The diary shows that I had a fair understanding of many structures and that I longed for informal input and interaction most of all. I was able to generate peer interaction during an all-school after-class activity: I planned, wrote, and performed a satire of the school along with three other students. This turned out to be a success, especially in terms of our creative use of language – the whole school was impressed.

By the fifth week in Mexico I was comfortable enough with my status as an accepted friend of the teacher group to converse easily when teachers and students were together.

Week 5:   I really feel like I'm an "in" person now and I love it. My Spanish competes with many other students in the school. I'm finding it easier and easier to talk to the teachers.

Week 5:   There were few students at school yesterday because a lot of them went to Zihuatanejo (on my recommendation). We students who did show up were standing around and Helen said we should ask to have a fun day of conversation instead of class. We had class for an hour, then sat around drinking cokes and talking for three more hours. It was nice. It was easy for me to talk and make jokes with the teachers and students. I'm feeling very good about it. I feel like I'm seen as having a personality. I've been driving at it and I think I've gotten there.

By the sixth week (when three-fourths of my time in Mexico had passed), I was frequently associating with the close group of teachers without other students present, but I sometimes felt like an outside observer, not totally involved.

Week 6:   The school party went on all afternoon. By about 7:00 P.M. all the students had gone. Just before the last of them went, Tito asked what I was going to do that night. I returned the question and he invited me to Pepe's or somewhere. . . . We talked some. . . . Then he went back over to where the teachers were and sang more. They were really enjoying themselves singing. I enjoyed watching, but I was definitely on the outskirts watching.

In such situations I was not always speaking, but I was not uncomfortable, and was able to listen and follow the gist of many conversations. The more time I spent with the group, the more familiar the context became, the clearer the various personalities became to me, and the clearer the relationships among those personalities became. The group's pattern of drinking, joking, singing, and dancing became repetitive, and eventually it seemed that the same linguistic forms occurred over and over. By the end of the sixth week, I felt less like an outsider and more comfortable with the teachers as a group, and possibly as individuals as well. At that point in time I felt a closer solidarity with the teachers than with the students, as seen in this excerpt.

Week 6:   I went around during break at school getting teachers' signatures on a birthday card for Mary Ellen. Again, I felt closer to the teachers than to the students. There are lots of new students and I can't handle all the new names.

212

By that time I loved the friendship with the teacher group and with individuals in it. I savored the lively atmosphere when everyone got together, and I reveled in having a boyfriend in the group.

Week 7:   Went to a fiesta [party] at school. . . . I talked to Oscar some. Then I talked to Guillermo and told him I didn't think he should become a priest like he has been talking about. . . . I clarified that it was his decision, but my opinion was that he could be religious without being a priest and that I thought that would be better for him. Later he said he really appreciated what I had said and considered me a good friend. . . . Tito and Jose played for quite a while and people sang. It was great. I wanted to try to capture it exactly in my mind so I could remember what they all look like and what that feeling with them is like. Tito passed the guitar on to someone else and we went up to the roof. . . . We had a nice conversation. For the first time we talked about how we felt about each other. When we went back down, everyone noticed our entrance. I loved it. We went outside with everyone. He played more. Passed around guitars. People told jokes. It was great. I never want to forget. Guillermo pulled us away from the group. . . . He was real drunk but lovable. He was babbling about how great Tito is, how he has a heart as big as this (and stretched his arms out as far as possible), and how I had won the lottery by being with Tito. I felt very close to Guillermo by the end of the evening.

For the last two weeks of my two-month stay in Mexico, I felt as though I was a good friend of the teachers. I felt more like their friend than their student, which made me an integral part of the group rather than an outsider when the whole group was socializing. It also enabled me to have conversations (e.g., the one with Guillermo regarding the priesthood in the preceding excerpt) in which the focus was on content rather than linguistic form. Guillermo was genuinely interested in what I was saying, and there was little or no concern for how I was saying it. I believe that this is exactly the type of situation which advanced my acquisition of Spanish the most.

There is, in fact, little indication in the last couple of weeks of my diary as to classroom language practice (except that we were studying present and past subjunctive verb forms) or other indicators of my language ability at that time. Instead, it is clear that I was much more involved in the many warm, friendly social events that occurred outside of class during that period, where I was developing arguments, expressing emotions, speculating on the future, accepting and downgrading compliments, and joining in on the general revelry of *fiestas*. The fact that this was all taking place in Spanish demonstrates the level of my language ability at the end of my two-month stay in Cuernavaca.

To summarize briefly, from the beginning of my time in Mexico I tried to become accepted and respected by a group of Mexican friends, which parallels my prior experience in Germany. As I was developing friendships with this group, I began to date one of its members. The general chronology of my association with the group of Mexican teachers shows that it was difficult early on relating to the group socially, but very gradually this seemed to become easier. Although I cannot pinpoint a breakthrough in my friendship with the group as a whole, it probably occurred midway through my stay, when I started dating Tito. Soon after, the diary indicates that I felt like a close friend of the Mexican teachers and was able to socialize with them very frequently, sometimes feeling like an outside observer, but soon enough as an active conversational participant. By socializing with the teachers as a socially equal member of their circle, I progressed in my acquisition of Spanish by using the language in meaningful and psychologically/emotionally charged situations.

Related studies

In an attempt to generalize the findings from my data to a certain extent, I surveyed other researchers' journals and analyses for similar issues. I found relevant documentation in the work of four other researchers and will present that here, along with relevant theoretical and quantitative evidence.

It must be noted that the information I will present is drawn from four case studies by individual language learner-researchers, each with very different backgrounds. Some similarities exist; for example, all of the diarists were university professors at the time of data collection, and all lived and studied in the target cultures. However, each studied a different language: Danish, Portuguese, Spanish, and Swedish. Some of the diarists present their data in a highly introspective manner with quite detailed observations; the data of others are less substantive. Moreover, some of the researchers have only made available discussions and analyses of their data and not the journal itself. All of this makes comparison of evidence in the intensive journals and drawing conclusions from those comparisons tasks that should be undertaken with caution.

As already indicated, the excerpts from my journal were, for the most part, representative examples of consistent trends in the data. That is not the case with the data to be presented from the other journal researchers. The major trends from their data are presented in their own analyses. The excerpts from their work are nearly exhaustive of the references to the issue. My purpose in citing these other journals is not to imply that the factors discussed were highly influential in the language learning of the diarists, but to provide further evidence for the major trends in my journal, namely how learners learn from social interaction with a group of friends who are speakers of the target language, and how prior language learning affects the new language learning experience.

Literature on out-of-class interaction

As visiting academicians at foreign universities, Burling (1981) and Moore (1977) discuss interaction with colleagues in their language learning diaries. Burling, expresses after two weeks in Sweden, longing for a group to associate with regularly.

> I remain vastly impressed by the social barriers to adult language acquisition: the high standards of English, the lack of interest in talking about simple "childish" matters, the failure to fully articulate the filler words, the assumption that if an adult does not know the language that it is not worth talking to him. . . . The most helpful thing for me now would be to associate with monolingual Swedes who really wanted to exchange information with me and who would patiently try. A few hours of that each day and my productivity would quickly rise. But it is almost impossible for an adult, in my situation, to meet such Swedes. (p. 48)

The Swedes with whom Burling had contact at the university spoke English, making it nearly impossible, as he says, for him to meet mono-lingual Swedes. His desire to find a group that "really wanted to exchange information . . . and would patiently try" is exactly what I enjoyed with my group of Mexican friends. Burling regularly had lunch with people from his office and considered this situation a linguistic challenge.

> If I can understand conference papers and if I could understand Ulla and Itzi last night, why does the lunch table conversation still pose so many problems? No doubt my lunch companions use a more "restricted code." They take more assumptions for granted and spell out fewer things explicitly. They speak briefly, cryptically, and that makes them harder to understand. (ibid.: 140–141)

Burling's analysis of sources of difficulty at the lunch table is notable. Indeed, any existing close-knit group, with past experience in common, has a restricted code which makes understanding by an outsider difficult (Bernstein 1972). However, if a learner is able to spend enough relaxed time with the group to be able to break the code, or, more likely, to realize that the code has somehow been broken, then it pays off in terms of linguistic and cultural input.

Although Burling never documented feeling either extremely fluent or at one with the lunch-table group, he realized advantages to associating with them. For example, the problem of Swedes being able to speak English so readily was sometimes solved when he, as the English speaker, was a minority in a group of Swedes.

215

When I have worked with other languages, it has always been much easier to sustain a conversation with a single individual than with several. In Sweden, since most of the people with whom I have regular contact speak English easily, conversation in Swedish with just one of them quickly becomes so silly that we both find it easier to switch to English. When two or three others are talking, however, they sustain Swedish among themselves, and it is natural for them to keep it going. I can then sometimes grin at the right places, respond to some questions, and toss in an occasional comment. (Burling 1981: 129)

Burling also describes such situations as being times when the language was "unforced," exactly my experience in Germany and Mexico. Here he notes such an example.

I participated in a good deal of Swedish conversation at the evening "Supe." I sat with people who seemed genuinely to prefer to speak Swedish with me, although they could certainly speak English. The occasions for using unforced Swedish gradually climb, and I can speak naturally with more and more people. (ibid.: 155)

Finally, after a weekend at a cottage with a group of Swedish colleagues, Burling characterizes the repetitiveness that occurs in group conversations over time. At this point, he seems to have cracked the restricted code.

My opportunities for using Swedish have been so limited that, when I do so, I have always been acutely conscious of the fact that I am, indeed, speaking Swedish. This weekend I came closer to using it without thinking constantly, "now I am speaking Swedish." It does help to use the language repeatedly in similar situations, to say the same things over and over again. Finally, that forces it to be natural. This is a drill aspect of learning that I abhor in class, but it has a certain usefulness in this natural situation. (ibid.: 174)

I sensed this same occurrence. The group of Mexicans I associated with definitely displayed a pattern to their banter, a pattern that elicited much of the same language over and over again.

In a situation similar to Burling's, Moore, a visiting professor at a Danish university, found conversation among colleagues most difficult. This is his lunch-table account.

I watch the speaker's faces, and probably my own expression to some extent mirrors theirs and gives the impression that I am following the meaning. Certainly when everyone laughs I invariably smile; it would feel stupid to sit poker-faced; but this must suggest that I understand more than I do. People usually seem surprised when they realize that I have not grasped the gist. . . . The sense of exclusion is greatest when everyone roars at a joke I have not taken in.

After trying in vain for some time to follow, one's attention inevitably wanders. The effort of trying to understand is so tiring and yields so little return that one opts out, simply to conserve energy. But this is an insidious and damaging course. (Moore 1977: 110).

It is interesting how obvious and important something becomes when it is lacking. Moore did not seem to be as frustrated about the linguistic difficulty as he was with the lack of social interaction with colleagues. He continued this analysis of his inability to easily converse at the lunch table and at other times with colleagues.

I had not realized before how importantly a satisfactory working life depends on being able to take part in casual discussion. Without it, one loses touch with events and never becomes aware of the currents of opinions among one's colleagues. One cannot contribute to the ongoing dialogue, let alone take any initiative, and increasingly feels isolated and debarred from playing one's proper part in the corporate life of one's working group. One may feel incompetent, resentful and depressed by turns, or may simply elect to withdraw from the fray and pursue one's own interests. The latter course may free time for productive work, but at the cost of social and professional isolation. (ibid.: 110)

Burling and Moore both found it difficult dealing with their groups of colleagues; nonetheless, they knew that the interaction was socially and professionally beneficial.

Like Burling and Moore, Schmidt and Frota's (1986) subject, R. (actually Richard Schmidt, himself), a visiting lecturer in Brazil, reports difficulty interacting with professional colleagues. However, he was introduced to a group with whom he spent most of his free time. He claims that the interaction greatly improved his comprehension and communicative abilities in Portuguese, as illustrated in these diary excerpts:

Week 17:   Two weeks ago, M. took me to a sidewalk restaurant in Copacabana to meet some friends. I've been back almost every night since. . . . Between eleven and one about twenty regulars show up for dinner. Everyone knows everyone, and there's lots of moving about and putting tables together. Later, smaller groups split off, either to party in someone's apartment nearby or to go dancing. I've seen a lot of sunrises, and I think I've found a place where I can really fit in. They have welcomed me, and there's a critical mass of very intelligent people whom I find very stimulating. The people I've met so far have been mostly writers (journalists, novelists) or theater people (actors, producers, directors). It's a big challenge. Part of the problem is cultural. . . . The language problem is severe. I frequently get so exhausted trying to keep up at least with the main topic of each conversation that I just drift off for a while. In spite of that, I've felt positively euphoric since I started to hang out there.

217

Week 22 [R.'s final week in Brazil]: The area where I think I've made the steadiest progress is comprehension. . . . I think the biggest help has been interacting with lots of people regularly at Trattoria. There I don't restrict myself to highly negotiated one-on-one conversations, but really strain to understand what everyone is saying. When I do get lost, usually someone will notice and will negotiate me back in. . . . Last night was my last there . . . U., who had been the harshest critic of my Portuguese, said I've improved a lot and my Portuguese is now almost as good as her English. (pp. 247–248).

My socializing with teachers, Burling's and Moore's attempts to socialize with their colleagues, and Schmidt's success at learning by socializing with his Brazilian friends serve as evidence for claims made by other theorists that learners in the society of the target language need a supportive group to rely on. Smith (1984: 8) referred to this as a desire to become a "member of the club." Larson and Smalley (1972) feel that in order to overcome culture shock and culture stress, "the learner needs . . . a small community of sympathetic people who will help him in the difficult period when he is a linguistic and cultural child-adult" (p. 46). Schumann (1975: 214) adds:

Whoever constitutes the family must be able to provide the learner with a sense of identity and help him to cope with his environment such that he finds culturally appropriate solutions to the problems he encounters. Also, the "family" must be willing to correct the alien's mistakes, provide him with access to the community-at-large, and serve as conversation partners and, where possible, language teachers.

Literature on the use of prior language learning experience

As mentioned earlier in this chapter, numerous second language transfer studies have demonstrated the effect of prior experience with or knowledge of language on new language learning, in terms of surface-level linguistics. Diary studies, too, have begun to add evidence to this area. Rivers (1983: 172) shows how she relied on her understanding of French cognates in her later Spanish study. She also felt that her knowledge of Italian helped her Spanish pronunciation (ibid.: 173). Likewise we find R. in the Schmidt and Frota (1986) diary study drawing on previous knowledge very early in his five months in Brazil. He used his French knowledge when reading public signs in Portuguese (p. 241); and Arabic initially helped him practice Portuguese pronunciation (p. 242) and usage of articles (p. 225).

In addition, experimental studies provide support for the importance of prior experience in a new language learning experience. Bialystok (1983) refers to a large-scale study at the Ontario Institute for Studies in Education, a study of inferencing and other communication strategies. The preliminary analysis indicated that adults who know three or more languages are more successful at inferencing in a new language – using the context and the structure of the new language as well as their knowledge of other languages – than adults who know fewer than three languages (p. 109).

Nation and McLaughlin's (1986) experimental study discusses the notion that experienced language learners know how to learn a language more efficiently than novice learners. Extensive prior language learning experience may enable people to draw out patterns from new language data simply by being exposed to the data, while less experienced language learners may need to be instructed to look for patterns that exist. Nation and McLaughlin suggest that language learning experience may develop in people something that might be characterized as either a linguistic sensitivity or more successful higher-order plans for working with linguistic information, or better automatic linguistic processing skills (pp. 52–53). Similarly, Larsen-Freeman and Long (1991) mention the possibility of streamlined hypothesizing about new languages by experienced learners speeding up their language-learning processes (p. 206).

Continuing on a more theoretical level, Wittrock's (1977) generative model of the learning process supports this discussion in that it assumes that the manner in which a person learns is consistent with his or her prior experience and prior learning. The model "predicts that learning is a function of the abstract and distinctive, concrete associations which the learner generates between his prior experience, as it is stored in long-term memory, and the stimuli" (ibid.: 623). The learner brings his or her prior experience to the learning situation and uses that experience along with the new information to create or generate learning. In my case, I brought to Mexico my prior experience of acquiring German from a German social group, and created my own optimal circumstances for learning by finding an equally social and friendly group in Mexico.

Conclusions

According to Wittrock (ibid.: 628) "[L]earners, especially their prior experiences, backgrounds, abilities, and attitudes, are part of our science and are crucially important in the equations for predicting learning." For this reason, I chose to observe myself as a learner by documenting in my language learning diary my experience in Mexico. From the emic perspective that such a study provides, it seems that my prior experience and attitudes determined the course of my Spanish language learning to an extreme.

I intentionally searched for a social group to interact with because of my awareness of its importance to me based on my prior experience with a group in Germany and because I was not entirely satisfied with the instruction I was receiving. In Germany I became acquainted with the group of German students more or less by chance; in Mexico, however, I set out to duplicate that social situation even though it meant taking risks. Having no detailed data on my experience in Germany, it remains unclear whether social salience was something I strove for there. My guess is that in Mexico I was trying a new strategy to achieve social status as a member of the Mexican group. Achieving that social status required effort on my part because of the imbalance of power between myself and the members of the group, all my teachers, and because of the solidarity within the group. As seen in Burling's (1981) and Moore's (1977) cases, too, it is very difficult for a foreigner to become a member of an established group of friends or co-workers; sometimes it just doesn't happen, and one remains an outside observer. If I had not had the experience in Germany of learning a language well by socializing regularly with a close group of friends, I doubt that I would have expended the effort that I did in Mexico in order to become a part of the Mexican group.

Until now, readers of this chapter have heard two voices: my voice as a language learner, sometimes complaining about and sometimes delighting in, my language learning experiences, as well as my voice as a researcher, analyzing my own and others' acquisition. At this point I would like to change roles to complete the discussion in the voice of a language teacher.

As teachers, we can see several pedagogical reasons documented in this study for socializing with our students. Students need to use their target language in many different situations and registers: in relaxed, informal environments, with ourselves and with others as interested interlocutors. Schmidt and Frota (1986) demonstrate R.'s improvement in comprehension once he was able to spend social time regularly with native speakers of Portuguese. Likewise, data from my diary and that of Burling (1981) show that many convivial occasions across time with native speakers of the target language encourage natural, sometimes unconscious language use and acquisition. In these types of situations, students are able to lose themselves in the joviality of the moment and practice the language without focusing consciously on form and without major inhibitions intruding. Students are also able to display their personalities more readily in congenial social situations than in the classroom, at least in cases where the social situations occur over an extended period of time. Demonstrating one's personality appears to be a need that concerns some adult students, especially if they are new to a country, as I was in Mexico, Burling (1981) was in Sweden, and Moore was (1977) in Denmark.

Even teachers who feel that socializing with their students goes beyond their professional responsibilities should realize from this study, among others, that their students may benefit affectively and sociolinguistically from communicative opportunities where the teacher sheds his or her teaching role. Students need to be treated with respect, as peers. In particular, adult students immersed in the target culture and the new language may spend much of their daily lives outside the classroom feeling powerless or subordinate, as I indicated in my journal, or feeling like a child, as Burling implies (1981). If the teacher interacts with these students as equals in social situations rather than maintaining the distance or superiority of the traditional pedagogue, the learners can eventually go far toward becoming autonomous individuals within the target culture.

In any case, the teacher's responsibility remains to help guide each student to develop language efficiently and effectively. This requires, above all, patience, what Burling (1981) longed for in a monolingual Swede and what I found in my Mexican boyfriend. Ideally, a teacher needs to become so familiar with each individual student that the teacher can guide the student's language learning progress, working with each learner as a whole person. It takes patience for a teacher to fully assess an individual's learning style in order to tailor teaching and feedback approaches accordingly. Such assessment has been demonstrated by Ellis (1989) and Tyacke and Mendelsohn (1986), who note that student diaries are crucial in language learning. It also takes patience for a teacher to become familiar enough with an adult student's prior language learning experience to be able to help that student exploit previously successful strategies. For years I have asked students by questionnaire on the first day of class how many languages they know, and to what extent. But I realize that this tactic only gives a superficial indication of prior language learning experience, and certainly no indication at all of the strategies used. To truly guide students to make conscious use of their prior language learning strategies, the teacher needs patience, insight, and commitment to individualized teaching. In order to understand an adult student's previous experience well enough to adapt teaching approach and feedback appropriately, the teacher must talk at length with each student, getting to know the person, probing the person's memory, and drawing out details of the language learning history and experience. Obviously, a full classroom and full teaching agenda rarely allow for such extensive individualized talk. There is no more opportune time or place to do this than away from the classroom over a cup of coffee or tea, students socializing with teachers.

References

Bailey, K. M. 1983. Competitiveness and anxiety in adult second language learning: Looking *at* and *through* the diary studies. In H. W. Seliger and

M. H. Long (eds.), *Classroom Oriented Research in Second Language Acquisition*. Rowley, MA: Newbury House.

1991. Diary studies of classroom language learning. The doubting game and the believing game. In E. Sadtono (ed.), *Language Acquisition and the Second/Foreign Language Classroom*. Singapore: SEAMEO Regional Language Centre, Anthology Series #28.

Bailey, K. M., and R. Ochsner. 1983. A methodological review of the diary studies: Windmill tilting or social science? In K. M. Bailey, M. H. Long, and S. Peck (eds.), *Second Language Acquisition Studies: Series on Issues in Second Language Research*. Rowley, MA: Newbury House.

Bernstein, B. 1972. Social class, language and socialization. In P. P. Giglioli (ed.), *Language and Social Context: Selected Readings*. Harmondsworth, England: Penguin Books.

Bialystok, E. 1983. Inferencing: Testing the "hypothesis-testing" hypothesis. In H. W. Seliger and M. H. Long (eds.), *Classroom Oriented Research in Second Language Acquisition*. Rowley, MA: Newbury House.

Burling, R. 1981. On the Way to Swedish. Unpublished manuscript, University of Michigan, Ann Arbor.

Ellis, R. 1989. Classroom learning styles and their effect on second language acquisition: A study of two learners. *System, 17,* 2, 249–262.

Gass, S., and L. Selinker. (eds.). 1983. *Language Transfer in Language Learning*. Rowley, MA: Newbury House.

Hudson, R. A. 1980. *Sociolinguistics*. Oxford: Cambridge University Press.

Jones, R. A. 1977. Social and psychological factors in second language acquisition: A study of an individual. In C. Henning (ed.), *Proceedings of the Los Angeles Second Language Research Forum* (Vol. 1, 331–341). University of California, Los Angeles, English Department, ESL Section.

Kellerman, E., and Sharwood Smith, M. (eds.). 1986. *Crosslinguistic Influence in Second Language Acquisition*. New York: Pergamon Press.

Larson, D. N., and W. A. Smalley. 1972. *Becoming Bilingual, A Guide to Language Learning*. New Canaan, CT: Practical Anthropology.

Larsen-Freeman, D., and M. H. Long. 1991. *An Introduction to Second Language Acquisition Research*. New York: Longman.

Moore, T. 1977. An experimental language handicap (personal account). *Bulletin of the British Psychological Society, 30,* 107–110.

Morris, M. 1988. *Nothing to Declare: Memoirs of a Woman Traveling Alone*. New York: Penguin.

Nation, R., and B. McLaughlin. 1986. Novices and experts: An information processing approach to the "good language learner" problem. *Applied Psycholinguistics, 7,* 41–55.

Rivers, W. M. 1983. Learning a sixth language: An adult learner's daily diary. In W. M. Rivers (ed.), *Communicating Naturally in a Second Language*. New York: Cambridge University Press. (Reprinted from *Canadian Modern Language Review,* 1979, 36, 1, 67–82)

Schmidt, R. W., and S. N. Frota. 1986. Developing basic conversational ability in a second language: A case study of an adult learner of Portuguese. In R. R. Day (ed.), *Talking to Learn: Conversation in Second Language Acquisition*. Rowley, MA: Newbury House.

Schumann, J. H. 1975. Affective factors and the problem of age in second language acquisition. *Language Learning, 25,* 2, 209–235.

Schumann, F. E., and J. H. Schumann. 1977. Diary of a language learner: An introspective study of second language learning. In H. D. Brown, R. H. Crymes, and C. A. Yorio (eds.), *On TESOL '77: Teaching and Learning English as a Second Language: Trends in Research and Practice*. Washington, DC: TESOL.

Smith, F. 1984. The promise and threat of microcomputers for language learners. In J. Handscombe, R. A. Orem, and B. P. Taylor (eds.), *On TESOL '83: The Question of Control*. Washington, DC: TESOL.

Stockwell, R., J. Bowen, and J. Martin. 1965. *The Grammatical Structures of English and Spanish*. Chicago: University of Chicago Press.

Tyacke, M., and D. Mendelsohn. 1986. Student needs: Cognitive as well as communicative. *TESL Canada Journal/Revue TESL du Canada*, November, 171–181.

Wittrock, M. C. 1977. Learning as a generative process. In M. C. Wittrock (ed.), *Learning and Instruction*. Berkeley, CA: McCutchan Publishing Corporation.

9 Sardo revisited: voice, faith, and multiple repeaters

Martha Clark Cummings

> Perhaps the extra knot that strangles my
> voice is rage. I am enraged at the false
> persona I'm being stuffed into, as into
> some clumsy and overblown astronaut
> suit. I'm enraged at my . . . friends
> because they can't see through this
> guise, can't recognize the light-footed
> dancer I really am.
>
> (Hoffman 1990)

The following are journal excerpts, in-class freewritings, and retrospective reflections on a ten-week, community college ESL composition course for "multiple repeaters." All twenty students had taken the course and failed the final exam at least twice previously. More than three failures required the students to withdraw from the school. Passing the course would allow them to enter Basic Writing in the English Department. After two quarters of Basic Writing, they would be eligible to take Freshman Composition and begin taking courses in their major. In the account that follows, the students' names have all been changed.

First I teach them freewriting to get them away from judgment, to get them away from trying to be perfect before they know what they want to say. I explain that freewriting is not really "free." There are strict rules. They will put their pens on the paper and keep going for ten minutes. They should not erase, not re-read, not worry about spelling or grammar or anything but getting their thoughts and feelings on paper. "If you don't know the word in English," I suggest, "write it in your own language." They look up, interested for the first time. "Is she serious?" they ask themselves. They see that I am smiling, but that I really mean it. "Is she crazy?" they wonder. I am, after all, the teacher who *asked* for this, the one who *wanted* to teach a class made up entirely of students who were repeating the course. They decide to go along with me.

"Remember this," I tell them. "Don't censor yourself. No one is going to judge this writing. You don't have to show it to anyone or share it with anyone if you don't want to. I will always ask you to share it with the person sitting next to you by reading it aloud. You can say no. I will ask you to share it with the whole class. You can say no to that too."

"Okay!" I tell them, sitting down at my desk and opening my notebook. "Are you ready?" I am startling them again. I am going to write with them. "No stopping. No reading. No crossing out. No erasing. Just writing for ten minutes without stopping. I'll tell you when to stop. Ready?"

They begin. They go along with me. This is a good start. Later, when I add "No thinking" to the list of rules for freewriting, they smile and keep writing. After a week, when I walk into class, some of them have already started writing. Freewriting is our time to feel safe with writing, to bring our concerns out into the open, to entertain and amuse instead of judge each other. Later, the students develop bonds with their classmates and freewriting becomes part of the social life they crave, part of why they are in school at all.

A class of twenty repeaters at a community college in urban America. One of many community colleges that has broken its promise (a career in two years) to its students who have immigrated to the United States hoping for new lives. Most of them are women. Half of them are over thirty. They have been in the United States and out of school from three to sixteen years, with an average of eight years. Many have a high school equivalency degree. They have already revealed these facts about their lives in the first "diagnostic" composition they wrote, an acknowledged but required exercise in futility. Since they have already failed this course, no matter how well they do on their first-day composition, they cannot, like other students at this level, be moved on to the next level if they do exceptionally well. They must stay where they are and pass. And if they don't pass, they must try again. After that, there are no more chances. The prospect is chilling.

Their first compositions reveal different levels of hope and despair. Current research tells us that hope is everything (see Snyder et al. 1991). I look for signs of it. Ronnie, the Indonesian girl, writes of her bitter disappointment at eating at a fast food restaurant alone on her birthday and then her great surprise upon returning home and finding all her friends waiting for her. If I were a Jungian psychologist and this were her dream, I would think that her chances were good.

Others are not so lucky. Mercedes writes about a party to which she invited all of her friends, but none of them came and she never found out why. Gladys writes about coming to America, falling into a deep and mysterious depression, only to realize that what she really wanted was to divorce her husband, run away from her children, and be utterly alone. Now she is a single mother of two boys, on welfare, attending ESL class, hoping to accept her fate instead of get what she needs. Her dark, deepset eyes are filled with longing.

225

Elena tries to write the story of her life in two and a half pages. The topic was, "Write about something that happened in the last year or two that made you very happy, angry, sad, excited, or upset. Please don't write about coming to America." Elena did not read the topic carefully. She writes about coming to America. Winton, who tells me that his parents meant to name him Winston but did not know how to spell it, writes about getting a job at the Holiday Inn as if it were achieving Nirvana. Jaime had his pocket picked on vacation. He gives his composition the title, "A Bad Vacation," and I recognize it as too familiar, one that he probably wrote in a previous semester for another teacher. This happens a lot with repeaters. The effort to start again where they have failed before is so colossal that they will do anything to avoid it. I understand this. I ask him to rewrite it anyway.

Zoraida tells of the time a woman tried to kidnap her child in New York's Central Park. Claudia tells of losing her fifteen-year-old daughter to stomach cancer. Rona writes about her best friend's suicide by swallowing acid because she got pregnant before she was married (this was in India, not here, she explains). Tony writes about his career in China as a radio broadcaster, which he gave up to come to the United States and work as a waiter in Chinatown, and the humiliation of serving dinner to one of his former professors who was visiting New York.

They are stories of defeat. Reading and writing skills have little to do with the problems these students face. But I am here to teach them about reading and writing. I continue.

When I sit down with their first compositions and I see the garbled prose, the mangled syntax, I say to myself, "What teacher in the world would *ask* to teach such a class?" Twenty people who have failed before will most likely fail again. The average failure rate in the ESL writing classes at this community college is 60 percent. The rate for repeaters is 75 percent. But I have my reasons. I want to teach them because I identify with them. I know enough about psychology to know this. In some sense I am one of them. I am not on welfare, not divorced, not a single mother, not Latina. But as a writer I am something of a slow learner. My history as a writer is one of repeated defeat and failure. It took me ten years to write my first novel. It was really my fourth. The first three, like the space shuttle *Challenger*, exploded, fizzled, reducing to cinders my belief in the power of my own voice. It was only because of my writing teachers, two or three generous people who believed in me, that I was able to keep trying. Gregory Bateson (1972) says it this way.

Some men seem able to go on working steadily with little success and no reassurance from the outside. I am not one of these. I have needed to know that somebody else believed that my work had promise and direction, and I have often been surprised that others had faith in me when I had very little in myself. I have, at times, even tried to shrug off the responsibility which their continued faith imposed on me by thinking, "But they don't really know what I am doing. How can they know when I myself do not?" (p. ix)

Now that I have finished one novel and am halfway through writing another, published a dozen short stories and several academic articles, all thanks to other people's faith in me, I have come to believe that if I can be brought back from failure, anyone can. I approach this task with evangelical zeal. My message, from one "repeater" to another, is this: To be a good writer you need two things. First, give yourself over to the act of writing. Second, have faith in your own voice. To get started, someone else must have that faith in you. I am teaching this course to be that someone else.

I require all of my composition students to write a composition for each day they are absent. I give them an excellent one as an example and tell them I want one just as good. They do not live up to this demand, but their writing about their illnesses and emergencies is the most powerful writing I get from them. Nelly tells me she is going to be absent for three days to have medical tests, and I tell her to write three compositions and make sure to get all the notes and assignments from one of her classmates, knowing full well that she will never be able to keep up with the class if she misses a week, not having the heart to tell her that her medical tests could lead to an *F*. She comes back five days later with all of her compositions written, all of her homework done, and a note from the Department of Nuclear Medicine at a large state-funded hospital. I don't ask her for details. She doesn't look at all well.

One day I try to do a freewrite in Spanish. They don't ask me to read it to them. I don't offer. I write about ten lines and then break into English. "I would go nuts," I write, "unless I spent several hours a day reading Spanish to have the words in my mind." I feel myself reaching and reaching for the words, and they are as far away as another planet. Somewhere far, far away are all the words I ever read or heard or spoke in Spanish, and when I reach for them and can't find them I feel blind, as if I am groping in a closet trying to figure out what to wear by the feel of it instead of by seeing its color or shape, instead of holding it up and looking in the mirror. I give them grammar lessons. We learn about the conditional. We discuss at length the difference between the future possible, "If you go to the store, get me a carton of milk," and the present unreal, "If I were rich, I would buy a house." We write sentences full of hopes and dreams, what we would do if we were mayor of the city, president of the United States, queen or king of the world.

Many of them want to feed and shelter the hungry. All of them want to buy houses for their mothers.

We continue freewriting. Claudia writes about women getting ahead, making great sacrifices to achieve their goals. Women can do all kinds of professions, she says. She gives the example of Geraldine Ferraro running for Vice President, and of the Secretary of Health, who is Puerto Rican. She knows that good writing requires examples. Gladys writes about men. Men are afraid of women, she writes, afraid of their intelligence. Men are lost in life and marry to have someone to help them find their way. Winton, the eternal optimist, writes about how important it is not to get mad about things you can't control.

We search for topics together, topics that we could all write about. "Love is not enough," emerges as their favorite. "Love is not enough to keep a family together, a couple together," becomes the midterm topic. "Are you sure?" I ask them. "Are you sure this is what you want to write about? Do you have lots of examples?" Of course they do.

Meanwhile Carmen keeps erasing and erasing and erasing, as if she wants to flick away every word on the page. On the other side of the wall, another teacher's chalk taps on the chalkboard, clicking out a message like Morse code.

The building we are in isn't finished yet. Across the hall, a member of the construction crew starts using a pneumatic drill to remove a narrow strip of marble from the threshold of the women's room. It must have been put there by mistake or be the wrong size. I go out into the hall to tell him that we are trying to have class and that we can't hear each other. "They told us you have lunch hour between twelve and one," he shouts. "They told you wrong," I shout back, but he doesn't stop.

Gladys reads her freewrite, which is all about how unhappy she is with the class. She didn't want to have to buy a book. She doesn't like big classrooms. She will never make any friends in this class, she says. I try to listen to her complaints calmly, but I am distracted by my hair. I feel it curving around my face like it's electrified, like it's full of static electricity, yet heavy on my head, like an old-fashioned floor mop. "This is how they feel," I think. "This is how distracting their lives are."

Liliana, who has bifocals and has been waiting for thirty years to go back to school, sits in the last row, craning her neck to smile at me, her dark eyes shining. She is so short that her feet don't touch the floor. She wanted to go to an Adventist college in Massachusetts, but someone told her it was very expensive so she'd better learn English in New York first. She is so short that I am only comfortable talking to her if she is standing up and I am sitting down.

We are reading *Love Life*, a collection of stories by Bobbie Ann Mason (1989), and it is too difficult for them but we are going on with it anyway. We are on the second story, "Midnight Magic." The discussion stalls at the point in the story where one of the characters brings up Sardo, the 1000-year-old American Indian who inhabits the body of a teenage girl. We sit in a circle trying to discuss the story, and our discussion keeps circling back to Sardo. They are fascinated by this. The Indian girl in class says that in India, too, they have a girl who is inhabited by a spirit. This gives everyone the creeps and we start talking about spirits in general. Carmen says that if it's a bad spirit, you're possessed and you have to go to an exorcist, but if it's a good one then you get to perform for people like the girl in the story. Jaime, as skeptical as the young man in the story whose girlfriend tells him that Sardo can predict his fate, scratches his beard and wants to know if we think it's okay for the teenage girl to drive a Porsche. "No, it's not!" Mercedes says firmly. "It's not okay."

"Why not?" we all want to know.

"Because she's only thirteen."

"Does it say in the story that she's only thirteen?" I ask.

Mercedes looks puzzled, hurt even. "It says she's a teenager. A teenager means she's thirteen."

Jaime becomes exasperated. A teenager, he explains, is from thirteen to nineteen, and anyway that wasn't his point.

"Oh," Mercedes says, "then it's okay."

"But what about the money?" Jaime wants to know. "Where does she get the money to buy such an expensive car?"

Ronnie suggests that maybe she was already rich.

I say that I think she collects money at the Sunday night meetings and that's how she paid for the car and is *that* okay? Everyone acts like what I say is law and it must not be okay or I wouldn't have brought it up and I'm sorry I said anything.

Winton says that the religion in the story is not like the Catholic Church, it isn't a real religion where they are supposed to give money to the poor, so it's okay. Several people around the circle squawk about his mentioning the church. Since when did the church ever give money to anyone, they want to know. I am more interested in his other point.

"How do you know when something is a real religion?" I ask.

Liliana, still smiling, still happy to be getting educated at last, her short legs dangling, raises her hand and waits politely for me to notice her.

"Liliana?"

"It's not a religion," she says. "It's a cult."

"A cult," several of the other women around the circle echo her, glad to be reminded that this word exists. "It's a cult."

"What makes it a cult instead of a religion?" I ask her.

Gladys, the Brazilian woman who is studying mortuary science and looks a little like a cadaver herself, leans forward, ready to give speaking to this group a try.

"They talk about God in a religion," she says. "Sardo says good things will happen to you if you look for answers in yourself, not God."

This leads us to a discussion of Buddha and Buddhism and if Buddhists talk about God. Ronnie explains that Buddha was a king and he sat like a yogi for a long time until the spirit came down on him. The word *spirit* sends a shiver through the group again and before I can stop it, we are back to Sardo once more.

At the end of class, Liliana comes up to my desk once more, smiling. I notice that the little vest she is wearing hangs loosely from her broad square frame and is covered with food stains. I am surprised by this. She seems so prim and proper. The thought of her spilling food on herself day after day and not noticing gives me vertigo.

She presses her soft belly against my desk and confides, "If you read the Bible, you will understand why these things are happening more and more." She is smiling the same smile she has been smiling since the first time she walked into the classroom.

"What things?" I ask her.

"Things like Sardo," she says. "These are the last days."

She goes back to her seat to put on her coat.

Mercedes, whose heavy eyeliner makes me think of Cleopatra, gives me a composition about the death of her boyfriend, a composition that has no grammatical errors and that I swear I have read before. Is it possible that she copied it from one of my own former students? Today, our day in the computer lab, she tells me that she doesn't have children and couldn't possibly write about how to raise a difficult child – this topic has been requested by popular demand, so many of them have difficult children – so instead she has decided to write about the effects of drugs and alcohol on unborn children. Would that be okay? she asks, smiling sweetly. No, it wouldn't, I tell her. I am not usually so strict about adhering to the topic, but she has her diskette from last quarter in the computer. I do not want to ask her to show me her list of compositions from last quarter. I am certain that the one about the effects of drugs and alcohol on unborn children will be there. Instead I tell her that it doesn't matter if she has children or not. She was a child once herself, wasn't she? She slaps her forehead, as if she had forgotten.

Liliana approaches me nervously in the computer lab. I notice a few wild gray hairs in her thick black hair, the food stains still on her vest. "May I speak with you in private?" she asks. I can tell that this is a serious request and walk with her out into the hall. She takes off her bifocals and says that she thinks she might not be able to continue with the class because she has emotional problems. As she says this, fat tears splash onto her cheeks. "It's from my childhood," she says. "I had a terrible childhood." She continues. She is sobbing. I hand her a tissue and put my hand on her shoulder and wish we were standing somewhere else. I should have brought her to my office. I can't really understand what she's saying, she's crying so hard. We are standing near the doorway of the new cobblestone courtyard. There is a little black girl nearby who must be waiting for her mother. She informs us that it is raining. We know that.

Liliana continues, becoming more coherent. She doesn't like people looking at her, she says. She doesn't like to be looked at. "I'm a Christian," she says. "I love God. I want to love people." But people make her nervous. Her breath catches. She is sobbing again. People I know are drifting by and I watch them pass but I don't speak to them because I am trying to concentrate on what Liliana is saying even though she is not making too much sense. She says she went to a psychiatrist and told him she needed medication and he said she just needed to talk. The rain is staining the courtyard and this small, stout woman is telling me that she feels guilt and terror and then taking it back with the next breath. "I don't feel guilty. I've made some terrible mistakes but I don't feel guilty."

"We have all made terrible mistakes," I tell her.

She does not come back to class.

One day I suggest a topic. "There are times in life when we expect to be unhappy and we are surprised by joy. Write about a time in your life when you were sure you were going to have a terrible time and you didn't. What did you learn from this experience? What advice would you give to someone in a similar situation?"

They ask me for an example. "This class," I say. "When I signed up to teach this class, I was expecting to be unhappy. I thought you would be a group of people with a bad attitude. Instead this class has become my favorite. You have a wonderful sense of community here." As I say this, I feel my vision growing blurry. Tears are welling up in my eyes. I continue telling them anyway, about how I look forward to seeing them, about how it cheers me up to think of them. I do not tell them that they are sometimes the only thing standing between me and calling in sick. I am afraid they wouldn't believe me.

It's the truth though. Several colleagues and I are so close to getting tenure, have so much at stake, are feeling so competitive, that this classroom is the only place left in the entire college where people aren't trying to hurt each other, where there is caring and warmth. When I walk into this class I know that someone will perform some simple act of kindness: share her Colombian snack, show me a picture of her child, lean against me while we chat about her paper. This classroom feels like the only place left in the college where no one has anything to prove.

Yesterday Gladys told me that she couldn't stay in the computer lab because her son's school had called. He was having an asthma attack and she had to pick him up. She didn't seem to be in a hurry to leave though. She wanted to tell me about the onset of his attacks, how they start because he doesn't zip up his jacket and his lungs get cold. She demonstrated this by pressing the sides of her own red jacket together against her bony chest, smiling at me, eager to please. She talked about how much she wanted to get away from her children. She has two boys, one is nine and the other is four. Sometimes she works and sometimes she collects welfare or unemployment. She is a woman with a lively sense of humor, a woman with a great deal of spirit, a woman with intelligence and verve.

"I can always write," she told me once, "but I have to concentrate to read."

She can't concentrate. She has too many worries. She is always on her way to the doctor's or the dentist, for herself or for her sons. There is no time to relax. She wears glasses with heavy black frames, the kind you buy from a rack at the drugstore. She often wears the same heavy plaid flannel shirt, a thick white undershirt, the same pair of jeans, her hair in a ponytail pulled back tight.

What does any of this have to do with reading and writing ability? How can I interrupt all of this to talk about verbs?

Claudia, the one who came to school to recover from the death of her fifteen-year-old daughter, comes up to me during an in-class writing with a small slip of paper in her hand. "Martha," she says. "I confuse . . ." On the slip is written, "marriage, to marry, married." I lunge at this "teachable moment." I tell her I will explain it to the whole class and usher her back to her seat. She is a woman in her fifties wearing a royal blue sweatshirt. Mickey Mouse writhes on her chest. On the board I write examples of how to use the words on her list. Some of the others notice. The ones who can see. One of the things I have learned about them is that most of them need either new prescriptions in the glasses they are wearing or to put on the glasses they are not wearing. Most of them are just pretending to be able to see the blackboard. I have asked the school nurse to give each of them an eye test.

What does any of this have to do with intelligence or aptitude or ability in reading and writing?

Most of their problems have to do with what we can't control. It is a relief when all someone needs is new glasses. Gladys tilts her glasses at odd angles just to be able to read aloud to the class. Nelly, who has now missed seven classes because of her continuing appointments with the Department of Nuclear Medicine, does not seem to be able to see the book at all.

I put them in small groups, and Ronnie, the girl from Indonesia, tries to carry out the task I've assigned, which is to identify the three places in the story that they think are most important. Rona, the Indian girl, interrupts.

"Is that a new color lipstick you're wearing?" she asks.

"Yes," Ronnie answers her, but she's embarrassed. She knows I'm listening. Then Rona suddenly feels that something is amiss and turns to see what is happening over her left shoulder. It is me, large and looming. They go back to work.

Zoraida, the Colombian woman who used to be in a women's softball league in her country, gets up in the middle of class and walks out of the room with a shopping bag full of goods that she has sold to one of her friends, who is waiting for it at the door. Zoraida once brought in her photo album for me to look at. She showed the whole class pictures of herself and her teammates. She looked beautiful in her uniform, I told her. And she did. Young and slender and full of vitality. She was the catcher. The catcher cannot be afraid of the ball, she informed us.

A lot of buying and selling goes on in these classes. Many of the students are Avon ladies, or some Latina equivalent, on the side. And who can blame them? More than verbs, they need money. When I turn my back to write on the blackboard, I can hear the crackling of a plastic bag as they try to tempt each other with costume jewelry and cut-rate cosmetics. There are days when I don't even try to stop them. I sympathize with these people who cannot get what they want, who are always struggling, who have dreams but cannot achieve them, who *could* achieve them if they could unload their cares, but whose cares will always be there. We spend two hours together every day thinking about paths that we pretend are still open to them, but the doors we are trying to open were closed and bolted shut long ago.

There is something else. Something deeper than this. Pulling them away from their interaction with each other and concentrating instead on our work feels like tearing apart Siamese twins with my bare hands. What point would there be in such carnage?

They are always ready for a chat, always ready to linger, to sit close and feel a sense of community. We would be much better off at a resort than in a classroom. The other, the academic stuff, is too painful and difficult and more than anything, too lonely. The isolation of reading and writing is terrifying. They are people trained to take care of the physical and emotional needs of others. Their own intellectual needs are alien to them. They are numb to those needs or distract themselves from them every time they come near. The more time I spend with them, the more I sympathize. This is probably not what's supposed to happen. More and more I feel like saying, "Couldn't we just have coffee?"

I watch them taking their final exam. How can they write nonstop for two and a half hours? Why on earth aren't they finished yet? As they do finish, some of them re-read what they wrote. But they do it with uncertainty and shame, as if they are sure they are doing something wrong. When they hand in their papers, the course will be over. And if they pass, it will be as terrible, as impossible, as leaving home.

And then, like magic, like something only Bobbie Ann Mason's character Sardo would have dared to predict, it turns out that eighteen out of the twenty have passed. We alternate between being amazed and being assured.

"Of course we did," Carmen said.

"Yeah," echo the others.

But why? how? I ask myself. Upon reflection, here is what I think is the secret to our success. The final exam in this course is a personal narrative with topics along the lines of "Describe an important decision you once made," or "Describe a moment in the past that you would never want to relive." Since all we want to do in this class is listen to each other's problems, give each other advice, tell each other stories, I teach them how to turn their troubles into good stories. I teach them how to use their senses. I explain that good writing reaches the reader through her body, not her mind.

"Take me with you," I tell them when they describe a place. "Make me feel it."

I teach them how to slow down the action at the dramatic moments, to use metaphors and similes, to use direct speech effectively, to write from the heart, to trust the power of their own voices. Gladys experiments and writes: "My mother told me, 'Your body is so ugly. You have no butt! No breasts! You are as skinny as a fishing rod.' And I hated her!"

"Exactly!" I tell her. "We believe you. We're with you. Tell us more."

On the final these students have written the stories of their lives in ways compelling enough to carry the reader beyond sentence-level grammatical errors. Even the most vigilant of my colleagues stops counting missing-*ed* endings when confronted with a story of a gang member who describes being stabbed in graphic detail, concluding with the startling fact that watching the blood drain from his body was the most relaxing experience he had ever had.

"Don't bore them for a second," I tell them. "Don't confuse them with one single word. Your readers are tired." I say this again and again. They love hearing it. "They are tired, old, grouchy ESL teachers.

They have their own problems. Your composition is one in a pile of hundreds they have to read. Write something that will open their eyes." I pause dramatically. I am getting good at this. "Write something that will open their hearts! Make them laugh. Even better, make them cry."

On the last day of class I have to tell them that I'm moving to California. This is hard. Normally I would promise to be there for them for as long as they need me. Normally I would tell them: Come back any time. I will help you.

And in the past they have. Marjorie, who passed this course in 1989, and who has repeated every course in the English Department at least once, sometimes twice, still shows up at my office door regularly. "Do you have a minute?" she asks and I invite her in. Sometimes she has a paper she wants help with. Usually she just wants to tell me how hard it is for her. I listen. She is satisfied and goes back to try again.

But this semester I'm moving away. This year I can only say goodbye. I tell them I'm proud of them, I'm glad they were my last class, I will miss them.

"Will you write to me?" I ask and they all nod vigorously.

I write my address in California on the chalkboard.

"Do you promise?"

They do.

But I know I won't hear from them. And I don't.

References

Bateson, G. 1972. *Steps Toward an Ecology of Mind*. New York: Chandler Publishing Company.

Hoffman, E. 1990. *Lost in Translation: A Life in a New Language*. New York: Viking Penguin.

Mason, B. 1989. *Love Life*. New York: Harper & Row.

Snyder, C., C. Harris, J. Anderson, S. Holleran, L. Irving, S. Sigmon, L. Yoshinobu, J. Gibb, C. Langelle, and P. Harney. 1991. The will and ways: Development of a validation of an individual-differences measure of hope. *Journal of Personality and Social Psychology*, 60, 570–585.

235

10 Language learning diaries as mirrors of students' cultural sensitivity

Sabrina Peck

> I don't think I can fully enter the culture.
> . . . What does it mean to be bicultural?
> (Lawrence, Week 2)

This chapter is based on the diaries of adult learners of Spanish. As part of an intensive, seven-week Spanish course for thirty-four social workers who were advanced beginners and low intermediates, the students (European-Americans, Latinos, and others) were asked to keep weekly diaries about anything related to their language learning and study: emotional reactions to instruction, comparisons of their learning in the course with their learning in other courses, and so on. All of the Latino students were Mexican-Americans. All grew up in homes where Spanish was spoken, and all grew up in Southern California speaking English and attending English medium schools.

The purposes of the diary, as given on a handout distributed to the students, were "to make you aware of your own learning style" and "to help the staff to adjust to your needs and styles." As the academic director, I read the diaries each week, as did the two instructors in the course. These staff members had agreed to keep the contents of the diaries confidential, and not to quote from them or reveal the identities of the writers.

The diaries yielded many useful comments about the course, both negative and positive, which helped us, as the staff, to alter the balance of activities as the weeks went by. However, the diaries were particularly interesting because they revealed the students' sensitivity to Latino culture and/or their own culture. Several students wrote about the relationship between learning a language and learning a culture. Anglos (European-Americans) felt that they could never become bicultural; Latinos felt that they were in a sense "healed," or made whole, by learning the language of their parents. This chapter will describe students' diary comments about cultural sensitivity and discuss implications for other language courses, in particular, ways in which language teachers might

I am grateful to Marcela Dominguez and Claudia Parodi, instructors in the Spanish for Social Workers course, and to the students – for their insights and for allowing their diary entries to be quoted here.

set out to teach a language and to increase students' cultural sensitivity as well.

For this chapter, I excerpted diary references to cultural sensitivity, and I secured permission to quote such entries from the writers. Cultural sensitivity is defined here as an awareness that one's own culture and another culture are different. Following Robinson (1985), culture is defined as ideas, behaviors, or products which are shared by members of a group. In studying culture, behaviorists focus on what is observable, while "functionalists focus on the underlying structure or rules which govern and explain observable events" (ibid.: 2). For cognitive anthropologists, in contrast, culture is an internal, computerlike mechanism "for organizing and interpreting inputs" (ibid.). Culture is made up of values, beliefs, attitudes, customs, and traditions. More specifically, culture includes hierarchies, rules, time and space relations, verbal and nonverbal communication strategies, and so on.

In other second language acquisition work, researchers have analyzed diaries kept by second language learners to better understand variables that are thought to contribute to language learning. These include the learners' reactions to pedagogical techniques, cognitive styles, motivational factors, sources of stress, and affective factors (Bailey 1980; Bailey and Ochsner 1983; Campbell, this volume; Hilleson, this volume; Schmidt and Frota 1986; Schumann 1980). Bailey and Ochsner point out that diary studies are valuable research tools that can be helpful to learner-researchers as they evaluate themselves, their frustrations, and their language learning techniques. While most of the diary researchers have touched on students' own sense of cultural identity and their reactions to the target culture, no published diary studies to date have dealt directly with how (or whether) a group of students gains in empathy for the target culture, or cultural sensitivity, through a language course.

The language learning diaries kept by the students of Spanish differed in two key ways from diaries that have been analyzed by other second language acquisition researchers (Bailey 1980; Bailey and Ochsner 1983; Schmidt and Frota 1986 Schumann 1980;). First, the diarists were social workers, not language teachers or language teachers-in-training. Social work entails primarily the following tasks: brokering and linkage; counseling and problem solving; formal intervention with individuals, families, or groups; and client status assessment (Sheafor 1982). As social workers, the Spanish students were unfamiliar with the concepts of second language acquisition but were at home with the terms and concepts of psychotherapy. Unlike many language teachers, they had not had formal training in cultural awareness. Second, the diaries were written for a different audience – for the staff of the course, not for the individual diarists themselves. Thus the diaries functioned more as memos to the staff in reaction to the course than as self-analyses for the original writers.

The Spanish course included a variety of activities, many of which, implicitly or explicitly, could have taught students about Latino cultures. As explicit instruction, the course participants heard lectures in Spanish on mental health and social work topics, given by professionals who were originally from the Southwestern states of the United States, or from Puerto Rico, Mexico, and other Latin American countries. Other activities implicitly included instruction about culture. For instance, students viewed role plays of typical social work tasks and performed their own role plays. They also observed Spanish-speaking social workers in action. Thus, the students were exposed to different varieties of Spanish and different perspectives on social workers and their Latino clients.

In addition, they studied vocabulary and grammar that was relevant to their social work tasks. They chatted and made small talk in Spanish in two weekly *almuerzos en español* [Spanish lunches], and for two hours per day they spoke with the community aides, two monolingual Spanish-speaking homemakers originally from Mexico. They played communicative games, cooked a Mexican soup, and sang Spanish songs. All of these activities were conducted in Spanish, and students were encouraged to guess and to take risks (Terrell, et al. 1986). For one hour per week, the students discussed in English their learning strategies and emotional reactions to their learning.

The course objectives were that the students would (a) be able to carry out many job tasks effectively and sensitively in Spanish, (b) improve in listening and speaking, and (c) develop strategies for continuing to learn Spanish after the course. (For a detailed description of the course, please refer to Peck 1987.)

As the academic director, I had several roles in this new course. I met some of the students months before the course began, during the needs analysis when I observed them or their colleagues at work. During this stage, many social workers and their supervisors talked about how frustrating it was for them, with their limited Spanish, to deal with Spanish-speaking clients. Many said that learning about culture was as important as learning more Spanish. My role was to listen, mull over what I heard, make tentative hypotheses, and ask a few new questions on my next visit. After designing the course, hiring two teachers, and deciding on placement tests, I helped to decide whom to admit. During the course, I counseled students with all sorts of problems (everything from parking to study skills) and administered the course (dealt with supervisors, oriented guest lecturers, warned students about excessive absences). In sum, I had two major roles: administering the course and being in touch with the students' and instructors' needs. Reading the diaries was one part of carrying out that second role.

The setting for the course was the University of California, Los Angeles (UCLA) campus in the summer. It was like a country club: The grass was thick and green, and jacaranda trees were full of light purple blossoms. The cafeteria had tasty, reasonably priced food: tacos, pizza, sushi, and so on. The classrooms were newly remodeled, cool, and well lit. The bookstore, tennis courts, swimming pool, jogging paths, and the UCLA hospital (where the students had their practicum) were all nearby.

At the end of the course, the students evaluated their progress on a scale of one (not true) to six (very true). In response to the prompt, "I have increased my cultural sensitivity to Latinos," the mean was 4.82 with a standard deviation of 1.31 ($n = 28$). The prompt confused some Latino students, two of whom gave a rating of six while noting that they were sensitive before the course. (One ignored the question.) Many students commented that they had learned about culture as well as about language. It thus seemed worthwhile to look at the diaries to see what students had learned about cultural sensitivity and how they had learned it.

Diary entries dealing with cultural sensitivity

Over the seven-week course, I asked the students to turn in one diary entry per week. The thirty-four students handed in a total of 177 installments, or an average of 5.2 entries per student.[1] Of these, thirty-five included some reference to cultural sensitivity. Eighteen of the thirty-four students made at least one mention of cultural sensitivity. The eighteen included five Latino students and thirteen non-Latinos (Anglos, African-Americans, a native speaker of Japanese, and a native speaker of Armenian). For the Latinos in this group of eighteen, the average number of diary assignments dealing with cultural sensitivity was 2.5 entries; for the others the average was 1.7. Figure 1 depicts the number of references to cultural sensitivity on a weekly basis.

The most frequent mentions of cultural sensitivity per week were in weeks two, three, and four, around the time of the cultural identity meeting. In week six, there were no references to cultural sensitivity. I do not know why this occurred; perhaps students were concentrating on their language skills, keeping in mind that the course would soon be over.

1 All of the diary entries are given here as originally written, without corrections. English translations of the Spanish are bracketed, and do not reflect any infelicities in Spanish.

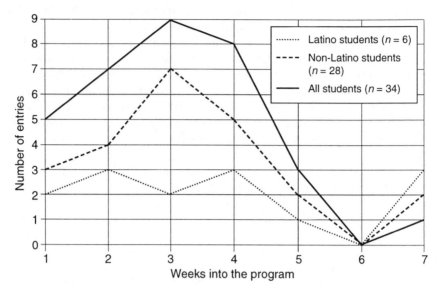

Figure 1. Diary entries with reference to cultural sensitivity.

The students with the most references to cultural sensitivity were Lawrence (a non-Latino) and Julio (a Latino), who together organized a special meeting about cultural identity in the third week of the course. Lawrence and Julio asked me if they could run this meeting in place of the whole-group program planned for the following Friday. Both felt that they were growing in their understanding of cultural identity and wanted to share their ideas and questions. All of the students attended the meeting. They concentrated their attention on the topic to a degree that the atmosphere was almost tense. The consensus was that all students, even European-Americans, have cultural identity problems. The students did not agree on whether an adult can become bicultural.

As we look at the thirty-five entries, several themes emerge. In every entry except one, the students seemed to accept cr welcome their increased cultural awareness. The themes that arose in my analysis are discussed herein under three main categories: those that were specific to the diaries of Latino students, those dealing with increased cultural sensitivity, and those dealing with a feeling of closeness to humanity.

Themes in the diaries of Latino students

Three themes occurred only in the diaries of Latino students: (a) a feeling of pressure to speak Spanish well because they were Latino, (b) a consciousness of being Latino, but growing up with American (Anglo) influences, and (c) higher self-esteem as a result of learning Spanish and returning to their roots.

The Latino students were extremely aware that other students, the staff, and the patients at the medical center expected them to speak Spanish well. They felt that because of their appearance, others assumed that they could speak Spanish:

Pero creo que la habilidad de estar bilingüe es importante a mi porque soy Chicana y muchas veces, otras personas creen que debo saber la lengua de español. [But I think that the ability to be bilingual is important to me because I'm Chicana, and a lot of the time, other people think that I must know Spanish.] (Maria, week 2)

I sometimes get scared and angry at the same time, by people's expectation that I should speak Spanish because I'm Mexican. I really wish I could and I am embarrassed by the fact that I don't speak fluently. (Lisa, week 2)

I believe it's easier for non-Latino students to feel comfortable taking risks [in speaking Spanish] because there isn't an added expectation that Latinos have – that is, because you are Latino, regardless of where you grew up, you *should* speak Spanish fluently and naturally!! (Lisa, week 5)

This burden of others' expectations apparently lightened somewhat as the course continued. Some students reported to the staff that they felt more relaxed when they spoke Spanish, and more willing to make mistakes than they had been earlier.

At the same time, these students acknowledged that their parents had encouraged them to speak English, and that they had in many ways grown up in an Anglo society. As Lisa wrote during the second week, "I realize that I grew up here and the American influence invaded my space." In sum, the students felt that they were Latinos, but also members of North American culture.

At the start of the course, some Latino students described the joy and relief of speaking Spanish and "returning to their roots."

In the depths of my soul, I've longed to speak my native language ever so long. To me this is a lifetime goal being fulfilled, a great accomplishment, a dream come true. I'm feeling great pride and wish to share my daily experiences with my family. (Frankie, week 1)

I think this course will also help to increase my self-confidence as a Chicano, as a Mexican. In returning, so to speak, to my cultural roots, I hope to face and deal with some of the blockages and splits I have felt in being a man from two different worlds – from two different countries. Most of my life I have been seeking to unite these two worlds into a harmonious whole, and I believe this course will add an additional bridge to this end. (Julio, week 1)

At the end of the course, Julio felt that he had indeed found a bridge to his Chicano roots.

... I have learned so much in speaking the Spanish language, ... but I have also learned even more to integrate my own life experiences in order to more fully relate to and help La Gente Hispanico [the Latino people]. ... I have felt a strengthening of my ethnic pride and self-esteem – surely qualities of positive transitional changes which will help my clients.

A week ago, my wife and I visited my father. He and I spoke Spanish almost en total. It was a surprising joy for both of us. We sealed a bond of unspoken cultural heritage and pride. (Julio, week 7)

Thus, the Latino students taking this course had to integrate two contradictions: first their Latino appearance with their lack of Spanish proficiency and, second, their two cultures. Their diaries indicate that these students were able to integrate these contradictions as they carried out the course activities.

Increased cultural sensitivity

At the same time that the Latino students were writing about one or both halves of a bicultural identity, all of the students were writing about becoming more sensitive to cultural differences. These diary entries covered four subthemes: (a) an appreciation of the importance of culture and of the ways in which language and culture are subtly entwined, (b) the consciousness that non-Latinos are different from Latinos and cannot become bicultural, (c) the students' awareness that they were becoming more knowledgeable about Latino culture, and more sensitive to it, and (d) the desire to become more culturally sensitive in the future.

In the first three weeks, five students commented on the subtle and important relationship of culture and language. The following comment is typical: "It seems possible that even when I understand the words I will not understand the person's true message" (Toni, week 1). Some comments were intellectual in their tone. In them I heard echoes of what social work administrators and professors had told me when I interviewed them while planning the course. Likewise these students stressed the connection between language and culture.

I don't believe that language can be taught to human service workers without also exposing them to the culture. Language and culture are interrelated, they depend on each other. (Brenda, week 2)

Not only is understanding cultural nuances important to acquiring a new language but it's essential for understanding the contextual framework of the language. (Jenny, week 3)

The sensitivity to culture that these comments reflected seemed more intellectual than emotional.

On an emotional level, the Anglo students reflected on their awareness of being non-Latino, and that no language or culture training could make them fully bicultural. These comments were most frequent immediately before and after the student-organized meeting about cultural identity. Jenny, an Anglo, wrote about her dream.

. . . tuve un sueño tocante a la clase de español. En el sueño, había muchas personas latinas, y yo era solamente la persona angla. El profesor dijo que (en inglés) yo era una estudiante nueva y tambien (en inglés): "Jenny is our new caucasian student. It is up to the class to decide whether or not to let her stay in this class." [I had a dream about the Spanish class. In the dream there were a lot of Latinos, and I was the only Anglo. The professor said (in English) that I was a new student and also (in English): "Jenny is our new Caucasian student. It is up to the class to decide whether or not to let her stay in this class." (Jenny, week 1)

The following comment is from Lawrence, who would soon be one of the organizers of the group meeting about cultural identity.

I don't think I can fully enter the culture. I tried to do that in the Peace Corps – complete with tattoos and earrings – and it didn't work. Anglo in a Latin sea. What does it mean to be bicultural? (Lawrence, week 2)

A week later, he had partially answered his question: "I can become culturally competent but not bicultural. And what I will learn re: culture will be learned very gradually" (Lawrence, week 3).

Another student, Aleia, accepted the inevitability of cultural differences and felt that they made life interesting.

Sometimes I think we Anglos expect too much of ourselves and then fail to appreciate what we do have or have accomplished. No, I'll never be Hispanic, nor do I feel a need to be. . . . I'll never have early childhood memories of growing up in that culture because I didn't, but I can sure enjoy Frankie or Maria or someone else sharing theirs with me. And hopefully vice versa. . . . So far . . . [this attitude has] pulled me through a lot of cultures – Black, Jewish, Polish, Catholic, Hispanic, etc. It's also pulled me through a lot of work situations – alcoholism, . . . single parenting, homosexuality. . . . I can understand if I allow myself to be human and to be touched . . . by another – no matter my race or age or sex. There are always points where there are differences and that is for me what makes life so interesting. (Aleia, week 3)

Thus, with acceptance or with apparent pain and confusion, these students expressed the idea that Anglos could not be bicultural.

From the second to the seventh week, non-Latinos and Latinos wrote that they were becoming more sensitive to Latinos, or more knowledgeable about Latino cultures. Several commented on a presentation by an Argentine teacher who gave her perspective on the differences between Anglo culture and her own. Several mentioned the group meeting that Frankie and Lawrence organized. One student, in reference to a lecture about an advice column for Chicano teenagers, commented, "There is a whole unknown world out there to be yet discovered!" Barbara, who had participated in many courses and seminars on Latino culture, analyzed how the present course had made her more culturally sensitive.

I never gained a level of insight such as now. This happened with a combination of opportunities given to us: the Conferencia speakers . . . [the instructors, the community aides,] the videotapes (Department of Children's Services and Department of Mental Health) and experiences shared by classmates. (Barbara, week 7)

In the seventh week, many students commented that they planned to continue learning about Latino cultures after the course.

I'm reading Joan Didion's *Salvador* and bought Carlos Fuentes' *The Old Gringo* and Richard Rodriguez' *Hunger of Memory* Anglo vs. Latin culture. Yo quiero aprender la cultura Latina. [I want to learn Latin culture.] (Lawrence, week 7)

I fully expect to learn many things from my clients (as I already have) – in terms of the perfection of the Spanish language, as well as in the cultural variances and nuances. (Julio, week 7)

In sum, the students who wrote about cultural sensitivity discussed the relationship between language and culture, and their own insights about cultural differences. They felt that Anglos could not become bicultural, but they all (the Anglos included) believed they were becoming more sensitive to and knowledgeable about Latinos as a result of the course. Several made plans to learn more about culture after the course.

Closeness to humanity

In weeks three, four, and five – around the time of the group meeting – six students commented that they felt closer to humanity in general, regardless of a person's culture. For example, in the fourth week, Laurence wrote, "For me this program is like a healing gift." Other entries have a similarly expansive tone.

[about the group meeting] I felt close to the group, as a whole. I felt the feelings of "apoyo" [support] were predominant. I gained a greater appreciation for feelings of "la corazón" [love, affection] not only among our group, but for all of humanity and for my hispanica familia especialemente [Hispanic family especially]. (Julio, week 5)

Frankie, who helped to set up the group meeting, wrote in week 3: "I just feel so exhilarated by being part of making it happen. . . . I have sensed a deeper feeling of unity and togetherness bringing the two groups together."

These six students, who wrote about closeness to humanity in a strongly emotional and personal way, seemed to be acknowledging cultural differences, but saying that people of different cultures still share a great deal. Thus, the students' self-evaluations and the diary entries of eighteen students suggest that both Latinos and non-Latinos had become more sensitive to their own cultural identities, and to the differences between Latino and Anglo cultures.

Discussion

In this study, diaries kept by students in an intensive Spanish course for social workers were examined for themes relating to cultural sensitivity, or, more specifically, to a student's degree of realization that his or her own culture differed from a Latino or non-Latino culture. Latinos in the course wrote about their biculturalism: being expected to speak Spanish well and being members of both the Anglo and Latino cultures. Non-Latinos wrote about their growing sensitivity to cultural differences, along with their realization that biculturalism was an impossibility for them. Some noted that language and culture are entwined, and that they wanted to continue growing in cultural sensitivity. For some students, both Latinos and non-Latinos, these insights emerged along with some pain and confusion.

Two key points emerged in reviewing the diaries. First, for some students, learning to speak a language was seen as being connected with becoming more empathetic to the target culture. Second, it was beneficial for both Latinos and non-Latinos to be in the same class. Non-Latinos grew in their awareness of Latino culture through discussions with Latinos, who, in turn, were more willing to take risks and make mistakes in Spanish even though they had non-Latino classmates. (The Latino students told me this repeatedly and some also wrote about it in their diaries.)

The course seemed to have increased the students' cultural sensitivity through a combination of opportunities, as stated by Barbara in week seven: "[the lecturers, the instructors, the community aides,] the videotapes . . . and experience shared by classmates." And yet, every opportunity mentioned by Barbara involved a person (except for the videotapes), so a key to increasing students' cultural sensitivity might be exposing them to a variety of people from the target culture. The increase in cultural sensitivity could also be explained through some of Robinson's (1985) principles of teaching cross-cultural awareness: Culture is transmitted gradually through many learning modes, when teachers encourage their students' positive self-concept and their subjectivity, when both field-sensitive and field-independent methods are used, and when the sameness of cultures is emphasized.

In terms of multicultural education, the course included features of what Sleeter and Grant (1994) call the "Human Relations Approach." These features were group process, role playing, and community action projects (observing social workers). The course also included features of Sleeter and Grant's "Single Group Studies": It was focused on a single group, Latinos, and made use of guest speakers. The course discussed in this chapter was less similar to "Education That Is Multicultural and Socially Reconstructionist," Sleeter and Grant's recommended approach, whereby students are encouraged to think critically, analyze varying viewpoints, and learn and use social action skills. This Spanish for Social Workers course explicitly taught language and implicitly taught culture. Cultural learning emerged through a variety of activities and as a result of the students' own interest in cultural issues.

Implications

This study has implications for Spanish language courses in the United States which have as objectives both cultural sensitivity and language proficiency. First, cultural sensitivity can increase when Latino and non-Latino students are in the same Spanish course, and when time is set aside for students and staff to discuss their cross-cultural awareness, in English if necessary. Second, cultural sensitivity can increase when staff members and content lecturers represent different realizations of the target culture (in this case, Latino) and are available to discuss cultural differences with the students. Third, students' language learning diaries provide teachers with useful knowledge about how and how much students are growing in sensitivity to the target culture.

Directions for further research

Further research might expand on this study and provide more specific guidelines for promoting cultural sensitivity. The diaries from this first-year pilot course can be analyzed and compared with those from subsequent years. Questionnaires could elicit student and staff opinions of the implications already noted. Students could critique this chapter and devise a set of cultural questions that they might deal with in their language learning diaries. In addition, Zanger's (1984) workshop approach (in which an Anglo student interviews a Latino) could be modified so that a Latino and a non-Latino would be paired and would interview each other on cultural topics. Thus, the questioning would be reciprocal, not just directed to the Latino member. An evaluation of this activity could be conducted through diaries and questionnaires.

246

Through such approaches, we might begin to distinguish how personal interactions in a language course contribute to growth in students' cultural sensitivity. Knowledge about such interactions could be taken into account when second or foreign language courses are designed. The goal of the design process would thus be to develop courses that foster growth in cultural sensitivity along with linguistic skills.

References

Bailey, K. M. 1980. An introspective analysis of an individual's language learning experience. In R. Scarcella and S. Krashen (eds.), *Research in Second Language Acquisition: Selected Papers of the Los Angeles Second Language Acquisition Research Forum*. Rowley, MA: Newbury House.

Bailey, K. M., and R. Ochsner. 1983. A methodological review of the diary studies: Windmill tilting or social science? In K. M. Bailey, M. Long, and S. Peck (eds.), *Second Language Acquisition Studies*. Rowley, MA: Newbury House.

Campbell, C. (Chapter 8, this volume). Socializing with the teachers and prior language learning experience: A diary study.

Hilleson, M. (Chapter 11, this volume). "I want to talk with them, but I don't want them to hear": An introspective study of second language anxiety in an English-medium school.

Peck, S. 1987. Spanish for social workers: An intermediate-level communicative course with content lectures. *Modern Language Journal*, 71, 4, 402–409.

Robinson, G. L. 1985. *Crosscultural Understanding: Processes and Approaches for Foreign Language, English as a Second Language and Bilingual Educators*. New York: Pergamon Press.

Schmidt, R., and S. Frota. 1986. Developing basic conversational ability in a second language: A case study of an adult learner of Portuguese. In R. R. Day (ed.), *Talking to Learn: Conversation in Second Language Acquisition*. Rowley, MA: Newbury House.

Schumann, F. 1980. Diary of a language learner. A further analysis. In R. Scarcella and S. Krashen (eds.), *Research in Second Language Acquisition: Selected Papers of the Los Angeles Second Language Acquisition Research Forum*. Rowley, MA: Newbury House.

Sheafor, B. W. 1982. *Social Work Practice in New Zealand: An Analysis for Education and Training Curriculum Development*. Palmerston North, New Zealand: Massey University Social Work Unit.

Sleeter, C. E., and C. Grant. 1994. *Making Choices for Multicultural Education: Five Approaches to Race, Class, and Gender*. New York: Macmillan.

Terrell, T., M. Andrade, J. Egasse, and E. M. Muñoz. 1986. *Dos Mundos: Instructor's Edition*. New York: Random House.

Zanger, V. V. 1984. *Exploracion Intercultural: Una Guia para El Estudiante*. Rowley, MA: Newbury House.

11 "I want to talk with them, but I don't want them to hear": an introspective study of second language anxiety in an English-medium school

Mick Hilleson

> At times our strengths propel us so far
> forward we can no longer endure our
> weaknesses and perish from them.
> > (Nietzshe)
>
> I have a new philosophy. I'm only going
> to dread one day at a time.
> > (C. Schulz)

The realization that teaching does not cause learning has led to a growth in the popularity of qualitative, process-orientated research into the conditions that make learning possible: "In an age when both pedagogy and curriculum development have recognized the learners' central role, it is appropriate that researchers should also bring the learner into the picture" (Bailey 1991: 87). In this study, I focused upon learner anxiety as one factor that could affect language learning and acquisition. In collecting my data, I encouraged a cohort of sixteen-year-old residential students to evaluate their own reactions to the learning situation. Analysis of their common experiences would, I hoped, lead to a heightened awareness of their needs.

Methodologically speaking, research by teachers within their institutions should lead to professional growth and "validate experiential knowledge or beliefs" (Brindley 1992). The research should also benefit the learner and provide information for curriculum planners. Sensitivity to the needs of the student is crucial if the curriculum is to facilitate efficient learning.

Context of the study

The starting point for the present research was the observed behavior of a group of students attending United World College of South East Asia (UWCSEA), Singapore. The United World College movement is characterized by its belief that students of different nationalities should be given geographical mobility, through scholarships, to encourage a global perspective in their education. Their pursuit of academic knowledge should be complemented by boarding life in an international environment. Student selection is undertaken exclusively on a merit basis, but the criteria state that while students should be of high overall academic standards, selection should not be restricted to applicants whose English is already good at the time of application.

The learners discussed in this chapter were recipients of such scholarships and are referred to throughout as scholars or students. As nonnative speakers of English, they were embarking upon the very demanding International Baccalaureate Diploma course. Since the language of instruction is English, each classroom is a language classroom for the scholars.

What's the problem?

The scholars were understandably sensitive to their responsibilities to the United World College movement. Their linguistic disadvantage, however, stretched beyond the classroom since they had to function in English for all social purposes, both in the boarding house and in the wider Singaporean context.

Observing the students' preoccupation with language issues, I was drawn to Bailey's (1991: 90) question: "What language factors lead to debilitating anxiety and how can such anxiety be managed?" Bailey hypothesized that:

language classroom anxiety can be caused and/or aggravated by the learner's competitiveness when he sees himself as less proficient than the object of comparison, and that as he perceives himself as becoming more competent (that is, better able to compete) his anxiety will decrease. (ibid.: 71)

This comment implied that attempts to study these students should be longitudinal, examining anxiety over a period of time. I felt that to address my questions about anxiety a combination of diary study and interview would be suitable for data collection.

What is anxiety?

Young (1990) pointed out that the definition of anxiety has frequently changed with the purpose of the research, and that "comparisons across research are often hindered by a lack of consistency in anxiety research" (p. 540). Scovel (1978: 34) noted that anxiety was not a "simple unitary construct, but a cluster of affective states influenced by factors which are intrinsic and extrinsic to the foreign language learner." A review of the literature reveals that researchers have indeed used different con-

249

structs for their anxiety research. These are the most significant elements of the conceptual framework for this study.

1. *Trait anxiety* (Scovel 1978) is described as an inherent, long-term, personality characteristic. This concept could apply to "born worriers" and suggests that some people are more prone to anxiety than others.
2. *State anxiety* (ibid.) refers to anxiety induced by a particular temporary phenomenon. In the literature, the term applies to specific situations, such as language classrooms.
3. *Communication anxiety* is a specific example of state anxiety. Someone communicating, whether in the first or second language, experiences stress as a result of having to communicate publicly.
4. *Foreign language anxiety* (Horwitz, Horwitz, and Cope 1986) occurs when students have to perform tasks in a language that is not their own. While this is, in some ways, similar to language shock (see number 6), I have treated it as a task-related phenomenon.
5. *Foreign language classroom anxiety* (Bailey 1983; Gardner and Smythe 1975) highlights anxiety induced by the need to perform classroom tasks in another language. This concept frequently refers to phenomena connected to speaking and is a situationally specific form of foreign language anxiety.
6. *Language shock* refers to negative self-perception (Schumann and Schumann 1977). With this form of anxiety students feel they cannot function properly within the community since they have been deprived of their real personality and are embarrassed to display a self that is fundamentally incompetent.[1]
7. *Test anxiety and fear of negative evaluation* (Horwitz, Horwitz, and Cope 1986) concern students' predictions of how significant others will react to them. Fear of negative evaluation is likely to manifest itself in students' insecurity, passivity, and performance deficits.

Research design

The way in which human beings learn languages is largely invisible, taking place inside the mind of the language learner, where researchers cannot follow. Bailey (1983: 67) states, "[T]he tasks of defining, manipulating and quantifying affective factors pose serious problems for researchers. A case in point is anxiety." In examining the situation of learners who have the dual task of both learning in a second language

1 Schumann (1978) pointed out that the learner has a self that is perfectly capable of behaving normally in the right linguistic and cultural setting but is forced by the circumstances to display a self that is fundamentally incompetent.

and performing in that language, the researcher is faced with a complex range of behavior and attitudes.

This research project differs from prior research in three important ways. First, the student respondents are not predominantly language learners. They directed their efforts toward general academic and social success through the medium of English. Second, the research is not primarily classroom-based. The questionnaires, diaries, and interviews relate to an immersion language experience beyond the classroom. Finally, the diaries themselves are not written in the first language of the respondents. Some of the diarists had relatively low proficiencies in English, and it was a new experience for them to express deep feelings in a second language. This aspect of the study made triangulation a crucial element of the design.

Data collection and manipulation

The research design allowed for triangulation through multiple source data collection: diaries, interviews, observations, and questionnaires. Following guidelines, from Allwright and Bailey (1991: 190), the diary entries in this research were not "corrected," thus encouraging the diarists to write freely. Students were told that the data would be used for research purposes and that through syllabus planning, they could help future students. Students' diaries were read and responded to after five weeks, and collected at the end of ten weeks. Students were asked to write as often as they could and, if necessary, to make comments in their first language. I assured them of the confidentiality of the information.

Since students were not writing in their first language, diary entries were followed up by interviews to allow fuller exploration. My approach was to use structured but open-ended questions, providing some uniformity across interviews but still allowing students to volunteer information and pursue interesting lines of discussion. Prompts and probes were geared toward anxiety-related phenomena, but students had free rein to discuss any aspect of their language experiences which they deemed important.

While I was not focusing exclusively on the classroom, I was able to observe the behavior of three students in my own classroom and could discuss behavioral features of all the students with academic, counseling, and boarding staff members. By taking observations of students' behavior into account, I hoped to further validate insights gleaned from the introspective data provided in the diaries and interviews. Conversely, I could recognize contradictions between students' reported behavior and my own observations.

A self-assessment questionnaire influenced by Horwitz, Horwitz, and

TABLE I   PARTICIPANTS IN THE RESEARCH PROJECT

Name	Language 1	Test place\ratings	Higher subjects
Maki	Japanese	61\22322	Math, Phy, Chem
Wayan	Indonesian	62\32243	Math, Phy, Chem
Adele	Italian	82\45454	Bio, Eco, Mus
Karen	Norwegian	86\56777	Bio, Math, His
Axel	German	92\77777	Bio, Eng, Ger

Cope's (1986: 127) Foreign Language Classroom Anxiety Scale provided a stimulus for early interviews, and the diaries themselves formed
the subject of later interviews.

The participants in the research

To facilitate the collection of initial data, I arranged to meet the UWC
scholars who had recently arrived during their first week. I asked for
their cooperation in the study and administered a simple proficiency test
and an affective questionnaire.

Information about the students who participated in the study is given
in Table 1. The names are pseudonyms. The "Test" column refers to
scores on the proficiency test administered during the first meeting.
"Place" is the student's percentage score on a simple placement test,
and the "Ratings" column lists are marks out of seven for fluency,
grammatical accuracy, sentence pronunciation, interactive communication, and vocabulary resource, as assigned by five different raters.
Cambridge First Certificate descriptors were used in the assessment
process.

All the students were between sixteen and seventeen years of age
when the data were collected. Maki, Wayan, and Karen were involved
in the English Subsidiary B course, which was designed to answer the
needs of ESL students who desired minimum English syllabus content,
while concentrating on other areas of the curriculum. Axel was in the
more demanding English B course. Adele was not taking a formal English course. Her Language A was Italian, and she had chosen to take
Japanese as her Language B, while conducting studies of all other subjects in English.

Supplementary information was collected from two additional students (Kato and Yasmin), who discussed their experiences retrospec-
tively. Kato (a Japanese) reflected upon his early insecurity shortly
before leaving Japan to take up a course in mathematics at Cambridge
University, United Kingdom. I also interviewed Yasmin (an Indonesian),

whose teachers were very concerned about her well-being in the early stages of the course.

Finally, further insights were gained from five non-residential students in my Subsidiary B class. Although they were not part of the actual cohort, I have included certain relevant quotations from them. I will refer to them by the pseudonyms Kei, Nato, Natsuko, Kazui, and Eri.

The data analysis categories

For the purposes of this study, I simplified the definitions found in the literature into three broad areas of anxiety to divide the data into manageable chunks. Learner comments discussed in one category could sometimes be justifiably placed in another area. These definitions were used to categorize the data:

1. *Language shock.* Anxiety caused by a move to an environment in which the native language is no longer the language of interaction or instruction. In this category were comments related to self-perception, facilitating and debilitating anxiety, total immersion, and the transition period.
2. *Foreign language anxiety.* Anxiety induced by the need to perform tasks in an unfamiliar language.
3. *Classroom anxiety.* Anxiety related to performance expectations within the classroom and in academic activities. All classrooms were viewed as second language classrooms.

Data are grouped in these categories. Quotations are identified by the pseudonym of the respondent. "I" indicates that the data were collected in interviews and "D" signifies diary data. Student comments are recorded in their original form, allowing some idiosyncratic language.

Language shock

While it is perfectly natural for young people leaving home and moving into a distant boarding environment to feel homesick, the feeling was particularly acute for these second language students. Often they were realizing, for the first time, the scale of the task ahead of them. As Kato said, "When I came here, of course I realized my English was bad. I had to do something. But we know the goals, we don't know how to start." Students reported that initially they had considerable difficulty in understanding simple conversation. This caused anxiety at an interactional level when attempting to develop relationships with other students. As Wayan said in an interview, "I'm afraid if I'm talking then they listening to me. I'm not shy in Indonesia; but I see my English really really poor." Maki felt the same:

253

I don't feel I talked to other new scholars. I just sat and listened to them. I think, I didn't talk. I couldn't understand anything on the first day. I was disappointed. I'd learnt English for four years in Japan. I know it's not enough but still I can't write or read well. I know my English is not so good but I really wanted to talk along. . . . [W]hen I met a new person I'd never met before it's hard to communicate. Actually I'm not too shy, but nervous. But I can speak Japanese well. (In Japan), usually I like to be with friends.

Maki's comments suggested that she was experiencing anxiety of the "state" rather than the "trait" variety and that it was definitely language related. It seemed to be influencing both the intake and output of language. Her comment illustrates Foss and Reitzel's (1988) connection between communication anxiety and foreign language anxiety: "Foreign language anxiety seems to share certain characteristics with communication anxiety, for example, high feelings of self-consciousness, fear of making mistakes, and a desire to be perfect when speaking" (p. 438). They suggest that "competence is a matter of degree, and perceptions of competence can vary from situation to situation and even within a particular episode. . . . a communicator is competent if perceived so by self and/or others" (ibid.: 441).

Kato pointed out that some people were more prone to anxiety than others. This would be an example of trait anxiety:

Kato (I): Some people don't care about these things (problems), it depends on people. I sometimes think too serious. Being introverted makes you less relaxed.

Wayan explained how the differences between a one-on-one conversation and a group discussion were a surprise to him.

Wayan (I): I imagine it's not difficult to get involved in life in different language. It's really difficult I have to be patient. . . . I just watch and listen I can't active. I just know a little. Between friends it's easy, in a group it's difficult.

From the initial tests, I knew that Maki and Wayan were the students with the lowest level of English proficiency at the outset of the course, but Adele (a more proficient student) explained similar problems in an interview: "In the beginning, I was very quiet, when we used to sit down at the table, to have lunch, I didn't used to speak at all. It was very strange for me." Other students also felt frustrated that interaction which would have come naturally in their native language eluded them. As Natsuko said in an interview, "I wanted to make everyone laugh, but I couldn't think any jokes."

The psychology of functioning in their second languages and the effects on self-image were discussed at length in both the students' diaries and their interviews. These were evidently preoccupations across the ability range. The students' frustration at not being able to communicate their true identity was succinctly stated in a number of comments, including Karen's diary entry: "I don't tell as many jokes or make fun because I am afraid that people don't understand. Therefore I have become much more serious." In an interview Kato said,

I don't think people could get to know me. I looked a shallower person, narrower minded, less knowledge with less experiences. Of course, I couldn't talk about philosophy. I could talk about how's Japan or how's the weather. I sometimes felt sad I don't appear to them as I am. I was especially sad when people said, "Why you so quiet, so unsociable!" In Japan I was noisier than other people. I tried to explain but they didn't believe it. That was sad.

Sometimes the students were worried about more than communicating their character. They started to doubt whether the original character still existed. As Wayan said in an interview, "I hope I have same character as before but till now I still can't find." Maki echoed this sentiment in her diary after two months: "I have decided to go back to Japan and I can see what happened to me so far. I want to know how and what I'm changed."

In her diary, Karen also discussed her frustration at losing her linguistic identity, as recorded in the following entry.

I am just back from the Norwegian Seaman's Mission. The reason why I choose to write in this diary now is because I really had problems with talking in Norwegian. I suddenly find myself thinking in English . . . Now I don't speak any language fluently. . . . When I first came to Singapore, to find myself, I had to talk to myself, inside my head in Norwegian because that was the real "I." I don't do this anymore because talking in Norwegian is unnatural and so is it in English. . . . I don't know if this is changing my personality or what. . . . I don't actually feel I speak a language fluently; I think in English definitely. . . . I have lost the sense of being myself.

Karen also felt that she was cut off from information in her own language. Part of her personality that had been important when she had access to this information was "starved."

Karen (D): I am still interested in what is happening [in the world] of course, but it is so much harder to understand [from the media] so sometimes I just give up. This would not have happened if I was still living in a Norwegian speaking world.

Students were also aware that the image they conveyed to other people was sometimes perverted by their language use. As Axel said in an interview, "Sometimes I sound ruder than I mean to in lessons. It sounds too frank – 'that's wrong' for example." Karen related this perception to vocabulary inadequacies. In an interview she said, "We couldn't express ourselves sometimes; there are just words missing."

As predicted in the literature, this awareness of performing badly in a second language seemed to indicate a loss of self-esteem. When comparing herself to Singaporeans she met, Maki suffered extreme self-doubt:

Maki (D):   I went to social service today. The school is for children who have a mental problem. But still they can speak English. I don't mean I looked down on them, just I thought why I'm here. Sometimes I don't know why I'm here. Of course I'm studying but I don't want to stay here just for studying. But I don't know what I should do. Sometimes it makes me bad feelings.

As Bailey (1983) reported, comparisons with others are related to anxiety, and in the preceding quotation, Maki is comparing herself negatively to children with "mental problems." Her self-image is extremely low and she seems to be contemplating giving up. She was not the only student to compare herself to others. Supplementary respondent Natsuko, who took her social service in a nursery school, wrote in her diary, "I felt a little ashamed because I was older but my English was not perfect." A similar comparison arises in an interview comment from Wayan, who said, "I always compare myself with others. I never satisfy with myself. Even with good grade, I compare myself and think maybe I get better." Since this comparison is with students who inevitably have a higher level of proficiency, it was demoralizing. Young (1990: 541) suggested that pupils with low self-esteem have high levels of anxiety. In this case the low self-esteem seemed to be situationally induced.

Wayan (I):   Before, in my previous school, my English was best. I got nine. . . . No I thought my English was okay. Because it was, compared to my friends (in Indonesia). But when I came here, I got a little bit sad. That's when the feeling of worrying came and I can't help.

It was difficult for this student to experience a sense of achievement and recognize progress.

Wayan (I):   Before I just want to have the ability to express myself to other people. Now I have that ability I wonder how to get my language better so people can see that I can do the same thing that other people can.

The confusion between real and perceived identity became clear in this interview exchange in which two more proficient students, Karen and Adele, were talking about Maki.

Karen (I):   There were many things she didn't understand. She couldn't express herself. When we went out we could talk to her. She didn't really understand what she was saying. Maybe she is a bit shy.

Adele added (in an interview), "It's not a problem of language – it's her personality." These quotes indicate that even those involved in the trauma of language shock may not understand the difficulties of another person trying to establish an identity in a second language. Subsequently, Adele admitted that her initial perceptions of Maki were wrong, and as they became close friends she realized that Maki was not, in fact, shy.

Students are aware that they are being evaluated by their peers and teachers, and this is a source of anxiety when they think that they are not presenting a good, or fair, image, as indicated by the following comments.

Kato (I): Some teachers just look me down and treat me as if I don't know anything. That made me really sad. At the same time I felt that can't be helped, that's my fault or in the social environment.

Wayan wrote, "I just don't want people to notice me because I can't speak fluently. That's why it seems to be better to keep silent and laugh if there is something funny." Perhaps the most telling of all the interview quotes comes from Maki, who inadvertently provided the title of this chapter when she said, "I want to talk with them, but I don't want them to hear."

Anxiety also existed at a transactional level when students were worried that there was important information that they were not receiving. They felt that they were almost second-class citizens, not because they were discriminated against as "foreigners" but because they did not have the means to access appropriate information.

Adele (I): In the beginning even the house meeting or the assembly was a problem for me. If you ask in the meeting they explain really briefly and you understand even less.

As a result, they did not get involved in the college publications, debates, or artistic performances in the early part of the term.

Kato (I): I felt sort of separate from the real life that is going on in this college. . . . When I first came here I felt like a half member of the college just because of the language.

For Maki, her inability to understand instructions caused her miss an important performance.

Maki (D): Today I missed the concert I was going to play with other violin and cello and piano. I was looking forward to it. I just heard Mr. P . . . say we had to meet by eight. I'm so sad. Next time I'm going to check everything definitely.

When students looked back on their first weeks, they reported distress associated with transition. For instance, Axel said, "In the beginning it was awful," and Wayan wrote, "I'm not homesick anymore as I've felt before." In an interview he said,

After 3 days I want to go home because in my last school I had lots of friends and they all respect me and I don't know how to make new friends and how they know I am. . . . I didn't sleep well. . . . I thought about everything. I compare to my last school. Oh God! It's really different.

Maki said, "I couldn't write to my parents because if I write I must say how I feel." This feeling was compounded by the effects of living and working in a second language environment.

Yasmin (I):   First month I really wanted to go back to Indonesia. It was so hard, all in English. First and second month I slept at 2 A.M. because of work [better after Christmas].

Wayan said in an interview, "When I came to class I feel like a small kid where all adult are. I feel very unconfident." In his diary he wrote,

Even though I've been here for 3 weeks I still worried or scare. I feel like I starting for studying since yesterday. . . . More than one month passed. I've started forgetting how hard I got used to life in my new school when I was just coming. I forget I wasn't communicated to other people. I remember the first time coming into class, I almost couldn't catch up what the teacher said. I can't keep listening any more. I will be bored. In first two weeks this commonly happened.

This language shock stage was, by definition, transitional, allowing passage to a more stable state. It was interesting to note how long the period lasted. For many, the return after the Christmas holidays (after four months) marked a huge leap in confidence, as noted in the following comments.

Kato (I):   I didn't feel my English was improving, so I was getting worried that my English might not ever get better. After Christmas it just jumped and I felt more comfortable with my friends.

Yasmin (I):   After Christmas it was better, I can even write an essay without using dictionary . . . but still a bit shy for me to speak. I didn't really speak much last year.

Wayan sums up this feeling in his diary: "After Christmas long holiday improve myself and my confidence, everything."

Williams (1991) suggests that one way to research foreign language anxiety would be "a diary study of the anxiety [the students] perceive during a semester (or longer) of studying a foreign language" (p. 26). Indeed, looking back at the first term from the perspective of having successfully completed the course, Kato said,

Now I've graduated I think about those 2 years but the 1st term is really strange. I can't recall it. It just passed. My mind is in a different state, like drugged, I think I was constantly just tense, although I didn't realize it at the time.

Even Axel, the most language-proficient of the cohort, stated "Yes, of course. I couldn't cope at first. The teachers spoke too fast. It wasn't demoralizing, it was kind of challenging." This is perhaps the clearest statement of facilitating anxiety, suggesting that students of higher proficiency may find the anxiety positive. An interesting observation came from Wayan.

Wayan (I): When I look at this term, when I feel worry, something push me to get it off the worry. I push myself to finish so I can get it off the worry. If I worry it's better that I don't ignore it.

Chastain (1975), Kleinmann (1977), and Scovel (1978) divided the anxiety concept into "facilitating and debilitating anxiety." The former "motivates the learner to fight the new learning task; it gears the learner emotionally for approach behavior. Debilitating anxiety, in contrast, motivates the learner to flee the new learning task" (Scovel 1978: 139). Williams (1991: 21) suggested:

[T]he emotional state of facilitating anxiety may be equivalent to a low-anxiety state that diverts the student's attention only slightly from the learning task. On the other hand, debilitating anxiety would represent a high-anxiety state that diverts a substantial amount of the student's attention.

Following McGrath (1982), Williams (1991) applied the inverted U model to the facilitating/debilitating continuum. Arousal is "a state of alertness and readiness for action" and the model states that

when arousal is low, performance is low. Then for a time, as arousal increases, so does performance to an optimal point. As arousal increases further, performance falls ultimately to zero. (p. 26).

Teacher observation and Axel's own self-reports suggest that he could have been experiencing facilitating anxiety. This comment is from a teacher:

Axel is now happier with the imprecision of English. Initially he was very pedantic, wanting to know the meaning of every new word. With more language confidence, he has developed tolerance for ambiguity, to the relief of his fellow students.

Parkinson and Howell-Richardson (1990) found a significant correlation between "rate of (language) improvement and the amount of time which students spent (using English) outside the classroom" (p. 135).

259

The boarding house at UWCSEA played a major part in building a security that counteracted transition anxiety.

Adele (I): I think it was important to live with other people. In the beginning I was really quiet. It was partly the language and partly I was an only child. But in the boarding house everyone is brother and sister.

Wayan (I): I think it's much better in the boarding house because a lot of friends and if I were living in a family it would hard. In boarding house it pushed me to speak English.

It would appear that the advantage of residential life is not just the opportunity to use the language, but the effect that community life has on debilitating anxiety. As Kato said, "It was the boarding house that helped me. I pity students living at home!"

Foreign language anxiety

The second major analytic category, foreign language anxiety, is rather amorphous, since it could embrace much of the anxiety experienced by these students. I have concentrated on the social environment in this section and discussed the classroom environment in the next. The frustration of not being able to translate concepts and communicate emotions is basic to the whole study; as Young (1990) suggests, it is best examined by considering the different language skills.

Speaking

Much of the research mentioned earlier focused on oral/aural anxiety. This preoccupation was, to some extent, reflected in responses from the students. Kato made the point that he did not find speaking more difficult than listening because he was in control of the conversation: "For me active English was easier because I use it. I control the language. . . . It's my pace." Frequent mention was also made of nervousness when speaking, as in the following diary entry from Maki: "I don't like it [speaking]. Of course it's a good way to know someone's opinion and to practice English but it's very hard for me and make me nervous." Some students linked performance to personality, which may be related to trait anxiety or general reticence.

Maki (D): But on the other hand it's not good for some people, like me, because of their personality. Some people are very friendly and like to tell what they think and some people are not.

Some students felt very self-conscious about their pronunciation in particular and thought that their English accent was a subject of amusement for others. Kazui said, "I felt that my pronunciation had not improved since I started learning English." Adele wrote, "My accent? It's terrible. I know it and everyone makes fun of it. . . . I know a lot of words because I read them, I can't pronounce them." Axel recognized accent as being a stress-related phenomenon. In an interview he said, "I think the more fluent you get, the less your accent becomes. If I stumble, I have a strong German accent. When you are tired, you have more accent." Success in pronunciation was cause for celebration. As Adele said, after a close friend's return, "The first thing she said was that my accent had improved and I felt really happy." It was also a great relief to be able to function in one's own language. In an interview, Natsuko said of her classmates in the Japanese class, "They are Indian and Pakistani so I don't need to worry about my strange accent when I talk to them. . . . Japanese lessons will be my oasis."

Trying to "jump into" a discussion was frustrating. Maki said, "By the time I want to speak and I have the sentences, the conversation is going on and the topic is changed. So I just quiet." In her diary Natsuko wrote, "There were many people so it was a bit difficult for me to speak out because while I was thinking what to say, other people spoke what I wanted to say." Searching for vocabulary or appropriate syntax was perceived as one factor that caused the delay. As Karen noted in a diary entry,

I am so irritated at myself right now because I have just had a discussion on Palestine/Israel with Daniel and I feel that I am not able to say what I want in English. It bothers me so much. . . . I do not take part in as many discussions as I used to because I am not always able to say what I want to.

Sometimes an attempt to use what was perceived as the correct language was a stumbling block. Kato said in an interview, "He asked me so many questions but I could not answer 'cos so many thinking going on in my head. I was trying to find long words because I didn't know easy way to say it." However, a certain defiance was exhibited by Adele in an interview.

It wasn't my fault. I tried hard to speak English so they couldn't say I was boring. So it wasn't my fault! . . . We could speak and listen to other people and even without telling what we feel, we could understand. . . . I feel that some persons can understand what I want to say without listening to my words.

This pseudo-telepathic effect could be an aspect of living in a close, mutually committed community such as the boarding house.

Axel mentioned that previous language teaching had not prepared him for making small talk. He was therefore experiencing more frustration than his proficiency would indicate. In an interview he said, "In

261

Germany we were discussing about very high topics, very difficult things like politics – we were not trained to do small talk." Lennon (1989), in his study of German students at a British university, made similar comments. His subjects reveled in the opportunity to learn the art of informal interaction, feeling that they were already well trained for formal transactional interchanges.

Communicative apprehension can induce negative affective feelings toward the language. As Adele said, "I don't really like English. In Italian we have many words to say the same thing and I miss the subtlety." However, students found great satisfaction as they achieved communicative success. At the end of the first two-week period, which marked a peak before a trough in Wayan's perception of his own ability, he wrote, "Suddenly, all the things that I worried before is disappeared. I strongly speak English in discussion. I've begin to talk to anyone actively." But then, two days later, this entry was made in his diary.

Today I feel terribly again. I got tired. There are a lot of homework I have to do. When I speak I still think and arrange what I want to say. But my listening is better than last week.

These contrasting comments underline the non-linear nature of anxiety. Students would feel satisfied with their progress one day, and the next they would feel that their speaking proficiency had not changed since their arrival. They seemed to have no fixed reference point.

Listening

Speaking and listening are complementary, and students were equally forthcoming on the subject of anxiety connected with listening. Requesting repetition proved a problem in one-on-one conversations when the students were concerned about taxing their new friends' patience.

Kato (I): When I was speaking to one person it was fine but in the boarding house we had meals together. I can't say, "Oh Christophe can you say that again; can you speak more slowly."

Kei (D): The most embarrassing thing is that when a friend or teacher says a thing to me, but I can't understand what they are saying. So I had to ask them again and again.

Asking for clarification was felt to be awkward. As Axel said in an interview, "I don't understand what the other pupils say – they mumble. You find yourself asking some stupid questions."

The inability to be selective in listening was also perceived to be a major problem. Maki wrote in her diary, "I sometimes can't understand what Mr. X says so I was very sleepy during classes. It was hard to keep my eyes open. I'm sorry not to listen to what he said." In an interview, Adele said,

I am so upset. I watched two videos in Economics and I didn't understand a thing. My teacher asked me a question and he was not pleased because he thought I wasn't paying attention.

This phenomenon is mentioned again in the section on classroom anxiety, but was also relevant in a social context.

Kato (I):   You get very tired if you listen to each word . . . so words passing through my head, if he comes to some important point, then I listen very carefully. When I first came here I asked each word if it had nothing important to me.

Often, listening problems were linked to vocabulary. Karen wrote, "I hate it if I don't understand some words that kids are using, but actually, by now, my vocabulary has gotten a lot better." In an interview Kato said, "There was a lot of slang going on. Words like Dhobi, Prep and Carrel [situation specific words] – I'd never heard them before." Adele felt that listening was one of a range of social difficulties, some completely unconnected to language.

Adele (D):   Only once I really felt bad because I couldn't speak English. People were talking American round me and I only understand some sentences because they were speaking so fast. . . . Actually I was the only girl. I'm sure the problem of language can be overcome if it's the only problem around.

Despite Adele's general optimism, she is clearly aware that language difficulties form only one of a group of more general problems inherent in moving to a new environment.

Reading and writing

Apparently, reading and writing did not play a major part in these students' social interaction. In an interview, Axel made an interesting point about vocabulary: "Sometimes if I have a German term I get many associations very quickly. That is missing in English – no automatic associations." This comment illustrates the role of language as a carrier of culture. One word will open different mental files for people from different cultures.

Wayan mentioned that reading and writing were extremely time consuming. These students compared themselves to native English-speaking students and felt disadvantaged. Their social life was affected because they spent more time in individual study instead of social interaction. This had a detrimental effect on both their language development and their affective states. As Wayan said, "Reading is first problem. A lot of words I have to look up in dictionary so it makes me bored so I just leave it." And, as Karen lamented in her diary, "It took me ages to write seven hundred words." Students became preoccupied by the amount of time required to do the preparation necessary for written assignments.

Kato (I):   When I was writing essays it took double the time. I had to read five or six articles. It took me a whole weekend to read. . . . and I have one hour for English then I wrote poor essay with so many mistakes.

Maki (D):   I have to write essay of History, about seven hundred words. I know it'll be hard for me because I wrote essay of English yesterday. It was only about four hundred words but it took me to do it about three hours. And it's not so good. I got three (out of seven) for a History essay. I guessed it but I was shocked. It took me three or four days to write it.

Kato pointed out that English "looked serious" and induced the feeling that he had to understand everything:

Kato (I):   When I first started the courses I found everything hard because I had fixed ideas that everything in English was very intelligent. It looked really serious, really hard. I talked with my friends and they said same thing.

With oral language it was difficult to apply repair strategies, but for the graphic skills students felt it necessary, and possible, to understand everything. Because they were spending inordinate amounts of time with texts and dictionaries, however, they felt that they were missing the social interaction that was necessary for their happiness and crucial for their oral English development. This theme is continued in the next section.

Language classroom anxiety

The final analytic category is language classroom anxiety. In this study, all classrooms were, in a way, language classrooms: Since UWCSEA is an English-medium school, each lesson presented its own language problems. A major aim for these students was to improve their English as the route to success in their studies. However, because they spent a maximum of only two hours per week in the English classroom, English was acquired in different areas of the educational institution. In the case of the learners in the present study, they sometimes felt encouraged not to communicate orally in the classroom, since the teachers were not focusing on their language proficiency and could interpret their reticence as a personality factor, rather than a language factor. Reading and writing also had greater importance for these students than for some of those quoted in earlier studies, since these scholars are following an academic course of study in which the English language is the medium and not the object of study.

While students can, perhaps, opt out of speaking in their classes, at some stage they must offer some writing for assessment. Much written language work will occur outside the classroom in the boarding house, where texts are read, dictionaries are used, and peer assistance is engaged. As Wayan said in an interview, "When I came to class, I feel like a small kid where all adult come. . . . I just worry about my English because my English worst."

Thus classroom learning was a major part of the students' lives. Their responses to this situation are covered herein under the different skill categories.

Listening

Listening was an area that students fastened on as being of major concern. Maki wrote, "I hope I will be able to understand classes before Christmas." Natsuko's diary says, "I was very nervous in every lesson because I could not understand some teachers." In an interview, Yasmin said, "I didn't know what was going on in the class. I had to catch up every single lesson and I'd ask something from a friend . . . I couldn't ask, because not only one point but every point I didn't understand."

In coping with listening situations, an understanding of the course content helped. This allowed the students to fit the new information into an existing schema and to fill the gaps in listening comprehension from previous knowledge. As Wayan said, "I think I don't really understand what the teacher talk about but I can guess what they are talking about because most of my subjects I have already studied in old school."

Signs of improvement in listening were noted and welcomed, as when Maki wrote, "When I had History class first time I couldn't understand anything – but today I could." Likewise Karen wrote in her diary,

In class I don't always get what the teachers are explaining and, in the beginning, I got very frustrated. Now I have learnt not to worry as much about it or I would get totally nervous. Also when I read or do homework I have learnt not to worry too much.

Mixing aural and graphic skills made great demands on the learner, as Nato noted in a diary entry: "I'm trying to write and listen at the same time but this is hard." Natsuko also commented on the competing demands of listening and writing in this diary entry: "If I concentrate on listening I cannot make notes and if I concentrate on writing I miss what the teacher said."

Mick Hilleson

Speaking

Classroom oral production has been highlighted by a number of researchers as being particularly anxiety inducing. Bailey (1983: 69) suggested that "[i]nhibition occurs when learners must publicly produce new responses which are not yet well learnt." However, in language classes it is not unusual for students to be called upon to perform during the early stages of learning. Horwitz, Horwitz, and Cope (1986) suggested that speaking in class provided the greatest emotional challenge to second language learners. Kleinmann's (1977) study found that oral performance was positively affected by facilitating anxiety. On the debilitating side, Phillips (1990: 541) found a "negative relationship between several measures of anxiety and the quality and quantity of foreign language speech." In other words, the type of language used may be related to the level of communicative anxiety. Students were reluctant to speak in class. As Maki said in an interview, "I don't want other students to hear me in class. . . . I've never spoken in class, never asked a teacher. Sometimes I have to answer but I don't like it because I know my English is not so good." Wayan echoed this sentiment in his diary: "About speaking, I feel I am the worst in the class. . . . I forget how to say it in English. . . . If I am in this situation I become nervous to continue what I talk." Kei's diary entry stated,

I felt quite nervous when I make an opinion when the discussion was held between class and the simple word was not found during the speech. . . . In some cases I started to tremble and couldn't say a word.

It is interesting to note that role play provided an opportunity to take on another persona. Eri said, "The activity which I felt the most comfortable was 'role play.' There are no reasons to it but I think I can do this the best." This comment is at variance with the findings of Young (1990), who classifies role play as one of the most stressful of activities.

Writing

Response groups in writing allowed students to compare their own work with others. This seemed to contribute to insecurity for many of them. Kazui wrote in a diary entry, "I felt my essay was really bad. When I read others work I thought (wished) if I could write as good as them." Other students also reported that it was in the field of writing that the formal language instruction was important. As Wayan said, "It does make a difference in writing skill because, before, I don't learn writing much but now I get much more from the lesson." Adele, who did not study English formally, felt handicapped in her studies only in

266

this area. She said, "Nobody corrects my written English. Speaking and listening is all right now. It was one of my problems at first but now I can follow a lesson." There was definitely a feeling of classroom competitiveness, bearing out Bailey's (1983) hypothesis mentioned earlier.

Kato (I):   Of course I look at other people. I find their English really good. I didn't think I was inferior because there were Japanese who had been in school for some years and I thought if I practice then my English would be like that. . . . I didn't like this school because people care about grades so much. In Japan you just take an exam, that's it. We didn't compete.

Maki also said in an interview: "Sometimes I compare myself to others. I didn't need to compare in Japan, now I think I need to."

This feeling of competitiveness may have been particularly acute for a "scholar." As Adele said, "Scholars are different. Everyone look at you and think you must be very clever." Maki echoed this sentiment when she said, "Many Japanese scholars are very good. They expect me to be good. I feel pressure."

Reading

The whole problem of studying in an unfamiliar language caused anxiety. Several students commented on this issue.

Adele (I):   Studying in English is very difficult. But you can force it. Economics I was shocked. I've never studied in English before, slowly me get used to it.

Wayan (D):   I don't know exactly how to read and think back easily, especially text books. Sometimes students could not perform adequately in tests because their reading skills were limited.

Natsuko (D):   I could not understand what the questions were saying in the test. It's a very big problem for me.

Classroom anxiety became extreme for Maki and Wayan, the students with the lowest proficiency. Maki wrote, "Today I was crying when I was doing the homework." Each class presented new challenges and the anxiety seemed to be debilitating. As Wayan said, "Actually everyday I come to school I feel Oh God! I just . . . if on Friday I get a little bit less depressed than other days. Sunday afternoons I start to think. . . ." This anxiety is often directly related to the pre-class period. As Wayan said in an interview, "I get nervous before a class but if I am in the class I forget about it. Walking up the drive to school is bad, especially if I walk alone."

Kato noted that English as a subsidiary subject was not as important for him as math, physics, and chemistry. Since English was not perceived as a content-based subject, it could take a lower priority when the pressure was on. This led Kato into truancy in a number of occasions. He had either not produced English work by a deadline, or had "more important" tasks to undertake. This is an indication of how the students were prioritizing their own needs in a way that could bring them into conflict with the institution, as shown in the following comment.

Kato (I):   I wanted to avoid English classes. English teacher look at poor second language speakers and think they have to spend a long time but we can't commit ourselves to English. English you can jump. Maths you can't jump a step.

Similar behavior was noted in the case of Kazui, who wrote about physiological signs of anxiety: "I couldn't impress myself into everything because of English. I don't know what happens to me. Stomach ache, maybe, too many pressure. And maybe take rest. I took days off. I get the headache Sunday." There is obviously a need for support and reassurance among these students in the early months of the course. In an interview, Wayan said, "I just want someone that can make me sure I will not fail after two years."

There was certainly anxiety about future academic achievement, particularly among lower proficiency students. Wayan, one of the least proficient students, asked in an interview, "I just feel with this mark, can I get better after two years?" Some scholars expressed concern about what they were expected to do in examinations, and whether they would have time to do it with their slower reading speed. Adele speculated, "Maybe we'll have to read an article and make some comments."

A recurring theme, however, was that there was no time to worry about the future. As Kato said, "I couldn't feel worried about things in the future because I had things to do at the moment, right? I just keep going on and on and time just passed."

One hope was that the situation would eventually improve. Wayan wrote, "Although I'm still worried whether I can catch IB Diploma I not thinking too much about that, because if I do I will be depressed." The confidence that "everything will be all right in the end" seemed to be present for all the students in the study. The anxiety was uncomfortable, but short term. As Kato said, "I wasn't worried about the grades because I have a confidence in myself that I will eventually pick up." The confidence was based on the successful academic careers that the students had already had, on received knowledge from peers, and the feeling that there was simply no point in dwelling on the discomfort.

Discussion

A major methodological question that is often raised is how far the findings of an introspective study can be generalized. The idiosyncracies of individual learners, limited applicability to specific cultures or learning situations, and the subjectivity of the researcher are all factors that have led researchers to question the validity of such studies. Bailey (1991: 83) claims that the point of introspective studies is to "understand language learning phenomena and related variables from the learner's point of view." Generalizability is not the sole purpose of such research. The aim of the present research was to explore the affective state of a particular group of students so that teachers and planners at UWCSEA could be more aware of the students' individual needs in similar situations in subsequent years. It was also hoped that the participants would benefit from the opportunity to confront their feelings. Of course, the process is generalizable and the benefits of helping the students to feel involved in their learning were obvious.

How can these data help in future anxiety management? Foss and Reitzel (1988) describe a relational model of competence which "involves five fundamental components or processes. . . . Taken together, these components provide a comprehensive starting point for developing exercises to help students recognize and handle their anxieties as they interact in a variety of settings" (p. 442). Foss and Reitzel's five categories (motivation, knowledge, skills, outcomes, and context) have provided the framework for discussing responses to anxiety. In addition, throughout this discussion, I will make suggestions for programmatic responses to students' problems associated with anxiety.

Motivation

As observed by Bailey (1983), a negative affective approach to study can lead to avoidance. This in turn means the loss of opportunities to communicate in the target language. Learners can thus reinforce their own perception of incompetence. This behavior was observed in Maki (self-report and from teacher observation) and to a lesser extent in Adele. Many of the comments in the section on language shock illustrate the insecurity and the pressures to remain silent.

It must be remembered that these students were motivated enough to apply for scholarships and to travel away from home to attend UWCSEA. But Maki's comment, "I don't know why I'm here," indicates a loss of motivation. Wayan's statement, "I don't know where to start," perhaps gives a hint. Initial workshops, presented early in the students' career, could cover the formal differences between spoken and written language, study skills, selective listening and reading, prioritization, and other relevant skills. The sense of personal shame that was reported (that their language was not better) could be managed in this context.

Knowledge

In these data, in each category, there was an inverse relationship between the degree of overtly stated anxiety and language proficiency as observed at the outset. Students at different levels of competence had different preoccupations that were reflected in their diary entries, interviews, and questionnaires. The task of learning the new language could appear overwhelming, inducing inordinate tension in those who viewed themselves as incompetent. As students who had opted for the Subsidiary B course in English, they gave a low priority to formal English classes, while recognizing that their performance in other subjects was related to their language proficiency.

Foss and Reitzel (1988) suggested that the keeping of journals for intrapersonal reflection helps students to reach "a more realistic, positive sense of their progress" (p. 450). The diary entry they quote bears a remarkable similarity to the comments in my own study.[2] If teachers have access to the learners' journals, they can help the students to develop realistic goals through counseling. It is certain that the opportunity to discuss the process and perception of language acquisition was welcomed and perceived as helpful by the students in this study. A more positive attitude to their language achievements can only help the students succeed in their studies.

Skills

The frustration at not having the necessary skills to function according to one's self-image can be debilitating; for example, Axel's insistence on understanding everything to the evident irritation of his teachers and classmates, or Adele's frustration with her own accent, can be viewed in this category. As Wayan said, he felt like a little boy among adults when he went to class.

Some way must be found of helping the students deal with their sense of frustration. In my opinion, a skills-based workshop and an informed counseling system within which the students have regular, mandatory meetings, are vital. All students in this study benefited from examining

---

2 Foss and Reitzel (1988: 437) quote the following comment from an ESL student attending college in California: "Why can't I speak what to think a lot in English? I'm so bitter, trying hard. I'd like to speak a lot, however, I can't. Finally, I think my basis abilities of English ran short. I'm disgusted with myself."

case studies of former students who had started in a similar situation. In this way the type of reassurance demanded by Wayan can be provided. Students need not feel that they are the only ones.

Outcomes

This category relates to a realistic evaluation of second language performance. Students frequently compared their production to others', often damning themselves unfairly. Adele's awareness of accent, Karen's frustration in debate, Kato's scant written outcomes compared to other students', Maki's not wanting other people to hear her speak – all these patterns support Bailey's (1983) findings on competitiveness. In comparing outcomes one is comparing oneself to others. For these students, the comparison inevitably led to a loss of self-esteem. Group counseling is once again indicated as an option for managing this area.

Context

This category relates to the subjective dimension of the environment. Students experiencing boarding life for the first time might have projected their unhappiness into a dissatisfaction with the environment. Their comments, however, highlight the positive effect of living in a boarding environment, emphasizing the contribution the residential community made to their stress management and language development. It has been suggested that the sense of alienation experienced by someone immersed in a new language environment may be increased because they are having to re-learn the language and conventions needed for everyday life. Not only was the social intercourse a rich area for acquisition of the type of language skills the students deemed important, but the formal management of the boarding house ensured that students attended lessons even when home students may have been ill.

Possible implications

The comments thus far suggest a number of possible implications in the UWCSEA context. For instance, a specific study skills workshop in the early days of the course, complemented by ongoing group counseling, could be very helpful to students in the situation discussed in this chapter. Open discussion of anxieties could help the students to realize what others are going through, as well as help them to recognize their own anxieties as irrational and unproductive. A list of questions in worksheet form and subsequent discussion leading to support from peers could provide a satisfactory format. Foss and Reitzel (1988) also proposed the use of an anxiety graph to help students realize that anxiety

271

is not constant. By charting their own anxiety, the students could relate highs and lows to specific situations or activities. Students who participated in the present study felt that exploring their own experiences in the diary and discussing them in the interview were therapeutic processes.

It is helpful for teachers to understand the pressures felt by learners in the classroom. There is some dispute, however, about the type of classroom activities that should be seen as low-stress, positive areas. Foss and Reitzel (ibid.) suggested that knowledge and skills can best be dealt with through role play, drama, and oral interpretation. Through performing the works of others, thoroughly rehearsed in terms of both verbal and non-verbal language, the students experience less communication anxiety than if they themselves must generate their own target language utterances.

My respondents suggested that performance exposure is a crucial factor in anxiety. They required the right to remain silent, even though they often wanted to speak. The quiet time seemed to be a necessary stage, violation of which induced dysfunctional anxiety. The teacher must be sensitive to this need and attempt to protect students from demotivating experiences.

While oral activities were more stress-inducing than low exposure activities, the teacher's attitude to errors and the personal characteristics of the instructor (humor, patience, degree of positive feedback, etc.) seemed important to the learners. This applies across the curriculum since in this context the second language experience is going on in all classrooms. Sensitizing teachers to the problem via papers or in-service training workshops could be fruitful in focusing teacher attention on the individual.

Foss and Reitzel proposed that context-based anxiety could be alleviated by allowing the students to invest something of themselves in the environment. They suggest basing activities on familiar cultural artifacts. While this strategy is obviously relevant in the language classroom, it also has relevance for the whole school. The context of an international school allows for a certain amount of shared experience and solidarity. In their diaries and interviews, the students reported that the "United Nations Day," when they planned ethnic dances, sketches, and food stalls, was of crucial importance in confidence building and making contact with others.

The overall thrust of Foss and Reitzel's work relates to students' perceptions of themselves and their own performance. If they can be helped to see themselves more positively, they will be more successful in their studies. Young (1990: 550) also highlights self-esteem as an important variable related to fear of speaking in front of others and anxiety in making mistakes. (As Maki said, "I want to talk with them, but I don't want them to hear.") Young suggested that the learner should be given coaching in productive self-talk (e.g., I can handle this). She also emphasized the importance to the student of being able to prepare adequately, since "on-the-spot" activities were deemed anxiety inducing. My respondents saw themselves as successful academic students in their own language and therefore had faith that "it would be all right in the end." They benefited from people telling them this, and perhaps such reassurance needs to be built into the early days of the course.

A workshop to prepare students for the ways of learning can help learners develop a positive attitude towards the discipline in question. Learner training aims to help students consider the factors that affect their learning. Campbell and Ortiz (1988: 153) ran a foreign language anxiety workshop which included an attitudinal survey, discussion of an anxiety questionnaire, discussion of the ideal language learner, and instruction in language learning strategies. The authors instituted this program because they had identified "alarming levels of anxiety in postsecondary students enrolled in foreign language courses in competitive environments" (ibid.: 159). The advantage of this approach is that it can affect students from the first days of their studies and immediately puts the topic on the school agenda. Students can also tackle specific language skills, such as writing essays in their second language. In my data, Kato and Karen reported that they initially wrote essays in their first language and then attempted to translate. It is clear that discussion of appropriate strategies would help students not to adopt such time-consuming and unproductive approaches.

While many previous studies focused on oral communication, anxieties related to listening, reading, and writing must also be considered. Young's (1990) study placed reading silently and writing compositions at home among the least anxiety inducing activities. The present study suggests that the time factor is also an important element. For example, Kato reported endless hours poring over texts. In general, these students were taking considerably longer than native English-speaking students to read preparatory texts and were thus excluding themselves from relaxing or interactive social activities. This in itself was dysfunctional in language acquisition terms, since the social environment was crucial in language development. Comparing themselves to other students, my respondents were aware of the language handicap, and in the first weeks the task ahead seemed impossible to some. Wayan in particular reported his reliance on God to see him through.

Students at all proficiency levels reported an almost magical transformation when they commenced the second term (about four months after beginning the course). Many had been away on holiday, some in a non-English-speaking environment, but they all remarked on the difference in their attitude after the break. They felt as if a barrier had been lifted and suddenly their confidence had returned. This is more marked in the cases of Kato, Maki, Wayan, and Adele, although Axel noted that he was linguistically less demanding and more tolerant of ambiguity. Students were more relaxed after the break because the demands they were making on themselves were more realistic. This interpretation suggests that students need guidance in terms of realistic goal setting.

As residence outside one's own country becomes more common, and more students are educated in an international setting, the experiences discussed in this chapter will be repeated. This research was intended to lead to a better understanding of the individual needs of such students. Even though I recognize that generalizability is a problem inherent in introspective research, I would suggest that some themes which are relevant to any language learner traveling beyond his or her own culture and language can be identified. Because educational institutions and teachers must find ways to address the needs of their students, I hope that the research discussed here will contribute to a heightened awareness of the learners' experience.

References

Allwright, D., and K. M. Bailey. 1991. *Focus on the Language Classroom: An Introduction to Classroom Research for Language Teachers.* Cambridge: Cambridge University Press.

Bailey, K. M. 1983. Competitiveness and anxiety in adult second language acquisition: Looking *at* and *through* the diary studies. In H. Seliger and M. H. Long (eds.), *Classroom Oriented Research in Second Language Acquisition.* Rowley, MA: Newbury House.

1991. Diary studies of classroom language learning; The doubting game and the believing game. In E. Sadtono (ed.), *Language Acquisition and the Second/Foreign Language Classroom.* Singapore: SEAMEO, RELC, Series 28.

Brindley, G. 1992. Becoming a Researcher: The Role of Classroom Based Research in Language Teacher Education. Paper delivered at RELC Conference, Singapore.

Campbell, C., and J. Ortiz, 1988. Dispelling students' fears and misconceptions about foreign language study. Cited in T. B. Freyer and F. Medley, *New Challenges and Opportunities: Dimensions in Languages '87.* Columbus, SC: Southern Conference on Language Teaching.

Chastain, K. 1975. Affective and ability factors in second language acquisition. *Language Learning, 25,* 1, 153–161.

Foss, K. A., and A. C. Reitzel. 1988. A relational model for managing second language anxiety. *TESOL Quarterly, 22,* 3, 437–54.

Gardner, R. C., and P. C. Smythe. 1975. Motivation and second language acquisition. *Canadian Modern Language Review,* 31, 218–230.

Horwitz, E., M. Horwitz, and J. A. Cope. 1986. Foreign language classroom anxiety. *Modern Language Journal,* 70, 125–132.

Kleinmann, H. 1977. Avoidance behavior in second language acquisition. *Language Learning, 27*, 1, 93–107.

Lennon, P. 1989. Introspection and intentionality in advanced second language acquisition. *Language Learning, 39,* 3, 375–393.

McGrath, J. E. 1982. Methodological problems in research on stress. In K. W. Krohne and L. Laux (eds.), *Achievement Stress and Anxiety.* New York: Hemisphere Publishing Corporation.

Parkinson, B., and C. Howell-Richardson. 1990. Learner diaries. In C. Brumfit and R. Mitchell (eds.), *Research in the Language Classroom: ELT Documents.* Modern English Publications and the British Council.

Phillips, E. 1990. The Effects of Anxiety on Performance and Achievement in an Oral Test of French. Unpublished doctoral thesis, University of Texas at Austin.

Schumann, J. H. 1978. *The Pidginization Process: A Model for Second Language Acquisition.* Rowley, MA: Newbury House.

Schumann, F. E., and J. H. Schumann. 1977. Diary of a language learner: An introspective study of language learning. In H. D. Brown, C. Yorio, and R. Crymes (ed.), *On TESOL '77: Teaching and Learning English as a Second Language: Trends in Research and Practice.* Washington, DC: TESOL.

Scovel, T. 1978. The effect of affect on foreign language learning: A review of the anxiety research. *Language Learning, 28,* 1, 129–142.

Williams, K. 1991. Anxiety and formal second/foreign language learning. *RELC Journal, 22,* 19–28.

Young, D. J. 1990. An investigation of students' perspectives on anxiety and speaking. *Foreign Language Annals, 23,* 6, 539–553.

Section III Questions and tasks

1. Each chapter in this section is based, in part, on journals kept by learners or teachers. Do you find diary data to be convincing? Why or why not?

2. Chapter 8 describes some of Campbell's experiences studying Spanish in Mexico. As in her previous experience, learning German in Germany, the importance of a group of friends who speak the target language emerges as a powerful factor in her language learning. Thinking back to your own experiences as a language learner, what has been the role of social interaction (as opposed to classroom learning) in your target language development? Give clear examples to illustrate any generalizations you may make.

3. Chapter 9 illustrates what Freeman (this volume) has called "teacher's knowledge as stories." In the introduction we said that this book was a collection of *research* papers. Is Cummings' chapter a research paper, or is it "just a story"? What would Freeman say?

4. The students Cummings describes are "repeaters" – people who have already failed the course at least once. If you were the teacher, how would working with a group of repeaters differ from working with students taking a course for the first time? If you were a student repeating a course, how would you like the course to proceed?

5. The students in Chapter 10 were all adults studying Spanish in order to use it professionally in their jobs as social workers. Some were Hispanic and some were not. According to the diary data and Peck's analyses, how did the learners' ethnicity interact with their learning of Spanish?

6. Peck finds evidence of developing cultural sensitivity in the Spanish students' diary entries. Can a person learn a foreign or second language without becoming culturally sensitive? Can a person become culturally sensitive without learning the language? Finally, where do you stand on Lawrence's question quoted at the beginning of Chapter 10: "I don't think I can fully enter the culture. . . . What does it mean to be bicultural?"

7. The students depicted in Chapter 11 were all living in an English-speaking environment, studying their secondary school subjects in English, their second language. Have you had any experiences similar to these students, or Cherry Campbell's (Chapter 8)? What were the circumstances? How did you react to the pressures of being in a total-immersion situation?

8. If you could talk to Campbell, Peck, Cummings, and Hilleson, what questions would you want to ask them?

9. What could the teachers in Tsui's study (Chapter 6) learn from reading Hilleson's chapter or by talking to his students? What

could the students in Hilleson's chapter gain by talking with the teachers in Tsui's?

10. Imagine yourself in the role of a language learner. What would you be likely to learn if you kept a journal of your experiences? If you are studying a language right now, try keeping a diary every day for a full week. Then re-read your entries. What notable patterns do you see in the data?

11. Imagine yourself in the role of a teacher. What might you learn by keeping a journal? If you are teaching now, try making daily journal entries for a week. Then re-read your journal and see if you can find any patterns. If you were a teacher, what would you have learned by reading language learning journals kept by the students in your class?

12. Imagine yourself in the role of a researcher. Under what circumstances would you keep a journal for research purposes? If you were analyzing diary data provided by language learners other than yourself, what guidelines would you give the diarists about making their journal entries?

IV Curricular issues

The chapters in this section all articulate a vision of curricula, with a particular focus on the effects of innovation on language learning and teaching. As in other sections of this volume, these chapters are drawn from a rich diversity of contexts. In Chapter 12 Ian Harrison explores the pedagogical effects of large-scale curriculum change within the Sultanate of Oman. In Chapter 13 Ann Snow, John Hyland, Lia Kamhi-Stein, and Janet Yu look at the reactions of Mexican-American students to curriculum innovation in junior high schools in Los Angeles. Peter Shaw also takes learners' perspectives on curriculum change as the thematic concern of his study, Chapter 14, although his interpretive focus is slightly different (i.e., the role of the ethnographer as an agent of change). Likewise, in Chapter 15 Peter Sturman considers the learners' perspectives, but in this case regarding the placement and registration procedures in two private language schools in Japan.

Substantive issues

Harrison examines changes in learner and teacher behaviors as a way of evaluating a large-scale curriculum renewal project in the Middle East. The focus of the investigation is whether learners' classroom language behavior changed as a result of the introduction of a new EFL curriculum with new textbooks and a new examination system. The data for the study include lesson transcripts, inspector's reports, interviews with inspectors, and reports from teachers' meetings. Harrison concludes from his investigation that simply changing the raw materials of the curriculum – that is, the materials that teachers and learners use – will not necessarily effect a change in language behavior. The study reinforces the truism that there can be no curriculum development without teacher development, as we see from following two teachers, "Ali" and "Sheikha," over a two-year period.

The chapter by Snow, Hyland, Kamhi-Stein, and Yu describes a project to improve teaching and learning in junior high classrooms in six schools in the heart of the Mexican-American community in Los Angeles. Through oral interviews conducted in English and Spanish, the study focuses on the reactions of the students to the instructional processes introduced in the curricular innovation. The researchers also elicit

279

data from students on the strategies the learners themselves believed to be successful in coping with the academic demands of school. The project is underpinned by the notions of the "helping interview" (Benjamin 1981), "action research" (Kemmis and McTaggart 1982), and the "instructional conversation" (Tharp and Gallimore 1988). Data were collected from sixty-six students through focused interviews based on elicitation (via a card-sort task and a role-play prompt). Students expressed a significant preference for classes where (a) the teacher uses cooperative learning (as opposed to classes where students work alone), (b) students are given opportunities to keep journals in English and Spanish (as opposed to classes where there is no journal writing), (c) they are active participants, and (d) they are expected to take notes. Students also expressed a strong preference for experiential learning activities, such as projects and experiments.

The chapter by Shaw investigates the role of the ethnographer as a curriculum change agent. Data for this study came from an evaluation of an innovative foreign language curriculum offered to graduate students in an international policy studies program. These were adult language learners who wished to work in cross-cultural and multilingual environments. The voices we hear are those of the participants (both teachers and learners) in these "content courses," where the learners studied subject matter related to their academic degrees but presented in a foreign language.

The chapter by Sturman investigates an important topic which has seldom been addressed: learners' initial impressions of a language program. Sturman solicits the learners' viewpoints of their first contacts with the teachers and the administrative staff through the schools' registration and placement procedures. The data are open-ended written comments and quantified categorical responses derived from questionnaires administered by Sturman at two British Council schools in Japan. The categorical data are subjected to a cross-tabulations analysis to reveal their underlying associations with students' attitudes about other instructional factors (e.g., their satisfaction with the school). The resulting statistical and interpretive account reveals the importance of learners' early contacts with a program.

Methodological issues

The studies in this section are methodologically heterogeneous. Data are admitted as evidence in the form of lesson transcripts, inspectors' reports, interviews with teachers and inspectors, responses to questionnaires, reports from teachers' meetings, focused interviews with students, role plays, ethnographic fieldnotes, and professors' and students' diary entries. But despite the diverse contexts, issues, and procedures of these studies, they all employ elicitation devices of one sort or another in the form of focused interviews, questionnaires, and role-play prompts.

As a device, elicitation is probably the most commonly employed data collection technique in applied linguistics. (In a meta-analysis of fifty classroom-oriented studies, Nunan [1991] found that over half of these employed elicitation.) Elicitation techniques have been used in second language acquisition research since the morpheme order studies of the early 1970s. The advantage of employing elicitation is that it can "speed up" the process of getting appropriate information by providing data which may be extremely slow in coming to the researcher who is relying exclusively on observation of naturally occurring events. Purposefully eliciting data can also enable the researcher to focus on issues and concerns which may be present but diffuse in a purely observational study.

There are, of course, several dangers inherent in the use of elicitation. Research based on elicitation techniques differs from naturalistic observation in a number of important respects. In particular, the researcher determines in advance what will be investigated (Allwright and Bailey 1991). Researchers need to be aware of two possible threats to the validity of such investigations. The first is that by determining in advance what will be considered relevant, the researcher may overlook other potentially important phenomena. The other danger, and one which needs to be considered when evaluating research utilizing such devices, is the extent to which the results obtained are an artifact of the elicitation devices employed (Nunan 1992: 138–139).

The researchers whose work is represented in this section found distinct advantages and some disadvantages in the use of elicitation. Snow et al. found that the oral interview, as a research technique, enabled them to engage in an "instructional conversation" with the students in a way which revealed the perceptions of the learners on the nature of effective teaching and learning. Harrison and Sturman both incorporate quantitative and qualitative data in their chapters. Both utilize data from a number of sources which were not entirely under their control (e.g., Harrison's use of school inspectors' reports in the Sultanate of Oman, and Sturman's use of questionnaire data in both open-ended and closed-question formats). Each of these authors candidly discusses the problems that arose in their attempts to integrate data gathered from a combination of elicitation procedures.

Shaw, however, found that his personal involvement was an issue in trying to enact the traditional role of an ethnographer. As a colleague of those under investigation, he was a stakeholder in the enterprise, and this is a problematic concern in studies of this kind. Viewed more positively, Shaw's expertise as a curriculum and pedagogy specialist put him in the position of being a resource to the learners and teachers in his study. As a result of this experience, Shaw develops the concept of a "consulting ethnographer" – one who is available to interact with his cohort to their advantage as well as his own.

References

Allwright, D., and K. M. Bailey. 1991. *Focus on the Language Classroom: An Introduction to Classroom Research for Language Teachers.* Cambridge: Cambridge University Press.

Benjamin, A. 1981. *The Helping Interview.* Boston: Houghton Mifflin.

Kemmis, S., and R. McTaggart. 1982. *The Action Research Planner.* Victoria, Australia: Deakin University Press.

Nunan, D. 1991. Methods in second language classroom-oriented research. *Studies in Second Language Acquisition, 13,* 2, 249–272.

1992. *Research Methods in Language Learning.* New York: Cambridge University Press.

Tharp, R., and R. Gallimore. 1988. *Rousing Minds to Life: Teaching, Learning and Schooling in Social Context.* Cambridge: Cambridge University Press.

12 Look who's talking now: listening to voices in curriculum renewal

Ian Harrison

> I thank you for your voices, thank you.
> Your most sweet voices.
> (Coriolanus, II.iii)

In 1988 a curriculum renewal project was initiated in the Sultanate of Oman with the aim of renewing "the ELT [English language teaching] curriculum in the school system through materials production and concomitant teacher and inspector development and revision of the English language examinations system" (Project Framework 1988). Expectations were that there would be an improvement in students' ability to use English effectively in a variety of pedagogical tasks which would approximate the real world tasks that they would engage in after their course of study.

What actually happened? Did pupils' classroom language behavior undergo a change? In this chapter I will explore the extent to which it is possible to make statements about the effect that curriculum renewal had upon one aspect of classroom language behavior of elementary students: the skill of speaking. Qualitative data are examined to see to what extent changes in student behavior are attributable to such curriculum renewal. I also examine data from the classroom to discuss whether conclusions can be drawn regarding changes in teacher behavior during, and possibly because of, curriculum renewal.

The study

The background

The Sultanate of Oman is a young country, the modern state having only been established in 1970. There were three schools then, but now there are approximately 800 schools and 2000 teachers of English. Initially the system depended upon expatriate teachers from other Arab countries from South Asia and Britain. The development of teacher training colleges and the education faculty at Sultan Qaboos University, however, has meant that elementary-level classrooms are now almost entirely staffed by Omani teachers and that there is an increasing proportion of Omani teachers at the lower and upper secondary levels.

An English Language Teaching Department was established in the Ministry of Education in 1974 to handle all issues concerned with the teaching, learning, and testing of English, including the professional activities of the English language inspectorate. Inspectors in each of the administrative regions ensure that schools are equipped with the requisite number of textbooks, and that formal examinations are conducted and graded according to approved guidelines. In addition, they conduct teacher development workshops and advisory visits to classrooms. Teacher appraisal and program evaluation are further aspects of their work.

Initially, materials based on a structural syllabus were used by expatriate teachers trained in grammar-translation or audiolingual methodology. Subsequently (from 1979) a set of specially developed materials (derived from a more skills-based and more functionally organized syllabus) was introduced with the aim of encouraging more communicative classroom activities with a focus on use as well as on form.

Class size typically varies between fifteen in smaller schools to forty-five in more urban areas. Schools are segregated along gender lines, although in some rural areas, elementary classes are occasionally mixed. English is introduced as a compulsory subject at age nine, when pupils receive four lessons of English per week, each lesson lasting thirty-five to forty minutes.

The curriculum renewal effected from 1988 onwards was extensive and included the development of student books, teacher guides, sets of ancillary materials, audio and video materials, television programs, examination reform, orientation programs for all teachers, special teacher development programs for Omani teachers and inspector development programs. The new elementary course materials, focused on in this study, were introduced into the school system in the 1990–1991 academic year.

The new materials aimed to "enable learners to leave the school system . . . in possession of a 'core' of the English language" (*Our World Through English: Fourth Elementary Teacher's Book B*, 1990: ii). Learners could then develop "specialized knowledge and skills in English, according to their varying occupational and study needs after school" (ibid.). Teachers and inspectors were asked as part of the evaluation to focus on the learners' involvement, since "the materials are designed to give the highest possible percentage of learners the chance to participate in classroom work" and since "the highest possible percentage of learners" would be obtaining and giving information about different topics in a variety of settings (ibid.: iii).

The data

In this study I have drawn upon four types of data. First, I examine baseline data from written reports on what the inspectors during the 1988–1989 academic year considered to be the strengths and weaknesses of the course materials which had been in use for nine years. I compare these reports with audio-recorded interviews with inspectors in the spring of 1992, during which I elicited opinions on the success or failure of the curriculum renewal with regard to pupils' oral skills.

Accounts of lesson observations, part of the evaluation of the new trial course materials, form the second type of data set analysis. During the trial year of the new materials at each level, I asked inspectors to observe two teachers using the new materials for a period of two to three weeks. Each inspector produced a number of narrative accounts of different lessons given by the same teacher in the same class. I examine these accounts as well as the report written at the end of the observation period on the inspector's view of the effectiveness of the materials – again, focusing upon the speaking skill.

I also examine the reports of meetings of groups of elementary teachers in different parts of the country as part of the materials evaluation process. (See Ministry of Education, minutes of April 1, 1991 meeting in Rostaq, and minutes of April 8, 1991 meeting in Muscat.) These reports provide information on whether teachers felt that changes had occurred in the oral behavior of their students.

In the main part of the study I examine videotaped recordings of teachers in their classrooms, which were made as part of the collection of baseline data at the start of the project. I recorded the same teachers using the new materials two years later. These recordings were examined in order to compare students' speaking behavior when using the former course materials and the new course materials – both quantitatively and qualitatively, as well as to examine changes in teacher behavior.

What regional inspectors think

I obtained baseline data from regional inspectors in the 1988–1989 academic year by requesting detailed written reports on the perceived strengths and weaknesses of the course in use. These reports provide a varied and comprehensive account of the baseline situation prior to the implementation of the new curriculum, viewed from the perspective of the inspectorate. Extracts from the inspectors' remarks are quoted verbatim. They contain comments on grammar such as, "There is too much grammar which is confusing for the pupils" (Report: Inspector 1). Another inspector said, ". . . more and more complex structures, taught for a short time and then left and then obviously forgotten" (Report: Inspector 7). On vocabulary, one inspector said, "The amount of vocabulary piled into the Elementary stage is a bit too much. There is also a lack of vocabulary which has a direct bearing upon the children's daily life" (Report: Inspector 5). The inspectors had the following to say about the effectiveness of the speaking component of the former elementary materials:

... a lack of a strong foundation which in turn results in poor language attainment at the higher levels. (Report: Inspector 5)

Speaking takes an important part in the syllabus but ... it is wrongly exploited as the teachers are the answerers even when group or pair work in rows or files are practical. (Report: Inspector 9)

... [They are] listening to and producing alien sounds and utterances in more or less meaningful situations. (Report: Inspector 10)

The interviews I conducted in the spring of 1992 involved a representative sample (taken from four of the nine administrative regions) of eight inspectors who had been working in Oman for a number of years and were familiar with both the former curriculum and the new one. Inspectors have to conduct advisory visits to as many as forty teachers, three times a year, to observe their classroom teaching. They are thus in a position to provide an impressionistic opinion of students' oral proficiency. In each interview, I explained the purpose of the study and allowed five minutes for reflection on the issues that would be focused on during the interview. These were the same issues that inspectors had been asked to address three years before, when they produced written comments on the former curriculum.

Inspectors generally felt that with the introduction of the new course pupils were able to say more in terms of utterance length. For example, Inspector 6 was asked to compare the former and the new course materials.

Inspector: Here, better. Pupils concentrate more and practice more than in [the previous course materials].
Interviewer: Can they say more?
Inspector: Yes, they can of course. In all levels. They can talk, for example, about themselves. A few sentences. But in the [former course] it was not there. They were very reluctant. Now they are able to talk a little about anything.

When asked to interpret why this was the case, Inspector 6 gave thematic choice as the main contributing factor.

At the elementary level, the topics are chosen very well, very carefully. The first thing they talk about is themselves, various interests. They talk about myself, my brother, etc. Omani topics most of them, Omani subjects concerned with Omani culture, surroundings.

Both Inspectors 3 and 7 similarly thought that pupils could speak better than previously.

I feel so because there the nature of the tasks before were just responses to certain stimuli, short answers, but here they are encouraged at sentence level, paragraph level. It's much better but there [previous course] mere responses, maybe short answers, but here they have been provided with the opportunity of talking at paragraph level and sentence level. (Inspector 3)

It is really great to see pupils right from the elementary level speak not just one or two words . . . rather sentences the moment they see the visual stimulus card – they just come out, you know, spontaneously. The students can really speak connected sentences. They may be guided but even then I mean it is still done far better than the [previous course]. (Inspector 7)

Inspector 2 focused more on the quality than on the quantity of what pupils were able to say, considering that pupils were now "more fluent" and had "better pronunciation." Half the inspectors interviewed said that overall fluency had improved. Some inspectors consider pupil pronunciation to have improved as a result of the new course. Inspector 2 also raised the interesting issue of pupil confidence: "You feel they are a little more confident when they stand up to say something. You can see that the students, she or he can say it."

Assessing gains other than language gains is problematic and thus often ignored, but the preceding subjective remark indicates that such gains might usefully have been evaluated more fully. In this study, two inspectors felt that learners had gained in confidence, one felt that there had been no change, and five made no comment. Table 1 summarizes what the inspectors felt about the pupils' speaking ability in the new curriculum, as compared with the former. Overall, inspectors perceived that the pupils' speaking proficiency had improved, both qualitatively and quantitatively. For example, although one inspector considered the situation to be worse with the introduction of the new curriculum, the majority of the inspectors considered that learners could now speak for longer periods of time. Some inspectors also felt that the quality of the students' spoken utterances had changed for the better – four of the eight inspectors interviewed felt that fluency had improved, although four made no particular comment. The inspectors' perceptions of changes in the students' pronunciation and grammatical accuracy are less obvious. Although three inspectors felt there had been an improvement in both aspects, no inspector considered the situation to be worse in the new curriculum, and no comment was made by half the number interviewed.

TABLE 1   INSPECTORS' PERCEPTIONS OF CHANGES IN PUPILS' ORAL
PROFICIENCY AT THE ELEMENTARY LEVEL ($n = 8$)

	Improved	*No change*	*Worse*	*No comment made*
Length of sustained utterances	5	1	1	1
Fluency	4	0	0	4
Pronunciation	3	1	0	4
Grammatical accuracy	3	2	0	3
Confidence	2	1	0	5
Realistic, genuine practice	3	1	2	2
Quantity of speaking opportunities	5	1	1	1

While inspectors felt that the new curriculum materials provided an increased number of opportunities for learners to speak, fewer inspectors (three) considered the nature of the speaking practice to have improved in terms of realism and naturalness. The current study would probably have been enriched if I had obtained more information from the inspectors in the interviews. These findings, however, need to be examined in relation to evidence coming more directly from the classroom. In the three sections that follow, I discuss examples of such evidence.

Inspectors' observation of teachers in the classroom

In this section I look at the narrative accounts of lessons observed by regional inspectors and at the reports made at the end of their observation period. The course materials were divided into segments of units, each segment being assigned to two of the nine administrative regions for detailed classroom trial, including inspector observation of two teachers for the whole period of the segment. The segment of materials under scrutiny thus has two sets of reports from two different regions to examine.

The reports of Inspector 4 contain little evidence of any major change in the students' oral ability. In the observation of a speaking exercise recycling past tense verb forms, he wrote about the pupils' difficulty with some verbs, but "despite that, recycled evenly and most pupils enjoyed it." When observing a similar exercise later, he wrote, "positive with good pupils; average and weak pupils found it difficult. Vocabulary ungraded and above their standard" (fieldnotes of Inspector 2, spring 1991). The written summary report describes the "teachers' conception of the material" as "quite positive" but mentions again "ungraded vocabulary," and words which "are difficult to pronounce." When interviewed, the same inspector, however, had no doubt that the new curriculum materials were more effective in getting pupils to speak: "In elementary level, they are far more effective. They have more of a chance to listen and also to speak. . . ." Reinforcement is mentioned as one contributing factor: "I think all these reinforcements help the pupils to reinforce the language in their minds, and to practice the skills thoroughly, more thoroughly than in [the previous course]" (interview of Inspector 2, spring 1992).

There is an indication from the observations of Inspector 1 that students were able to speak in a guided and prompted way. The notes of one observation, for example, state that "groups in chorus said the sentences for the pictures, then individuals." This type of controlled preparation for individual speaking is commonly used in classrooms in Oman. The end result was, however, that pupils could retell a story when prompted with a picture or action cues: "One girl did the action while four girls said the sentences for each picture." In a subsequent pair work exercise using the same pictures, the teacher was observed as having "asked the pupils to say to each other the sentences for the pictures" (fieldnotes of Inspector 1, spring 1991).

The other teacher that this inspector observed as part of the trial procedure similarly followed the teacher's book guidenotes fairly closely: "When she covered all the sentences, she asked pupils to practice in pairs the sentences." In a later exercise, she "elicits sentences for the pictures" (on the blackboard). Pupils in this class were also apparently able to retell the story: "Pupils in pairs practiced the story orally" (fieldnotes of Inspector 1, spring 1991).

Although these remarks describe guided and controlled oral practice, this has to be compared with the typical Omani elementary classroom prior to the introduction of the new curriculum where, in the words of one inspector, "the teachers are the answerers." The report of Inspector 1 (spring 1991), indicates that "in terms of language skills, generally pupils did better in this course book. Most pupils can describe things in simple language."

What teachers think

In this section I look at the minutes of the meetings that were part of the procedures set up to evaluate the effectiveness of the new curriculum, particularly the new materials. These "evaluation meetings" were designed to involve classroom practitioners as much as possible in the development and revision of new course materials. Rea-Dickens and

Germaine (1992: 25) point out the importance of involving teachers, since they "have a key role to play in the curriculum renewal and development process" not least because "it is the teacher, rather than the 'tester' or the evaluation 'expert', who has most information about specific classroom contexts." After completing a segment of the materials, teachers were asked to respond to questionnaires before attending the evaluation meeting. To help triangulate the data, the segments assigned for evaluation by teachers were the same as those assigned for intensive inspector observation.

Unfortunately I find it difficult to state with any certainty whether or not teachers felt that the students' speaking ability had indeed improved. The minutes of the first teachers' evaluation meeting mention "positive remarks in general" and that "the teachers noted that the pupils have a positive attitude towards the materials – pupils like the materials because they touch their lives." This correlates with what Inspector 6 (from a different administrative region) put forward as one of the reasons for pupils doing better with the new curriculum materials (i.e., the appropriate choice of topic). The second group of teachers also felt that the pupils are "highly motivated and they like the subject very much and this shows the connection between the material and their environment." The minutes of the first meeting mention, however, that "some phrases are too long and too difficult for the pupils." In contrast, the teachers at the second meeting felt that the development of speaking was "adequate," but I cannot really say that this was particularly informative.

There was thus no clear indication of teachers' views on whether the pupils' speaking ability had changed with the implementation of the new curriculum. There may be a number of factors contributing to this lack of clarity. For example, teachers were not specifically asked to compare the new course with the former course, and this may have resulted in their not thinking in terms of change in student behavior. Another reason may be that, despite an established procedural format, the right kind of atmosphere for frank and open discussion may not have been created, or there may have been domination of the meeting by a limited number of voices. Or perhaps the right kind of questions may not have been asked or the minutes may have been incompletely taken. What is clear, however, is that obtaining information from practitioners about what happens in the classroom is not straightforward. Moreover, although "the uniqueness of each classroom setting implies that any proposal – even at school level – needs to be tested and verified and adapted by each teacher in his own classroom," getting a clear picture of how a new curriculum has been implemented is a very complex issue (Stenhouse 1975: 143, cited in Rea-Dickens and Germaine 1992: 68).

TABLE 2   TEACHERS AND CLASSES IN THE STUDY

Teacher	Lesson	Date	Class size	Duration
Ali	1	January 1990	33	30 minutes
	2	February 1992	43	34 minutes
Sheikha	1	January 1990	44	36 minutes
	2	March 1992	41	42 minutes

Some evidence from the classroom

In this section I describe the results of my analysis of video recordings of two teachers in their classrooms. In 1989–1990, the proportion of Omani teachers working at the elementary level was very much lower than expatriate teachers (16 percent vs. 84 percent). However, the increasing number of teacher training colleges – three in 1984, six in 1987, nine in 1990 – would soon ensure that English teaching at the elementary level would be staffed almost entirely by Omani teachers. I felt it inappropriate, therefore, to choose expatriate teachers for the study. The data base for each teacher is depicted in Table 2.

The two Omani teachers who were videotaped both taught in the Muscat (capital) region and were approximately twenty-three years old in 1990. In order to obtain a balanced data set, one male teacher and one female teacher (and, therefore, one class of male students and one class of female students) were identified. The teachers were videotaped at the beginning of the second semester in both academic years, 1989–1990 and 1991–1992. The pupils observed had thus received more or less the same number of hours of English instruction. (Pseudonyms have been used for the teachers, both of whom graduated from teacher training college in 1988.)

The type of analysis selected was Brown's Interaction Analysis System (BIAS) (Brown 1975, cited by Malamah-Thomas 1987: 48). Although this instrument was not designed specifically for analysis of the language classroom, I considered it a simple and useful tool for analyzing verbal interaction and, thus, particularly useful for examining lessons involving oral practice. Furthermore, it provides both quantitative and qualitative information in its analysis of the amount of time spent in the lesson on different types of oral interaction. The system involves marking a time-line display for every three seconds of the observation according to six categories. These categories, which are a simplified version of Flanders' (1970) descriptive categories, are given in Tables 3 and 4.

In this analysis, results are given for each teacher separately, since the idea was not to compare teachers but to compare behavior in the same

291

TABLE 3   ANALYSIS OF CLASSROOM VERBAL BEHAVIOR: TEACHER I – ALI

	Lesson 1 January 1990 30 minutes	Lesson 2 February 1992 34 minutes
Teacher lectures, describes, explains, narrates, directs.	42%	29%
Teacher questions about content or procedure, which pupils are intended to answer.	33%	24%
Teacher responds, accepts pupils' feelings; praises, encourages; accepts or uses pupils' ideas, builds upon pupil responses.	4%	9%
Pupils respond directly and predictably to teacher questions and directions.	12%	28%
Pupils volunteer information, comments, or questions.	0%	0%
Silence. Blackboard work without accompanying teacher talk, writing activity.*	9%	10%

*Note that this last category has for the purposes of this study incorporated Brown's (1975) last category of "unclassifiable."

teacher's classroom at two different times. Although the main focus is on the pupils, there is some discussion of teacher behavior: Had it changed? If so, did this change have any demonstrable effect upon pupil performance?

As shown in Table 3, Ali's pupils showed a marked change in terms of the *amount* of time that they spent talking. In the 1990 lesson they spent only 3.6 minutes talking (12 percent of the total lesson). Considering that the predominant nature of the lesson was oral (revision and practice of the body parts as preparation for a song), this was a surprisingly small proportion of the lesson.

The discourse is typified by the following transcript, in which "A" represents Ali (the teacher); "S1" and so on stand for an identified student; and an opening bracket indicates overlapping speech.

A: What is this? (Pointing to head, ears, nose, etc.)
S1: My head.
A: What are these? Yes . . .
S2: Ears.
A: What is this?

S3: It's a nose.
A: What is this? Yes, (S4's name).
S4: Mouth.
A: What are these?
S5: Hands.
      [
S6:   Hands.
A: What are these?
S7: Shoulders.
A: What are these?
S8: Toes.
A: Good.

In 1992 the proportion of Ali's lesson during which the pupils spoke was higher – 28 percent. In addition, the quality and length of individual utterances was much greater. In place of the simple one-word responses that they were making in 1990, pupils used a greater number of phrases and sentencelike combinations, as Inspector 3 and Inspector 7 reported when interviewed in 1992. In 1990, for example, pupils were struggling to say phrases or sentences above the level of one word responses, such as "ears," "mouth," and "hands."

A: I will give you the word, you give me the sentence. Listen: Shoulders.
S1: These . . . shoulders.
A: These are my shoulders.
S1: These . . .
      [
A: These are
S1: These are . . .
      [
A: These are my shoulders.
S1: These my shoulders.
A: OK. These are my shoulders. Now you (S2's name). Help him.
S2: These . . .
      [
A: are
        [
S2:   are . . .
          [
A: my shoulders
            [
S2:   my shoulders
A: Good. These are my shoulders.
S2: These are shoulders.

293

A: These are my shoulders
S2: These are shoulders.

Although there are still a number of one-word and hesitant responses in 1992, both the pace of response and the quality of individual utterances have improved.

A: Hold up your cap (pointing at S; S holds up his cap). What color is his cap?
S1: Green.
    [
S2:   Green.
        [
S3:   Green.
A: Yes? Whose cap?
S1: His cap
    [
S2:   green
S1: His cap is green.
A: Good. Hold up your cap. (Student holds up his cap.) What color is his cap?
S5: Blue and white. His cap is blue and white.
A: Yes. His cap is blue and white. Hold up your bag. (Student holds up his bag.) What color is his bag?
S6: His bag is red and white.
A: Good. Yes. His bag is red and white. Hold up your cap. (Student holds up his cap.) What color is his cap?
S7: His cap is green and white.

Students produce comparatively complex utterances ("Blue and white. His cap is blue and white") as well as simple sentence level responses ("His bag is red and white").

Ali's teaching behavior had also changed in the intervening period. I feel that excessively long teacher talk, when setting up classroom activities, although possibly beneficial in some respects, does not further the aim of providing maximum opportunity for the pupils to practice talking. In 1990 Ali spent 43 percent of the lesson directing and explaining, for example:

A: Now please, if I say a word, you put your hand on that part of your body. (Pause) Head . . . Don't speak please. (Children point to different parts of their body while teacher says the word.)

and (later):

A: Now I will give you the word, listen to me first, try and understand – then you will give me a sentence. Shoulders – listen to me first –

These are my shoulders. (Pause) Nose. This is my nose. Listen to me. Look at me. (Pause) Eyes. These are my eyes. (Pause) Now who can do the sentences again? I will give you the word, you give me the sentence. Who can do the sentences?

In 1992 explaining and directing took up 29 percent of the lesson – still quite high but definitely a reduction from two years previously. For example, in the following 1992 lesson extract, Ali is comparatively succinct.

A: Look at the pictures, please. Who can tell me what the first picture is? What is the first picture?
S10: A pen.
A: Yes. A pen.

Ali appears to have trained his pupils. In 1992 there are occasions when he does not actually ask a direct question, but the pupils know what is expected of them.

A: Look at this.
Ss: A bag.
A: What color (is) my bag? What color (is) my bag?
Ss: Brown.

It is difficult to say what caused this change. It may be that in 1990, Ali, as a new and inexperienced teacher in his first year of teaching, was overcompensating for a possible lack of response from his pupils. He could have been trying too hard to ensure that his pupils understood what they had to do. Or he could simply have been nervous because of the camera in the classroom, although videotaping of lessons had been a regular part of his training college course. In addition, his inspector would have made only a maximum of two classroom advisory visits at the time of recording the 1990 lesson and, therefore, may not have focused on this aspect of his classroom behavior.

By 1992, as a more experienced and confident teacher, Ali avoids an excessive amount of direction and explanation. The nature of the teacher's book guidenotes in the new curriculum may also be a contributing factor, although there are in fact frequent occasions when Ali does not follow these closely. One of the design features of the guidenotes was the insertion in bold type of suggested teacher classroom language:

Tell me about this picture.

Briefly elicit the language that the pupils can produce about these pictures . . .
(*Our World Through English: Fourth Elementary Teacher's Book B* 1990: 18)

This kind of guidance may possibly have had an effect upon Ali's classroom style.

A further aspect of Ali's teaching behavior that had changed, although less obviously, was the time spent on pupil responses. In 1990 he spent only 4 percent of the lesson attending to pupil responses; in 1992 he spent nearly double this amount on encouraging and building upon his pupils' responses. (The symbol "S?" indicates an unidentified student.)

A: Yes, good. After a blue pen?
S3:   An apple.
A: Yes. After an apple?
S17:   A rat.
A: A rat. Yes. Well done.
S16:   A box.
A: A box. Yes. Last picture?
S13:   Bottles.
A: No not bottles. Try again.
S?   Tins.
A: Yes, good. Tins.
Ss: Tins.

Between 1990 and 1992, it is fair to say that Ali's teaching style has changed for the better, according to the value system described earlier, and that his pupils' performance in oral classwork, while not necessarily totally reflecting currently accepted "good" practice, has also improved. The same cannot, unfortunately, be said of the second teacher, Sheikha, involved in the study. Table 4 provides information on the verbal behavior in Sheikha's classroom in 1990 and 1992.

Although the amount of time that Sheikha's students speak has increased from 16 to 24 percent of the lesson, this is much less of an increase than we saw in Ali's lesson. In addition, an analysis of the language indicates that the quality and length of utterances have not improved.

In 1990, Sheikha's lesson was characterized by the type of exchange illustrated as follows. "Sh" represents Sheikha; "Ss" represents a group of students; "S?" indicates an unidentified student; "S1" and so on stands for an identified student.

Sh: Are they short legs or long legs? Are they short legs or long legs? Are they short legs?
Ss: No.
Sh: OK. Has it got a long neck? Has it got a long neck?
S?: No.
Sh: No?

TABLE 4   ANALYSIS OF CLASSROOM VERBAL BEHAVIOR: TEACHER 2 – SHEIKHA

	Lesson 1 January 1990 36 minutes	*Lesson 2 March 1992 42 minutes*
Teacher lectures, describes, explains, narrates, directs.	38%	31%
Teacher questions about content or procedure, which pupils are intended to answer.	34%	29%
Teacher responds, accepts pupils' feelings; praises, encourages; accepts or uses pupils' ideas, builds upon pupil responses.	6%	8%
Pupils respond directly and predictably to teacher questions and directions.	16%	24%
Pupils volunteer information, comments, or questions.	0%	0%
Silence. Blackboard work without accompanying teacher talk, writing activity.	6%	8%

S?: Yes.
Sh: Look at the neck. Is it long or short, [S1]?
S1: Long.

In the 1991–1992 academic year, despite a series of one-day in-service seminars and regular advisory visits from her inspector, Sheikha's approach has not changed much. As a result, the pupils did not say more than one word at a time and the lesson was still very teacher-centered, as the following extract indicates. The teaching guidenotes were not followed; Sheikha wrote the verbs on the blackboard first rather than eliciting these from the pupils as indicated in the teacher's book.

[Sh. writes the following past tense verbs on blackboard: *covered, arrived, saw, thanked, saw, stopped.*]
Sh: Look at this one. [Points at a verb.] Look at the first one. What is this? Try to do it. [S1], come on. Try. Never mind. . . . Well, what is it? OK. What about this, [S2]? Yes, [S3].
S3: Arrived.
Sh: What is this?
Ss: Arrived.
Sh: Arrived. Thank you. What about this?
Ss: Sew.

Sh: No, not sewing. Saw. Saw. Very good. Say it together.
Ss: Saw.
Sh: [S2].
S2: Saw.
Sh: Saw.

Sheikha dominates the proceedings while the students produce only one-word responses to her questions – mainly in chorus and only individually when called upon. There is no evidence, even later in the lesson when they are supposed to be retelling the story, that they can produce utterances of more than one or two words. (The names that Sheikha uses are characters in the story or random names she selects as a pedagogic device.)

Sh: Look at picture number 1. Who saw? Who saw? Me and Bilquis?
Ss: No.
Sh: Who saw? Who saw?
Ss: Badr and Maymoona.
Sh: B. Capital B for . . .
Ss: Badr.
Sh: M for . . .
Ss: Maymoona.
Sh: So Badr and Maymoona saw. Covered. Who covered? Who covered? Badria and Abbas?
Ss: No.
Sh: Najma and Ali?
Ss: No.
Sh: Maymoona and . . . ?
Ss: Badr.

Two specific aspects of Sheikha's teaching behavior that had changed very little were her questioning and explanation techniques. The amount of time taken up with the teacher's questioning was almost the same in both lessons – in 1990, 34 percent; in 1992, 29 percent. The amount of time spent in directing and explaining likewise did not change much from 1990 to 1992 (38 percent vs. 31 percent of the lesson).

It is interesting that in all the recorded lessons (from both Sheikha *and* Ali), the amount of time that pupils volunteered information or questioned the teacher remained constant. The pupils never initiated any of the classroom moves. Two possible explanations are the comparatively formal atmosphere of the Omani classroom, where the teacher is seen as the controlling dispenser of information, and the young age (ten) of the pupils.

Discussion

In this section I widen the discussion and relate the data examined previously to broader issues of curriculum renewal. The problems involved are discussed, and some suggestions made for alternative procedures in future projects.

Problems of curriculum renewal

As a number of writers have noted, effecting curriculum renewal is a complex process. Putting a new curriculum in place does not necessarily mean that a change in classroom behaviors will occur. Nunan (1988: 138–141), for example, discusses the frequent mismatch between what was planned (the *planned* curriculum) and what actually occurs in the language classroom (the *implemented* curriculum). He also emphasizes the importance of establishing the degree of mismatch (the *evaluated* or *assessed* curriculum). White (1988), citing Sockett (1976: 22), continues the latter's metaphor of comparing a curriculum with the plan of a house, but takes the metaphor further, saying that the curriculum is three things. First, it is the plan which is "directed towards an objective yet to be realized." Second, it is the plan of *how* to build the house – "the systems that are needed in order successfully to build the house." Third, he says that curriculum also has to include the view of the house after it has been completed – and how it matches up to requirements and expectations. This important evaluative aspect provides a feedback loop so that "planned and actual outcomes can be compared and appropriate remedial action taken to repair failures or deficits" (White 1988: 4).

How does this relate to the data from the Omani curriculum project examined? As indicated, the curriculum *planners* provided new materials designed specifically for the Omani context, as well as a program of teacher and inspector development courses. Attempts were also made to *evaluate* in a formative way the *implemented* curriculum from a number of viewpoints. In the next section, I examine the problems that arise during this evaluative loop of curriculum renewal.

Problems of evaluation

Who should be involved in the evaluation of the implemented curriculum has been the subject of some discussion. Indeed, as noted by Alderson and Beretta (1992: 60), "The insider-outsider issue is currently hot in the evaluation literature." Rea-Dickens and Germaine (1992: 67) point out that once "it was widely held that evaluation could only be conducted by outsiders because this was the only way in which objectivity could be achieved." They also note that this concern over biased data led to the belief that "an insider such as a classroom teacher or an inspector was unsuitable because their judgements would be too subjective" (ibid.).

Alderson and Scott (1992) argue for a collaborative approach:

Participatory evaluation is the most satisfactory, because it is the most complete way of carrying out evaluation. It is also evidently a more democratic way of proceeding than the JIJOE ('Jet-In Jet-Out Expert') model. (p. 54)

As they point out, however, such an approach "necessarily involves a lot more time and effort, because of communication between all interested parties" (ibid.). Alderson and Beretta (1992: 60) indicate that although insider evaluations might be more trusted and therefore actually used, "one of the principal arguments in favor of an outside evaluation is that it might provide a *fresh* perspective."

Alderson (1992: 282) sums up the current debate on a different aspect of evaluation: "One of the most vexed questions in evaluation about which would-be evaluators feel unsure is how is the evaluation to be conducted." Lynch (1992: 94) feels that a combination of both qualitative and quantitative approaches is the most effective. Long (1984) similarly argues that without a process-oriented approach to evaluation, any analysis of the product (student performance) presents an incomplete picture.

One of the problems inherent in a descriptive, data-based process approach to evaluation is that the conclusions reached can be different according to the source. This is the case with the data obtained during the current study. Qualitative research of this type must therefore use a variety of sources in order to enable triangulation of the data. An advantage of such evaluation, however, is that it need not be threatening but can be both an awareness-raising process and a professional development activity. Evaluation is complex and it would be unrealistic to always assume that things will happen as expected. As Alderson and Beretta (1992: 272) say:

[I]n the real, messy, political, ever-changing world of education, educational politics and personalities, compromises are the order of the day, where ideal designs for evaluation studies have to be sacrificed at the altar of undefined aims, where hopes and fears abound, and where evaluation methodologies and foci are arrived at all too often 'on the hoof' – in a rush, without deliberation or negotiation and in some confusion.

Next, I examine whether the evaluation process obtained the desired information and make suggestions for areas that, with 20/20 hindsight, would have benefited from further study.

Implications

What lessons can be learned from this study that might be generalizable to the evaluation aspect of projects elsewhere? Acknowledging Alderson's (1992: 274) warning that it is impossible to find the "One Best Way of conducting an evaluation," did this evaluation of curriculum reform provide conclusive evidence of success or failure in improving either students' speaking performance or teachers' classroom behavior?

There is a reasonable indication that there has been a *perceived* improvement in students' speaking performance. Inspectors consider with little dissension that this is indeed the case. However, I feel that this perception is only an indication and that I cannot draw summative conclusions. A useful follow-up to the evaluation process would be to discuss with the inspectors (either individually or as a group) the videotapes or the transcripts of the lessons analyzed in this chapter.

It is unclear whether teachers see an improvement in students' speaking skills – either the format or conduct of the meetings of teachers may have contributed to this lack of evidence. A different and interesting set of data might have been obtained if interviews had been conducted with a sample of teachers familiar with both the former and the new course materials.

The video evidence is only partially indicative of improvements in pupil and teacher behavior. It seems that Ali has settled down as a teacher and that his pupils are allowed to talk much more than previously. He appears more relaxed and recognizes the need for opportunities for pupils to talk, although his lessons, reflecting the norm in Omani classrooms, are teacher- rather than student-centered. It seems that Sheikha's classroom behavior, on the other hand, has undergone little change, with the perceived result that her pupils' oral participation does not improve very much over time. Further interesting research would be to discuss the videotaped lessons (including lesson plan objectives) with the teachers and then to see whether there is change in subsequent lessons.

The teachers were involved in a variety of professional development activities (e.g., regular classroom advisory visits by inspectors and a series of short orientation courses conducted before and as the new courses were introduced). But we do not have sufficient information on whether Sheikha would have responded to a different model of professional development. It is unclear whether an approach encouraging Sheikha to reflect more upon her teaching (by using audio or videotape recordings, for example, or by keeping a diary) might have been more effective. Although Ali seems to have benefited from the various professional development experiences available, Sheikha may have been more responsive to a different type of experience.

It is perhaps this last point that is most important. New courses can be devised, new materials written. Inspectors and teachers can contribute to the development of these courses and materials and can be invited to provide evaluative comments based on subsequent classroom experience. In addition, essential professional development can take place in various ways, but what is actually important is what happens in individual classrooms – in the interactions between teachers and pupils.

These classroom interactions must be monitored, and not just by occasional external visitors. Getting teachers and learners to reflect upon their own teaching and learning, in a systematic and structured way, has the potential to provide valuable insights into the effects of curricular changes. Moreover, an approach to professional development involving both self- and peer observation can become the very vehicle for implementing such curriculum change – the information emerging from such observations can be promulgated through small group discussion so that an increasing number of individuals in the network are involved. Such procedures were lacking in the curriculum innovation that I have briefly described. Teachers were asked to reflect on a regular basis upon the materials they used, but less regularly on *how* they used the materials. Such an addition might well have been a useful part of the battery of formative evaluation procedures and instruments.

Conclusion

Planning, implementing, and evaluating curriculum renewal is a complex process, dealing with people's beliefs, interests, expectations, feelings, and emotions. It is difficult, if not impossible, to "get it right" all of the time, both in terms of process and product – and in the evaluation of both. I felt it important, however, to document what happened in one aspect of the Omani curriculum project, in the hope that it may be useful to practitioners working elsewhere. The various voices mentioned in this chapter – inspectors, classroom teachers, and learners – have provided the data which have made the study possible; my thanks and acknowledgement must therefore go to all those people involved.

References

Alderson, J. C. 1992. Guidelines for the evaluation of language education. In J. C. Alderson and A. Beretta (eds.), *Evaluating Second Language Education*. Cambridge: Cambridge University Press.

Alderson, J. C., and A. Beretta (eds.). 1992. *Evaluating Second language Education*. Cambridge: Cambridge University Press.

Alderson, J. C., and M. Scott 1992. Insiders, outsiders and participatory evaluation. In J. C. Alderson and A. Beretta (eds.), *Evaluating Second Language Education*. Cambridge: Cambridge University Press.

Brown, G. 1975. *Microteaching*. London: Methuen.

Flanders, N. A. 1970. *Analyzing Teaching Behavior*. Reading, MA: Addison-Wesley.

Long, M. 1984. Process and product in ESL program evaluation. *TESOL Quarterly, 18*, 3, 409–425.

Lynch, B. 1992. Evaluating a program inside and out. In J. C. Alderson and A. Beretta (eds.), *Evaluating Second Language Education*. Cambridge: Cambridge University Press.

Malamah-Thomas, A. 1987. *Classroom Interaction*. Oxford: Oxford University Press.

Ministry of Education, Minutes of Muscat Region Fourth Elementary Evaluation Meeting, 8 April 1991, Muscat.

Ministry of Education, Minutes of Rostaq Region Fourth Elementary Evaluation Meeting, 1 April 1991, Rostaq.

Nunan, D. 1988. *The Learner-Centred Curriculum*. Cambridge: Cambridge University Press.

Our World Through English; The English Language Course for the Sultanate of Oman: Fourth Elementary Teacher's Book B. 1990. Sultanate of Oman: Ministry of Education.

Project Framework: Memorandum of Understanding Signed Between the Governments of the Sultanate of Oman and the United Kingdom. 1988.

Rea-Dickens, P., and K. Germaine. 1992. *Evaluation*. Oxford: Oxford University Press.

Sockett, H. 1976. *Designing the Curriculum*. London: Open Books.

Stenhouse, L. 1975. *An Introduction to Curriculum Research and Development*. London: Heinemann.

White, R. V. 1988. *The ELT Curriculum. Design, Innovation and Management*. Oxford: Blackwell.

13 U.S. language minority students: voices from the junior high classroom

Marguerite Ann Snow, John Hyland, Lia Kamhi-Stein, and Janet Harclerode Yu

> Dare if you can to share through our
> eyes to find lost dreams within darkened
> skies . . .
>
> (Otteson 1993: 4)

The voices one hears in this chapter are in English and Spanish (although only the English will be presented in the interest of space). They come from language minority junior high school students, ages twelve to fourteen. Some were born in the United States and others immigrated from Mexico and Central America. The schools they attend are located in two distinct communities of Southern California. Five of the schools are located in the heart of the Mexican-American community in East Los Angeles; the other can be found in Central Los Angeles, an area characterized by a mix of ethnic populations and languages. The problems of the urban landscape are reflected in the schools. For teachers, they are viewed as "difficult" places to work; for students, the pressures of the home and the community spill over into the classroom. Test scores are low and student transience is high. These teachers and students are participants in a project aimed at improving instructional services for language minority students in five areas: (a) achieving English proficiency; (b) improving student role efficacy; (c) mastering math, science, and history; (d) developing the primary language to refine English literacy; and (e) demonstrating study skills for academic study and for productivity in work and careers.[1]

This chapter describes a staff development model which sought to create an instructional environment conducive to effective teaching and productive learning. Within this context, a study was undertaken to examine the reflections of students attending the classes of project teachers. Through an oral interview conducted in both English and Spanish, we recorded the voices of language minority students as they

· 1 Funding for this project was provided by a grant from the Title VII Transitional Bilingual Education Project (#T003A80343), Office of Bilingual Education and Minority Languages Affairs, U.S. Department of Education.

rated the instructional practices to which they had been exposed and described successful strategies for coping with the academic demands of school.

Theoretical underpinnings

The project incorporated both practical understanding of the school setting and a theoretical basis for implementing instructional change. It was not based on any single model of instruction or staff development, but incorporated both theory and practice. Key organizational settings and activities for ensuring the successful improvement of the program were teacher teams, training seminars, training for project advisors, active involvement of school site administrators, and close collaboration with university scholars. Taken by themselves, none of these was new. Rather they were selected because both experience with staff development in project schools and careful study of the literature on improving schooling suggested them as powerful settings and activities for the implementation of enduring innovations.

Work from three diverse sources informed the theoretical foundation and day-to-day workings of the teacher training project. The first cornerstone is in Benjamin's (1981) *The Helping Interview*. Benjamin defines techniques that assist individuals to become aware of their own needs. The assumption is that change cannot be forced to occur. Thus, it is a question of how to guide individuals into an awareness of their own needs. We believe the helping interview process, or its close analog, is fundamental to significant educational change. Any staff development effort must be humanistic and receptive to teachers' needs while simultaneously trying to promote positive change for those individuals. Benjamin's ideas address ways an individual can best assist others in change processes.

The second cornerstone, *The Action Research Planner* (Kemmis and McTaggart 1982), sets out a cyclical procedure for professional problem solving which teachers can use as they make essential changes in their teaching. This guide provides a modus operandi for implementing incremental change and embodies a procedure that teachers can use to systematically examine their teaching. Our assumption is that action research provides the means to integrate the pedagogic innovations into current classroom practice. In action research, teachers are encouraged to work together in an informed, systematic way to identify what to change, attempt a change, evaluate the attempt, and cycle new understandings into further change. Individuals are taught to avoid issues about which they can do nothing, and to focus on a realistic and manageable field of action. Thus, through incremental action research cycles, significant change can occur over time. The action research process, we believe, is also fundamental to significant educational reform in the classroom.

While *The Helping Interview* and *The Action Research Planner* served as operational guides for the project, Tharp and Gallimore's *Rousing Minds to Life* (1988) formed its theoretical rationale. Tharp and Gallimore define teaching as assisted performance by a person who is a more "capable other." Learners acquire knowledge and skills in the presence of a teacher who has the role of assisting the learner by "means of assisted performance." The means of helping learners to perform with new knowledge and skills are modeling, feeding back, contingency managing, direct instruction, responsive questioning, and cognitive restructuring. These occur in a particular "activity setting," which must be consciously organized to support the assistance of learners.

According to Tharp and Gallimore, learners come to understand new knowledge and acquire skills through the "instructional conversation," an all encompassing notion of language and literacy. Sustained learning occurs to the degree that the activity setting is organized and designed in such a way that the means of assisted performance can genuinely take place.

The instructional conversation is the medium through which assisted performance occurs; it is both the end product and the vehicle that leads to it. The concept itself contains a paradox: 'instruction' and 'conversation' appear contrary, the one implying authority and planning, the other equality and responsiveness. The task of teaching is to resolve this paradox. To most truly teach, one must converse; to truly converse is to teach (ibid.: 111)

If language minority students are expected to become active members of the U.S. school culture, then a reciprocal process must take place. These students have to gradually develop an understanding of the values and structure of the new school system; at the same time, teaching practice must become more responsive to the needs of linguistically and culturally diverse students. The study, therefore, sought to answer the following questions:

What instructional practices do language minority students view as effective?

What is the role that they see themselves playing in the transmission of school values?

How can the school environment help language minority students to socialize into the new school culture?

In what ways can language minority students help their peers become successful in the new school system?

Oral interviews

The oral interviews were designed to gauge student attitudes toward the new instructional techniques that were being implemented by project teachers and to better understand student role efficacy – how they viewed their roles as students. Sixty-six students drawn from the six junior high school sites took part in the oral interviews. They represented a cross section of the schools' language minority populations.[2] Each of the sixty-six students was interviewed individually outside of class in a quiet location; all interviews were audiotaped for later analysis.

Each interview commenced with a warm-up activity in which the students were asked to fill in the captions of two cartoons. The interview consisted of two different activities. The first was a card sort activity, conducted in English, in which the students were asked to create a "recipe" for the ideal class by selecting among a set of "ingredients." The following pairs of descriptors were printed on the opposite sides of index cards.

1. A class where I write journals in English or in Spanish.
   A class where I do not write in journals.
2. A class where I can speak English if I want to.
   A class where only English is spoken.
3. A class where the teacher is the center of attention.
   A class where I participate a lot.
4. A class where the teacher uses cooperative learning.
   A class where I work by myself.
5. A class where I learn only from the teacher.
   A class where I learn from my classmates.
6. A class where I have to take notes.
   A class where I am not expected to take notes.
7. A class where I help my classmates edit what they write before they write a final version of an assignment.
   A class where I am the only person who reads what I write before having my teacher read my assignment.

As students chose between the two descriptors on each card, they explained why they had selected these ingredients. By having students discuss their choices, we could see whether or not they understood the

2 Students are reclassified from LEP (limited English proficient) to FEP (fluent English proficient) status when they pass the district exit exams. FEP students are then mainstreamed into regular English and content-area classes. The sample included recently arrived LEP students, students who had been reclassified as FEP, students still classified as LEP despite the fact that they have been in the United States for several years, and native speakers of English from bilingual backgrounds.

instructional technique in question, and we could gain more insight into the students' needs and preferences. Students then added two ingredients of their own, again explaining why they added these items while the interviewer wrote the student-generated items on new cards. In the final step, the students arranged all the cards (including their own two ingredients) in order, from the most to the least important ingredient for the ideal class.

The second part of the interview consisted of a problem-posing activity with the same students who took part in the English portion of the oral interview. In Spanish, students were asked how they might orient a new student by explaining what he or she would need to do to be successful. The students responded to the following hypothetical problem:

Eu tu clase hay un alumno nuevo que habla muy poco inglés. Tú eres el consejero de ese alumno y debes ayudarlo. ¿Qué es lo que ese alumno tiene que hacer para convertirse en un buen alumno? ¿Cómo tiene que estudiar para un examen? Recuerda que tu debes aconsejar a tú nuevo compañero. ¡Su éxito depende de ti! [In your class there is a new student who speaks very little English. You are his advisor and you have to help him. What does the student have to do to become a good student? How does the student have to prepare for an exam? Remember that you have to help your new classmate. His success depends on you!]

The students, in general, responded readily to the task. They quickly assumed the role of the experienced student, offering advice to the newcomer. In some cases, the interviewers had to repeat parts of the question and prompt the students to respond to all parts of the situation. Five of the sixty-six students said that they could not perform the task in Spanish. They responded in English; however, their responses were not included in the analysis, since one objective of the task was to see if the students could communicate their meta-notions of student role efficacy in Spanish.

Findings of the card sort activity

After the interviews were completed, preferences chosen in the card sort activity were analyzed using a chi-square analysis. In addition, the ingredients added by the students were sorted and arranged thematically. Statistically significant preferences were found for the following descriptors of the ideal class:

A class where the teacher uses cooperative learning.
A class where I write in journals in English or Spanish.
A class where I participate a lot.
A class where I am expected to take notes.

A class where I help my classmates edit what they write before they write the final version of the assignment.
A class where I learn from my classmates.

No statistically significant preferences were obtained for the choices, "A class where I can speak English if I want to" or "A class where only English is spoken."

The reasons given by students for their choice that only English should be spoken were interesting. Some students indicated that they could learn English better if they had to use it. Others said that it would be rude or unfair to speak Spanish since some of their classmates did not understand Spanish. Some also said that it would be impolite to speak Spanish in a class where the teacher did not know what they were saying. One student indicated that he would speak Spanish only if he wanted to say something he did not want the teacher to hear.

Among the ingredients for the ideal class suggested by the students themselves, several themes emerged. The category that contained the most student-generated responses dealt with the role of the teacher. Twenty-three responses focused on teachers' attitudes and behaviors.

A class where the teacher could help you more often – the teacher can give you more quality time and work with you until you get it.
A class where the teacher can be your friend.
A class where the teacher is nice.
A class where teachers have positive attitudes.
A class where the teacher is patient.
A class where the teacher cares – where the teacher is on your back whenever you fool around.
A class where the teachers are more open and more fun.
A class where the teacher makes the class fun.
A class where the teacher helps students when they need help.
A class where I can get extra help on something I may find difficult.
A class where the shy people are encouraged to participate.
A class where everyone is encouraged to try.
A class where teachers explain the assignments well.
A class where the teacher is clear about assignments and deadlines.
A class where the teacher doesn't give too much work but gives it correctly with enough information.
A class where the teachers don't have to refer to the textbook so much.
A disciplined class where the teacher teaches well and understands.
A class where things work well; teachers help students improve their education.
A class where the teacher assigns a lot of work.
A class where teachers show you tests ahead of time to help you get a good grade.

A class where the teacher asks questions before a test so that everybody is forced to study.

A class where the teacher gives homework three times a week.

A class where teachers want you to help them when they make errors.

The second most popular category dealt with the need for student participation in class activities. One of the most frequent ingredients suggested was the need for class or group discussions. In this vein, students added the following ingredients.

A class where students talk about their feelings or emotions.

A class where we talk about students' opinions.

A class where there's time to discuss the lessons in groups.

A class where you participate in group discussions.

A class where there are more discussions about wars – anything.

A class where I can speak out and say my opinion about something I heard.

A class where you can discuss a subject.

A class where everybody participates.

A class where activities have a purpose.

A class where the students teach.

A class where students play together – like math games.

A class where I can help my classmates solve problems.

A class that has many activities and games.

A class where the teacher could be included in the groups.

A class where we do fun things.

A class where we do work.

A class where sometimes you can do a problem that you make up.

A class where the student can evaluate his own work – like in art class.

A class where you have choices.

A class where we do different assignments – variety.

A class where the kids do their own work and then get into groups to check it.

Sixteen responses reflected concern about peers' attitudes and behaviors and revealed the belief that students should be courteous to each other and follow rules for turn taking and good behavior.

A class where people are friendly and nobody says anything bad.

A class where everybody is quiet.

A class where you don't get interrupted when you're talking.

A class where students behave better.

A class where everybody cooperates.

A class where everyone cooperates.

A class where there is no peer pressure – no judgments.

A class where the students finish the work on time.

A class where everybody speaks to one another – where everybody respects one another.
A class where students do not make fun of you.
A class where there is competition with friendship.
A class where the kids don't talk while the teacher is talking.
A class where there is no speaking in Spanish if the teacher does not understand it.
A class where the kids do their homework.
A class where students are good people and not gang members.
A class where teachers and students get along.

Many responses focused on student preferences for experiential learning activities, including projects and experiments.

A class where they do more projects instead of book work.
A class with projects.
A class where we do more experiments.
To do a lot of experiments – work in groups.
A class where students are taught how to do experimental projects.
A class where there are more projects and you learn new things.
A class where you have more hands-on equipment.

A number of students made suggestions pertaining to specific school subjects, including a preference for art classes.

A class where art is taught.
A class where students draw pictures.
A class with art and painting.
A class where the students are taught how to work with wood.
A class where we make neat things like graphic arts where we made note pads.
A class where Fridays have art or music.

Other students made suggestions for social studies activities.

A class where the teacher shows historical movies to help you understand why there's freedom.
A class where we see more films.
A class where you write reports on Presidents. You learn about people's lives.
A class where I can learn about different cultures.
A class where there are history hours.

Still other students expressed ideas related to reading and writing in language arts or foreign language instruction.

A class where students write book reports.
A class where you read in groups.

A class where you do a lot of writing.
A class where there is more reading and writing.
A class where you read in English and Spanish.
A class where you can write stories about yourself.
A class where I can learn other languages.

Other suggestions for diversifying school activities included:

A class where there's a choir.
A class where you have guest speakers.
A class where you have field trips to museums and parks where you study nature.

Four students expressed a desire for fewer restrictions.

A class where there is free time to talk to other students.
A class where there is time to relax.
A class where I can listen to a radio.
A class where there is more freedom in the classroom.

In an era of large classes, several students raised the issue of class size in their portrayal of the ideal class.

A class where there's not too many people, ten to fifteen.
A class where you receive a better education – fewer students and smaller classes.
A class where there are fewer students and the teacher can help students more.
A class with 20 students per class.
A class where the teacher could help you more often – the teacher can give you more quality time and work with you until you get it.

Other comments which did not fit into the general themes just listed included the following.

A class where we wouldn't have to carry books.
A class where I like the teacher.
A class where I have a lot of friends.
A class where I like the subject.
A class with fewer exams.
A class where we could write in the books – or calculate right in the book – like worksheets.
A class where there is a psychologist to talk to.
Have more classes.
A class where the teacher has an assistant.
A class where your grade is based on many factors.
To have a lot of books in class.
A class where you read if you want to.

A class where you can speak without permission.
A class where seats are assigned.
A class where I can help my teacher.

While the students suggested varied ingredients, the findings of the card sort activity revealed that the ideal class is characterized by an atmosphere of involvement and consideration. For these students, the ideal class promotes experiential learning in the context of a disciplined environment.

Findings of the problem-posing activity

The students' responses emphasized two topics that they would share with the new student they were advising. They were (1) the need for cooperation among students, students and teachers, and students and parents; and (2) the need to understand the academic demands of the new environment. The following excerpts provide a flavor of the students' advice to the hypothetical new student.

During the interviews, most of the students emphasized the importance of cooperating with new students in order to socialize them into the school culture. Because they come from a home culture where cooperation is encouraged, they often find it difficult to enter a school culture that promotes competition (Kagan 1986; Trueba 1989). Therefore, the patterns familiar in the students' homes might help teachers and students understand the importance of promoting an atmosphere of cooperation in the classroom (Trueba 1983; Trueba and Delgado-Gaitan 1988). Luz's account (translated from Spanish to English) is an example of the importance students placed on cooperation.

I would tell my new classmate that if he needs help, I will show him how to get to his classes. I would help him in whatever I can. If he wants me to, I will introduce him to my friends, I would teach him what a good friend is.

By working cooperatively, language minority students often learn to cope with the anxiety often embedded in schools. A student named America was outspoken about the significance of sharing knowledge among students: "He should ask other people for help; in this way he can share what he knows with other people and in this way they can help themselves."

Parents are also important in the school socialization process of language minority students (Heath 1992). The family environment seems to provide students with the encouragement that results in an increased desire to do well in school. Students often attribute their success in adjusting to the school culture to their parents' mentorship (Trueba and Delgado-Gaitan 1988). Josefina's comment illustrates some of the stu-

313

dents' beliefs in the power of parental support: "The new student's parents should help him a lot; they should advise the student; they should advise the student what to do, so that he gets good grades."

For many of the students, the teacher has an important role in helping them to understand the rules of the school culture and assisting them to acquire knowledge. As Milena put it: "If he has a problem, he should ask for help from those teachers with whom he feels most comfortable."

Most of the students corroborated Trueba's (1983) finding that an understanding of the classroom structure and requirements is critical because it helps new students perform under less threatening conditions. Evelia emphasized the importance of socializing students into the rules of the classroom culture as a means to foster academic success: "The student has to complete all the assignments and study a little bit in school so that the tests are easier to take."

As Trueba (1989) argues, when language minority students are placed in the classroom they may notice that classroom activities are controlled by the teachers. Many of the students concurred with Aileen's remarks: "The new student has to pay attention to the teacher and not distract the class with jokes. He has to remember what the teacher says."

Some of the students' feelings toward tests revealed that they saw tests as events that judged the students' academic performance (Deyhle 1987). As Edgar put it, "I have to tell my classmate to study to get good grades. I would tell him to study and review his notes until he has learned them, then in the test he can get an *A* or a *B*."

Contrary to Tyler's (1979) earlier notion that children from lower socio-economic classes do not take testing seriously, many of the students in this impoverished urban setting emphasized the importance of preparing for tests. For instance, America explained how she would help her new classmate prepare for a test.

I am going to help my new classmate prepare for all the tests by studying all day long. I am going to tell him to do all the problems that are going to be on the test so that he can learn them well.

Josefina, among others, emphasized the importance of teaching her new classmate study skills to be used in preparing for a test.

I would tell my new classmate that he can read the book he is given, especially those parts that he thinks he does not know, he underlines them, and then studies them. Then, he tells a friend to help him explain what the book says, or he can ask his parents, brother, or sister. If he does not remember a word, he should skip it and return to it later.

Finally, many of the students felt strongly motivated to graduate from high school and continue studying at the university. Amilkar, among

314

other students, stated, "My classmate has to study. This is the only way to become somebody in life. He has to bring to class all that is asked for, his books, his homework, and he has to do the work there in class."

In summary, the findings of the problem-posing activity show that students may play a critical role in helping their peers' transition from home to school and that the students interviewed are aware of learning strategies which promote school success. Finally, the students' cooperative orientation emphasizes the importance of creating a school environment that promotes cooperative modes of learning.

Discussion and conclusion

The project in this study was designed around a set of activities which our experience and study of schooling literature suggested would improve in the instruction of language minority students. These ideas and practices resulted in a comprehensive teacher training program which focused on such instructional techniques as cooperative learning, sheltered English, journal writing, and other communicative language activities. Teachers also designed individual action research projects involving the implementation of the instructional practices introduced in the training workshops. In a study of the action research model used in the project, Moran (1994) looked at four project teachers considered "high level" and "low level" action researchers. She found that the two teachers who participated fully in action research – particularly in observation, reflection, and collaboration – were the more successful classroom innovators. The high level action researchers also had a prior attraction to research and sought "excitement" in their work. The low level action researchers were less intrinsically motivated and sought "comfort" in their work.

The oral interview findings revealed that the students liked the instructional techniques they had been exposed to in the project. They rated such activities as journal writing, cooperative learning, peer editing, group work, and notetaking highly. It is also obvious from the student-generated ingredients that these language minority students had much to say about ways to improve instruction. They expressed high expectations for their teachers, offering many suggestions for the ideal role teachers might play. Clearly they embraced a learner-centered classroom, calling for increased student participation, more hands-on projects, and opportunities to discuss issues of concern. These students, in spite of their at-risk academic status, generally displayed maturity and facility in articulating the features of the ideal class. They sought organized, disciplined classrooms where students were polite to each other and respected their peers and teachers. Few of the comments were friv-

315

olous or glib; rather, emanating from the interviews was a sense of seriousness about their education and a validation that instructional activities which involve students actively are highly valued.

The findings of the problem-posing scenario involving the hypothetical new student demonstrate that the language minority students interviewed are acquiring learner role efficacy: They are able to articulate strategies for success in school even though their previous academic records have been, at best, spotty. Through the role play, we can see that the students are developing metacognitive awareness of appropriate learning strategies, as discussed by Chamot and O'Malley (1987), which contributes to academic success. It should be noted that we were interested in the students' reactions to classroom practices and their perceptions of student role efficacy as part of the development of metacognitive awareness. We are, therefore, making no claims about actual classroom behavior based on these data. Findings from Moran (1994), however, indicated that teachers' observations of increased student motivation and achievement as a result of project participation encouraged them to continue with the instructional innovations being implemented.

On a more practical level, the findings also indicate that students believe they can play an important role in helping new arrivals socialize into the school system. Language minority students' experiences in the educational system can be used to promote a newcomer's awareness of the academic demands. Furthermore, the students' cooperative orientation underscores the need for administrators and teachers to promote an atmosphere which will ultimately lead not only to more effective academic socialization, but also to the design of learning experiences which tap students' strengths.

The oral interviews allowed us as researchers and teacher trainers to engage in an instructional conversation with the students, in which they revealed their insights into effective instruction and their perceptions of strategies for successful academic behavior. Curiously, seldom are students' opinions solicited at this age level, yet they are the ultimate consumers of the techniques and practices we present to teachers during in-service training programs. It is our hope that the findings of this study will provide direction to teacher trainers and curriculum developers. Moreover, we hope that similar studies will be conducted with other language minority populations so that teacher training can truly be a cyclic process – bringing students' voices into the loop.

References

Benjamin, A. 1981. *The Helping Interview.* Boston: Houghton Mifflin.

Chamot, A. U., and J. M. O'Malley. 1987. The cognitive academic language learning approach. *TESOL Quarterly,* 21, 2, 227–247.

Deyhle, D. 1987. Learning failure: Tests as gatekeepers and the culturally different child. In H. Trueba (ed.), *Success or Failure? Learning and the Language Minority Student*. New York: Newbury House.

Heath, S. B. 1992. Sociocultural contexts of language development. In P. Richard-Amato and M. A. Snow (eds.), *The Multicultural Classroom: Readings for Content-Area Teachers*. New York: Longman.

Kagan, S. 1986. Cooperative learning and sociocultural factors in schooling. In *California State Department of Education Beyond Language: Social and Cultural Factors in Schooling Language Minority Students*. Los Angeles, CA: Evaluation, Dissemination and Assessment Center, California State University, Los Angeles.

Kemmis, S., and R. McTaggart. 1982. *The Action Research Planner*. Victoria, Australia: Deakin University Press.

Moran, M. A. 1994. A Case Study of an Action Researched–Based Staff Development Effort: Four Teachers' Stories. Unpublished doctoral dissertation, University of California, Los Angeles.

Otteson, C. C. 1993. *L.A. Stories: The Voices of Cultural Diversity*. Yarmouth, ME: Intercultural Press, Inc.

Tharp, R., and R. Gallimore. 1988. *Rousing Minds to Life: Teaching, Learning and Schooling in Social Context*. Cambridge: Cambridge University Press.

Trueba, H. 1983. Adjustment problems of Mexican American children: An anthropological study. *Learning Disabilities Quarterly, 6*, 395–415.

1989. *Raising Silent Voices: Educating the Linguistic Minorities for the 21st Century*. New York: Newbury House.

Trueba, H., and C. Delgado-Gaitan. 1988. *School and Society: Learning Content Through Culture*. New York: Praeger.

Tyler, R. W. 1979. Educational objectives and educational testing: Problems now faced. In R. Tyler and S. H. White (eds.), *Testing, Teaching, and Learning*. Washington, DC: National Institute of Education.

14 Voices for improved learning: the ethnographer as co-agent of pedagogic change

Peter A. Shaw

> Calvin Coolidge didn't say much, and
> when he did he didn't say much.
>
> (Will Rogers)

> See all, hear all,
> Say nowt;
> Eat all, sup all,
> Pay nowt;
> And if tha ever does owt for nowt,
> Do it for thisen.
>
> (Old Yorkshire saying)

This chapter describes changes in the patterns of learning and teaching which took place subsequent to the introduction of a new curriculum. The curriculum discussed here is the advanced level foreign language component of the International Policy Studies program at a graduate school which trains bilingual professionals. The chapter is written from my point of view, as the ethnographic researcher given the responsibility of monitoring the new courses and reporting on their effectiveness. My intention is to show how my privileged position, with access (both inside and outside the classroom) to all participants, permitted me to combine the muted murmurs of individual concern into one voice, thus allowing the clear identification of certain problems and the positing of appropriate solutions. In other words, by attending to classroom events and by listening to students' and teachers' views and interpretations of these events, I was able to occasionally intervene and attempt to expedite and comment on possible improvements.

Ethnographers are traditionally silent observers, as typically unforthcoming as U.S. President Coolidge or my tight-lipped ancestors in Yorkshire. Nevertheless, in this chapter I will also explore the role of the

I would like to thank all the teachers and students who participated in this project for their endless interest and unblemished cooperation. I truly appreciated the opportunity to be there, and I commend them all for their hard work and creativity.

318

researcher as agent of change, as it came about in this project.[1] It was my intention to use the data obtained from these classrooms to fulfill the basic requirements of such research – namely, to develop a narrative account of the curriculum renewal process and to furnish a basis for assessing the effectiveness of the new approach. However, it became clear to me quite early in the process that a number of factors were pushing me into a more active role. These factors are explored herein, but first, the background circumstances must be presented.

The program

The Monterey Institute of International Studies (MIIS) encapsulates its purpose in the following mission statement:

> MIIS is an academic community committed to preparing innovative professionals able to provide leadership in cross-cultural, multi-lingual environments.

Its programs in management and policy studies have substantial foreign language components (admission requirements of significant previous experience with the foreign language and a minimum of twelve units of further study). In recent years, it became apparent that traditional foreign language courses in literature, culture, and thought; advanced grammar; and advanced conversation were neither appropriate nor sufficient, and interest developed in the notion of content-based instruction (CBI), in which business, economics, and political subject matter would be delivered in the students' foreign language. This approach was favored in terms of practicality (the experience would facilitate future professional performance) and motivation (students would be more interested in language classes which are a vehicle for content relevant to their professional interests). The belief was that advanced level language learners could best proceed to higher levels of proficiency by addressing the language as a means of communicating ideas. Practice is provided in CBI courses in all four skill areas, and learning is boosted by the interest and motivation generated by the subject matter. Support for a CBI approach also came from a needs analysis conducted among MIIS students. The results confirmed the students' strong interest in CBI, their preference for increased fluency and communicative skills over accuracy, and their dissatisfaction with traditional instructional formats.

The program involved in the work discussed here is International Policy Studies (IPS), which consists of a core of courses in policy analysis, economics, international relations, and area studies. Students then

---

1 For discussions of researchers' competing roles in other contexts, see Delgado-Gaitan (1993), Elliott (1991), Heath (1987), Maxwell (1992), and van Lier (this volume).

select a specialization, usually a regional expertise appropriate to their foreign language. The goal of the program is to produce graduates who can do policy research in at least two languages.

At this point, the resources available to curriculum planners were considered. These consisted largely of faculty: either language professors with background, expertise, and interest in relevant subject areas, or IPS professors who were capable of offering or participating in instruction in a language other than English. A grant from the Pew Charitable Trusts allowed faculty the necessary release time to develop a new curriculum.

Curriculum

One of the outcomes of the early thinking and planning for the new curriculum was the realization that the most effective deployment of resources (in particular, the knowledge and skills of the faculty) would involve multiple instructional formats rather than one particular kind of course. Thus, some featured a solo instructor, others a team of two or more. Some were conducted entirely in the foreign language, others featured the foreign language and English, while a third category involved English and multiple foreign languages. An example of a simple format was *Kokusaikasuru nihon* (the Internationalization of Japan), taught entirely in Japanese by an IPS professor who is a native speaker of Japanese. A more complex design was seen in The Comparative Politics of Western Europe, which featured a plenary session taught in English by an IPS specialist. In the plenary session, for example, legislative systems were surveyed and examples were drawn from various countries. The foreign language sections (in French, German, and Spanish) each followed up with detailed consideration of the legislature of one country. These classes were led by language faculty with sufficient background in politics and government.

The distinctions among the different instructional formats are not significant for this paper and are not pursued here. (See Baker [1992] for additional information). The learning problems identified in the ethnography were common to students in all types of course organization.

While there is typically considerable interaction among the faculty of MIIS on a variety of issues (including curriculum content), there is usually little or no discussion of classroom instructional practices. Thus, the planning meetings I attended were characterized by prolonged and detailed consideration of three issues: selecting and grading course content, identifying appropriate written and audio-visual materials, and setting the ends and means of assessing student learning. In interviews with subject matter instructors, I discovered a fairly uniform reliance on a standard pedagogical package: assigned readings, instructors' lectures, question-and-answer sessions, class discussions, and individual student presentation of projects, with a written version due at the end of the semester.

Research components

In order to monitor the progress of the new courses and to establish a data base for the subsequent assessment of their effectiveness, the following activities were undertaken.

1. *Ethnographic observation.* For selected classes, the fieldnote record is intensive, with an observer assigned to almost all class sessions. However, most courses were observed on random occasions, averaging approximately every third class meeting. The voice of the ethnographer is represented here by excerpts from the fieldnotes.
2. *Student diaries.* Roughly one student in four kept a diary. They wrote about their learning experiences inside and outside the classroom. Guidelines and focus questions were provided at the outset, and every two or three weeks I read and responded to the entries. My responses were intended to maintain the focus on crucial issues, to ask clarification questions, and to ask for further details, as well as to provide encouragement to students. The voice of the students appears here in excerpts from these diaries.
3. *Debriefing interviews.* Individual professors, instructional teams, single students, and groups of students participated in interviews (partly structured and partly open-ended), both during particular courses and at their conclusion. These participants' voices appear in direct quotations from these interviews.
4. *Tapes and transcripts.* Class sessions were recorded (some on videotape, most on audiotape) and transcriptions were made. The voices of students and professors are presented in these excerpts.

These activities provided representative samples of classroom events (activities one and four) and of participants' feelings about and interpretations of those events (two and three). I hope to show here, by quoting from all four data sets, that together they provide a richly textured chorus of voices, with a message-laden lyric, although not always completely in tune with one another.

The ethnographer's dilemma

I mentioned at the outset that I had been pushed into a more active role in this study than is normally accorded to an ethnographer. The factors exerting this pressure included the following.

321

1. As a member of the MIIS community and of a team involved in the implementation of a new curriculum, I had a commitment to these particular learners and teachers at this specific time. Developing an insight in private and informing the world later would not help the classes already in progress.
2. My aim as an ethnographer was different from that of the traditional cultural anthropologist: I was not there to record a culture for posterity but to document the implementation of a new idea and to provide feedback.
3. While the plan was strong and relatively complete in terms of curriculum content and assessment, pedagogic details were not planned and, in part, had to be created en route. It was not unexpected, therefore, that my role relative to curriculum content would be different from that vis-à-vis pedagogy.
4. It is not currently the nature of applied linguistics to produce narrow specialists. It is unusual, I believe, for someone trained in the field as an ethnographic researcher not to be conversant with current methodological practice. In this case, I did not throw the ethnographer's cloak over my methodologist's uniform and go in disguise; I was always both, because they are in the final analysis inseparable (see, for example, Boomer 1987).

While the great majority of the adjustments made in these classes were achieved by the participants alone, from time to time, in the face of certain interesting problems, I was asked for suggestions or advice.

Thus arose what I am calling the ethnographer's dilemma. Just as sportswriters cannot enter the field of play, just as judges cannot help lawyers with their cases, so, I had always assumed, the ethnographer records, describes, and analyses but may not interfere. Our lot is to be there and to tell the tale. Judges, I am sure, often see missed opportunities and, in their own minds, reformulate botched arguments; sportswriters are full of bright ideas on Monday to prevent Sunday's loss. But judges must keep their ideas to themselves and sportswriters must stay in the press box. Can ethnographers legitimately participate in a process they have been hired to observe?

I believe that the dilemma has two components in this case. One is the institutional ethnographer's dilemma: As part of the team, a stakeholder in the enterprise, can one pass up an opportunity to suggest an improvement simply because one is not a primary participant? The second is the dilemma of the ethnographer with relevant expertise: Is it not surely more difficult to keep quiet when one's suggestions are based on experience and expertise pertinent to the problem at hand?

I shall return to these questions later to propose the notion of the consulting ethnographer, a researcher who is an active member of the curriculum renewal community and who exploits a unique perspective to strengthen the process.

The four cases

To establish the pattern of the learning improvement process, four cases are briefly described, those of (a) jigsaw reading, (b) a process approach to writing, (c) learner training, and (d) the use of group work. In each case, the particular problem is defined, the data sources are catalogued and exemplified, and the solution is described. The voices from these classrooms will thus be heard first complaining or describing problems, then nominating or reacting to suggested solutions, and finally discussing the effectiveness of actual solutions.

The case of jigsaw reading

This section sketches various difficulties related to reading authentic material in the foreign language and shows how one specific solution emerged – namely, the use of the "jigsaw reading" technique, whereby individual students or small groups are assigned one article or chapter and asked to study it closely enough to be able to instruct their class-mates in its key points, thus freeing students from the burden of having to read everything assigned (for jigsaw theory and practice, see Aronson [1978] and Slavin [1990]).

PROBLEM

In some cases, instuctors set the normal reading load, making no concession for the fact that all reading materials were not in the students' native language. In addition, the courses were set up under the traditional graduate school norm that all students read all materials. Consequently, the reading load became, in some cases, a major challenge, and in others, overwhelming to most or all students.

DATA SOURCES

Information detailing the reading load problem came from three sources: student diaries, classroom observations, and student interviews. It is an axiom of graduate education that students read a lot; in fact, all students are responsible for all the set reading for each class session as well as their own library research and background reading. However, the early diary entries in all courses contain many complaints about the reading load, and such comments were frequent in student interviews. Even when instructors had consciously selected a relatively lighter load because of the language circumstances, students often found it unmanageable. The following are typical comments from student interviews. (The language of instruction is given in brackets when not otherwise apparent.)

The reading load is enormous and varies a lot in difficulty. This last week I spent 4 hours on a ten-page article. [Spanish]

The readings are very long and dry. [German]

I'm spending as much time on the reading for this class as for all my other classes combined. [Japanese]

The difficulties generally sorted themselves into three basic issues: sheer volume, vocabulary load, and discourse problems, usually with identifying main points. The following diary entries were typical.

The next reading looks really long and difficult – the amount of new vocabulary is so overwhelming that I'm not even taking it in. If I were taking only this class I could afford the time to study each word and make it part of my active vocabulary, but it's impossible in this situation, unfortunately. Words don't reoccur naturally that much because we're switching topic each week, so I can't depend on reinforcement. [Spanish]

Major headache with the book. Frustrating! First I read it normally and then I practice sight translation with it – it's fine as the terminology is all there and the style is, to say the least, direct. But there's so much of it! [French]

The vocabulary issue seemed to encompass background knowledge as well as simply knowing first and second language equivalents. A Spanish instructor pointed out to me how often his solicitation of vocabulary questions is met with silence, yet this is clearly a major obstacle. A few days later, the following incident in his class was documented in my fieldnotes.

There is another long silence following this question, which is wryly noted by the instructor: "Silencio completo." It prompts him to ask if there are any questions about vocabulary in this text; there are none, though F7 comments that when she looked up the words she didn't know, she didn't know the English words either. There is sympathetic laughter at this.

Many students stressed how the vocabulary problem has a negative impact on classroom events, causing instructors to change plans in order to remediate knowledge gaps caused by reading problems. The following comment is from a student interview.

The problem is that we don't have enough time to do the primary reading, so setting background material to read doesn't help. So the instructor ends up using class time to give us a context for the reading – which is sort of crucial but takes time from discussions. [Spanish]

A number of diarists reported necessary compromises with regard to the literature.

The readings seem to have gotten progressively longer and more difficult and so hard to keep up with. I have had to limit myself to only those materials which will be useful to me when writing my paper and learn about the other countries through the lecture and presentations. I don't know if this is a good way to go about things but it's the only way for me to get a handle on my work load. [Spanish]

An interesting perspective on the reading issue came from students who were native speakers of the languages of instruction. Here, in her diary, a native speaker of Japanese relates the reading difficulties of her American classmates to discourse differences between the two languages.

Today's content was hard for even Japanese to understand enough. How do Americans understand the content? When I read Japanese articles, sometimes I wonder why Japanese structure is so ambiguous that you cannot understand what it want to say. It is obvious even in one sentence. In English the result which you want to say comes first, then the reason why you think so follows. So, since you can know first the result, it is easy to follow the following sentences. However, in Japanese, because the result comes last, you do not know what the author want to say consequently. In other words, you have to guess the result to follow the sentences until last paragraph. Moreover, because some sentences are very abstract, even though you guess a result for the article, the sentence make you confuse.

This account is strongly echoed in comments from American students. Here is a typical remark made during a mid-semester interview.

When things are presented logically in Japanese – er and that's not very often – my western mind seems more capable of following them. Some of the readings and some sentence and paragraph structures are a real struggle for me and I lose the flow of argument or the central point. Then my motivation to keep reading goes way down.

In summary, students voiced frequent complaints about the required reading, citing three broad problems: the overall amount, the lexical challenge, and the discourse complexities.

SOLUTION

Responses to these difficulties were varied. Some instructors lightened the load, making certain texts optional. Others urged greater concentration and application. One or two made suggestions for more effective reading strategies, stressing that total comprehension of all texts was not necessary and skimming for main points was sometimes appropriate. The most successful response, however, was to make some arrangement whereby responsibility for covering the reading material was distributed among the students, that is, to use the technique of jigsaw reading.

In one case, in a debriefing interview, the instructor of the German section of Comparative Politics of Western Europe indicated that he would reduce the reading load the next time the course was offered to two articles per week and give time in class for the students in two groups (one group per article) to prepare their positions on this material. Class discussion would then follow. This way, he felt, the students would "do the work themselves" and free him to add his own emphasis and focus, rather than have to lecture extensively on material few students had read.

In a second example, in *Movimientos sociales en america latina,* one pair of students was assigned to each of the set readings. The pairs then had the responsibility of reporting the main points to their colleagues. This approach was initiated by students, who addressed their concerns to me very directly in their diary.

The reading load is killing me, all of us in fact. Can you give us any suggestions we can take to the instructor? It's all obviously interesting and important stuff, but we simply can't handle it. When we raise the issue, [the instructor] just says there's nothing that can be omitted.

My response was to suggest a jigsaw arrangement with individual students or small groups each responsible for one of the readings and class time allocated for sharing the main points and insights. The instructor proved happy to accept this suggestion, and the system was praised by all participants. One student commented in an exit interview:

The funny thing is I feel as confident about some of the material I didn't read it as the stuff I did get to. Somehow, it's much clearer when someone else explains it to you.

This kind of arrangement was also reached by the students themselves, acting independently outside of class. One diary entry states, "I occasionally meet with other students in the German section to discuss our readings – one of us will take one chapter and then we swap information." The value of this strategy is seen not only in dealing more effectively with the reading load but also in facilitating class discussions by providing what the students described as a "ground clearing service," leaving the instructor free to focus on key specifics. In another case, students not only took the initiative in forming discussion groups out of class time, but also invited native speakers of the foreign language, in this case Japanese, to join them as an extra resource. The diary reports:

The Americans decided we wanted to get together with at least one or two Japanese to discuss the reading by [X] that was so vague and abstract. [Two Japanese] showed up and we ended up having a very interesting and informative discussion. . . . The two Japanese were more outspoken than they'd ever been in class before, and I understood what the discussion was about much better than usual.

With respect to reading issues, the voices of concern were never entirely stilled. In some courses, the volume and the level of difficulty were objects of complaint and remorse until the end; in most, however, these plaintive solos were drowned out by the chorus of creative solutions.

The case of a process approach to writing

In this section, students voice their concerns about writing papers in the foreign language and call for a more process-oriented approach, with students receiving different kinds of feedback on various drafts of their paper.

PROBLEM

Through the influence of advocates such as Elbow (1973), ideas about writing as a process have been widespread for some time. However, college professors in the subject areas still tend to focus on the product, the final draft of students' papers. In the case of these courses, some instructors made concessions to the fact that students would not be writing papers in their mother tongue (and, therefore set shorter assignments than normal, for example); others pursued the normal graduate school practice of setting one due date for the final version of the paper and having no concern for the process whereby it would get written. With very few exceptions, students experienced significant difficulties with the task, which caused a good deal of frustration and anxiety.

DATA SOURCES

The nature of this problem became clear from assembling data from four sources: professor interviews, student diaries, classroom interactions, and student interviews. Specifically, the issue may be separated into three components.

First, when students submitted only a final draft of a paper in the foreign language and linguistic errors were marked, they felt resentful. They suggested that the instructor had not paid enough attention to their ideas and that their grade was based on *how*, rather than *what*, they wrote. One student commented in an interview:

327

I was devastated when I got my paper back. There were red marks all over it – all correcting language errors. When I looked for comments on the ideas, all I could find was one short phrase at the end. So I have to figure my grade is about the French. But maybe I wrote A+ ideas in B– French! I thought this was a content course.

Even when the assignment consisted of a series of shorter papers, the same complaints were found. This is from a diary writer studying politics in Italian:

I got my second paper back and the grammar/language corrections were massive, filled with comments about incomprehensibility, and careless word usage and lack of time spent on it, enough to make me think [the language instructor] hadn't understood a damn thing I had said and that it was horrible. And then [from the content instructor] the only thing written was "excellent!" and he understood perfectly what I was saying . . . so it's just bizarre.

Second, when students submitted a paper in the foreign language, some professors felt they could not do justice to the ideas because of their difficulty with inaccurate or inappropriate language. One instructor likened this situation to trying to assess the merit of a painting viewed through very dirty glass.

To be fair to the student, the glass has to be wiped clean so that the ideas stand out as clearly as possible to be judged. I don't think we can trust ourselves not to be prejudiced by language mistakes. Plus, how can you be sure that you're getting their real meaning?

Third, students complained about the excessive amount of time which had to be devoted to writing papers in the foreign language; these comments were particularly strident in the Japanese and Chinese classes. These are typical diary comments:

As the due date for the paper draws nearer every minute, the class time itself doesn't seem important. I don't care if I participate, I just want to get the paper done! [Chinese]

I was so tired today because I stayed up so late trying to finish the paper due today. Thank God it's over and done with! . . . I need more help in writing, especially with organization, so it's a pity we didn't write two or three shorter papers, rather than one big one. [Japanese]

SOLUTION

In some cases, the second edition of a course featured an earlier deadline for a draft of the written paper in order to provide feedback in terms of appropriacy of discourse, sentence-level accuracy, and word choice. In others, adjustments were made on the spot when students openly acknowledged their difficulties. Faced with the papers written in Japanese by American students, one professor extended the deadline and agreed to treat the papers as early drafts, commenting on language problems and areas of murky logic. Meetings with students resolved many of these difficulties, and the final drafts could be fairly graded on the basis of content. In addition, the native speakers of Japanese were recruited to assist in the process, as one Japanese student's diary states:

> Today the professor suggested that native-speaker should read and help non-native speakers' papers which we handed in first draft. This paper is all related to Japanese internationalization. Some people chose Japanese internationalization in terms of labor, some other people chose internationalization in terms of media, and so on. The length of the paper suppose about 20 pages. It is difficult for non-native speakers to write perfect sentences. That's why the professor suggested it.

In fact, as I learned from debriefing interviews, only a couple of the half-dozen native speakers were able to offer help because of their own time constraints. This fact led to the suggestion that students could trade help with written papers as the Japanese natives were having comparable difficulties in writing papers in English for other classes.

The case of learner training

Part of effective curriculum renewal involves orienting students to the new program and training them to be effective participants. This need for learner training emerged clearly in the data.

PROBLEM

This is not an issue which could be addressed within a given semester. Rather, when students in the initial versions of these courses encountered struggles and difficulties because of lack of resources and strategies for studying complex subject matter in a second language, solutions were sought to apply to subsequent presentations (about half the courses were taught more than once during the research period). Experience indicated that students who treated these classes as either just another subject matter class or as just another foreign language class were likely to experience difficulties.

At various times, it became apparent that students needed help with the following: reading skills, interactive listening skills, organizing and expressing ideas in writing, organizing their own learning, identifying and deploying successful language learning strategies, and seeking and dealing with appropriate feedback on their performance. Three issues are briefly touched on here: reading skills, dealing with vocabulary deficiencies, and sociolinguistic competence.

DATA SOURCES

The four chief sources detailing student learning difficulties were student diaries, classroom observations, written comments in end-of-course evaluations, and student interviews.

The problems in terms of volume and complexity of text are clearly compounded by students' inadequate repertoire of reading skills, quite possibly in any language. Exit interviews indicated that they had not consciously developed strategies – either original or modified from their first language habits – for dealing with the foreign language reading task. In addition, there is some evidence that students held inappropriate objectives in terms of reading comprehension: frustration was often discussed in terms of failing to understand everything. This diary writer discussed reading authentic texts in Japanese.

Today's class was back to the usual level of frustration . . . The content of the article wasn't that difficult – but I nonetheless had trouble distinguishing what the most important points were. . . . I had marked some areas in the article which I agreed or disagreed with, but I hardly have time to get through them once, much less go back and really pin down the main points. [The instructor] said that if we could get 60–70% of the article, that would be sufficient, but there's a perfectionist part of me that wants to understand it all.

Very often, of course, the principal obstacle to effective reading was perceived as a lack of vocabulary. This feature also emerged as a problem in spoken expression. In a typical diary entry one learner of French wrote, "One time I could not think of the word for *reflect* in the middle of a sentence, so I used the word for *show* instead." Some students showed an awareness that lexical deficits may be lamented. In an interview with students in an Italian course, one said, "I understand almost everything, but I still have trouble expressing myself. Sometimes I don't know a key word and I don't have enough vocabulary skill to get around such a word." A student studying Francophone Africa in French wondered in her diary why she so rarely shared her insights into the literature the class is reading. She wrote, "The more I analyze this, the more I decide that it's the vocabulary that gets in my way." There were also frequent occasions in class when instructors and students directly confronted a vocabulary issue, sometimes without immediate result, as in this exchange from a politics class in Spanish.

S1: . . . hablaron de . . . de *impeachment*. Como se dice *impeachment*? [. . . they talked about *impeachment*. How do you say *impeachment*?]

S2: Veto? [Veto?]

S3: Denuncio? [Denunciation?]

S4: Acusación? [Accusation?]

S1: No se. [I don't know.]

P: Yo tampoco. Tendremos que buscar. . . . [I don't either. We'll have to find out. . . .]

Usually the students were successful, as here (same class):

S1: . . . las vamos a poner en contr-contr- co- [. . . we are going to contr- contr- co-]

S2: contraposición [literally, "we are going to put them in contrast"]

S1: contra-pos-ición. Contraposición? [S1 repeats the word, once broken down and once with rising intonation]

S2: Si. [Yes.]

S1: Gracias. [Thank you.]

Participants helped each other in this way quite often, though a number of students could never fully accept these prompts as an acceptable, normal phenomenon. Every instance was a brief reminder of their imperfection, as in this diary comment:

Today I got into a sentence and couldn't remember the word for "judge" (*Richter*). It just wouldn't come, and eventually one of my classmates came up with it (it took them a moment too). So much for my fluency; but I was obviously confident enough to start a sentence and speak as I thought. [German]

Communicative competence at the discourse level was also an issue. A number of students mused over the gap between their own spoken production and native speaker norms. Often, the problem is simply that of activating passive knowledge, as seen in this interview excerpt, where "S" represents the student's speech and "I" the interviewer's.

S: I blank when I speak out loud.

I: Which means?

S: I use simple vocabulary and grammar. Afterwards, I think I could easily have used the correct grammar.

I: By correct, do you mean accurate, no mistakes?

S: No, I mean more like native speakers. I don't have the native ability, but I have an intuitive grasp of what's right and what's wrong. I have the knowledge to use it, but it's passive knowledge.

In other cases, however, the issue is more complex. Thus, in a Japanese class, a journal writer discusses the puzzle of how the Japanese (specifically, as represented by the instructor and four native-speaking students in the class) can be at once so logical and practical yet so vague, indirect, and intuitive.

The degree to which these fluctuations are reflected in the Japanese language – or should be reflected when spoken properly – is something I'm trying to grasp. I'm also trying to determine *when* to use which approach: in which situations it is kosher to be more direct or logical, straightforward. Most times, I try to be *clear* and grammatically correct (a challenge in itself), although I do notice that I tend, when speaking Japanese to use more qualifiers or statements which "discount" my main point, such as "hakkiri wakaranai keredo" [I'm not sure but . . .] or statements to elicit support: "ja nai desu ka/to omoimasen ka" [isn't it true that/don't you think that].

Another student in the same class described in his diary how he consciously developed a strategy for expressing ideas.

Be polite, use some qualifiers to soften what you say, but then say it anyway and follow with "don't you think" or "what do you think?" In a sense, it's using a more feminine, intuitive, relational approach to what you're saying, to communication. This is very appealing to me in any case, but I do want to know that I *am* clear, since I'm speaking a foreign language.

SOLUTIONS

From listening to the students' issues and concerns, I was able to propose an initial learner training component for subsequent versions of these courses. Often, raising the awareness of anticipated difficulties and suggesting a range of strategies and solutions could be achieved through the voices of previous students. Quotations from diaries and interviews were used to directly inform and advise, giving the procedure greater validity and impact. In many cases, these quotations emphasize the joyous complexity of the learning process by raising questions and offering answers all in the same breath, as in this diary entry from a Spanish class:

I make vocabulary lists, which are immensely helpful. I would be interested in a brief training program for the articles – they are quite difficult but very beneficial to read because I push myself to widen my vocabulary in order to understand the material. The only disadvantage to this is that it takes a lot of time.

Some suggestions are also delightfully creative and might never surface without this mechanism. This example is from an interview with a student from a class in Spanish:

What I do before I have to write in Spanish is listen to Spanish music with Spanish lyrics for about twenty minutes. Crazy as it seems, it does help.

The case of group work

The issue of group work is more complex than the previous three. Instead of one particular difficulty, it involves a cluster of related problems, largely concerning the processing of material. The solution to these problems was the introduction of some form of small group work in the classroom. This, in turn, generated other problems, some of which remain unsolved. The problems are defined through material from a range of sources: classroom observations, transcripts of class sessions, student diaries, professor diaries, student interviews, professor interviews, and end-of-course assessments.

In all cases, the solution to the problem was some form of cooperative team work. These solutions were implemented during the course or from the beginning of a second or third offering of a course, usually with advice from the ethnographer and, in one or two cases, with the active involvement of the ethnographer.

One such need surfaced in the diaries and student interviews and was readily confirmed from the fieldnotes, namely the lack of appropriate affective conditions in a large class (more than twelve students, say) for effective student participation. Anxiety, hesitation, and restraint were common themes when diarists wrote of whole group discussion.

After the movie, we had a discussion which predominantly concerned the role of women in African society. Unfortunately, I did find myself resisting the impulse to participate. I would respond in my brain, but not vocally, which I would like to try to overcome eventually. Basically, I felt it was due to insecurity about my French, although I know that is pretty ridiculous.

My main problem currently seems to fit into the area of fluency and confidence. Today, I paused in the middle of a sentence looking for the word I wanted to say. . . . I would then either remember it or choose an alternative form of expression, which of course lessened the impact of my statements. [German]

I was so frustrated by my inability to get out coherent sentences today. I could get out the first part but then sort of got stuck as if I were over-monitoring what I was saying. I didn't feel I was translating from English to Japanese what I wanted to say – I don't use that as a strategy. I prefer to turn on the Japanese and think only in Japanese as I find it comes out more fluently. But not today.

Once small group activities had been introduced, students were then able to compare the two experiences. This comment is from a French class diary:

I found that I used more fragmented sentences and worse grammar when I spoke to the large group. I guess because I felt less intimidated and more

333

willing to take my time to formulate sentence structure and search for words in the smaller group.

Eventually, almost all students came to relish the opportunities to practice their speaking skills, and performance before the whole class was fostered, almost rehearsed, in the small group setting.

A great class today. The group discussion brought in a lot of people who were silent earlier in the semester. . . . As far as vocabulary and ability to speak and be understood in a content course, I think this course has been very successful. [Spanish]

I felt pretty comfortable with the language during my presentation today and in class generally. I can tell that I'm growing more confident and that my skills are improving. I still make mistakes, of course, but my general ability to participate in complex political discussions is improving, especially in a small group setting. [German]

From the faculty side, particularly for the subject matter teachers, came the need to deal with the size of the class in terms of participation opportunities. The introduction of the foreign language focused much more attention than usual on the nature and frequency of student participation. Once in progress, this discussion led naturally to the use of small groups and to seeking appropriate formats and tasks.

The use of the technique of putting students in groups of three to five and setting a problem to resolve or an issue to discuss arose, then, as a response to the issues of class size and the need to permit all students to participate and express their ideas. Thus, the instructional team of Francophone Africa, faced with an enrollment of well over twenty students, began, two or three weeks into the course, to form small groups and set tasks based on the material of the day. Here is an example from the professor's log.

The movie *Afrique Vivante* was shown. The class was then divided into five groups of four students each and given fifteen minutes to identify the cultural values of African village life that were identified in the film. They were to find one specific instance of each value in the film and one example from *L'Enfant Noire* [the novel being studied at that point]. After the break, the various groups reported the values they had identified and these were listed on the blackboard. From these various lists, the most common values were identified: Family, Community or Group, Nature, Work, and Education/Instruction. These themes were then explored further in a discussion of *L'Enfant Noire*.

Related strategies also emerged. For instance, once the students had read a particular text, five topics were listed on the blackboard, and a student was assigned to lead the discussion on each topic. The rest of the class selected the topic of greatest interest, with a maximum of five permitted in each group. In other cases, students were placed in three groups, one for each major segment of the political spectrum (left, center, right) and asked to prepare policy statements in particular areas. Alternatively, after general discussion of a text, the class brainstormed a list of relevant issues; from this list, students self-selected into groups and prepared a report, including appropriate quotations from the book.

The reaction of students was generally very positive. (The exception is noted herein.) They valued the opportunity for participation and for using the target language under less stressful circumstances, as noted in these diary comments.

It's easier to talk in the small groups. I really feel that to be part of a small group and to be responsible for its successful presentation of viewpoint in class helps me to participate more . . . because the stress to perform and sound intelligent about the topic overrides the stress of my fear of making mistakes in my speech. In the large group, my fear, or feeling of intimidation becomes stronger and I tend to shut up. [French]

In terms of language usage, today was one of the first times that I really participated in class. Just as I had assumed, the more intimate group setting facilitated communication. Our group was comfortably divided in terms of language level. . . . As a matter of fact it was one of these two [students in the group less proficient than the writer] who volunteered to be spokesperson for our group. . . . I hope we will have more time to hash out the material covered in class in this manner. [German]

Not only is there an effect in terms of quantity of participation: Professors and students agree that the quality of work is superior in the small group format. As noted in a French course diary, "The work in small groups continues to be very helpful. Much richer thoughts flow out of the groups as a general rule."

Two problems with small group work are found in the research record. The first is that success is directly correlated with the specificity of the instructions given: One cannot simply tell students to get into their groups and discuss something. They need clear guidance, normally a specific desired outcome. In the French example just quoted, for instance, the student groups emerged with a list of values and two examples for each, one from the film, one from the novel.

In the absence of such a brief, the results were disappointing. Here are two comments from the same student diary, the second a month or so later than the first:

This group thing isn't working. Our discussion goes all over the place and no one seems to know what we are doing.

Today we were given specific questions to answer and the groups worked much better. I actually enjoyed the experience and participated a lot in the discussion.

The second issue is the capability of students to undertake small group tasks. A number of student diaries refer to unsatisfactory sessions in which their colleagues fail to take responsibility for the work of the group or where inappropriate interactive styles ruin a promising discussion by souring the atmosphere. These kinds of problems should be addressed in learner training sessions.

Conclusion

In this chapter, I have attempted to demonstrate the value of training the various voices of the classroom on one set of ears: those of a methodologically aware ethnographic researcher. I suggest that one should look beyond the dilemma posed at the start of this chapter, and that the ethnographer's duty in a case like this includes making all relevant information available to the parties concerned. And, when invited, the consulting ethnographer should assist in interpreting these data, both to clarify problems and to identify appropriate solutions. The classroom ethnographer, therefore, need not be the taciturn Coolidge, offering the occasional content-free remark, or the old Yorkshire figure, tight-lipped as well as tight-fisted, never offering free advice.

However, given that curriculum renewal can and should be a continuous process, the larger lesson is how to achieve the same results in the absence of such an individual. How, in other words, can teachers and students working together find their own ethnographic voice? The answer may be pursued by examining possible parallels to the different means of investigation described here: learner diaries, classroom observation, interviews, videotapes of lessons, and questionnaires. By finding the most appropriate form and application of these devices, I believe that teachers and learners together can effectively explore problems and find solutions.

I would like to express, in conclusion, my sense of wonder and of encouragement at the cogency, clarity, and creativity of the voices I have tried to represent in this chapter. This search for improvement, this pedagogy-as-problem-solving, is only possible when all concerned speak out frankly and, in turn, listen attentively. I believe that the role of the ethnographer-facilitator is a useful, though not indispensable, one.

References

Aronson, E. 1978. *The Jigsaw Classroom.* Beverly Hills, CA: Sage.
Baker, S. J. 1992. The Monterey model: Integrating international policy studies

with language education. In M. Krueger and F. Ryan (eds.), *Language and Content*. Lexington, MA: D. C. Heath.

Boomer, G. 1987. Addressing the problem of elsewhereness: A case for action research in schools. In D. Goswami and P. Stillman (eds.), *Reclaiming the Classroom: Teacher Research as an Agency for Change*. Portsmouth, NH: Heinemann.

Delgado-Gaitan, C. 1993. Researching change and changing the researcher. *Harvard Educational Review, 63*, 4; 389–411.

Elbow, P. 1973. *Writing Without Teachers*. Oxford: Oxford University Press.

Elliott, J. 1991. *Action Research for Educational Change*. Milton Keynes: Open University Press.

Heath, S. B. 1987. A lot of talk about nothing. In D. Goswami and P. R. Stillman. (eds.), *Reclaiming the Classroom: Teacher Research as an Agency for Change*. Portsmouth, NH: Heinemann.

Maxwell, J. A. 1992. Understanding and validity in qualitative research. *Harvard Educational Review, 62*, 3, 279–300.

Slavin, R. 1990. *Co-operative Learning: Theory, Research, and Practice*. Englewood Cliffs, NJ: Prentice Hall.

van Lier, L. (Chapter 16, this volume). Conflicting voices: Language, classrooms, and bilingual education in Puno.

15 Registration and placement: learner response

Peter Sturman

> ". . . I have spent so much of my time in studying at these schools." "Alas!" said Nasrudin, "you have studied the teachers and the teachings. What should have happened is that the teachers and their teachings should have studied you."
> (Steinem 1992: 152)

This chapter looks at the registration and placement procedures involved in joining a new school, both the procedures themselves and the importance of the human interactions that take place during their administration. I will show that the registration and placement procedures, and the way they are administered, are strongly associated with students' degrees of satisfaction with the schools, the teachers, and the lessons and the students' images of the schools. The untested assumption here is that higher levels of "satisfaction" are associated with better learning, however defined. The study uses data from two sources: the written comments of a sample of students who had just joined the two schools involved in the study, and quantified data from a questionnaire that these students completed. The contrastive use of these two data sets will show the effects of the registration and placement processes from different but complementary perspectives. While the actual results may only be directly appropriate to the type of schools that were involved in the study (British Council Language Schools in Tokyo and Kyoto), the implications of the results might be relevant to most EFL institutions and programs.

My interest in registration and placement developed over the four years I worked at the Tokyo school. Indeed, my very first job there was to photocopy and laminate copies of the written placement test. Like

This study was made possible by the assistance of the staff and students of the British Council schools in Tokyo and Kyoto, and financially supported by a grant from the British Council, London. I am indebted to Dr. Sara Delamont of the School of Social and Administrative Studies, University of Wales, College of Cardiff; Ms. Mary Whitsell and Mr. Takeo Kimura for translation; and Mr. Stephen Nowak and Mr. Tony Brown for technical support. It is no exaggeration to say that without the help of all these people, this chapter could not have been written.

all the teachers, I was involved on a rota basis in the registration and placement systems: smiling in what I hoped was a welcoming manner at potential students who approached the reception area, walking with them to the written placement test, helping to settle them down to take the test, then briefly interviewing them, and finally recommending a suitable class for them at the reception desk. The whole process was fraught with opportunities for misunderstanding and embarrassment. Many potential students obviously could not understand most or any of what I was saying; some of them were nervous, some flustered, some confident, some amused; and I met several who were quite obviously confused, upset, frustrated, bored, or generally put out by the whole process. To the school's credit, however, there were many formal and informal meetings to improve the system and make it more encouraging and less intimidating. There was even a videotape series of teachers interviewing "prospective students" (all volunteers), as well as meetings to standardize the interview process.

In first meetings with new classes, we (the teachers) would meet the students new to the schools (the results of the placement system) and the "continuing" students (those who were progressing through the school curriculum). In many cases there seemed to be big differences between the two groups in terms of ability, expectations, and attitudes to studying. The differences were sufficiently consistent – and some students were rather vocal about them – that we often felt that either the registration and placement system or the "promotion" system was not working as well as it ought. The aim of the original research, then, was to look at the effect of the placement and registration procedures and of the people who administered them. This took place in 1991, so the results may have little or no relevance to the current practices of the schools. (I no longer work there, so I do not know.) Nevertheless, I hope that teachers involved with placement and registration anywhere will find this chapter interesting and informative, and be able to compare their own processes with the ones described here.

Literature review

The central areas of interest in this study are registration and placement processes, the students' experience of them, and whether or not the processes might affect students' levels of satisfaction with lessons, teachers, and the schools.

Placement and registration

One of the few writers on students' experience of registration is Fielden (1977). In a report of the responses of thirty-two students enrolling in courses undertaken as part of the Nottingham Diploma in Adult Education, Fielden notes that "there is no excuse for not treating the adult student as an adult" (p. 353). The following quotation from an adult attempting to enroll may give you a feeling of what registration procedures can be like.

I could not find clear instructions as to how to enroll, nor could I identify anyone to ask for clarification. The presence of purposeful adults seemingly knowing what they were doing confirmed my impression that the whole set up was OK for the initiated who knew what I could not see written up anywhere. I passed into the enrollment room. There were several queues leading up to tables where I saw forms being handed in. Several people were sitting at tables filling in forms. No-one was speaking to anyone else, except those at the end of the queues. My feeling of not knowing what to do was increasing and I was sorely tempted to ditch the whole exercise. (ibid.)

Brown (1989) has written on student placement, noting the differences between continuing students and newly enrolled students. He once mentions the possible student reaction to placement: "The first contact that many students have with an ESL or EFL program is the cold and detached experience of taking some form of placement examination" (p. 65). Both Fielden and Brown suggest, respectively, that registration and placement procedures can produce anxiety and may lack warmth and encouragement.

The importance attached to the students' experience of the placement and registration processes may depend upon how responsive the institution is to the student as a person, or (bluntly) to the student as a customer. The economic importance of students differs according to the type of institution.

Different types of institutions

In an issue of *Educational Research* devoted to differences between private and state education, Hannaway (1991: 464) succinctly describes the ethos of private schools:

Private schools offer their services in a competitive marketplace where choice by consumers supports and regulates the system. Survival depends on responsiveness to client preferences. If a school is not responsive, clients go elsewhere.

Or, in short, "He who pays the piper calls the tune" (ibid.).

Mee (1980) argues that educational criteria are rarely applied to evaluate the success of adult education, and that administrative criteria are often used instead – budgets that are usually dependent on enrollments, for example. Clark (1958) believes there is a danger of functioning

within such an "enrollment economy" and argues that whenever enrollment becomes the dominant criterion, the teacher becomes very
(too) sensitive to the demands of the established clientele. As Salisbury
(1986: 63) says, "the chief task of adult education teachers, if they want
their classes to survive, is of 'pleasing the students.' " Newman (1979:
67) also believes that "[a]dult education teachers must be good with
people. They must be capable of moulding disparate collections of
adults into working groups and of creating a relaxed and friendly atmosphere."

While these comments are obviously aimed at the teacher in the classroom, it is during placement and registration that prospective students
first meet the teachers and form their first impressions of the schools.
In a competitive environment, students are quite prepared to change
schools if they are not happy with the institution, the teachers, the methodology, or the other students. As a result, there is intense pressure on
institutions and on teachers to satisfy the students, and the economic
power of the student-as-consumer is certain to influence the way institutions respond to student needs and wants.

Foreign language anxiety

Performing in an interview situation in a second language may be highly
stressful. Second language students suffer "risk to self" when they cannot
present themselves fully in the new language: "Adult language learners'
self-perceptions of genuineness in presenting themselves to others may be
threatened by the limited range of meaning and affect that can be deliberately communicated" (Horwitz, Horwitz, and Cope 1986: 128).

The placement interview is often the first time many of the students
have to interact with a native speaker of English – creating anxiety
about what will happen and what to do. Given the reticence to make
mistakes that is typical of many Japanese students of English, an interview may not be an ideal situation for enabling students to respond and
feel that they have done their best. The assembly-line nature of interviewing students at the peak of a registration period might also make
it difficult for the teacher to be genuinely interested in the new interviewee, or even to put on an appearance of such interest.

The role of the teacher

Although the teacher who conducts the placement interview may not
be the eventual classroom teacher, there is evidence that the actions of
individual teachers in the classroom can reduce (or increase) the students' stress; they can influence many factors that affect the learner's
receptivity to language learning. (See Allwright and Bailey [1991: 164–

341

TABLE I   REASONS GIVEN FOR STUDYING AT THE SCHOOLS

| | Important | | Unimportant | | |
	Very	Fairly	Fairly	Very	Neither
What was your reason for studying at this school?					
To enjoy it.	53.5	36.5	1.9	0.6	7.5
To learn English.	88.7	8.8	0.0	0.0	2.5
To make friends.	28.9	43.4	7.5	0.0	20.1
To learn about other cultures.	58.2	29.7	0.0	0.6	0.0

165] for the identification of eight such factors.) I believe that the student's receptivity to language learning is also affected by the administrative systems of an institution and the attitudes of the staff and teachers who are encountered during these procedures.

Christison and Krahnke (1986) asked a group of eighty non-native students at five different U.S. universities to define what constituted a good teacher. While 25 percent of the respondents cited "professional" characteristics such as organization, preparation, experience, teaching style, and fairness, 35 percent cited "personality" factors such as whether the teacher was patient, kind, interested, caring, cooperative, enjoyable, stimulating, and helpful. A successful registration and placement procedure needs a combination of personality factors, to enable the students to relax and respond, and professional factors, for accurate placement.

Language study in Japan

The results presented in this study may only apply in Japan. The learning of English in private language schools in Japan must be set within the context of the aims and expectations of the students, as well as the cultural context of Japan itself. Research on the attitudinal orientation of Japanese people toward learning English is inconclusive. Stone (1989) and Hildebrandt and Giles (1980) suggest an instrumental orientation; Chihara and Oller (1978) and Benson (1991) argue for integrative and personal reasons; and Skehan (1989) notes the limitations of the distinction between "integrative" and "instrumental."

For the purposes of this chapter it should be noted that students come to the schools to enjoy themselves, to socialize and date, and to learn English – for whatever purpose; some students are highly motivated to study and some are not. Table 1 shows the relative importance of four different reasons for studying at the schools. (This table uses information from all the respondents in the original sample, both students who have just registered and continuing students.) Teachers in other private language schools both in Japan and elsewhere might recognize elements of these data.

Summary

As we can see from this brief literature review, registration and placement procedures are recognized as potentially cold and discouraging. The role of the student-as-consumer may vary according to institution, but private schools need to be responsive to student needs and wishes in order to survive. In addition, trying to communicate in a foreign language is stressful and people may get frustrated when they cannot express themselves as well as they would like to – a feeling that may be all the more acute in an interview situation. Students' receptivity to learning may be influenced by the teacher; students value the personal characteristics of teachers as highly as they do the professional ones. It has also been noted that the results may only apply to private language schools in Japan. Finally, the general motivation of Japanese students to study English is not well established and was not used as a variable in the study.

Methodology

A closed-question questionnaire was designed, translated into Japanese, and validated to the extent possible in the Japanese community in Cardiff, Wales. Spaces for open-ended questions were left for each section of the questionnaire. The portions which are pertinent to this chapter can be found in the appendix. The responses of 116 students who had just registered at the Tokyo and Kyoto schools were eventually used. The written comments were translated back into English and collated. The data from the questionnaire were entered into the SPSS/PC+ statistics application, and subjected to cross-tabulation using the chi-square statistic.[1] A full description of the chi-square statistic and the

1 The cross-tabulation procedure enables you to determine the probability that two (or more) variables are independent (i.e., not related to each other). More frequently, however, statements are made about how sure one is that the variables are related to each other and that this association is not due to chance. In this study, probability figures (p) are given when $p \leq 0.05$, which means that the particular variables are statistically associated and that there is less than a 5-in-100 chance that the association was due to chance (or, alternatively, that it was more than 95 percent certain that the association was *not* due to chance). The essential thing to bear in mind, however, is that even if a statistical association is demonstrated, it does not necessarily mean that a causal relationship has been established.

343

problems involved in its interpretation can be found in any good statistics textbook (I recommend Everitt [1977]).

The next section of the chapter reports on the students' reactions to the registration and placement procedures. Owing to limitations of space, only essential statistical details will be given. Interested readers can find full details in Sturman (1991).

Registration and placement procedures

In the registration and placement systems when the data were collected, a potential student would approach the front desk where a staff member would explain the registration and placement procedures and give out promotional literature. A teacher then accompanied the individual to a room for the first of a two-part written exam. This would be marked and the student would either do a second, more advanced test or have an oral placement interview elsewhere. The interview would start with non-demanding questions to relax the student, and then become increasingly difficult at the discretion of the interviewer. The grades for the written and oral components of the test would be compared and a suitable class recommended. The oral interview grade was supposed to take preference in determining the appropriate class for the student, as the chance to practice and improve spoken English is emphasized among language school students in Japan. The student would then return to the main desk and the administrative procedures would be completed – arrangements to pay the school, the gathering of additional personal details, and recommendations about the purchase of textbooks.

While the system is designed to be as reliable as possible, there were still several ways in which a student could end up in the wrong class. The teacher's judgment of the students' oral ability was occasionally influenced by the written test marks. Some teachers felt that the students should be placed in "challenging" classes, while others preferred "confidence-building" classes. Many based their decisions on their knowledge of students in a particular class or level they were teaching, and then worked backwards and compared them with the person being interviewed. Finally, the interviewee might not feel that he or she has done as well as possible, for a variety of reasons, as the following quotations make clear. (Each quote is preceded by the student's arbitrary identification number.)

18. Aren't there some people who come to the school without knowing anything about a placement test or interview, who consequently panic, rush through it and end up in a lower class than they should be?
21. When we took the test, we were all in one room and I couldn't

concentrate because of the rustlings of all the papers. I'd like to see this changed.

22. I was terribly nervous during the placement interview, partly because I couldn't understand one word of what the teacher was saying. If only she could have spoken a little more slowly and easily, I really think I could have done better and been placed in a more appropriate class.

Furthermore, the recommended class may not meet at a convenient time, or all the classes at the recommended level may already be full, or there may not be a class at the recommended level because there are not enough students to make it viable, as in the following comments. (Glosses are given in brackets.)

23. Because of my job, there is only one time I can attend. I'd like there to be more classes during the late night period.
24. I wish there were a larger range of class divisions.
25. In the course schedule it looks as though there are plenty of classes to choose from. However, for beginners who want to finish before 6:00, there is only one!

There are also students who insist on joining a certain class, simply because a friend is in it or because it is taught by a particular teacher. One student (#38) wrote, "Please make it possible to choose our own teachers ahead of time."

Finally, there are students who simply feel they are in the wrong class, whatever the placement instruments say.

16. I'd like to know exactly why I was allocated to a particular class, what my English lacked for me to be put in this level, what we will study, what important points we will focus on, etc.
17. Please explain why students are assigned to particular levels.
20. The class levels are not clearly fixed. I'd like the chance to discuss my aims and the evaluation of my own level.

The problems encountered with continuing students can be even more acute, and the teachers aren't the only ones who are aware of the differences.

32. In every class there are new students as well as continuing students. (This was written in a disapproving tone.)
34. Even for repeat students there should be repeat tests with appropriate review classes.

There is considerable pressure on the teachers and registration staff to allow continuing students to go on to the next stage, even when this might not be in the students' best interests. The assumption that a student progresses from point A to point B over the course of ten weeks is rarely borne out in practice, and developing achievement examinations for all levels turned out to be an impossible task. Moreover, repeating a course meant exactly that – doing the same things again, as there were no alternative courses. In all, it would be difficult to maintain that the apparent objectivity of the system was always upheld in practice.

The students' criticisms and comments on the placement and registration system relate to (a) comments about the system and the results of the system, and (b) comments about the people who administer the system.

Criticism of the system and its results

The comments can be broken down into the following categories: those that state or imply (a) that the focus or style of the classes is not what they hoped for (#s 13, 19, 31, 36); (b) that the whole system was inefficient (#s 27, 28); (c) that the placement system lacked necessary components (#s 14, 37); (d) that the interview was problematic; and (e) that the placement system was inaccurate (#s 15, 16, 17, 18, 20, 21, 22, 26, 33).

13. Placement should be based on BOTH ability and aim in learning English.
14. In placement – have separate speaking, listening, reading and writing parts.
15. The interview was over so quickly that I really wondered if it was possible to judge a person's ability in such a short period.
19. People's reasons for studying should also be taken into consideration when allocating to classes. Office workers and housewives might like a more relaxed atmosphere that they could enjoy more.
26. Although there are supposed to be 18 levels, there seems to be a wide range of students in any one class. The office people are NOT polite on the telephone. One would expect a little more politeness.
27. The registration and placement procedure is not at all efficient and took a lot of time.
28. Registration seemed to take forever. I was made to wait such a long time due to errors such as miscalculating the amount I had to pay, etc. It really wasn't efficient at all.
31. Divide classes into speaking classes and listening comprehension classes.
33. It is difficult to change classes.
36. Students should be given advice according to their reasons for studying English.
37. It would be good to include a listening component in the placement test. I appreciated being shown the textbook and everything was politely explained.

The design of the study enables us to look further at three of these categories: the accuracy of the placement system, the efficiency of the

TABLE 2   THE PERCEIVED ACCURACY OF THE PLACEMENT INSTRUMENTS

	Yes	No	Number of respondents
Were the placement instruments accurate?			
Test	83%	17%	99
Interview	82%	18%	107

registration and placement systems, and the nature of the placement interview.

THE ACCURACY OF THE PLACEMENT SYSTEM

It is fairly clear that at least nine out of the thirty-nine students who wrote comments (24 percent) feel that the placement system was not accurate. As this is the largest category, we will consider the quantified data for this category first. Students' assessments of the two instruments' accuracy are summarized in Table 2.

The accuracy of the placement system is questioned by just less than 20 percent of the sample. There are no objective criteria to say whether 20 percent is a good or bad level of people who feel that the placement system is not accurate. Any institution would, presumably, hope to have as many of their students as possible believing that they are in the right classes. The perceived accuracy or inaccuracy of the placement instruments is not randomly distributed throughout the sample, and for some reason it is the male students who are more likely to find the placement test inaccurate ($p = .0490$). If there is an unconscious gender bias in the written test, this would warrant further study. The alternative is perhaps an unfortunate reflection on Japanese men.

The importance of the accuracy of the placement instruments is also reflected in the statistical cross-associations. Perceptions of the accuracy of the interview were positively associated with satisfaction with the school ($p < .0000$), the teachers ($p < .0000$), and the lessons ($p = .0002$); as well as with images of the schools as consumer-oriented ($p = .0030$), professional ($p = .0057$), of good value ($p = .0003$), and flexible ($p = .0086$). Perceptions of the accuracy of the written placement test were also positively associated with satisfaction with the teachers ($p = .0141$) and the lessons ($p = .0397$), and with images of the school as consumer-oriented ($p = .0250$). None of these results should be taken as implying causal relationships, however.

TABLE 3   EFFICIENCY-RELATED MEASURES OF THE PLACEMENT
AND REGISTRATION SYSTEM

	Yes	No	Number of respondents
Was the . . .			
registration too long?	4%	96%	102
test too long?	8%	92%	100
interview too long?	2%	98%	102
test too short?	17%	83%	100
interview too short?	37%	63%	103
registration efficient?	75%	25%	106
registration relaxed?	83%	17%	102

THE EFFICIENCY OF THE SYSTEM

Table 3 displays the students' responses to the yes/no questions about the efficiency of placement and registration. Twenty-five percent of the sample felt that the registration process was not efficient, although this does not seem to be directly related to the time it took, but rather to how that time was spent. This perception varied by school: Kyoto school students were significantly more likely to find the process efficient than students at the Tokyo school ($p = .0219$).

It is interesting to note that 37 percent of the students felt the interview was too short, as opposed to only 17 percent who felt the test was too short. The perception of the interview varied with age, with students in the fifteen to nineteen years category likely to say it was too short, and students in the twenty-five to thiry-five category the least likely to feel it was too short ($p = .0178$). The importance of the placement interview might suggest the value of varying the amount of time given to the interview – taking a little longer with younger students. The view of the test being too short varied by gender, with male students more likely to feel this way than female students ($p = .0330$). Likewise, intermediate level students were notably less likely to think the test was too short ($p = .0353$). Presumably, if male students were allowed more time to complete the test, they might be less inclined to feel the test results were inaccurate. It might be worth reconsidering the length of time allocated to the test and allowing students to take as much time as they want, or trying to determine whether doing so has any effect on performance.

The importance of the efficiency of the registration and placement procedures was drawn out by the cross-association results. An efficient registration system was positively associated with satisfaction with the

TABLE 4   FURTHER MEASURES RELATED TO THE PLACEMENT INTERVIEW

	Yes	No	Number of respondents
Did you feel the placement interview was . . .			
necessary?	100%	0%	113
intimidating?	13%	87%	105
enjoyable?	69%	31%	103
encouraging?	69%	31%	106
interesting?	54%	46%	102

teachers ($p = .0219$) and the school ($p = .0444$) and with an image of the school as professional ($p = .0094$). A relaxed registration system was positively associated with satisfaction with the lessons ($p = .0028$) and images of the schools as welcoming ($p = .0448$) and professional ($p = .0077$). The perception that the interview was too long was negatively associated with satisfaction with the schools ($p = .0439$). In sum, students' perceptions of the schools' procedural efficiency are statistically associated with long-term attitudes about the schools. We now focus specifically on the placement interview.

THE NATURE OF THE PLACEMENT INTERVIEW

Summary data concerning the students' views of the placement interview can be found in Table 4.

The strong emphasis that adult learners place on spoken English in Japan, and perhaps the role of the student as a consumer, might partly explain the surprisingly dominant view of an interview as necessary. Few students stated that they found the interview intimidating, which could either be seen as an endorsement of the way the teachers do the interviewing or a criticism of how easily I thought the students could be intimidated. Perhaps it was just me that seemed to be intimidating students!

Perceptions of the placement interview as encouraging varied with the level of the students. Students in intermediate level classes and above were less likely to find the interview encouraging ($p = .0124$). Lower elementary students were more likely to find the interview interesting ($p = .0121$). Possibly, students who were eventually placed in the intermediate level had taken both parts of the written placement test, but were unsuccessful on the (more difficult) second half. They might have started the interview in a poor frame of mind, having spent twenty to thirty minutes trying to do a test that was too difficult for them. This is an aspect of the placement system that could be improved.

The importance of the interview was brought out by the results of the statistical cross-associations. An interesting interview was positively associated with satisfaction with teachers ($p = .0472$); an encouraging interview and an enjoyable interview were both associated with an image of the schools as professional ($p = .0349$ and $p = .0004$, respectively).

Discussion

The other written comments lead to some valuable insights into the students' experience of the placement system, such as the need for students to understand why they are allocated to certain levels or the importance of their aim in studying English. Four comments implied that the classes were not really what the students had hoped for, and perhaps a more relaxed or less academic focus was what a certain proportion were seeking.

The two different types of data give different types of information. Perhaps it would be too easy either to dismiss uncomfortable statistical information, if there wasn't also written evidence of a problem, or to consider written comments to represent the views of just one or two disgruntled students, without further statistical evidence to determine how widespread the views are. The advantage of the written comments, however, is that they allow the students' depth of feeling to be expressed, and are an opportunity for students to point out new problems that the researcher, or school, was not aware of and that were not addressed in the design of the research instrument (and therefore unlikely to ever have been discovered). By contrast, the advantage of the quantitative data is that it gives us the opportunity to see how representative the written comments are and whether these comments are distributed randomly through the sample.

As mentioned before, this study has assumed a relationship between satisfaction and effective learning. If this is the case, then determining which problems to address by looking at the students' relative degrees of satisfaction could be justified on academic grounds. Otherwise, such an approach could still be justified on economic grounds. It would be nice to synthesize these two sides of teaching, though this may seem like the economic pot of gold at the end of the academic rainbow.

Criticisms of the people who administered the system

The comments that follow were all from students at the Tokyo school. They are critical of the Tokyo registration staff but supportive of the teachers there, and I would like to stress that these comments in no way reflect upon the current operation of the Tokyo school. However, the following discussion should help to point out the importance of the people administering placement and registration systems. (Some of the following comments refer to question 6 of the questionnaire [see appendix].)

1. Teachers get YES for all, administrative staff get NO for all except 'efficient' (refers to question 6).
2. A number of my class-mates have very negative opinions of the receptionists, although I don't myself.
3. The teacher in the interview created a very relaxed atmosphere and spoke clearly – that was great, but the man at reception was abrupt and unfriendly. Also one woman receptionist – they should be told.
4. When I first entered the school, I had to change class. The teacher very kindly advised me about this, but the receptionist seemed taken aback/bothered/put to trouble.
5. Before the interview, I was nervous but the interviewer was polite and considerate and made me feel relaxed, which I appreciated.
6. I did not answer Q#6 as it would vary depending upon instructors and receptionists. Generally the teachers have been kind and given me an impetus to try harder.
7. The person who interviewed me was chewing gum and this gave me a bad impression.
8. One of the receptionists 'laughed down his/her nose' (derisively/disrespectfully) at someone going through the registration system, though I have not had any bad experiences myself.
9. The office people do not seem to be familiar with the registration procedure and give ambiguous answers, or run off to ask a superior in the back office. Even after 6 months, I still get evasive answers.
10. When I first enrolled the person on the desk was a little intimidating and scary.
11. I felt the office people/front desk people were cold.

On a positive note, the comments do give further confirmation that the teachers managed the interviews extremely well. It has to be admitted, however, that the comments are negative toward the registration staff during that particular session. Unfortunately the quantitative data do not distinguish between teachers and staff, but apart from the gum-chewer (who was offered the school's service revolver), the information given in Table 5 suggests the students did not feel the teachers and staff were too rude.

As Table 5 shows, over 90 percent of the respondents felt the teachers and staff were polite. However, the percentage of students who found the teachers and staff to be kind, helpful, considerate, friendly and encouraging is lower than one might like.

Such perceptions are not uniformly distributed throughout the sample. Full-time students outside the British Council schools, students in

TABLE 5 ATTITUDES TOWARDS THE BRITISH COUNCIL TEACHERS AND STAFF
DURING THE REGISTRATION AND PLACEMENT PROCEDURES

	Yes	No	Number of respondents
Do you think the teachers and staff were . . .			
polite?	91%	9%	105
efficient?	85%	15%	101
kind?	82%	18%	107
helpful?	78%	22%	102
considerate?	70%	30%	93
friendly?	67%	33%	98
encouraging?	60%	40%	99

the younger age brackets, and students who have not attended other language schools are more likely to have positive perceptions of the teachers and staff. Obviously the three groups are linked: Younger students are more likely to be full-time college or high school students and, perhaps, less likely to have attended other language schools.

The importance of the students' perceptions of the teachers and staff met during the placement system is again revealed by the statistical cross-associations. Perceptions of the teachers and staff as kind, helpful, considerate, friendly, and encouraging were all positively associated with satisfaction with the schools, teachers, and lessons; and a professional school image was associated with teachers and staff who were seen as polite, efficient, kind, helpful, and encouraging. A consumer-oriented school image was associated with teachers and staff who were polite, efficient, helpful, considerate, and encouraging. Full details can be found in Sturman (1991).

The essential point is that the attitudes of the teachers and staff during placement and registration are closely associated with the students' degrees of satisfaction with the schools, the teachers, and lessons, and the students' images of the schools as professional and consumer-oriented. As a result, institutions might want to put greater stress on appropriate interpersonal relationships in all aspects of their operations.

The results also suggest that students draw their images of a professional school or a consumer-oriented school from a wider range of aspects than we might expect; the idea that the "teaching" and "business" sides of an institution are entirely separate is mistaken. A tentative conclusion is that neither side should be "managed" by people with little or no experience of the other, and institutions should look at their procedures from an organic, holistic perspective, rather than treating each aspect as a separate entity.

Conclusion

I hope that this study has established that there are relationships between the students' experiences during registration and placement and the students' satisfaction with the schools, teachers, and lessons, as well as with the students' images of the schools. I have suggested that the type of students involved in the study might draw their images of schools as professional and consumer-oriented from a wider range of aspects than we might have previously supposed. The study provides some evidence of the importance of excellent interpersonal relationships especially in the registration and placement procedures, which might be where the students' first images of the school and its staff are formulated. Finally I feel that institutions should resist the temptation to split into business, administration, and teaching sides, and consider how these processes overlap.

Perhaps more important, I hope the study has demonstrated the advantages of collecting both students' written comments and quantified data. The two types of data can be used to confirm or deny each other, but also to give different information – information that could not have been collected using only one or the other approach. I appreciate that translation increases the cost of the research, but in my view the advantages of collecting comments written by the students in their first language justify the cost.

Several areas for further study are raised by this chapter.[2] For example, one could investigate the influence of the students as consumers on the institution's practices and on the nature of the teacher-student relationship. Other questions could probe to determine why certain groups of students find particular aspects of registration and placement more problematic than others; whether an institution consciously or unconsciously adapts its practices to the believed needs of the majority of students (in this case younger female students); the links between school experience and language learning; and ways in which the cultural experiences of students and a different set of expectations on the part of the school might affect the experience of learning at the school. It would also be interesting to know (a) whether the impressions the students have of the school and teachers from the registration and placement process influence their experience of the first few lessons and (b) whether the associations noted in this study are only true immediately after registration and placement. Finally, of course, it is necessary to test the assumption made throughout this study that higher levels of satisfaction with aspects of the institution's operations are associated with better learning.

2 I am grateful to one of the anonymous readers of this chapter for some of the ideas expressed in this section.

Appendix: Registration and placement portions of the questionnaire

3. When you joined the school, you were given a placement test. What were your opinions of this test? Did you think the test was:

necessary?	Yes	No
accurate?	Yes	No
enjoyable?	Yes	No
encouraging?	Yes	No
intimidating?	Yes	No
too lengthy?	Yes	No
too short?	Yes	No

4. When you joined the school, you were given a placement interview. What were your opinions of this interview? Did you think the interview was:

necessary?	Yes	No
accurate?	Yes	No
enjoyable?	Yes	No
encouraging?	Yes	No
intimidating?	Yes	No
too lengthy?	Yes	No
too short?	Yes	No

5. When you joined the school, you also had to register. What were your opinions of this registration procedure? Did you think the registration procedure was:

enjoyable?	Yes	No
encouraging?	Yes	No
intimidating?	Yes	No
efficient?	Yes	No
too lengthy?	Yes	No
relaxed?	Yes	No

6. When you joined the school, during the placement test, interview, and registration procedure, you met some of the school's teachers and staff. What were your opinions of the people you met? Did you think they were:

helpful?	Yes	No
kind?	Yes	No
considerate?	Yes	No
friendly?	Yes	No
polite?	Yes	No
encouraging?	Yes	No
efficient?	Yes	No

Please write any comments you have about the placement and registration processes and the staff and teachers you met at that time.

References

Allwright, D., and K. M. Bailey. 1991. *Focus on the Language Classroom: An Introduction to Classroom Research for Language Teachers.* Cambridge: Cambridge University Press.

Benson, M. J. 1991. Attitudes and motivation towards English: A survey of Japanese freshmen. *RELC Journal, 22,* 1, 35–45.

Brown, J. D. 1989. Improving ESL placement tests using two perspectives. *TESOL Quarterly, 23,* 1, 65–83.

Chihara, T., and J.W. Oller, Jr. 1978. Attitudes and attained proficiency in EFL: A sociolinguistic study of adult Japanese speakers. *Language Learning, 28,* 1, 55–68.

Christison, M. A., and K. J. Krahnke. 1986. Student perceptions of academic language study. *TESOL Quarterly, 20,* 1, 61–81.

Clark, B. R. 1958. *The Marginality of Adult Education.* Boston: Chicago Center for the Study of Liberal Education for Adults.

Everitt, B. S. 1977. *The Analysis of Contingency Tables.* London: Chapman and Hall.

Fielden, D. 1977. The student voice. *Adult Education, 49,* 6, 351–358.

Hannaway, J. 1991. The organization and management of public and Catholic schools: Looking inside the black box. *Educational Research, 15,* 5, 463–481.

Hildebrandt, N., and H. Giles. 1980. The English language in Japan: A social psychological perspective. *JALT Journal,* 1 and 2, 44–55.

Horwitz, E. K., M. B. Horwitz, and J. Cope. 1986. Foreign language classroom anxiety. *Modern Language Journal, 70,* 2, 125–132.

Mee, G. 1980. *Organization for Adult Education.* London: Longman.

Newman, M. 1979. *The Poor Cousin.* London: Allen and Unwin.

Salisbury, J. 1986. Classroom Interaction in Higher Education. Unpublished MEd Thesis, University of Wales, College of Cardiff.

Skehan, P. 1989. *Individual Differences in Second Language Learning.* London: Edward Arnold.

Steinem, G. 1992. The pleasantries of the incredible Mulla Nasrudin. *Revolution From Within.* Boston: Little, Brown and Co.

Stone, R. 1989. Considerations for Japanese ESL learners prior to intensive ESL programs in the United States: Three case studies in awareness and motivation. *Cross Currents, 15,* 2, 39–49.

Sturman, P. 1991. An Evaluation of Students' Responses to the Processes of Learning About, Registering at, and Settling into the British Council Schools in Tokyo and Kyoto, Japan. Unpublished MEd thesis, University of Wales, College of Cardiff.

Section IV   Questions and tasks

1. Chapters 12–15 are all related to curricular concerns. Think of a curricular change that you are familiar with, either as a teacher or as a student. What was the curricular change? How did the innovation affect you personally? How might an outside observer have discovered the effects of that change on you as a teacher or learner?

2. In Chapter 13, Snow and her colleagues used a card-sort task and a role-play prompt to discover students' opinions. If you are teaching, try their card-sort task and their question (about helping a new student) with your own students. How do your students' answers compare to those of the learners in this chapter? What other sources of data would you want to gather to supplement this information and provide a basis for triangulation?

3. The learners in Chapters 13 and 15 responded to the research prompts in their first language. What are the advantages and disadvantages of having learners use their native language in providing research data?

4. Chapter 12 includes the "voices" of inspectors by considering their reports. What are the differences, if any, between the perspectives of such supervisors and the perspective of an external researcher? Is it important to include school inspectors' viewpoints in research on large-scale curricular change? Why or why not?

5. Imagine a conversation between the two teachers Harrison compares, "Ali" and "Sheikha." What do you think these two teachers would say to one another about the new curriculum in the Sultanate of Oman?

6. In Chapter 15 Sturman utilized an extensive questionnaire to gather his data (only a portion of which is discussed in the chapter). The questionnaire included both open-ended prompts and closed questions. What are the advantages and disadvantages of these two types of elicitation procedure?

7. Sturman makes a strong case that learners' initial impressions of a school (gained through the placement and registration procedures) are related to their satisfaction with the school and several other long-term factors. Think of a time when you entered a new program as a student. What were the intake procedures? How did you feel about them? If you have teaching experience, describe a typical first-contact experience for you and your students.

8. The learners in Chapter 14, like those in Chapter 11, were studying their academic subject matter through the target language. Have you ever taken a nonlanguage course in a language that is not your mother tongue? If so, how similar or different were your experi-

ences from the experiences of the students Shaw quotes? Give examples to explain.

9. Shaw describes two potentially competing roles – that of the involved curriculum and pedagogy specialist who helps teachers cope with curricular changes, and that of the ethnographer who listens to and objectively records the voices of the participants in the curricular change. Shaw's solution is to adopt the role of the consulting ethnographer, which allows him to combine the two roles. What might be the advantages and disadvantages of taking this combined role?

10. Imagine yourself in the role of a student in any of the four settings described in these chapters. What would you like to ask or tell the chapter authors, from the student's point of view?

11. Imagine yourself in the role of a teacher who has been teaching with a grammar-based syllabus. How would you feel if your program adopted a content-based curricular model, as described by Shaw in Chapter 14? What changes in your teaching would be necessitated by the curricular changes?

12. Imagine yourself in the role a researcher who has been hired by your school to investigate some aspect of the curriculum. What would you choose to study? What questions would you try to answer? What research procedures would you want to use?

V Sociopolitical perspectives

The four chapters in this final section, in some ways, could hardly be more different: Leo van Lier deals with the politics of being a "foreign expert" in a bilingual education project in the Peruvian Andes, Ralph Adendorff explores the code-switching behavior of teachers in a Kwazulu boarding school in South Africa, Patricia Duff looks at dual language school classrooms in Hungary, and Denise Murray examines the strategies teachers use for dealing with the vast cultural and linguistic diversity represented by ESL learners in California. Although the location, environment, and scope of these contributions are quite varied, each shares a central concern – that is, the sociocultural context in which language learning and teaching take place.

Substantive issues

In Chapter 16, van Lier describes the language use of children and teachers in a Spanish-Quechua bilingual education program in Peru. He presents a vivid picture of an attempted educational innovation, along with his own concerns about whether the program and its accompanying research agenda could be sustained over time. The chapter illustrates the use of focused ethnographies and underscores the value of "portrayal" as a method; it also presents "understanding" as a goal of educational research (see van Lier [1988] for further discussion).

In Chapter 17 Adendorff explores the sociocultural context of code switching. His data are derived from situations in which teachers switch between Zulu and English in their interactions with native Zulu-speaking students in South Africa – that is, various classrooms and a school assembly. Adendorff builds his analysis on Gumperz's (1982) and Tannen's (1985) interpretations of code switching as "contextualization cues" and demonstrates that such switches are significant, both academically and socially. Adendorff also explores the implications of code switching for language teacher education.

In Chapter 18 Duff investigates the socialization of discourse competence in two different instructional environments in Hungarian secondary schools. One is a traditional monolingual school in which the dominant pedagogical strategy is that of recitation. The other is a dual-language school in which the instruction occurs mainly in English. The broad goal of Duff's research is to analyze the impact of the massive social changes wrought within the educational system with the end of Soviet domination in Hungary. The data base includes approximately fifty videotaped lessons, as well as written and oral comments from teachers and students. Duff uses her data to highlight issues of educational and linguistic reform in a rapidly changing political environment.

Chapter 19 takes its data from previous studies by Murray herself as well as work by other researchers. Murray's illustrations are drawn from linguistic minority children and adults in California, where portions of the white majority population have recently felt increasingly threatened by emerging minority groups and non-native speaking immigrants. It is in this social context that Murray addresses the concept of diversity. Whether the learners are studying in ESL programs, in college composition classes, or in graduate courses in sociology, the cultural diversity that they represent causes challenges for their teachers. Murray, in a positive, hopeful vein, argues that such diversity should be viewed as a resource, rather than as a source of problems. Her chapter ends with a number of helpful suggestions for teachers along with eloquent excerpts from the students' own emerging voices as authors.

Methodological issues

If anything, the authors in this section paint with an even broader methodological brush than those in other sections of the book. Their research methods include classroom observation, videotapes, transcriptions and close analyses of classroom interaction, fieldnotes, ethnographic narratives, teacher interviews, and examples of learners' writing. What draws these studies together methodologically is the emphasis on the sociopolitical context and the broad interpretive perspective the authors take. In a sense, these studies, among all the chapters in this volume, come closest to being truly ethnographic in character.

A great deal has been written and said about the essential characteristics of ethnographic research (see, for example, Watson-Gegeo 1988). To qualify as ethnographies, studies must be at the very least contextual, unobtrusive, longitudinal, collaborative, interpretive, and organic. We believe that the contextual condition should underpin all naturalistic inquiry (and that is certainly the case in the studies reported in this volume). Of itself, an emphasis on context is therefore not a defining characteristic of ethnography. Being unobtrusive is more difficult. It is also a relativistic and subjective notion, for what is unobtrusive to one individual may be highly obtrusive to another. Ethnographic research is also relatively long term. While this requirement is also subject to a variety of interpretations, it is certainly incompatible with the "quick fix" approach that characterizes a certain amount of classroom research. The notion of collaboration (with the participants in the setting) is also apparent in the four studies reported here. Finally, the analyses are richly interpretive, and there is evidence in these chapters of an interaction between the questions posed and the data collection and interpretation. None of the researchers emerges at the end of his or her study untouched by it.

In a sense, all of these pieces bear out Freeman's (this volume) insight that "to tell the story, you have to know the story." Each chapter is deeply embedded in the sociopolitical, cultural, and educational contexts in which it is located, and an appreciation and understanding of the findings is impossible without the in-depth knowledge of the context which these authors provide.

References

Freeman, D. (Chapter 4, this volume). Redefining the relationship between research and what teachers know.

Gumperz, J. J. 1982. *Discourse Strategies.* Cambridge: Cambridge University Press.

van Lier, L. 1988. *The Classroom and the Language Learner: Ethnography and Second Language Classroom Research.* London: Longman.

Tannen, D. 1985. Cross-cultural communication. In T. A. Van Dijk (ed.), *Handbook of Discourse Analysis.* (vol. 4: Discourse in Society). London: Academic Press.

Watson-Gegeo, K. A. 1988. Ethnography in ESL: Defining the essentials. *TESOL Quarterly* 22, 4, 575–592.

16 Conflicting voices: language, classrooms, and bilingual education in Puno

Leo van Lier

> On the altiplano, at altitudes of 4000
> meters or more, the air is clear and
> sights and sounds carry far. It's a vast
> and windy plain, and from time to time
> you can see small dust-filled whirlwinds
> (torbellinos), the size of a person, race
> across the dry flat pampa, appearing out
> of nowhere and disappearing without a
> trace. The campesinos say that these
> might be troubled souls, and you must
> avoid them crossing your path. A gringo,
> recruited by an agency to be a "foreign
> expert" in some project, might think at
> times that among these dust devils there
> are the ghosts of projects past: foreign
> aid, agricultural experiments, irrigation
> projects, educational innovations. . . .
> Perhaps the bilingual education project
> described here is one of these: once a
> fleeting presence, now vanished without
> a trace, leaving nothing behind except
> some uneasy memories.

In this chapter I describe the language use of children and teachers observed and recorded in many different classrooms while I was working as a "foreign expert" in a bilingual education project high in the Peruvian Andes, in southern Peru. (The names of students, teachers, and schools have been changed in order to protect their anonymity.) I begin with a brief description of the physical setting and the use of the Quechua, Aymara, and Spanish languages in the region. To promote a flavor of authenticity I also use some common local terms.

Some readers may be familiar with the project described here from the work of Hornberger (1988), who was doing her doctoral research in collaboration with the project during my participation. This chapter intends to complement Hornberger's detailed descriptions, as well as an earlier paper (van Lier 1989) and an internal report (van Lier 1984).

Some years ago Bailey wrote a paper entitled "If I had known then what I know now" (1985), a title which would admirably fit my feelings as an ex-"foreign expert" (the phrase seems to *require* quotes). So often, it seems, hindsight painfully highlights all the things one should have done, might have tried, could have changed . . . if only one could have a second chance! This feeling is probably familiar to all those who have worked in one-shot projects, and it dramatically shows how inefficient such attempts at innovation tend to be. It may be familiar also to many thoughtful teachers and teacher educators who have felt this way after a lesson, a course, an observation, or an action undertaken in response to an unexpected occurrence.

Hindsight implies that it is too late to remedy the situation in question, hence the connotation of uselessness that the term carries with it. It is only when we can sufficiently shorten the lag between the hindsight and the actions it refers to, or if we do get that second chance – or multiple chances, in the case of a teacher – that hindsight becomes useful.

My experiences in the bilingual education project of Puno (hereafter PEEB, from the project's official title: Proyecto Experimental de Educación Bilingüe) have contributed considerably to my strong interest in and advocacy of the principles and practices of *action research* and, beyond that, the *theory of practice* outlined in the work of Bourdieu (1977; 1990). This kind of research, and this way of theorizing, carries the hope of turning hindsight into foresight by way of insight, while one is actually still on the job. I did not have that way of working available to me when I was in the project, and I was therefore continually torn between conflicting demands of (primarily ethnographic) research and pedagogic action. As a result of my experiences I am convinced that the only worthwhile reform and innovation is that which combines research and action in principled ways (as do the theory of practice, action research, and critical pedagogy), and that this way of working must be designed into a project right from the start.

I suggest that the reader keep these comments and caveats in mind in the pages that follow. My aims in this chapter are twofold: first, to describe an educational reality which, though different, may nevertheless provide much food for thought and perhaps even lessons to be learned. Second, I hope that this chapter will provide strong arguments for the application of action research in educational settings everywhere.

Puno

I first visited Puno in the late 1970s and remember being impressed by the great lake Titicaca. It's the highest navigable lake in the world, stretching between Peru and Bolivia. The Urus live on the lake on floating islands constructed, like their graceful boats, from reeds that grow in the lake. I had no idea then that I would end up working in Puno for two years.

Puno lies at an altitude of 3800 meters, and most visitors suffer from *soroche* (altitude sickness) for the first few days. The area around the lake has a fairly mild climate, is well suited for agriculture, and is comparatively densely populated. The countryside around Puno is rather flat and barren and is called the *pampa*. There are many small villages (*pueblos*) and even smaller communities (*comunidades* or *ayllus*) where the main activity is subsistence farming.

In Puno and the neighboring city of Juliaca the main language is Spanish, but in the markets and small shops one also hears much Quechua and Aymara. Once outside these cities, especially away from the main roads, the predominant languages are Aymara to the south and around the lakeshore, and Quechua on the rest of the pampa and in the Andean mountains to the north and west (the *cordillera* or *puna*). Quechua is what the Incas spoke, and to this day various dialects of it are spoken all along the Andes, from Chile to Ecuador (Lopez 1988).

Quechua

Quechua (also called *Qhishwa* or *Runasimi*) was the language of the Incas, a sophisticated civilization which stretched from one end of the Andes to the other. The Inca empire was eventually destroyed by Spanish invaders, but the Indians of the high plains, the *Altiplano,* overwhelmingly still speak Quechua and have kept many of their age-old traditions, such as communal work, weaving, distinctive agricultural practices, and ceremonies. The Aymara speakers around the lake and in parts of Bolivia are a different race, never completely dominated by the Incas. The two languages, though related, are very different, but I will refrain from giving a linguistic description. I will mainly discuss the Quechua area, since that is where I did most of my work.

In the rural communities of the Altiplano, the children are overwhelmingly monolingual in Quechua or Aymara when they enter the first grade (between 80 and 100 percent, depending on the size of the community, its proximity to a main road, and other factors). In the absence of sporadic bilingual education experiments like the one described here, all schooling has traditionally been conducted in Spanish, with varying degrees of tolerance of the native language in the first three grades, ranging from a total ban (including punishments for speaking it, and signs in the classroom saying *prohibido hablar Quechua* [speaking Quechua prohibited] to occasional use when children obviously don't understand something or break down in tears. It is an unwritten rule, clearly observable to this day, that from the third grade on all children should address teachers in Spanish and vice versa.

During the revolutionary government in the late 1960s and early 1970s, there was a strong push for the revaloration of indigenous languages and cultures, and in 1975 Quechua was declared an official language alongside Spanish. The sociocultural optimism of those days was well expressed by the prominent Peruvian sociolinguist, Escobar (1976: 15).

The officialization of Quechua in the country, giving it equal rank to Spanish, is a decisive act of cultural politics. This act does not pretend to substitute Spanish, which is the language that offers us the greatest communicative range inside and outside the Republic, but must rather be seen as a choice in linguistic planning, directed towards the reorientation and rectification of the asymmetrical interchange between the Spanish and Quechua-speaking segments of the population of Peru. (my translation)

The project

It was out of this optimism that the PEEB was born, in an agreement between the Peruvian and West German governments. However, by the time the project began to be implemented, the government and the public mood had changed, and equality between Spanish and Quechua was as remote and unlikely as it had ever been. Even so, the project was implemented as planned, starting around 1980, staffed by foreign and local educators and experts (Jung 1992). Though initially favoring a transitional model, it came to strongly advocate a maintenance and enrichment model of bilingual education, in which the native language would be maintained throughout the elementary school and the pedagogical materials would consciously try to bolster the language by resuscitating native grammar, vocabulary, and expressions wherever possible. Moreover, indigenous wisdom, knowledge, skills, and traditions were respected and given prominence in the curriculum, through stories, discussions of medicinal herbs and the Incaic abacus (*yupana*), ancient irrigation systems, and so on. The aim was to give the children reason to be proud of their language and their heritage. To my knowledge, everybody involved in the project was committed to these ideals and goals, and this created a unique spirit of idealism and concerted action. Yet, many of us worried that the project – with its explicit objectives and planned actions – might not succeed, that it might disappear, once the foreigners disappeared and the funds were withdrawn. This is what many of us thought (see also the conclusions expressed in Hornberger [1988] and van Lier [1989]). Was this an unduly pessimistic view? PEEB participants Jung and Lopez (1988) indicate in their survey of the project's activities that the end of the official project sponsorship signals the beginning of "a new phase" of bilingual education in Puno. There were hopes, therefore, that the project would continue, perhaps transformed or reconfigured in some way, fueled by local energies. In addition, there may be important, lasting effects in unexpected, intangible, delayed, or dispersed ways, in individuals and groups, near or far away.

The dynamics of working in a situation like this are perplexing and themselves worthy of study. I cannot do full justice to them here, but my description may give a flavor of them, and perhaps remind readers of correlates in their own experiences. Returning to the concrete tasks of the project, I now proceed with a brief summary of its developments and major activities.

The project's main tasks can be summarized as follows:

1. The design, production, and revision of syllabi and educational materials in two vernacular languages without a well-developed literary tradition to draw on.
2. The development of a syllabus for teaching Spanish as a second language and the production of materials for this new subject.
3. The enrichment of native languages and cultures through the recuperation of linguistic forms and expressions and the inclusion of native cultural content and knowledge.
4. Teacher training in native-language literacy and grammar, second-language methodology, and general pedagogy.
5. Convincing teachers, parents, children, and authorities of the benefits of a bilingual/bicultural approach.

In addition to being on the production team for two of the Quechua textbooks, and participating in regular training courses for the project's teachers, I was involved in the overall evaluation (monitoring) of the project for the two years I was there. As part of these various duties I frequently visited communities in which the program was implemented in one or more elementary classrooms. In particular, I often spent an entire week at two schools which constituted one of three sets (or pairs) especially chosen to assess the effectiveness of the project on a longitudinal basis. One of these, *Tiyaña* was a project school (i.e., bilingual education was implemented there). The other, *Qotokancha*, was a "comparison school" in which there were no bilingual grades. These two communities were located a few miles apart.

During these visits I administered (sometimes with colleagues' help) entry and exit tests to all children in bilingual grades and comparison grades, both in Quechua and Spanish (spoken and written), observed classes, and talked to teachers, parents, and students about many issues, pedagogical and otherwise. We also played volleyball and *fulbito* (a variety of soccer) and attended community meetings. On one occasion I participated in the annual *pago a la pachamama*, a ritual payment to Mother Earth, to enlist her collaboration for the new school year.

In the remainder of this chapter, I focus on the classrooms, the teachers, and the students in the Altiplano. I try to make my description as realistic as possible so that the reader can form a mental picture of the setting and the role of language in it.

The school: the daily grind

In this section I reconstruct (from my fieldnotes) a typical visit to Tiyaña and Qotokancha. On Monday morning some colleagues and I leave from Puno in one of the project cars. I am dropped off first, then my fellow passengers continue on to other destinations to conduct tests, teacher training, or observations in other schools. The trip takes about four hours, depending on road conditions. We usually pick up several people who need a lift, including teachers on their way to various schools.

We arrive in Tiyaña just after eight in the morning. The school, consisting of three classrooms (adobe walls and corrugated tin roof) and a storeroom (*almacen*), which the *director* (the principal) has converted into his living quarters, is still locked. There is no community center as such (apart from the school itself), just a scattering of low adobe houses strewn across the pampa, with tilled fields in between the houses and further out, against the low foothills of the *Cordillera*. Gradually the children and the teachers (three in total) begin to arrive from various directions. Meanwhile the *awicha*, or grandmother, a tiny old woman living in a small house next to the school, comes over for a chat in Quechua, from which I cannot gather much more than that the teachers are good-for-nothing layabouts and drunks, the children are a nuisance, and the weather continues to be awful.

When the teachers arrive, one by one, we greet, exchange news, and discuss plans for the week. Around nine o'clock the *profesor de turno* (teacher-on-duty; this week it's Gerardo's turn) whistles for the *formación*. The children line up, grade by grade, facing the school. The students receive a pep talk, general announcements about meetings or various community activities, sing a couple of songs (including the national anthem), perhaps do a bit of marching in place. All this is in Spanish, with a few comments repeated in Quechua for the benefit of the smallest ones (*los más chiquitos*).

Students continue to arrive in dribs and drabs throughout the *formación* (many of them having to walk up to an hour from their widely dispersed homes across the pampa). Around 9:30 the students are marched into their classrooms. In Tiyaña there are three teachers, which means that every teacher has two grades. The director, Luis, has the first and the sixth grade, which is unusual (adjacent grades being the rule in combination classes). I begin by observing a couple of classes, and plan to start the oral entry test for the first grade after lunch.

The classroom is fairly spacious, with barely adequate light from two rows of small windows in opposite walls. About half of the window panes are broken. There is no electricity (or running water or other amenities) in the school or in Tiyaña as a whole, for that matter, and the room is quite cold early in the morning. The sixth grade students (ten children) sit at one end of the room, facing the back wall, the first grade students (seventeen children) at the other, facing the front.

At 10:30 there is recess, and Luis and I stand outside against the wall which is now warmed by the sun to warm ourselves for a while. Then the teachers, several of the biggest kids, and I play volleyball after putting up the net. It is almost 11:30 before the director declares that it is time to go in again. Another lesson follows, and at 12:15 it is lunchtime.

The children take their plate or mug and go to the back of the school where the kitchen is. Several sixth graders and a few *madres de familia* (mothers, who do this voluntarily, in turns) have prepared *el quaker* (oatmeal) which they dole out to the children.

At about 1:30 Gerardo blows the whistle for *formación*. At that moment, the *Teniente Gobernador* (the elected leader of Tiyaña), Don Anselmo, arrives on his bicycle. We talk a bit, and he makes some announcements to the assembled children about vaccinations for cattle, the importance of hygiene, and the need to study hard in school. He speaks in a mixture of Spanish and Quechua, with Quechua predominating.

Around two o'clock the children march into their classrooms again. Assisted by an older student, I start the oral Quechua test (about five to ten minutes per child), using a structured interview format. At three o'clock there is another recess which lasts 'til four, and then the children are sent home. One teacher, Ignacio, rides home on his little motorbike. The other teacher, Gerardo, walks across the pampa to a house where he rents a room.

Later on, Luis fetches a bucket of water from an open water hole behind the school, and I help him cook dinner (the inevitable *sopita*, or soup, made with potato, tomato, noodles, and a few other bits and pieces that happen to be available) on a primus stove, sharing some ingredients. Gerardo comes over to join us.

The other days proceed very much like the first one. On Wednesday I go to Qotokancha (Ignacio gives me a ride over on his motorbike), where there are only two teachers, each one taking care of three grades – but otherwise a similar routine is followed. On Friday afternoon I wait for the car to take me back to Puno.

369

Leo van Lier

Educational practices

It has been commented by many observers (see, for example, Hornberger 1988; van den Berghe and Primov 1977; Wagner, 1979) that traditional methods of teaching in Peru (as in many other places) rely heavily on copying, repetition, and rote memorization. Van den Berghe and Primov, doing research in the rural areas around Cuzco, a region not dissimilar to Puno, noted the following about educational practices there.

When in attendance, children learn little and slowly because of the enormous obstacle of learning to read and write in a foreign language and because of the rigid, authoritarian, and antiquated pedagogical techniques used. Teaching is by rote memorization, often without understanding. Spanish is taught largely by the repetition of songs chanted in chorus or by the recitation of memorized verses. Even the alphabet is learned through choral chanting. The success of the teacher is measured by how much of a theatrical performance of recitations and songs her pupils can produce for visiting school inspectors and other mestizos. In most instances, the children have little or no understanding of the meaning of the Spanish words they recite. Much school time is also devoted to such activities as making the children stand in military formation by order of height, inspecting them for cleanliness, singing the national anthem, or listening to exhorations by teachers. (1977: 167–168)

These authors blame the bad practices they noted on two main factors: the language is foreign to the students and the pedagogical practices in general are antiquated. That the poor quality of teaching cannot just be blamed on language problems is supported by the work of Wagner (1979) in northern Peru, where the native language of the students is Spanish.

The model of teaching – routine-based and without variation, whether oral or written – is based on repetition, learning by heart, copying texts and dictation. . . . By means of this method of repetition and memorization the teacher exerts a kind of pressure on the students which, throughout the years of schooling, becomes deeper and deeper. Moreover, this constant repetition causes in the children fatigue, boredom, and saturation, because the teaching is at times very abstract and formalistic, and the students are not given the opportunity to develop through free expression and play. (p. 150; my translation)

In her observations, Wagner suggests that one of the causes of this methodology is the use of contents and expressions which are alien to the reality of the children, and which signal a disdain for their own reality. This is so because the books invariably depict urban and suburban people and lifestyles.

Hornberger (1988) suggests a further plausible reason for these pedagogical infelicities. The teachers very often do not have books for all the students, and the only way to present the required materials is to write a text on the blackboard for copying, or to dictate from the teacher's book. Indeed, I have frequently observed that teachers, especially in the upper grades, use only one source, a fat book called *la enciclopédia* (the encyclopedia), which contains suggested material for all the subjects of a particular grade. The teacher reads from this or writes parts of it on the board. The content and the style of these encyclopedias do not seem to have been chosen with the levels of interest or comprehension of primary school students in mind, to put it very mildly. They excel in turgid prose and themes that bear not the remotest relationship to anything a rural child might need to know.

We have thus identified a school system for rural children which is seriously inadequate, and we have seen four reasons for the inadequacy: (1) the language of instruction is unknown to the students, (2) teaching methods are antiquated, (3) the subject matter of instruction is alien to the students, and (4) the teacher has no materials available for the students. The PEEB attempted to deal with these problems by making the native language the language of instruction (with a gradual increase in the use of Spanish, reaching 50 percent in the upper grades), by holding annual training courses and a program of follow-up on-site visits, by drawing extensively on native knowledge and crafts, and by providing materials for all students and teachers free of charge.

In the classroom

In this section I describe some typical classrooms, presenting a composite picture, but one which is designed to be realistic and representative. The resulting picture is derived from my observation notes (made at each classroom visit) and from my transcription of audio recordings.

Let's first enter Luis's room. The reader will recall that this contains both the first and sixth grade. There are about seventeen children in the first grade, and about ten in the sixth grade, facing different ends of the room. The first graders have the "good" blackboard, whereas the sixth graders have a makeshift one made of a piece of sheet metal. The students sit at tables about three to four feet long, on low benches without backs or boards placed on concrete blocks. Girls and boys always sit at separate tables. One student is standing by the wall because there is no convenient place for him to sit. All the children in the first grade (I will ignore the sixth grade for the moment, difficult though this is given the noise they make) have pencils, but in some cases they are down to the last inch. Two little children have their pencil tied around their neck with a string (indicating how valuable pencils are here). Unfortunately the string is so short that they practically strangle themselves when putting the pencil to paper. All children have lined notebooks, in some cases inherited from siblings who were in first grade before them, with some blank pages left.

As we settle down, two students are trying to fix one of the tables which collapsed. Luis comes over and takes a look at it, then tells the students (in Quechua) to take it outside. The first-grade Quechua textbook *Kusi* is distributed. Luis puts a colorful picture on the board, of a little girl taking an armload of wool to the lake (*Kusi gochaman willmata apan*, reads the text underneath). Luis writes the word *willma* (wool) on the board, pronouncing it several times, then divides it into syllables: *will - ma*. He writes and pronounces *ma* separately, then writes *ma mi mu me mo* with a circle around each one. The students get instructions (in Quechua) to copy these syllables many times. He models writing the letter *m*, counting the legs *huk, iskay, kinsa* (one, two, three), as he draws them. When the children start writing he goes over to the sixth grade. I go around helping here and there. It strikes me that the children appear to have had no guidance in how to hold a pencil. Most of them find it impossible to stay between the lines, and their often diminutive pencil stubs or the strings around their neck obviously don't help. I guide some of the children's hands and model how to hold the pencil.

We now move to Qotokancha, where there is no bilingual education, and all classes are therefore in Spanish. We enter the grade 1-2-3 combination class, where young Teófilo is the teacher. There are sixteen children in the class. The teacher has written two sentences on the board:

Papá trabaja en el campo. (Dad works in the field.)
Mamá cocina en la casa. (Mom cooks in the house.)

Underneath these two sentences he has written:

pa - pe - pi - po - pu
ma - me - mi - mo - mu

The students are asked (in Spanish) to copy the two sentences many times. I walk around and note similar problems to the ones I mentioned in Luis's class. I note many errors such as reversals of letters and words (*ne* instead of *en*), and much atrocious handwriting. Then I notice something quite peculiar. Many students have written *canipu* or *canipo* instead of *campo*, every time they have copied the word. This is a very puzzling error, until I take a good look at the blackboard, and notice a small spot on it, just above the third leg of the letter *m* in *campo*. Since *canipu/-o* is not a word in Spanish, this is clear evidence of how mechanical the students' copying activities are.

A little later in the lesson, students are called to the front of the classroom one by one to read the sentences on the board. It is clear that the students are not actually reading, but rather repeating from memory what it says up there. The last little girl who has to come forward is very small and appears very shy. She does not want to move. The teacher has to go to her seat, take her by the hand, and lead her to the front. The little girl speaks some scarcely audible words while the teacher holds her hand, all the while speaking reassuring words to her in Quechua. After that, two boys are called to the front for some recitation, then the whole class sings several songs (in Spanish) in a spirited performance designed to impress the visiting *misti* (Westerner).

It might be worth mentioning that during this lesson, which lasts about one hour, several bigger girls from the other class (where the teacher appears to be absent) crowd into the open doorway of the classroom, in order to check out the *misti* and observe the lesson, causing considerable disruption. Every five minutes or so the teacher goes to the door to kick them out, but they promptly reappear, giggling and whispering behind their hands. One boy makes the eminently sensible suggestion: "¡*Cierre la puerta*!" (Close the door!) but it is ignored, and the disruption-eviction-reappearance cycle continues until the end of the lesson.[1]

The next lesson is on addition. First there is some recitation, an extract from which follows. "P" represents the teacher (*profesor*) and A (A) represents student (s) ("*alumno (s)*").

1	P	*cinco más tres*	five plus three
2	AA	*ocho:: / ocho:::*	ei::ght / ei:::ght
3	P	*siete más dos*	seven plus two
4	AA	*nueve: / nueve:*	ni:ne / ni:ne
5	P	*cinco más dos*	five plus two
6	AA	*shete:: / shete::*	sheve::n / sheve::n

(Lines 7 through 12 have been left out.)

13	P	*tres más cinco*	three plus five
14	AA	*tre:::::s / seis*	three::::: / six
15	P	*mentira*	not true
16	A	*qué cosa es pué*	what is it then
17	P	*es ocho*	it's eight
18	AA	*ocho:::*	ei:::ght

1 One of the characteristics of the rural classroom is its interruptability. The school is truly the property of the community, and *comuneros* feel free at all times to walk in and strike up a conversation with the teacher, or to call the teacher out to discuss something in the *patio*.

We can note two things here. First, the teacher (in line 17) gives the correct answer without finding out if the students themselves can do it. Second, it appears that the sums have been learned entirely by heart. The students have no trouble with "five plus three" (lines 1 and 2), but they stumble over "three plus five." The teacher does not use the opportunity to point out to the students that $5 + 3 = 3 + 5$. After the recitation, a row of sums is put on the blackboard:

$$
\begin{array}{ccc}
8 & 9 & \\
+2 & +3 & \ldots \text{etc.}
\end{array}
$$

When the teacher has finished writing all the additions on the board, he proceeds to add all the sums to them. Then he instructs the class: *Vayan haciendo eso en sus cuadernos* (start doing this in your notebooks). He does not erase the sums, so the students merely copy the numbers, without getting any practice in addition. After some time of copying, another row of additions is put on the board and a student is called to the front to do the sums. None of the children are paying attention, and over in the corner a few girls start playing *yaquis* (jacks) on the floor. The teacher sits at his desk, turned toward the blackboard, talking to the girl who is – unsuccessfully – trying to do the sums. He apparently does not notice the rapid deterioration of order in the classroom.

We next peek into a bilingual classroom in another school, where a teacher is teaching a lesson in Quechua. He draws different sizes of objects on the board: chairs, balloons, *phushkas* (spinning tools). He asks the students to copy the drawing of the chair, which appears an impossible task, especially since many students do not actually have a notebook. He starts pointing to the chairs and so on of different sizes and says: *Más hathun* (more *grande*) and *Más huch'uy* (more *pequeño*). These are the Quechua words for big and small, with the Spanish comparative modifier *más*. Sometime later the teacher points to the medium-sized chair on the board, and proclaims: *Ni huch'uy ni hathun – chawpi*. In other words, "neither small nor big – medium," another example of code mixing (*ni* is Spanish for neither; the adjectives are Quechua).

Back in Tiyaña, it is time to observe Gerardo's grade 3-4 combination class. During *recreo* I ask him what his next lesson is going to be. He walks over to the weekly schedule on the wall and points to Monday. "Let's see. . . ." I remind him that it is actually Tuesday. "Ah, social studies." This indicates that the next lesson is unlikely to be carefully planned. Gerardo writes on the board: *Autoridades de la comunidad* (authorities of the community). All the authorities are listed, with their titles, and the students are asked to copy. I now notice a writing practice which one sees with some regularity in other schools as well, and which we might call "vertical copying." Let's say that the students have to copy sentences like this:

Teniente Gobernador: Sr. Juan Pumpilla
Presidente de la ASPAFA: Don Pedro Mamani Pari
El Director: . . . etc.

The students will copy T - P - E - . . . on successive lines, then next to these letters they will write, again starting at the top and working their way down, e - r - 1 . . . , and so on. They are therefore not copying words, but rather an amorphous multitude of letters, in a way that seems most efficient to them. In the final product, words are run together and spacing of letters and lines looks strangely chaotic – strange, that is, until one realizes that the text has been vertically constructed. As a result the text is virtually unreadable. However, this does not appear to matter since one does not get the impression that it is actually ever *meant* to be read.

Before leaving this section a few qualifying comments are in order. My examples give a rather gloomy, and some would say unfairly negatively biased, picture of pedagogical practices in the Altiplano. One might observe also good lessons, even excellent ones. During my final year in the project I observed a beautiful lesson on telling the time taught by a new teacher in Qotokancha. Although this was not a project class, she used Quechua in an exemplary way to scaffold her instruction, at the same time modeling Spanish with an evident concern for its comprehensibility. However, in my notes and recordings such lessons, whether bilingual (in the "official" sense) or not, are extremely rare. This may have been the result of my particular assignment. My colleagues certainly reported observing excellent teaching now and again. Hornberger (1988), while generally noting very much the same educational practices as those described in my vignettes, observed a qualitative (as well as quantitative) improvement in the use of Quechua in the project schools as compared to non-project schools (p. 158). I personally saw as much, if not more, responsible use of Quechua in non-project schools as in project schools, paradoxical though it may seem. This means that, in the schools in which I did most of my observing, the project was not implemented in ways intended by its designers. Further, one might even say that for some teachers the formalization of Quechua in the project syllabus actually resulted in more artificial and less beneficial native-language use than the haphazard, unpremeditated use of Quechua which they had hitherto employed.

Leo van Lier

Whistling in the wind?

The project started out with the aim of implementing bilingual education in 100 schools, equally divided between the Aymara and Quechua areas. By 1982, however, it became clear that the goal of 100 schools was extremely unrealistic. We based this on widespread observations that in many schools that were officially on our list, the project was implemented only partially or not at all. Further, given the lack of personnel, the difficult traveling conditions, and inadequate transportation, it was impossible to provide even the barest minimum of in-service backup, monitoring, and training. To make matters worse, our timetable was to add one grade every year, and in addition to native-language instruction and Spanish as a second language, we were developing curricula for mathematics, science, and social sciences. This meant that we might soon have to observe and train teachers in all six grades for five different subjects, a task which vastly exceeded our capacities.

We decided, therefore, to do a complete and exhaustive survey of all the schools on our list, and over a two-month period we produced a detailed report on the state of the project (Lopez, Stack, and van Lier 1982). We found, among many other disturbing, though not wholly unexpected, circumstances that the project was appropriately implemented in only fourteen of the eighty-six schools then on our official list, with a further twenty-one schools in which the project was partially implemented in at least one grade. The remaining fifty-one schools applied the program ineffectively (based on observations, interviews, and examination of students' work) or not at all.

We determined many different reasons for this state of affairs, too many to discuss in detail here. Among them were the frequent and unpredictable transfer of teachers, and the fact that, in their haste to assemble the magical number of 100 schools, the initiators of the project had chosen some schools in urban centers or along main roads, where the influence of Spanish was too strong to establish bilingual education. Perhaps most seriously of all, we felt that in many schools bilingual education had been implanted without the full conviction or informed consent of the teacher(s), the principal of the school, or the community's parents. We came across many teachers who did not appear interested or who had not been properly trained. In many communities we noted a definite suspicion and resentment among the parents, at times bordering on scarcely concealed hostility, restrained only by the free materials provided by the project. We thus faced an additional task: diffusion of the ideals and goals of the project and consciousness raising among teachers and parents.

As a result of this study, and after much soul searching and discussion, the team decided to reduce the number of schools to around forty, a number which during 1983 further decreased to around thirty-five (see also Hornberger 1988: 42ff). We hoped that, with this more manageable number, we would be able to visit each school twice a year and observe every classroom and subject taught bilingually at least once a year. However, my report of 1984 showed that we were not able to visit 49 out of 124 bilingual classrooms even once in the first half of 1983 (van Lier 1984). To compensate somewhat for our inability to provide adequate in-service and on-site backup, we instituted several week-long training courses for project teachers prior to the beginning of the school year in 1983 and 1984.

Searching, researching, . . .

If the description so far has given readers the impression that we were like amateur jugglers throwing more items into the air than we knew how to catch coming down, then they have a fairly accurate picture of the situation. Amidst our ongoing duties of teacher training and follow-up, diffusion, materials production, testing, and coping with broken-down cars and impassable roads, we had an ambitious program of longitudinal research.

I mentioned earlier that we had chosen three project schools matched with three similar nearby non-project schools, and we used these three pairs to obtain longitudinal comparative data regarding the functioning of the project. In these schools we observed and recorded classes, tested all incoming and outgoing students in each bilingual and comparison grade using a variety of specially designed or adapted measures of proficiency and scholastic achievement, talked to parents and other community members, and so on. One such research visit has been briefly sketched (the description of Gerardo's class).

In addition to this structured research activity, for which three of us set aside several weeks each school year, we engaged in a number of ad hoc data-gathering activities to obtain specific kinds of information. A brief enumeration and description of some of the more salient activities follows.

Classroom observation: Checklists, duties, possibilities

In order to carry out the *seguimiento* (on-site follow-up and guidance) throughout the school year, teams of locally appointed specialists traveled to all the schools to assess the implementation of the project, observe classes, attend community meetings, deliver materials, and give pedagogical advice. We devised an observational instrument (*la ficha de observación*) which was intended to fulfill the dual purpose of providing pedagogical advice to teachers as well as basic research data.

In my evaluation report of 1984, which covered the preceding eighteen months of monitoring work, I repeatedly emphasized that classroom observation should be the cornerstone of our program evaluation and that a major weakness in our evaluation was that analysis of classroom work was given lower priority than all sorts of other activities (van Lier 1984: 104). This comment highlights the difficulties of balancing day-to-day jobs and emergencies with longer-term monitoring/research requirements. In addition, some members argued that giving too much emphasis to follow-up and evaluation activities would be a luxury limited to the "privileged few of the early hours" (ibid.), which could not be sustained once the project was generalized all over Puno, and which therefore should be rejected as being unrealistic. In other words, there is no point in doing a better job in a pilot project than you can expect to do in its eventual generalized implementation, a defeatist position which the project as a whole never bought into. However, it turns out that the research aspect was generally sacrificed for practical concerns. Most unfortunate (from my own perspective) was that the six-school monitoring project, designed especially so as not to forget research in the hustle and bustle of daily activity, was discontinued altogether. Jung and Lopez (1988: 291), in retrospect, offer the following comment:

[W]e regret the discontinuation of the longitudinal study, begun in 1983 by a linguist member of the team, which only got as far as to cover the first two grades in a few project schools. Under the coordination of Leo van Lier, various members of the team collected information in six schools, three with bilingual education and three comparison schools. In spite of its short duration, this study gives a closer view of the educational processes, and, in this way, permits us to interpret and understand better the results of these processes as they relate to scholastic achievement. (my translation)

Increasingly, therefore, research and practice, monitoring and action, had to be combined into one single job. Turning once more to my report of 1984, I recall my conviction that it was impossible to combine activities of in-service training with investigation and monitoring. I found support in a report on program evaluation in bilingual education (Cohen 1979: 25):

During classroom visits, members of the evaluation team should not examine or evaluate the performance of the teachers or aides. Rather, they should investigate the instructional processes of bilingual education, especially those that differ from the processes in traditional education locally. (my translation)[2]

2 In my report (1984: 110) I translated this from English to Spanish. Now, being unable to trace the original document, I must translate it back into English. I hope that, in spite of these translational peregrinations, the quote still resembles Mr. Cohen's original text!

TABLE I   TEACHERS' LANGUAGE USE

Greatest L1 use	%	Greatest bilingual use	%	Greatest L2 use	%
With own parents	76.5	With students	72.3	With own	
With students'		With spouse	45.3	children	64.0
parents	71.8	With colleagues	42.4	With colleagues	57.6
With local		With own		With friends	48.2
authorities	58.8	siblings	37.7	With own	
With own family		With local		siblings	46.5
members	50.6	authorities	36.5	With spouse	40.0
With friends	25.9	With own		With own family	
With students	23.5	children	32.0	members	28.9

That powerful generator of rationality – hindsight – is once again kicked into action to see if it can churn out some suggestions that might resolve this research-practice conflict. I now think that the way of working known as action research can very usefully be pressed into service in situations such as the one described here. According to Kemmis and McTaggart (1982: 5), "action research provides a way of working which links theory and practice into the one whole: ideas-in-action." Had we read this sentence in 1982, we might have designed our activities around this organizational concept, and perhaps created a research/practice dynamic that could have withstood the multiple pressures of the situation. Our actual activities might not have turned out all that differently, but perhaps an action research focus could have given us an ethos capable of turning constraints into resources. Who knows?

Survey of teacher demographics and attitudes

In spite of the daily onslaught of urgent tasks, we managed to assemble a few snippets of research that are noteworthy. One of these was a small survey of all the project teachers ($N = 85$ to 90) in terms of their circumstances of life and work, language use, and attitudes toward a few relevant phenomena (for one part of this survey, see Hornberger 1988, App. 5). The following findings are of particular interest in the context of this chapter.

LANGUAGE USE

We asked the teachers to indicate when they mostly used their L1 (Quechua or Aymara), L2 (Spanish), or a mixture of L1 and L2. Table 1 shows some of the reported functional separation of the two lan-

Leo van Lier

guages. In particular, note the discrepancy between the teachers' predominant use of L2 with their own children, and the required (by the project) use of L1 with the students in school.

In addition to these self-report data, an attitude survey (see Hornberger 1988: 255) elicited frequently contradictory statements from most participating teachers, indicating considerable sociolinguistic instability in the teachers. Moreover, in conversation teachers would often use the term *despierto* (being awake) when referring to students who spoke Spanish or manifested other Westernized traits.[3] One bilingual teacher admonished his students by threatening that unless they paid attention they would forever be stuck *en este lugar* (in this place). Although all our teachers showed a keen interest in their native language and unanimously supported our efforts at its preservation, they evinced numerous signs of the constant sociocultural pressure of Spanish in their environment. A teacher whose name was Donaldo Mamani Rodriguez would sign his name Donaldo M. Rodriguez, rather than the more usual Donaldo Mamani Rodriguez, or Donaldo Mamani R., thus highlighting his Spanish name and downplaying his Indian name. (Mamani is one of the most common Quechua surnames.)

RESIDENTIAL PREFERENCES

Of the teachers we polled (84 percent were male, and 87 percent were married), 38 percent lived in Puno or Juliaca, although only 9 percent had been born there, indicating the urbanization trend among educated people. Furthermore, virtually all teachers apply for relocation every year. In an earlier paper I wrote about this as follows (van Lier 1989: 523; see also Hornberger 1988: 43):

The teacher's place of work is rarely his preferred location, and each year, as a recurring ritual of hope, he files his application for transfer to a school in the town where his family lives, or to a school closer by, or to a school closer to the main road. Placement is assessed by way of a list of rankings of points, based upon experience, family situation, years of service in the rural area, professional activities, and potentially a host of other less predictable factors. Inevitably, the best teachers tend to be the first to leave the rural areas.

Although only a minority (probably less than 20 percent) succeeded in this endeavor in any one year, teacher transfer was a major cause of instability in the project, particularly since it often occurred in the middle of the school year, and at a moment's notice.

3 See Montoya (1984) and van Lier (1989) for a discussion of the concept of "becoming awake" in Andean culture.

380

SEXISM

We had the strong suspicion that differential treatment of boys and girls was endemic in the rural school system. Consulting my notes and observation reports for 1983, I came across a dramatic shift in participation levels in boys and girls over the duration of the first grade. At the beginning of the year there was no difference between the levels of participation of the two sexes: Girls were just as likely as boys to raise their hand, shout answers, and climb on their tables in sheer scholastic exuberance. In fact, the sharpest and most bright-eyed children in my entry tests were often little girls. At the end of the first grade, however, things had changed dramatically. Most girls had gravitated toward the back of the room, many of them had become remarkably shy, and one might often see little groups of girls playing under a table or in the corner without being reprimanded by the teacher. During the year these girls had clearly received and internalized a message, whether hidden or overt, regarding the expectations of their success in school. We did not obtain sufficiently fine-grained data to examine the educational processes whereby this differential was created, though it would no doubt have been extremely useful to investigate the phenomenon in depth.

In one of our questionnaires we decided to ask teachers the open-ended question as to whether they treated boys and girls differently, and if so, how and why? We knew full well that the teachers were aware of our egalitarian values in this respect, and might therefore be expected to conceal any biases they might have. We were surprised, therefore, that over half of the teachers (forty-eight out of eighty-nine) indicated clear differences in their own treatment of boys and girls, and stated their reasons for this quite baldly. Here are some characteristic replies:

The boys are more *despiertos* (awake) and the girls are more silent.
A boy is extrovert and a girl is introvert.
The female student knows little and the male student achieves normally.
Because the boys learn more rapidly.
Yes, a boy tends to be a leader, but a girl is more subservient.
Yes, it's different, the girls form little groups amongst themselves, the same as the boys, the girls in the lower grades stick together, withdraw, do not converse.
Yes, it's different, because a boy acts almost naturally but a little girl is more timid.

We can note in classroom observations and in comments such as these that societal role configurations are reconstructed with great efficiency in the educational process.

TABLE 2 COLORS IN L1 AND L2

	Entry		Exit	
	L1	L2	L1	L2
Knows/says all colors on test	48%	17%	50%	17%
Knows/says some colors	43%	47%	38%	61%
Doesn't know/say the colors	9%	36%	12%	22%

TABLE 3 COUNTING IN L1 AND L2

	Entry		Exit	
	L1	L2	L1	L2
Counts up to seven	21%	31%	20.5%	74%
Counts up to three	49%	22%	33.5%	16%
Doesn't know/say numbers	30%	47%	46.0%	10%

Children's language maintenance and attrition

I mentioned earlier that in a six-school sample we conducted a battery of entry and exit tests for all pupils in the first and second grades. The results of these tests told us far more about the individual teachers than about any significant differences between project and comparison schools. However, as a byproduct they provided interesting glimpses of several educational issues, such as language dominance. A cursory glance at the data showed that as the students were learning Spanish, they were *unlearning* Quechua. In other words, a process of *subtractive bilingualism* was underway, with L2 gradually replacing L1. I had insufficient data to note any differences in this respect between bilingual and comparison schools, and a more in-depth investigation into this crucial issue was never undertaken, to my knowledge.

To illustrate the subtractive tendency, I present here Tables 2, 3, and 4, constructed post hoc from first-grade entry and exit tests involving around 135 students in three bilingual and three non-bilingual first grades. (Bear in mind that there were no significant differences in performance between the two sets.) The data are based on questions we asked the children in interviews in Quechua/Aymara and in Spanish at the beginning of the year and again at the end of the year. We asked the children to tell us the color of various objects, to count how many fingers we were holding up, to take a particular number of pebbles from a jar, to point to their nose, and so on. Crude though these data are, the tendencies of subtraction are clear (though less so in the colors table than in the others).

TABLE 4 BODY PARTS IN L1 AND L2*

| | Entry | | | | Exit | | | |
| | In L1 | | In L2 | | In L1 | | In L2 | |
	Rec.	Prod.	Rec.	Prod.	Rec.	Prod.	Rec.	Prod.
Uses all	96%	67%	9%	25%	30%	48%	20%	43%
Uses some	4%	16%	57%	29%	68%	17%	62%	34%
Uses none	0%	17%	34%	46%	2%	35%	18%	23%

*In this table a division into *receptive* and *productive* was possible. The fact that in L2 the productive use is greater than the receptive use is because different items were included in these test parts. The students had particular difficulty, in the receptive test with the items *brazo* (arm) and *pierna* (leg), possibly due to the fact that the native language does not make an arm-hand or leg-foot distinction. Careful retesting might have resolved these and other problems in the tests.

The logic of pedagogy

The pedagogical actions and the educational process I have described are not random effects of bad teaching practices. Rather, they are the result of rational responses to specific contextual problems. The following example is from a class of Spanish as a second language. The purpose is to teach the difference between the article in masculine and feminine plurals: *los* versus *las*. Note how the teacher (P) consistently gives the correct form before the students (AA) repeat in chorus, and, even more interestingly, how the students systematically fail to repeat the required item correctly at the required time. In line 1, the teacher gives the article *los* which is the object of the exercise; in line 2, the students connect the plural article to the singular noun; in line 3, the teacher models "the pencils" correctly; and in line 4, the students leave out the article but repeat the noun in the correct plural form. It is as if the teacher is a fisherman who, upon having caught two slippery eels, is trying to put them both in a small bucket but finds that whenever he finally manages to grab one and put it in it, the other one slithers out again.

1 P	Y aqui . . . <u>los</u> . . .	And here . . . <u>the</u> . . .
2 AA	<u>los</u> lápis	<u>the</u> pencil
3 P	<u>los</u> lapices	<u>the</u> pencils
4 AA	<u>lapices</u> ((etc.))	pencils

I have described in an earlier section how teachers rely heavily on rote repetition and mechanical copying. Reading and writing are taught on the basis of words and sentences which the student does not understand, linked to pictures which do not correspond to the child's reality. As a result, children cannot react in spontaneous, creative ways to the tasks put before them, with an understanding of the message represented by the words that are offered. In the past, teachers tried to deal with this by using the native language as a last resort, but in asystematic and officially proscribed ways. As a result of these difficulties, and to avoid utter instructional chaos, the teacher has developed the mechanism of answering his or her own questions before giving the students the opportunity to respond, as the only reliable way of obtaining the desired answer. Following the teacher's answer, the students repeat it in chorus, and the exuberance with which this is accomplished has become a major indicator of educational quality.

Bilingual education, by destroying the conditions which have brought the described educational practices about, might be expected to reverse these practices instantly and irrevocably. However, my observations indicate that we are dealing here with a profoundly internalized habit, which is, moreover, culturally normatized. I noted frequently that our excellent materials and our modest in-service training activities notwithstanding, teachers would ask a question, give the answer, and then call forth a choral repetition. On one occasion, during our annual teacher training course, we had put a picture on the board, and underneath it written words relating to the picture in Quechua. We modeled this and then illustrated how we would point to a word and ask students to read it. A *promotor* (a specialist in charge of teacher training for a specific district) became quite agitated and said, "You can't do it like that. The students are never going to read if you don't tell them the word first." A heated discussion ensued among teachers and project specialists, showing that this seemingly minuscule event, merely a pointing-before-saying instead of a saying-before-pointing, hit the center of the pedagogical nervous system. It appears that the teachers did not perceive the possibility of letting students think for themselves, look for the answer, and propose solutions. In this microcosm of pedagogical action lies the key for pedagogical success or failure. For me, at the time (as noted in van Lier 1984: 115), it prompted the realization that the use of L1 as the medium of instruction would only bear its promised fruit if at the same time one could effect a change in basic teaching habits. It would not, automatically or easily, bring about such a change by itself.

Conclusion

I have tried, briefly, to give a living picture of an attempt at educational innovation. Many salient issues have remained undiscussed, such as the drastically curtailed school year due to agricultural cycles which conflict with the centralized urban calendar, numerous *fiestas*, teacher absences, and so on. Equally neglected has been the description of the problems of a small group of foreigners living in a small town with plentiful opportunities to get on each other's nerves, or the problem of being a "foreign expert" whose very presence in a place like Puno expresses occidental arrogance.

After spending two years in that situation, it is appropriate to ask questions like: Was it a good idea? Did we do more good than harm? Did we get something started that will benefit future generations of Andean children? Presumably, these questions are also relevant to such diverse international workers as Peace Corps volunteers, British Council officers, and Foreign Aid workers. They may be equally relevant to any teacher, after a lesson, a semester, or a course. How do we answer such questions?

At the beginning of this chapter I expressed a fear that some of us in the project had – that every trace of the project might vanish as soon as foreign financing came to an end. However, I also speculated that the ideals the project stood for might survive in a number of different ways: transformed or diffused in ways undetectable by our accustomed methods of data collection and scientific explanation; or taken over by local people and developed in directions not envisaged by the original sponsors.

Publications relating to the PEEB (Jung 1992; Jung and Lopez 1988; Lopez 1988; Lopez, Pozzi-Escot, and Zúñiga 1989) indicate several interesting and promising developments since 1984. First of all, Lopez (1988) reports that in 1987 the project included forty schools, indicating a stable level of interest and participation since 1983 (although he also emphasizes adverse conditions and lack of collaboration from many parents, along with many of the other obstacles I have referred to in this chapter). Further, the University of the Altiplano in Puno, in collaboration with the German sponsor of PEEB, the Deutsche Gesellschaft für Technische Zusammenarbeiten (GTZ), created a postgraduate degree in Andean Linguistics and Education, in which local educators could specialize in indigenous linguistic, cultural, and educational issues. Lopez (ibid.) also reports that students in bilingual schools perform better in their L1 as well as in Spanish, and also outperform their peers in non-bilingual schools in math. In a later work, Jung (1992: 146) reports that results in math are contradictory.

It appears, in general, that at least up to 1988, the year in which official sponsorship by the GTZ came to an end, the project successfully carried out its mission, and even expanded its vitality by contributing to a cadre of highly trained local specialists.

It would be nice to end on a positive note. However, in January 1993

Leo van Lier

I visited Peru and talked to several people who had been involved with the project or observed its progress. It appears that it has been impossible to maintain the momentum, and by now bilingual education in Puno seems to have vanished virtually without a trace. Dr. Inés Pozzi-Escot, a noted Peruvian sociolinguist, informed me (personal communication) that for some years the project's materials continued to be reprinted and distributed under a special grant, but this has now been discontinued and the books are no longer available. The postgraduate program in Applied Linguistics appears to have been discontinued as well. The PEEB, it turns out, has after all become one of the *torbellinos* of the Altiplano.

References

Bailey, K. M. 1985. If I had known then what I know now: Performance testing of foreign teaching assistants. In P. C. Hauptman, R. LeBlanc, and M. B. Wesche (eds.), *Second Language Performance Testing*. Ottawa: University of Ottawa Press.

van den Berghe, P. L., and G. Primov. 1977. *Inequality in the Peruvian Andes: Class and Ethnicity in Cuzco*. Columbia: University of Missouri Press.

Bourdieu, P. 1977. *Outline of a Theory of Practice*. Cambridge: Cambridge University Press.

1990. *The Logic of Practice*. Stanford: Stanford University Press.

Cohen, B. H. 1979. *Evaluating Bilingual Education Programs*. Hingam, MA: Teaching Resources Corporation

Escobar, A. 1976. Prólogo. In A. Cusihuaman, *Gramatica Quechua: Cuzco – Collao (15)*. Lima: Ministerio de Educación.

Hornberger, N. H. 1988. *Bilingual Education and Language Maintenance: A Southern Peruvian Quechua Case*. Dordrecht: Foris Publications.

Jung, I. 1992. *Conflicto Cultural y Educación: El Proyecto de Educación Bilingüe-Puno/Perú*. Quito, Ecuador: Ediciones Abya-Yala.

Jung, I., and L. E. Lopez. 1988. *Las Lenguas en la Educación Bilingüe: El Caso de Puno*. Lima: GTZ – Deutsche Gesellschaft für Technische Zusammenarbeiten.

Kemmis, S., and R. McTaggart. 1982. *The Action Research Planner*. Victoria, Australia: Deakin University Press.

van Lier, L. 1984. *Informe de Evaluación Integral del Proyecto: Primera Etapa de la Evaluación, 1982–1983*. No. Proyecto Experimental de Educación Bilingüe: Puno.

(1989). Puno: Teacher, school and language. In H. Coleman (ed.), *Working with Language: A Multidisciplinary Consideration of Language Use in Work Contexts*. Berlin: Mouton de Gruyter.

Lopez, L. E. (ed.). 1988. *Pesquisas en Lingüística Andina*. Lima-Puno: Consejo Nacional de Ciencia y Tecnología; Universidad Nacional del Altiplano – Puno; GTZ – Sociedad Alemana de Cooperación Técnica.

Lopez, L. E., I. Pozzi-Escot, and M. Zúñiga. (eds.). 1989. *Temas de Lingüística Aplicada*. Lima: CONCYTEC, GTZ.

Lopez, L. E., J. Stack, and L. van Lier. 1982. *Situación Actual de la Aplicación de la Educación Bilingüe en Puno*. No. Proyecto Experimental de Educación Bilingüe – Puno (Convenio Peru – RFA).

Montoya, R. 1984. El mito contemporaneo de la escuela: Significado de la escuela en el pensamiento andino. In I. Seminario sobre Problemas de Educacion y Capacitacion en Comunidades Indigenas del Perú. Universidad Nacional de San Marcos, Lima, Peru.

Wagner, M. 1979. *Jedem das, was ihm gebührt? Eine Untersuchung über Bedeutung und Einfluss der Landschule sowie über Lebenswirklichkeit und Lebensvorstellungen von Campesion schülern im Nördlichen Hochland von Peru*. West Germany: Pädagogische Hochschule Rheinland.

17 The functions of code switching among high school teachers and students in KwaZulu and implications for teacher education

Ralph D. Adendorff

Yonke imlando ingethungwayo
(All great stories are woven with different
[colored] threads)

Imfula egcweleyo izenzela ngokuthanda
(Overflowing rivers choose their direction)

These are Zulu aphorisms drawn from Mazisi Kunene's *Igugu lika-Maqandeyana*, a collection of aphorisms currently in press. The first aphorism suggests something about the texture of the discourse employed in the classrooms I shall be describing. In the second aphorism one can read the overflowing rivers as analogous to communicative need. The rivers are innovative and unstoppable in the routes they take, in much the same way as the spontaneous use of English-Zulu code switching is in the classrooms.

Background to the investigation

Code switching is an area of sociolinguistic behavior which, while increasingly evident in public and social life in South Africa, is little explored or understood. Attention is sometimes drawn in newspaper headlines to instances of calculated code switching. One example occurred at the historic first meeting in 1990 at Groote Schuur between

I acknowledge with gratitude the assistance in particular of Bheki Simelane, a graduate student who, under my guidance, collected the data on which this chapter is based. I am grateful, further, to David Duma, Bheki Simelane and a number of other Zulu-speaking teachers, principals, teacher trainers, and graduate students who have helped to interpret or confirm my interpretations of the interactional data which are central to this study. I wish to thank Mphiwa Nkuku, a school principal and a past student of the boarding school where the data for this study were collected, for enriching my understanding of the teaching circumstances at the school described and those which prevail in Black education more generally. I also thank Keith Chick, Jane Boustred, Marina Savini-Beck, and Kathi Bailey for their critical feedback at various stages in the writing of this chapter, as well as Mazisi Kunene for his kindness in identifying, translating, and discussing the Zulu aphorisms which I have included.

the ANC and the South African government, when Mr. Mandela addressed the government in Afrikaans before switching to English for the rest of his speech. Another example was Margaret Thatcher's use of Afrikaans to greet the audience at the Rand Afrikaans University after being awarded an honorary doctorate. She, too, reverted to English thereafter. (These two instances of code switching are detailed in Adendorff [1993].)

Most code-switching, however, is spontaneous and goes largely unnoticed. The linguistic behavior of studio guests on programs screened on CCV-TV (Contemporary Cultural Values – Television), for instance, provides abundant evidence of spontaneous code switching, as indeed do many other so-called marketplace settings in which interaction occurs. Today, code switching is also a prominent feature of the discourse on the campuses of traditionally White, liberal South African universities. Zulu-English switches, for example, are a feature of the campus discourse at the University of Natal. Interestingly, many Black students in the Linguistics Department at the University of Natal at first deny that they code switch and disclaim any usefulness for code switching. In addition, I am surprised at the responses of Zulu English teachers to my questions about the prevalence of, and purposes behind, code switching in predominantly Black classrooms, bearing in mind that English is the language of instruction. They imply that code switching is an indecent, forbidden form of behavior. It seems that code switching is something many teachers are ashamed to admit to.

My overall purpose in this chapter is to show that, contrary to the popularly held view that these responses reveal, code switching is in fact highly functional, though mostly subconscious. It is a communicative resource which enables teachers and students to accomplish a considerable number and range of social and educational objectives. It is in Gumperz's (1982) terms a "contextualization cue," in Tannen's (1985), a "meta-message."

I shall first clarify what I understand by the notion *contextualization cue*, focusing in particular on how such cues guide participants in their interpretation of meaning in discourse. My main emphasis hereafter lies in identifying the academic and social functions which code switching serves by considering data featuring three Zulu-speaking teachers and the principal of a boarding school as they interact in English, largely, with students whose mother tongue is Zulu. Finally, I consider what the implications are of the findings of my investigation for teacher education in South Africa. My concern here is to motivate the need for consciousness raising and to suggest how this might be accomplished if teacher trainees are to appreciate how potentially rich a communicative resource code switching is in educational settings.

Ralph D. Adendorff

What is a contextualization cue?

As a means of answering this question, I shall refer first to the function of contextualization cues. Essentially, contextualization cues help to delineate the context (i.e., as it unfolds, as it changes, both in broad outline and in fine shading), thereby channeling or guiding interpretation and so giving additional meaning to what is said and done in a conversation. Contextualization cues enable those who are interacting to signal information such as:

1. The kind of activity they are engaged in (e.g., a chat or something requiring greater personal commitment).
2. The real meaning of what is being said.
3. How what is being said relates to what was said earlier or to what is still to come.
4. The role relationships and other social relationships implicated between those conversing.

Tannen (1985: 204) uses a helpful metaphor to explain the role of contextualization cues in interpretation. According to her, their effect is to provide an advance message of some kind about the message and about how it is intended, including information about the relationship of those who are interacting. A contextualization cue, in other words, is a meta-message.

Contextualization cues are signals which can take any linguistic form – a phonetic, lexical, or syntactic choice, for example, or a dialect, a register, or a formulaic expression of some kind, to name just a few. However, the crucial feature of contextualization cues is that they always signify a marked choice. This means that in choosing one, the speaker departs from what he or she would conventionally do in those same circumstances. All marked choices, in other words, have an important discourse function in addition to their microlinguistic function. Gumperz (1982: 119) emphasizes that the meaning of contextualization cues is also always implicit and tied to the context. Thus people who are outsiders to a particular conversation will probably not recognize the contextualization cues which are employed in it. They will not see them as salient (i.e., not recognize them as marked choices). By contrast, being able to interpret a contextualization cue appropriately presupposes that one shares knowledge and understandings with others in the interaction. Such knowledge and understandings are built up in the conversation itself, are carried over from previous conversations, derive from the shared setting in which the interaction takes place, or else derive from other avenues of shared world knowledge.

The data upon which this study is based

The data which I shall be discussing in this chapter feature the interaction of three experienced high school teachers with their classes. There is also a fourth interaction between the principal and the full student body. The high school is a well subsidized state school for Black students (all of whom are Zulu speaking). The students are drawn from a wide geographic area, and, because it has boarding facilities, the school is selective when admitting students. Girls at the school are dominant, statistically, and are all boarders. By contrast, all of the boys are day scholars. The school is staffed solely by Black teachers, most of whom are graduates. This fact further distinguishes the school from most others like it in South Africa. Moreover, unlike other such schools, it is adequately provided for in terms of teaching equipment and teaching facilities generally (e.g., it has a well-equipped science laboratory). The school has electricity, which again sets it apart from many other Black schools, and while classes are large, they are not overcrowded as tends currently to be the norm elsewhere. It is recognized that the school produces above average results, bearing in mind that final year results in Black schools have, for political and allied reasons, been particularly poor in recent years.

A senior member of staff at this school, Bheki Simelane, was a student of mine at the time I was assembling data for this study. I worked closely with him in planning the collection of data from his school. I have also worked with him and a number of others in piecing together necessary ethnographic information regarding the interactions and the settings in which they took place, and in translating the switches into Zulu. I have subsequently been at pains to discuss the translation and the contextual details with as many other teachers, teacher-trainers, graduate students, and others as possible in order to confirm or modify the translations and to characterize the learning context. In particular, I have sought people who are native speakers of Zulu and whose prior learning experiences and teaching circumstances overlap with those of the teachers and students in the data, thereby validating my interpretations. In my attempts to arrive at an understanding of what the implicit meanings are of the code switches in the exchanges, I have again been fortunate to have worked closely with both Bheki and other teachers. Their familiarity with the teaching circumstances illustrated has allowed me to reflect something approaching a participant's perspective on what the code switches mean rather than an observer's perspective.

As far as the details of the data collection are concerned, Bheki arranged for students in various classes to record an English, a biology, and a geography lesson, while he himself recorded the principal. These recordings were originally made without the knowledge of the teachers (and principal) for the following reason. Bheki believed, and I concurred with him, that this knowledge would significantly inhibit their code switching behavior, especially since they knew he was pursuing a higher degree in Applied Linguistics and he felt they might be suspicious of his motives and also see him as being critical of their use of language. This, he believed, would make them self-conscious. Subsequently, however, he played the recordings to them and obtained their permission to quote from the data.

The first teacher is the senior English teacher who was recorded while working through John Donne's poem "Death Be Not Proud" with his final year students. The second is a biology teacher who is recorded conducting a revision lesson which deals largely with blood corpuscles. The third recording features the geography teacher who is also conducting a revision lesson with a senior class. The lesson concentrates on the formation of flood plains, which is a topic he first covered the previous day. According to Bheki, all three teachers are experienced, energetic, and well respected by the students. According to him, too, all of them encourage their students to participate freely in their lessons. Such a stance is not typical in Black classrooms in South Africa.

The fourth source of interactional data is the school principal addressing the staff and student body at assembly. As is the convention in most state schools, the principal leads morning prayers before making announcements of a general nature. In this case, these announcements deal with upcoming examinations and with disciplinary matters. In contrast to the three classroom settings, where the atmosphere is generally "relaxed" (even "noisy" in the English lesson), the assembly is a noticeably formal event, and the student body is silent throughout.

The English lesson

"Death Be Not Proud" is a poem which is characterized by the use of an ingenious paradox, namely, that death will itself die. It is an intricate poem, requiring the teacher to unravel a very complex line of logic and to convey this to the students. What complicates this task are the circumstances in which the teaching takes place. The following facts would seem to be particularly significant:

1. The students are going through the poem for the first time with the teacher.
2. There are over sixty students in the class, which complicates the teaching task.
3. The students constitute two distinct groups, those who sit in the first two thirds of the room and are attentive and actively engaged, and those at the back who are generally inattentive and disruptive.

4. The lesson is conducted in English, which, according to a local teacher, connotes profundity on the one hand and students' feelings of inexpertise on the other.

For most of the lesson, the teacher is involved in what I can best describe as a form of exegesis – that is, painstaking unpacking, interpreting, and then reassembling of the poet's message. His principal concern is academic, though he does not ignore social relationships in the classroom. Exegesis is apparent in the following episode in the lesson. It centers on three lines from the poem which the teacher first reads aloud and then comments upon.

"Die not poor Death; / Nor yet Can'st thou kill me. / From Rest and Sleep. . . ."
When one is dead one is not actually dead but asleep. Therefore death would not have killed him. Therefore one would be asleep and dreaming. When we are asleep we dream and *yonke into oyiphuphayo* is recorded in our minds (". . . all that we dream about is recorded in our minds"). [There is laughter from the class when he code-switches.] You all dreamt last night. We always dream when we are asleep but we sometimes forget what we dreamt about. [Spontaneous discussion and laughter follows amongst the students over whether they dream in their sleep.]

Why, one might wonder, did the teacher switch briefly to Zulu? What is the implicit meaning which Zulu conveys? Clearly the words in Zulu *yonke into oyiphuphayo* (everything which you dream) add nothing new by way of content. This fact reinforces the likelihood that if the Zulu words are communicatively significant, it is not because of their semantic content but because they constitute a meta-message of some kind. Another possibility is that the teacher feels that the students might not understand his meaning, and it is for this reason that he uses Zulu. According to informants who favor the first interpretation, the switch is an attempt on the teacher's part to gain credibility from his students. What he is really trying to do here is not to advance his explanation of the meaning of the poem, but rather to encourage the students to believe his interpretation so far, and to believe in him, the teacher.

The following comments occur soon after the preceding data. The teacher is again closely involved in clarifying the poem.

"And soonest our best men with thee do go / Rest of their bones and soul's delivery!"
We are born and we die again. We live for a very short time and die. *Siphila isikhathi esincane siphinde sife futhi* ("We live for a very short time and thereafter we die.") *Njengaye lo* it looks *wayenesikhathi esincane ehleli emhlabeni.* ("Just like the poet he lived for a short time.") Therefore you must know that we are passers-by. But we will live again. *Umuntu ufa isikhathi esincane aphile futhi* ("One dies for a very short time and lives

393

again".) Therefore *akekho umuntu ofayo*. (". . . there is no one who dies forever.")

What is significant here is the greater prominence of switches into Zulu. The teacher builds up the students' understanding of the poem step by step. On first impression, Zulu is the language of direct translation and of paraphrase: The teacher resorts to Zulu because he feels that his students do not understand what he is saying. On another level, and in addition, Zulu is the code by which the teacher slightly advances his interpretation of the poem. We note the simple translation/paraphrase function of Zulu from *"Siphila . . ."* to *". . . futhi"* as well, interestingly, as the way the use of Zulu slightly extends the teacher's interpretation of the poem in the switch which starts with *"Njengaye lo"* and continues to *"emhlabeni."* Throughout, Zulu clearly fulfills an academic function. It is the code with which the teacher tries to interpret the meaning of the poem and to clarify the English he uses in order to make the poem accessible. What these data suggest is that Zulu is also the code of encouragement, which means that it also fulfills a social function. It intercedes between the complexity of the poem, the efforts of the teacher, and the morale of the students.

Code-switching fulfills another function later in these data, as the language of provocation. The question, *"Sikhona isihogo?"* ("Is there hell at all?") is provocative in that it raises an issue, namely, hell, which not all students agree exists. Moreover, it is a question which attempts to engage even the passive students, so it is provocative in a second way. The question *"Sikhona isihogo?"* is semantically full in a way that *"yonke into oyiphuphayo"* ("everything which you dream"), to which I referred at the beginning of this analysis, is not. But, just as Zulu had an implicit symbolic function earlier, so, too, does it here, since it is the code which reaches everyone in the classroom. Hence, it is the code of teacher-student unity.

In concluding my analysis, it is clear that if this interpretation is correct, the Zulu code switches facilitate the teacher's accomplishment of his academic and social agendas by enabling him, implicitly, to clarify information and to encourage, provoke, and involve his students.

The biology lesson

Switches into Zulu during the biology lesson appear to have rather different functions from those evident in the English lesson. One of these functions is signaled by the formula: *"khona"* suitably inflected for concordial agreement + noun class 2 prefix (typically plural). This formula is evident in the following sentences:

1. "[*Kukhona ama-red blood corpuscles*] that report heat to the brain *umakushisa*."
2. "And then [*kubekhona ama-main light corpuscles*] which are responsible for light touch; for light light touch."
3. "The main corpuscles are found in the skin and [*kubekhona i-crowsian corpuscles*] from crows."

An interesting variant on this formula occurs in the following formulation:

4. "Lastly, there is homeostasis [*i-homeostasis*] is nothing but the maintenance of the external environment of the body."

The formula itself is semantically empty and therefore relatively insignificant. But, phrased in Zulu, it is marked, because it contrasts with English, the code which surrounds it. The *khona* + noun-class-prefix code switches are brief contextualization cues, not unlike the intermittent flicker of a light, which for motorists and pilots is often a warning signal. What responses from Zulu informants revealed was that these mini-switches constitute advance (implicit) messages from the teacher to the students about the upcoming message. Implicitly they alert the students to the fact that what is coming up (i.e., what follows the *khona* + noun-class-prefix formula) is a key technical term, which is being introduced into the discourse for the first time. As such, this is a prospective signal (or contextualization cue). What makes the role of Zulu interesting in sentence 4 is that it is a retrospective signal, confirming what has just been said in English. The two references together mark the fact that "homeostasis" is also a key term in the discussion.

This advance marking of key terms serves the teacher's academic agenda. What the data from the biology lesson also attest to is that Zulu code switching is the means by which the teacher checks that the students are following. This is evident in *"Kuyezwakala angithi?"* ("Do you follow?"), a formulaic question which is never translated or paraphrased into English by the teacher. According to my informants, this strict use of Zulu is doubly significant because Zulu concurrently serves social functions on the teacher's part. It enables the teacher to express implicit encouragement to the students, equivalent to "You see, what I have said so far isn't so difficult!" Zulu, in the words of one informant, is the "I'm helping you, I'm on your side" code. As such, switches into Zulu mark solidarity with the students.

Zulu is also the solidarity code later on. We can infer this from the fact that it is in Zulu that the teacher overexaggerates, teases, and generally indulges in tension-relieving (and relationship-building) banter with the students as the lesson draws to a close. All are forms of solidarity politeness (Scollon and Scollon 1982). They are in evidence in the following teacher-student interaction and are confirmed by the students' laughter.

The population dynamics will give you a lot of marks. Alright, I have not done what I was called for. But you will all pass biology. It is only that you get into the examination room fascinated, excited, *ucabanga ukuthi into elukhuni inde futhi lento* (". . . then you will think that the paper is difficult and exceedingly long"). [The students laugh out loud. The teacher's speech is slow. He stresses every word and elongates the penultimate vowels.] *Uyabona? . . . we . . . bathule nje babone i-question exakile bathi we babe*!! ("Do you see? They will stare at the question paper and realize/there is the realization that it is one that they cannot attempt to answer and will cry out, Oh Father!!") [The students again laugh loudly. The teacher places heavy stress on *"babone"* ("realize/realization")].

The geography lesson

The geography lesson data again alert one to the academic and social functions which Zulu code switching accomplishes in the classroom. Unlike the earlier data, however, where the code switching serves academic and social functions evenly, the geography lesson illustrates the teacher's heavier reliance on Zulu to accomplish social objectives. First, let me deal with a case in which a switch to Zulu fulfills an academic function. I label it as such since it clarifies the theme of the classroom talk and so draws attention to important information which is part of the teacher's academic agenda. The substance of the switch is a partial paraphrase of what the teacher expresses in English, except that the Zulu is a more explicit statement of the lesson's theme than is the English expression.

Today we are going to revise the work that we did yesterday. Yesterday we looked at the formation of flood plains, *ukuthi akheke kanjani* (". . . how flood plains are formed").

Had the Zulu switch simply been a translation of the English, it would have been, "*Izolo besifunda ngokwakheka kwama i-flood plain.*"

For the rest, the geography teacher uses Zulu as the means of exercising classroom management, rather than as a vehicle for transmitting academic knowledge. Especially important is the manner in which the classroom management is carried out. The tape shows that Zulu is the language of extra loudness (i.e., on the part of the teacher). Superficially it is also the language of authoritarianism and of coercion. Seen through Eurocentric eyes, it seems to be an instance of a marked choice employed in order to establish authority (not solidarity). The teacher's choice of this code (Zulu) coupled with the students' responses, mainly of laughter, seems then to undercut the implied authoritarianism and in fact to signal solidarity with his students as well as his desire that they cooperate with him. Distance, however, is not necessarily to be associated with power. In fact, the teacher's behavior here is an instance of solidarity downwards and is consistent with Chick's (1985) characterization of Zulu-English interactional style, in which the more powerful person uses solidarity downwards, and the less powerful person uses deference politeness upwards. Clearly the message behind the message (i.e., the teacher's expressing solidarity with the students while requiring them concurrently to take seriously his classroom management instructions) requires inferencing which relies on considerable shared knowledge and assumptions on the parts of those involved in the interaction. The data which I believe support these contentions are the following.

1. *Musani ukuvula izincwadi zenu* ("Do not open your books"). [There is laughter from the class. When the teacher switches, he raises his voice.] *Hhayi bo, vala wena*! ("Close your books over there!") [Scolding tone. The students laugh.]
2. In what parts of sections of the river do flood plains form? *Ama*-flood plains *akheka kuphi emfuleni*? ("In what part or section of the river do flood plains form?") [Spoken with increased volume. There is absolute silence in the class, after which students start whispering answers to one another.] *Wo!* . . . *Wo!* ("Woo! . . . Woo!") [The teacher raises his voice.] *Wena* . . . *Wena* . . . *Wena* ("You . . . you . . . you"). [The teacher nominates students to answer, volume again raised. Students laugh.] *Abantu abangibuke abangabheki phansi* ("People should not look away from me. You must look at me"). [Students look away from him to avoid being pointed at. He raises his voice once again.]

There are two other noteworthy exchanges in the geography lesson. They suggest how diverse is the range of discourse-level functions which code switches can serve. The first is evident in the following data:

T: What is a flood plain, mh?
S: A flood plain is a heap of soil or sand which is deposited on banks of a river or a stream when the river or a stream has been in flood.
T: [Confirming the answer with raised volume.] Very good *Sigqueme-zana, uyasebenzake silwane* ("Sigqemenzana, you are really working very hard").

Zulu, the language generally of teacher-student solidarity, here carries the full weight of the teacher's approval of the student and his answer. Hence it signals the teacher's solidarity with the student (but also his greater power, given that politeness behavior in Zulu-English interac-

tional style between status unequals is asymmetrical – solidarity down
and deference up). Not only is it the code with which the teacher com-
mends the student (*"uyasebenzake silwane"*), it is also the means by
which the teacher encodes a praise name for the student, *"Sigqema-
zana"*, which literally means "person with a small head but with a big
brain." The *si-* prefix is normally attached to proper names, which
means that it is here elevated to the status of a proper name. The *-ana*
morpheme is a diminutive suffix which apparently carries the teacher's
praise. Taken as a whole, the teacher's affirmation of the student is
about as rich as it can be. Were it coded in some language other than
Zulu, however, the extent of its "richness" would be considerable reduced. Hence, it is the deep-seated and powerful endorsement of the
student's answer which Zulu contributes to the classroom discourse in
this particular instance.

Strong feelings, this time in the way of personalized appeal, are the
principal reason behind my isolating a further instance of code switching in the geography lesson. It is employed by the teacher as he concludes the revision lesson.

T: Next week we will take a walk, down to Mhlathuze River where we
   will see flood plains in reality. *Kufanele niyibone ngamehlo
   i-flood plain nihambe phezu kwayo* ("You really do need to see the
   flood plain and walk on it").
S: Yes sir. *Bazoholwa yimi* ("I will lead them").
   [The student shouts out, offering to lead this excursion.]

The teacher's switch into Zulu is the implicit means by which he
makes a special plea that students experience the fascination of a real
flood plain and, I presume, do not settle only for book knowledge about
flood plains. The switch here signals his desire that the students share
his enthusiasm for the experience. From the student's response indicated
in the transcript (as well as that of others), it is clear that they too are
enthusiastic.

The principal addressing the school assembly

The data recorded during morning assembly include considerably more
code switches than occur in the three lessons which I have discussed up
to this point. In the interests of brevity, I will not discuss these data
exhaustively. Instead, I shall point out briefly the range of discourse
purpose which the switches serve, noting at the outset that social relationship building and expressions of solidarity are conspicuously absent
in the data.

The principal is well respected by the students. He is also an authority figure who does little to challenge this perception of himself. It is for this reason, perhaps, that he does not see the need to work as much as others do in building social relationships. On his agenda are a number of issues: exhorting students to prepare for the upcoming exams; discouraging forms of misbehavior prevalent at the time; outlining school policy, specifically with respect to admissions; drawing attention to misbehavior at meal times. Throughout, code switching clearly is a conversational resource which he employs to considerable effect.

Code switches are a means by which the principal paraphrases his message, a strategy much in evidence in the English lesson. Consider the following extract from the principal.

You cannot start doing anything without being psychologically and spiritually prepared to work. *Kufanele umqondo wakho uwunikele futhi usemukele isikhathi se-examination* ("Your mind should be psychologically prepared to accept the examination"). *I-examination yisikhathi sokuthandaza* ("The examination period is the time for which we must pray"). When you do this you will become collected.

The communicative effect of this paraphrasing is no doubt to clarify the message and also to reiterate, and thereby reinforce, the points which he is making.

Code switching is also a vehicle for listing. The discourse motivation for doing so is to convey key information early on, as is done in writing when one provides a topic sentence as the first sentence in a paragraph. Such a topic sentence encapsulates the theme of the current "chunk" of information (in writing, the paragraph). Evidence of this includes the following:

1. *Okunye futhi okufanele nikuyeke ukuma esangweni nihleke abantu abadala* ("Another thing is that you should not stand at the gate and laugh at the elderly people passing by the school"). *Lokhu akuphele njengoba kuqala i-examination* ("This should come to an end as we begin with examinations"). I just wonder where do such people find time to stand at the gate instead of doing their school work. Most of these people who are doing this mischief are those that are repeating classes.
2. *Okunye okubi, ubuvila, phasa uye kwa-standard ten.* ("Another bad thing about you is that you are lazy." [There is laughter from the students.] "You must so work that you pass and proceed to standard ten").

Code switching is also the vehicle for reiterating important information. This is evident in the following two contributions, in which the principal enunciates school policy:

399

3. The following has to do with our school policy. You must listen very carefully to this so that you do not misquote us. *Abantu bafika basimisquothe* ("People misquote us a lot"). *Isikole asinayo i-policy ethi uma ufeyilile ungabe usabuya* ("It is not the policy of the school to reject the applicants who want to repeat classes"). [*He says the above with great emphasis.*]

4. Generally *okuyi-policy engiyichazayo njengamanje* ("... our policy that I am discussing with you now") we believe *ukuthi uma umfundi es esikoleni ahlale unyaka wonke akangaphumelela, kusho ukuthi* to a certain extent not *kuyo yonke i-extent* we have both failed ("We believe that when a student has spent the whole year and still fails, that means to a certain extent, not the whole extent, we have both failed"). [This is said with great emphasis.]

Code-switching is also a focusing device, akin in its function to the use of prosody in English to convey a "watch this" function. This function is evident in the following utterances.

5. Do not make the work of the hostel staff difficult. It's a fact *ukuthi uma umsebenzi we-hostel staff niwenza ube lukhuni* ("... if you make the work of the hostel staff difficult they will always come back to us"). *Ngicela ukuthi ni-co-opareythe nabo* ("Please cooperate with them"). [This was spoken with great emphasis.]

6. I have a complaint from teachers that *abafana basukuma kugcina* ("... boys are last to stand up when teachers enter the hall"). [He places great emphasis on the word *"abafana"* (boys; the literal gloss of the phrase would be "boys [they are] standing at the end/last").]

7. Mr. Zondi has told me that the three next Sunday church services will be communion services. It is very important *ukwazi i-meaning ye-*Holy Communion ("... to know the meaning of the Holy Communion"). [These words are spoken, again, with great emphasis.]

Implications for language teacher education in South Africa

The first and most powerful realization that comes as one reflects on the implications of these analyses for language teacher education must surely be that code switching is pre-eminently a form of sociolinguistic, contextualizing behavior. If teachers are to understand the role of code switching (i.e., as an interactional resource), priority must be given to consciousness raising, thereby developing sociolinguistic sensitivity in aspiring teachers. The content of a program which aims to develop such sensitivity regarding code switching must, it seems to me, focus squarely on fundamental insights sociolinguists have gained into the nature of language in general as well as its use in society. In what follows I will explain what I envisage by way of consciousness raising. In particular I will identify essential content knowledge and then offer methodological suggestions which teacher trainers might use to encourage sociolinguistic sensitivity in teachers of the future.

Consciousness raising: what it should entail

Consciousness raising should entail at least five procedures. First, it must entail contrasting prescriptive, essentially purist views of language and language use (which decry code switching), with empirical, descriptive ones, which approach code switching in a more balanced way. I would want teacher trainees to consider standard and also non-standard lects of English, such as Extreme South African English and South African Black English, as well as anglicisms (mini code switches?) and their relation to "suiwer" (pure) Afrikaans expressions. I would also encourage reflection on the relationship between so-called pure Zulu and Fanakalo, a Zulu-based pidgin which, in some of its varieties, shows strong influence from English. The reason is that teachers need to recognize the functional ends to which each of these codes is put and to understand the real-world benefits which derive from having a repertoire of languages and language varieties from which to choose. Teacher trainees should further understand that developing students' language repertoires should be a major language teaching objective once the trainees are in the classroom.

Second, teacher trainees need to be disabused of the idea that multilingualism is a curse in the South African context (so, too, bi- and multi-dialectalism); they should be encouraged to view them as riches, as communicative resources. They need also to be disabused of deficit notions of codes in general and of code switching, in particular – that it is dysfunctional and symptomatic of ignorance; that it is the product of insufficient target language resources; that it is something to be embarrassed about. These are views held by people unaware of the social context of language use, and are apparently driven by a purist perspective on language. Such people avoid and decry code switching because their own social identity is wrapped up in language preferences which do not employ code switches.

Consciousness raising will also entail sensitizing teacher trainees to the fact that it is misleading, though common, to view languages as neutral signaling systems. Languages are carriers of social (i.e., symbolic) meaning and express the identity value systems of their users. Teacher trainees should recognize that social meaning is largely a contrastive phenomenon: The symbolic associations of one group's speech are usually juxtaposed with those of some other competing group, and it is this juxtaposition which gives them their distinctiveness. It is because language is so symbolic and so full of associations (i.e., because it is so non-neutral) that people become emotional about language. This explains why they belittle the language of contrasting social groups (see Adendorff 1992), and why many are scornful of code switching. An understanding of social meaning is important, moreover, because it is itself a conversational resource: Conversationalists often exploit the symbolism of different codes in the process of signaling and interpreting "fine shading."

Further sociolinguistic information which teacher trainees need to understand if they are fully to understand some of the effects of code switching is the role which language plays in the exercise of power. Put very simply, learners need to recognize (and their own personal experience will almost certainly confirm this) that communicative power usually goes hand in hand with social power. Translated into practical terms: If one has communicative power (and this would include an ability to code-switch appropriately) one has a voice, one is listened to, one can argue one's case and persuade others, and one can also counter the deception and manipulations of others. In sum, it means that one is taken seriously. Language legislation and language planning, on whatever scale, facilitate acquisition of powerful codes for some members of a society, but can at the same time frustrate the aspirations of others. Some, in fact, are condemned to powerlessness. Teachers-in-training need to recognize these truths and be able to understand code switching in their schools in terms of the power it brings its users.

The message which emerges most strongly from my analysis of the English-Zulu code switching in the KwaZulu boarding school is that code switching is an extremely valuable resource. It should therefore not be legislated away at this school or at schools in general because such legislation would cut teachers and students off from a crucial communicative resource. Such a policy would be disempowering. Teachers need to understand that they are the ones, ultimately, who formulate and monitor school (including playground) language policy and their decisions must be rational and informed by sociolinguistic understanding of languages and their statuses in the school and in the community. The boarding school scenario referred to earlier suggests that if English is chosen as the medium of instruction, it is in the students' self-interest that it be promoted. Mother tongues should be promoted, too, but for somewhat different reasons. As we saw, the mother tongue is the solidarity code, the link language mediating between students' knowledge of the world (which is presented to them at home in the mother's tongue) and the preferred mode of representing that knowledge at school, in English.

How sensitivity toward code switching might be accomplished

The means by which I suggest teacher trainees might most profitably develop teacher trainees' understanding of what code switching entails is to turn them into ethnographers (see, for example, Heath and Branscombe 1985). By turning teacher trainees into ethnographers, teacher trainers will be able to capitalize on ethnographic method and, in particular, on the high regard in which ethnographers hold multiple sources of information, as well as the empirical manner in which such sources are assembled. By going through the process of collecting their data, teachers (as emerging ethnographers) will become sensitized to (a) the circumstances in which code switching is employed and (b) the effects which it achieves. In general they will become sensitized to sociolinguistic realities. In what follows I shall indicate very briefly some useful sources of code switching data and then suggest a few "discovery procedures" by which an understanding of the meaning of switches might be elicited.

SOURCES OF CODE-SWITCHING DATA

One obvious source of code-switching data is the press. Editorials, reports, and letters to the editor are often useful sources both of data and of public reaction to code switching. (For examples of a report and letters to the editor, see Adendorff [1993: 159–161].) Recorded interviews are likewise useful. Religious programs on television provide a ready source of spontaneous code-switching data. Cartoons often also hinge, in part at least, on code switches. Fine shading and emotional coloring are conveyed, too, in political cartoons simply because of the codes which are chosen in them. In this regard, see the account of the social meaning of Extreme South African English in the mouth of a security force member in Adendorff (1991: 208–210). Sitcoms often also employ code switches for comic as well as more subtle effects and can be profitably videorecorded and analyzed.

Additional data are available in the spontaneous interactions of people in the marketplace; teacher trainees simply have to have a tape recorder in order to tap into this source. Of course a good marketplace venue to start with would be the campuses on which teacher training is taking place. Code switching is also common in many households.

SOME EXAMPLES OF DISCOVERY PROCEDURES

Having captured their data and noted pertinent contextual information, teacher trainees need to analyze it and interpret the meaning of the code switches. This is where various discovery procedures are useful. For instance, having as individuals, in pairs, or as a group, assigned an analyst's meaning to the switches in a selection of their data, it is necessary to see how adequately the teacher trainees' interpretations match those of the original participants. Interviewing seems to be an obvious way of getting at this information but, given that code-switching behavior is largely unconscious, speakers (and people with similar backgrounds) could be unreliable commentators. For this reason, participants might be given "substitution frames" – that is, the researchers (the teacher trainees) would provide their informants with discourses in which there are two options in an utterance slot. These options would differ only in that one is cast in the dominant language (e.g., English in the boarding school case, which means that the entire discourse would be in English), while the other option is cast in the non-dominant code, thereby constituting a code switch. (Zulu was non-dominant at the boarding school.) Informants would make their choice in each case and try to justify the basis for it, in particular, what difference in interpretation choosing one rather than the other code has. Alternatively, teacher trainees might present informants with two versions of the "same" message, differing this time in terms of the background and the foregrounded language. Informants, once again, would give their interpretation of each version of the discourse.

Several other options come to mind as sensitizing activities to be conducted in the field. Teacher trainees could be presented with transcripts from naturally occurring data and be required to indicate the code switches. Thereafter, they could be given contextual information and be asked to work out what fine shading the code switching provides. Or, they might be given labels for discourse-marking functions (e.g., identifying topic, subthemes, new information, important information, and so on) and look for instances of these in the transcript.

The matched-guise technique (an indirect method of investigating language attitudes) offers the basis for another activity. In working out the communicative effect of code switches, informants might be presented with a scenario, "voices" (which employ different patterns of code switching), and a list of various judgments as to what the speakers were trying to accomplish; what the speakers' attitudes are toward their subject matter or to the hearer; and how coherent (i.e., well marked) their discourse is. This exercise attempts to establish what others consider to be the meta-message behind the code switching.

OTHER SENSITIZING ACTIVITIES

Other sensitizing activities could involve teacher trainees in choosing a written utterance from a list of alternatives to fit into the speech bubble of a character in a cartoon strip. They can also be presented with contextual information (including historical information, anthropological detail, folk knowledge, and so on) related to passages from literature which involve dialogue with code switches. Trainees would be asked to indicate likely speaker intent and would be restricted in their response to one line of writing. This is a deliberately restricted limit because teacher trainees are thus forced to distill the background information and the code-switching behavior into some kind of statement regarding the underlying intent of the speakers who code switch.

Conclusion

In this chapter I have offered an alternative view of code switching to that held by language purists, who reject code switching because they see it as leading to a lowering of standards, as well as by many teachers. Although teachers often engage in code switching, they are ashamed to admit doing so because they too believe that it is indecent to behave in this manner. I have treated code switching as a contextualization cue and, in close cooperation with informants, have interpreted switches in the data as delineating the context for those involved in the interaction in various ways. Switches are viewed as guiding the participants' interpretation of academic goals and intentions as well as their interpretation of social relationships in the classroom. The second part of the chapter dealt with the implications of my analysis of the interactional data with regard to teacher education in South Africa. Here I argued that prospective teachers' level of consciousness regarding language and its use in society needs to be raised. I concluded by suggesting that, as ethnographers of code switching, teacher trainees can be guided in various ways to explore and appreciate the functions of code switching, drawing on readily available data sources.

References

Adendorff, R. D. 1991. Political cartoons: Uncooperative forms of communication? In J. Prinsloo and C. Criticos (eds.), *Media Matters in South Africa*. Durban: Media Resource Centre.

    1992. The social meaning of English in South Africa (or: Don't you kick my teddybear!). *Crux*, 26, 1, 50–62.

    1993. Codeswitching amongst Zulu-speaking teachers and their pupils: Its functions and implications for teacher education. *Language and Education*, 7, 3, 141–162.

Chick, J. K. 1985. The interactional accomplishment of discrimination in South Africa. *Language in Society*, 14, 299–326.

Gumperz, J. J. 1982. *Discourse Strategies*. Cambridge: Cambridge University Press.

Heath, S. B., and A. Branscombe. 1985. Intelligent writing in an audience community: Teacher, students, and researcher. In S. W. Freeman (ed.), *The Acquisition of Written Language: Revision and Response.* Norwood, NJ: Ablex.

Scollon, R., and S. Scollon. 1982. *Narrative, Literacy, and Face in Interethnic Communication.* Norwood, NJ: Ablex.

Tannen, D. 1985. Cross-cultural communication. In T. A. Van Dijk (ed.), *Handbook of Discourse Analysis* (vol. 4: Discourse in Society). London: Academic Press.

18 Different languages, different practices: socialization of discourse competence in dual-language school classrooms in Hungary

Patricia A. Duff

> *Embert beszédéről, ebet szőréről*
> (People [are judged] by their speech,
> dogs by their fur)

It is break time between classes, and Hungarian students in one classroom are munching on sandwich buns as they nervously review their history notes and textbooks. In the few minutes remaining in the ten-minute respite from a long series of forty-five minute lessons, they speculate about the upcoming lesson: Who will be the next "victim" and what will the topic be? How are their marks so far? Do they really understand this material?

Down the corridor, in the same academic secondary school, other teenage students are milling about, eating, playing cards, listening to rock music, chatting, comparing fashions, and casually glancing over their history notes and textbooks.

Why the stark contrast between the two classrooms? In one, a *non-dual-language* (non-DL) class in a Hungarian-English school, the teacher is about to arrive and then will ask one student, unannounced, to recite the previous day's lesson in summary form in Hungarian, the student's first language (L1). The student's performance (*felelés*) will then be judged in front of her peers according to what she says and how she says it. In the other, a *dual-language* (DL) class, conducted primarily in English, the students' second language (L2), the teacher no longer believes in the utility of recitation. Instead, she will ask some review questions, which may generate some discussion, then there may be pair or small group work, perhaps a prepared student presentation (lecture), and later the teacher's lecture will continue.

This study examines differences between the socialization of discourse competence in these two types of instructional environment – the traditional and the non-traditional, the monolingual and the bilingual – and explores the impact of educational reform on school life and the ways in which students are inducted into academic discourse practices in the two contexts through different kinds of performance tasks. The

407

divergence of teachers in Hungarian-English DL schools from traditional Eastern European practices in assessment activities in English-medium history classes is discussed, along with important consequences of these differences. Ethnographic material from videotaped observations, interviews, and essays is included to capture the perspectives of teachers and students regarding changing practices within classrooms and corresponding changes in post-1989 Hungarian society (cf., Duranti's [1985] discussion about the ethnography of discourse and the *bridging* of related academic traditions; see also, Hammersley and Atkinson's [1983] description of ethnographic procedures and principles; Duff 1995).

Unless otherwise indicated, all student excerpts in this chapter come from DL students and were produced originally in English, their second language. These students are familiar with non-DL education, having for eight years attended non-DL primary schools where recitation techniques are prevalent. In addition to their DL classes, these students currently attend courses taught in Hungarian (e.g., chemistry, Hungarian language and literature), by what are considered to be fairly traditional teachers who also teach in the non-DL section of the school and who continue to use *felelés*. Non-DL students could not be surveyed in a comparable way because of the need for interpreters/translators and because the researcher's official role was originally assessment in the DL, not the non-DL, section. I have intentionally not edited these excerpts for inaccuracies in spelling, grammar, or other non-standard language features.

The socioeducational context: dual-language schooling

The dual-language or late immersion school system was established in Hungary in the second half of the 1980s, and at that time represented an innovation in foreign language education and a departure from the conservative, highly centralized Hungarian education system. These DL secondary schools, which now number more than thirty across the country, introduced not only a new medium of instruction (one of several possible foreign languages, such as English), and thus a new system of communicating, but more important perhaps, implicitly advocated a new Westward-looking worldview and set of practices, textbooks, teachers, and experiences. Students in the dual-language schools are given intensive instruction both in and through their foreign language, with the majority of their academic course (i.e., history, mathematics, biology, geography, and physics) taught in the L2.

This study grew out of a larger project initiated in 1989 to examine the efficacy of DL education in Hungary. The project, and my role in it, entailed the assessment of students' L2 abilities, the description of students' attitudes and motivation toward participation in the experimental programs, and observations of classroom practices (see Duff 1991a; 1991b). However, beyond characterizations of students' linguistic development and affective dispositions, some of the most interesting issues that emerged from the first years of the study were related to the impact of the dramatic changes taking place inside and outside of schools on observable sociolinguistic behaviors and events within classrooms.

In the first year of fieldwork leading up to the present study (1989–1990), a number of changes had taken place in Hungary. Within a short stretch of time the country was transformed from a controlled East-bloc country to an independent republic; Prime Minister Imre Nagy, who had orchestrated and been martyred for his resistance movement against Soviet domination in 1956, was posthumously "rehabilitated"; Hungary opened up its borders for tens of thousands of Eastern Germans seeking to cross into Austria, which led to astonishing further developments (e.g., the dismantling of the Iron Curtain, the dissolution of the Soviet Union); and the first free elections in forty years took place (see, for example, Banac 1992; Brown 1991; Echikson 1990; Garton Ash 1989, 1990; Kuran 1992; Ramet 1991). It is no wonder that Hungarians – young and old – were dazzled and unsettled by changes engulfing them both during and after that period and were excited by prospects of a brighter, more democratic future.

The Hungarian *felelés*

The focal point for this analysis is the speech event known as the *felelés*, the "oral recitation," which occurs daily in traditional Hungarian classrooms, but which from my early observations was conspicuously absent from many English-medium classes in DL schools. The *felelés* is not only a rich locus for language socialization (see Duff 1993; Ochs 1988; Ochs and Schieffelin 1984; Poole 1992; Schieffelin 1990; Schieffelin and Ochs 1986a, 1986b), but also a micro-level crystallization of macro-level changes and tensions pervasive in the school community and beyond. Indeed, its very presence in or absence from lessons has become a catalyst for change systemwide. That is, the practice (or ritual) of *felelés* and the school system (or society) in which it is practiced are mutually engendered or constituted (Bourdieu 1977; Giddens 1984; Ortner 1984), in that the system creates the ritual but the ritual also creates the system; hence, change in one is bound to effect change in the other. The recitation has been modified or even eliminated from many Hungarian-English DL school history lessons, but it has been reintroduced to restore order in some of the same schools experiencing instability, leadership problems, and student unrest. It is thus a significant activity, laden with social, historical, and political meanings, relationships, implications, and consequences.

In Hungarian classrooms, as in many Eastern European countries, the *felelés* (pronounced /fɛlɛleš/, meaning "answer") constitutes the standard means of assessing students' progress in their content classes. The word *felelés* refers to the abstract construct of recitation or oral examination, but here, the generic form will have both general and specific as well as singular and plural connotations.

The recitation approach to teaching is commonly associated with the name of Herbart (e.g., Herbart 1898) and the Prussian educational principles he advanced two centuries ago (e.g., see Alexander 1918). Originally, its purpose was to develop students' moral character; secondary goals, still upheld today, are to foster discipline, patriotism, conformity, oral self-expression, and the accumulation and review of knowledge presented in courses.

Like other assessments, the *felelés* is graded on a scale of one to five, where one is the lowest score and five the highest. A weak (i.e., hesitant, unprepared) *felelés* may either yield a poor score (e.g., one, two, or weak three) and criticism from the teacher, or may necessitate subsequent *felelés* or other make-up work from the student. To be eligible for top grades (i.e., four and especially five), students must know their material well, and teachers and students must jointly work at establishing the degree of mastery. This is accomplished through interaction, negotiation and, finally, judgment on the part of the teacher. Students are quick to point out that teachers have different standards for judging them; as one student reported, a teacher can say:

Well God knows it – the material for five. I know it for four, and you can only know it for three. . . . It depends on the teacher. He can say he knows it for five, or God knows it for five, or you can know it for five too if you learn what I've said.

Standards exist for discursive attributes of the *felelés,* which are seen as a manifestation of students' knowledge. Following eight years of experience at primary schools, secondary school students have a good sense of what constitutes criterion performance. They emphasized the need to "speak and speak and speak" without stopping; faltering was considered a sign of imperfect learning as well as discursive incompetence. One DL student explained:

And – if you say something very – very fast and you make like you knew something then you get a grade five. And if you say something like "Oh – uh – " but you know everything, then you get a three or – so it's not the best way to test a student. . . . *Felelés* is like you have to talk for ten minutes and you mustn't stop. And you have to talk fluently about the thing. [P: Why in *felelés* is it important that you speak quickly and fluently?] Because then the teacher feels that you know everything and – and he or she can't ask anything because you speak so fast that – and uh . . . and I have heard about when somebody made this *felelés* in history class and he didn't speak about history but about – he read his identity card or something and the teacher didn't notice it and ((laughs)).

The issue of whose "voice" is expected during a student's *felelés* is another important matter (cf., Aronowitz and Giroux 1991; Bakhtin 1981). Students identified (at least) two variants: in one, the teacher expects verbatim recitation of assigned texts; and in the other, students must be more creative, giving a more personal account and synthesis of material, combining the voices and perspectives of historical text writers, teachers, and the students themselves, which is a much more complex discursive task. One student reflected on the two approaches:

I think it's again up to the teacher. The Hungarian [literature] teacher wants something personal. Something uh – from me. My opinion. But I think most of the teachers want to know exactly what they have told us – so just give it back exactly the way it was given. Exactly – from the book and exercise books.

In my fieldwork, it was apparent that the *felelés* evoked a strong and often visible emotional response from those familiar with it – which was practically every Hungarian I met. Some teachers believed wholeheartedly in its usefulness. They reprimanded students who did not perform optimally and praised those who did. Others criticized it (but sometimes only half seriously) as a mindless "feudal" exercise aimed at terrorizing students and reducing teacher course preparation requirements; yet, some of these same teachers retained it nonetheless. Still others acknowledged its value but not when used in the traditional way, favoring and rewarding rote memorization. Rather, they encouraged personal reactions to and interpretations of content. Remarks from one teacher in this last camp follow:

I don't like that. Maybe it is a professional way of teaching. And very good for the last examination and very useful, but [students] are puppet figures in the hand of a teacher if they are – I don't like it. I'm teaching not for the last examination, but for life. [non-DL teacher, English in original]

Dual-language students interviewed, representing diverse primary school backgrounds from around the country, mostly dreaded it, gladly volunteering their most memorable *felelés* terrors. In an interview, one DL student described recitation procedures as follows:

When you have to learn new material, then in the next lesson, in the first ten to fifteen minutes someone from the class or from the group has to – to talk about the material. And – no one likes it. It's terrible. We get a mark for this and uh everyone is afraid of it. So for example in chemistry someone has to

411

make this *felelés*, and then he or she has to go to the blackboard. And it's terrible, and the whole class is watching him or her. Oh! And then you forget everything you learned. Especially in chemistry lessons because it's quite hard. And I study it and I forget everything because I'm nervous.

In short, everyone had something to say about this activity. Some DL teachers said they had used it in the past but had decided it was a waste of class time, a source of stress for students, and an ineffective way of getting students to integrate and reflect on the class material. However, if they didn't practice the *felelés*, what did they use in its place? How was students' oral discourse developed and evaluated – especially in their L2, in which many identified a need for more opportunities to practice? Furthermore, if the purpose of the *felelés* was to coach students toward performance on final oral matriculation examinations, how would the deprived DL students then measure up in the final analysis, that is, compared to well-rehearsed non-DL students?

Early indications from the examinations involving the first graduating class at one school did not bode well for others. One student there lamented:

And so far nobody who went to this kind of school passed the final exam, there is not an example, and we don't know how we should study and what we should study because there's nobody who could tell it to us, there's nobody who has already done it. . . . And when last year I heard that the first dual-language school students in [the town of Vidékiváros] [failed] the final exam, I got disillusioned. They did it miserably, it was a great failure.

At another school, a Hungarian language and literature teacher noted that his otherwise bright third-year students had difficulty expressing themselves even in Hungarian and that he had to do some remedial *felelés* work with them, from which they were really benefiting, in his opinion.

As it turned out, and despite earlier observations to the contrary, in the months of observations which followed, some lessons in DL classrooms did in fact contain *felelés* – but curiously, primarily in Hungarian-medium DL lessons at the third school, Vidékiváros, and then, generally in a manner distinct from non-DL lessons. Furthermore, in some schools, tensions which I had observed or heard about often resulted from teachers being firmly committed to a position at one or the other end of the highly simplified continuum shown in Figure 1.

Hence, this study analyzes speech generated by everyday assessment activities considered by participants to be locally, culturally, and academically relevant and, in some contexts, also susceptible to change. This focus on oral assessment activities was in part motivated by problems I had encountered designing or selecting appropriate content-sensitive EFL assessment instruments for this unique socioeducational

Figure 1. Continuum of approaches to instruction and assessment.

setting; also, assessment in this region favors the oral modality, and high school final exams and university exams give equal weighting to oral and written components. Thus regular classroom activities provided evidence of students' academic oral proficiency and also provided guidelines by which they are judged within their own school culture. The procedures and results of assessment are typically very public and are negotiable, with input from others in the class as well as from the teacher.

Data collection

In the spring and fall of 1991, I videotaped a total of about fifty secondary school history lessons taught by eight Hungarian teachers in three Hungarian-English DL schools. The schools were located in different regions of the country: in urban, rural, and provincial locations, which I refer to as Nagyváros, Kisváros, and Vidékiváros, respectively. Two of the schools (Nagyváros and Vidékiváros) house DL and non-DL programs under the same roof, and some of the non-DL teachers (especially chemistry and Hungarian language and literature, which are always offered in students' L1) taught classes in both sections. Non-DL lessons were conducted in the Hungarian language and DL ones were either in Hungarian or English, depending on the content, the school, and the teacher's L2 proficiency. When dealing with topics of Hungarian history, for example, some DL teachers chose to use Hungarian. Unfortunately, because of space limitations in this chapter, only English translations of Hungarian speech or excepts which were produced in English will be provided (i.e., Hungarian texts will not be included). I will, however, indicate whether the excerpt was originally produced in Hungarian or in English.

I isolated history as a content area because it is a compulsory subject in the Hungarian curriculum, is enjoyed by most students, and is rich in both interaction and in linguistic and cognitive structures (e.g., narrative, description, cause-effect).

Teachers were typically observed over a two-week period to permit thematic development and review within a given unit. Data were then transcribed and translated, where appropriate; additional information came from interviews with teachers, students, and administrators; student essays; discussions with consultants; and other observations.

The structure of history lessons and the *felelés*

The typical forty-five minute history lesson begins when the teacher (T) enters the classroom, the students (Ss) stand up to greet him or her, and the class monitor (*hetes*) reports on absent students. Then the previous lesson is briefly reviewed, recitations take place, and new material is presented in lecture format. The lesson concludes with the teacher assigning readings for the next lesson and then thanking and dismissing the class.

The portion of the lesson in which recitation is practiced comprises three components: the pre-*felelés*, initiation of a recitation topic, selection of student, and presentation of criteria; the *felelés*, student's recitation and related question-answer sequences; and the post-*felelés*, evaluation of the recitation.

I will illustrate the entire activity with a few examples from non-DL teachers' history lessons in Nagyváros and Vidékiváros (grades nine and eleven, respectively). (See Duff [1993] for a much more detailed deconstruction of the *felelés* and for the original Hungarian versions of these passages.) Example 1 clearly presents criteria for student speech which are shared by many teachers: that it should be relatively brief, coherent, and factual, and that the speaker should be visible and audible to all members of the class. (See the Appendix at the end of this chapter for transcription conventions.)

Example 1 (Nagyváros, Hungarian in original)

T: Now then, (2.0) these are the <u>great</u> changes happening. (1.2) I'd like to hear a – coherent *felelet* about that. (1.2) So to explain once very briefly – the time limit is about five minutes, that I'd like to spend on it, so once ((S coughs)) again – what kind of change took place in the Roman economy in the <u>literal</u> sense of this, so <u>from where</u> . . . Roman economy in the second – third century, I'd like to hear a – very nice *felelet* about this. My-E ((S name with endearment)) (3.0).

E: Shall I stay here? [Or?

T: [Come out ((up front)) please. There somewhere. There, so that the others can (see you) better. (1.8) ((S comes up to front)). ((E continues briefly))

T: Back a bit. ((S moves back two paces)) Okay? And louder. All right?

The reciter and topic have been named, the student is correctly positioned to present, books are closed, the class is quiet; now the *felelés* begins. Normally the first few minutes involve an uninterrupted stretch of talk by the reciter. During or after this time, the teacher may intervene for several reasons; because of errors of fact (dates, chronology, places, names); clarification of the topic for the class; restatement of the original question or introduction of another topic; verification of information sources; problematic language use by the student, including register; stylistic anomolies (e.g., too much or too little detail; rambling delivery); or because of other, unrelated disruptions in class. Then, if the topic warrants, quizzing of name, date, and time associations may ensue, generally with the reciter up at the map at the front of the room. The *felelés* ends when the teacher tells the student he or she may stop talking and the class then engages in post-*felelés* discussion.

From the outset, students try to include crucial information in a *felelés*: the topic; the names of main characters associated with that topic; dates; and a summarized narrative of events leading up to, following, or otherwise connected to the topic. If the account is accurate, the teacher will acknowledge the correctness of these features and signal to the student to carry on, by nodding his or her head or uttering back-channel cues such as "uh huh" and *igen* ("yes").

In Example 2, another student has been asked to speak about "the reaction to the Compromise" (Hungary's agreement in 1867 to a shared government with Austria). Besides including relevant facts, S represents the various perspectives on the Compromise associated with the main characters (e.g., Kossuth, landowners), that is, their reactions and explanations for those reactions. Notice that only one terminal (falling) intonation contour (indicated with a period) occurs during this long first turn.

Example 2 (Vidékiváros, Hungarian in original)

S: ((standing)) The diet which assembled in 1867 accepted the twelfth law about the Compromise, the reaction to this was quite different in the country the emigration rejected it with Kossuth in the lead, this is when Kossuth wrote his Cassandra letter to Deák, which actually accuses Deák of betraying the country, because according to him it's suicide to join with a country which is obviously in decline because it lost in the Italian and Prussian front as well this is a loss of prestige for the Austrians, and for uh uh Kossuth the main, so according to him the greatest mistake is that we agreed to have a common army so the army wasn't in Hungary anymore. (1.4) The big landowners and medium landowners who were in the new government accepted it as it was, they agreed with it, there was a group the centre left which accepted the Compromise, but they didn't like

the <u>way</u> it was made so that these common affairs were established, their leader is Tisza Kálmán,
T: Um hum
S: ((continues with turn of same length as first turn, at the end of which there is terminal, falling intonation)

The following excerpt begins at the juncture of a student's pre-*felelés* and *felelés*. The *felelés* begins very unimpressively, picks up somewhat, but then ends weakly as well. The teacher, with unmasked exasperation, provides an ongoing, and seemingly unrelenting, commentary and critique of the content and manner of B's presentation. Hardly a turn goes by that the teacher doesn't offer feedback of a negative nature, and yet neither the teacher nor student (B) gives up on this *felelés*. B is standing at his desk at the back of the classroom flanked by male friends; the teacher is sitting, standing, and pacing at the front.

Example 3 (Nagyváros, Hungarian in original)

B: So Diocletian divides the empire into four parts uh=
T: =We know that you are going to start from here. Right?
B: He nominates 2- 2 companion emperors to govern these parts (2.5) ((B looks down, perhaps at neighbor's notes?)) So uh (1.0) ((looks up)) later (1.0) when – (later I will mention it again) that Constantine the Great issues that Decree of Tolerance=
T: =Now. but you should talk about this, B. ((B looks down, shifting stance; one or two Ss turn to look at B)) (1.4) So <u>not</u> Diocletian, <u>but</u> [yes – what's after him. Well?
B: [(xxx) ((B looks up, then down))
. . .
B: At this time Christianity has already appeared, (3.0)
T: B (I don't know) if you have understood my question. I'd like to hear about Constantine <u>the Great</u>. This should be very [simple. ((B smiles weakly))
B: [(xx) ((one friend smiles at B))
T: Hm? (.4) ((B looks down)) So don't say such stupid things as the appearance of Christianity.

The post-*felelés* evaluation period allows the teacher to debrief the student and the rest of the class about the student's performance according to many of the same criteria introduced in the pre-*felelés* phase. Beyond the implicit socialization and evaluation that takes place throughout the activity, especially pertinent didactic material may be presented by the teacher at the end, ostensibly to accomplish the following: to teach the other students a lesson, to identify the student presenter as a positive or negative role model, or to reflect upon other qualities or weaknesses exhibited by that student (e.g., neatness of exercise book, lateness in submitting homework, absenteeism).

The rest of the class – who may or may not have been attending to the *felelés* – may also be called upon to contribute to the teacher's assessment and rendering of a mark for another student's presentation. They may be asked to guess what grade the reciter will get, generally when it can be assumed that the teacher plans to award a five, or they may be required to give frank comments, both positive and negative, about the observed *felelés*. Occasionally, a student may be asked to do a self-criticism or confess to being ill-prepared.

Example 4 highlights positive attributes of a *felelés* by E (the same student as in Example 1). The teacher remarks to the class that E has produced "very – correct, precise, nice, clever answers." Furthermore, the teacher refers to E's beautiful exercise book, which the teacher had praised at length at the beginning of the same lesson. The adjective "nice," (i.e., *szép*) is understood to be equivalent to a grade of five.

Example 4 (Nagyváros, Hungarian in original)

T: Well, all right. ((T sits down at desk)) Thanks. Thanks. ((E returns to seat)) (2.2) Not only is E's exercise book beautiful, (1.8) ((T opens up grade book)) but what she knows is too. ((E is now seated)) Yes, I think she has given us very – ((looks up at class, changing glasses to write in grade book)) correct, precise, nice answers here. Very clever. Very <u>nice</u>.

The foregoing examples are not atypical of *felelés* structure and format, although teachers may be more or less harsh with students. Teachers in non-DL classes were very much in control and yet they delegated some of the responsibility for evaluating, criticizing, and quizzing to other students. Students themselves did not normally self-initiate such comments or questions.

Assessment in DL schools: innovation and change in educational practice

As reported earlier, DL schools represent innovation and change in the educational, linguistic, and cultural status quo for a growing number of secondary students in Hungary. First proposed as an alternative model of L2 instruction by a few interested officials in the Ministry of Culture and Education, the schools have over time become increasingly independent and accountable to the needs and concerns of local councils, teachers, parents, and students. Hence, many changes are now introduced by the schools themselves, as situations may dictate, and the Ministry has, on the whole, been only marginally concerned with the schools' progress over the past few years of decentralization (Duff, in press).

It would be misleading to suggest that in their move away from educational authoritarianism and totalitarianism, the schools have embarked on a uniform course toward democratization, just as it would be wrong to suggest that all Eastern European countries have followed one single path in similar pursuit. Rather, a "plurality of transitions" have arisen (Bruszt and Stark 1992), again depending on local constraints, circumstances, and personnel. Yet commonalities exist across the schools (and countries) in the quest to exercise newfound freedoms and in the need to deal with unpredicted setbacks, opposition, and dated (and thus what are perceived to be "tainted") approaches to institutional management.

The students themselves represent a vocal and powerful constituency within the DL system, poised to be agents of change within the schools and in the community. Some consider themselves to be geniuses; most are also regarded as very clever by their teachers, families, friends at non-DL schools, and DL schoolmates. At some schools, they represent the top 3 or 4 percent of applicants who take the competitive entrance examinations, and after a short time of immersion at school they come to possess a very valuable commodity: a Western foreign language. This resource in turn often yields coveted work, travel, and study opportunities as well as a greater sense of connectedness with the Western world.

Thus, teachers have bright, idealistic students. The DL schools, being "elitist by merit," attract a large number of high achievers who, for the first time, can be very disappointed to find themselves in a class where, in the words of one headmaster, "*everybody* is the best," and "all of a sudden it turns out that you are the *worst* of the best."

Students' expectations are also heightened and sharpened by their exposure to a different world and to a range of diverse attitudes through EFL and through a (relatively) communicative approach to teaching which they experience in their first year at the schools. This year makes a tremendous impression on them, particularly in the five-year programs with intensive, highly interactive, foreign language instruction. In their small classes of twelve learners each, students are encouraged to express their opinions and grievances, to speak up and be heard, to make mistakes and to learn from experience and not just from teachers' lectures and textbooks. The teacher's role is often subordinated to that of the learners, who engage in role plays, small group discussions, debates and other activities meant to stimulate EFL development in an efficient, fun way. Officially discouraged in earlier years, the widespread social and political changes relevant to their lives and of interest to them can now be taken up quite openly in class. Many of the messages the new students appropriate from that year, such as how classroom communication can (or should) be carried out, and about their interactional roles and rights, they then carry with them into their non-DL lessons and future DL lessons as well. They speak out when they wish and ask imaginative questions about matters beyond the scope of textbooks. As one non-DL teacher reported, these students have difficulty adjusting to large classes after having been in smaller ones, and "the real difficult task is to make them understand how they can interact in a class of thirty-six in a polite way." The students also expect teachers to prepare materials that are supplementary to the textbooks. Hence, students attempt to *re-socialize* the more conservative teachers to more progressive, less rigid ways of teaching, based on their experience as EFL students in the DL schools.

Following are students' perceptions of differences between the two approaches, of the freedom and democracy they experience at the DL schools – and most dramatically in the entry-level year – compared with the austere atmosphere in primary school and in more traditional classes at the DL schools. (Excerpts are taken from Nagyváros essays of students completing their first year at the school, May 1991, English in original.)

Now I like my school. I love it. Because studying is only a part of the school. There is a good school group here and the teachers are young and friendly. When I was going to the primary school, I hated teachers. I thought they only lived because they wanted to give me a bad mark and destroy my life.

... the teachers talk with me like with an adults, and if I have a problem with a teacher I can solve it with the teacher together. We have younger teachers, then [sic] I had in a Primary School. It's interesting that I can say 'Hello', and not always 'Good Morning, Afternoon' etc. but it's not always good, because sometimes I feel that this school is not too serious, and then we write a Test, and I feel serious immediately. ... So I liked this school better, then [sic] the Primary school, because we have more freedom, and if you know the film Hair, you know what it means that the freedom and happiness are given.

As a consequence of their motivation, talent, and successful EFL learning experience, students are quite demanding about schooling practices, opportunities to further their academic goals and other aspirations, and their teachers' qualifications. The students' EFL skills often exceed those of their native Hungarian, content-area teachers after just a year or two; therefore, teachers must appear very competent in their subjects so as not to lose credibility. This risk, naturally exacerbated by the tendencies of adolescence, adds to the insecurity of new teachers, who must spend inordinate amounts of time preparing their lessons.

This curious mismatch between students and their teachers in terms of foreign language competence represents a twist in the normally accepted notion of teachers being *experts* and students *novices* (see Jacoby and Gonzales 1991) and that schooling provides apprenticeship chiefly for *pupils* – not for their *teachers*, and certainly not apprenticeship for the latter *by* the former. Dual-language students may correct (or criticize) their teachers' English skills, while teachers correct the students' re-presentation of historical dates, names, events, and so on; indeed, language socialization in these schools is a very dynamic, bidirectional process (Ochs 1988, 1990). Unfortunately, however, the potential cognitive *construction zone* (Newman, Griffin, and Cole 1989) often provides a *deconstruction* (or destruction) zone for DL students who are only too willing to analyze their teachers' weaknesses.

I do not want to insolt [sic] my teachers and I am not sure wheather [sic] I have the right to critisize [sic] them or not, but I feel that some of them don't speak English as much as I would expect them.

Non-DL teachers are quick to point out differences between the DL and non-DL populations they encounter. They must prepare more material for each DL lesson and can expect more questions and feedback. Sometimes teachers surmise that students' questions are intended to test them rather than to generate answers to sincere queries. Teachers also noted that they are subject to overt criticism by their DL students, which they strongly disapprove of. One non-DL teacher wistfully remarked (in English):

I have two [DL] classes at the third level. One is problematical, rather problematical. They are – our connection is not so good. It's not so interesting but they could speak much more in the last years than now. Uh they like – in this year – they like to judge, judge me. . . . To push me around.

Finally, although younger students at the DL schools tended to be quite happy with their education, during the times of perhaps the greatest change in the political and socioeconomic fabric of the country (e.g., 1990–1991) many students expressed grave concerns about their school experiences. Their doubts and frustrations stemmed from disillusionment with an educational system (and new government) that had perhaps promised more than it could fully deliver in its earliest years of implementation, leaving students' futures in the balance. Typical viewpoints from Vidékiváros and Kisváros students' essays (1990–1991) follow.

Our school is an *experimental* one so that it is a kind of adventure both for pupils and teachers. Adventures have both positive and negative effects on people. Attending to this school is exciting, the atmosphere is relaxed, we may get to know to other cultures and reach a high level in English.

However, attending to this school means many disadvantages, e.g., the level of education keeps *changing* all the time, neither teachers nor students have experience in this kind of school and the *lack of routine* causes many mistakes.

I feel uncertainty in school. The old curriculum turned out to be bad and unusable. The books are not about reality. But there're no new ones yet so the teacher has to educate us from somewhere else. They don't really know what to expect from us in terms of knowledge. We might have good ideas but it takes ages until they are put to work.

I was born in 1976, and I lived in the "Gulash socialism" as a child. It was exactly what I needed, quite silent and peaceful. When I became a teenager, in 1989 or so, I started to critizate [sic] my life, my school, my parents, and everything. And that was the time, when the real changes started in East-Europe. I wanted to be a piece of it. I wanted to take part in it. I started to go to political meetings, I read about politics, etc., and I felt I really am a member of the new system. A lot of people felt the same, but now they are disappointed.

I'm afraid these changes [toward democracy] haven't been reflected in our school. The leadership of the school is still the same and the methods they're using haven't changed. The headmaster has been reelected and most of the students' proposals are denied by him. On the other hand I believe we are a step closer to real democracy since now we students dare to do something against the authority, while earlier we were to agree either we liked it or not. And nowadays the headmaster wouldn't reject our proposal without explaining why he does so. So I suppose we are on the right path but we still have much way in front of us.

The *felelés*: under siege in DL schools?

Given the preceding description of DL students, it is no wonder that, despite their years of daily recitation at primary school, students may be quite critical of the chronic stress associated with the anticipation of numerous possible recitations everyday as well as the formality and rigidity of the structured interaction. Once exposed to instruction in which the traditional *felelés* is no longer practiced, students were especially vocal about its perceived abuses.

[The *felelés*] is an ordeal for children. "*Felelés*" is an act during which one person is exposed to the authority and power of the other, the former being the student, the latter the teacher. Situations like this apparently result in a confused relationship between the two. The cooperation of teacher and student could be enhanced by abolition of *felelés*. (Nagyváros, English essay)

The most horrible and I think very bad part of the Hungarian school-system is about giving daily-account [i.e., *felelés*]. Which means that from every subject a teacher can ask you to give an account about what you learned for

421

the day. This can happen any day from every subject. The teachers make up our grades from this. This means that in one half of the year we have about four marks only. And if you had a bad day and you have to give an account and you get a bad mark your grade is bad for that half of the year. My opinion is that this is no way to grade somebody. So the conclusion is that there are still a lot of things to change. (Vidékiváros, English essay)

I really don't like it because it means that – they – ask questions from you every lesson from the previous (x) or something like that and it means that you have to prepare for every lesson. And it's quite a stress. . . . Maybe if a class one day after each other, I have half an hour to learn the matter. Y'know. Then I will know tomorrow but then I forget everything. I think it would be much better if we would have tests in two weeks every two weeks or something. (Nagyváros, English interview)

Dual-language history lessons which did feature *felelés* differed from non-DL lessons in several respects, most of which are related to opportunities for DL students to make and act upon choices about (a) complying with a *felelés* solicit by the teacher; (b) self-selecting for *felelés*; and (c) negotiating the manner of conducting *felelés* (e.g., the modality, oral vs. written) as well as physical positioning (i.e., standing or sitting, at their seats or at the front of the room).

Dual-language students who felt they should *not* have to do the *felelés* because of lack of preparation or perceived lack of fairness in selection, contested teachers' solicits or excused themselves from the performance, without explanation. In one DL class, students asked the teacher to revise her method of selecting students to make it less predictable.

One situation I observed seemed particularly indicative of problems encountered when a liberal, democratic atmosphere is fostered (starting with EFL courses) in an otherwise conservative school system. In this rather mismanaged provincial school (Vidékiváros), the locally educated history teachers, quite unlike teachers observed at the other two schools, had consistently used *felelés*. However, the classroom dynamics and the negotiation associated with the recitation were often markedly different from those observed elsewhere in non-DL lessons and were frequently conducted in Hungarian. A bright seventeen-year-old student, LG, was told he must do both an oral and written exam during that period. This unanticipated decision upset LG, who believed that with his consistently superior performance (i.e., fives on tests), yet another display of his competence would be unfair and unjustified. As a consequence, he vehemently opposed the teacher's decision, leading to a lengthy and heated argument about LG's grade status and the past performance he defended. He challenged the teacher's authority, her calculations, and even her ability to write legitimate test prompts, before finally relenting. The teacher insisted, meanwhile, that an oral examination would be good practice for him, an aspiring history major.

This emotional scenario revealed an incongruous juxtaposition of the traditional, austere *felelés* (and the teacher's marked use of formal, symmetrical, address pronouns) on the one hand, and the manner in which the two were arguing on the other hand. Indeed, an ideological, political, and linguistic tug-of-war appeared to be taking place in this DL class, which I'm told would have been unthinkable in the past. What is more, at about the same time, the Vidékiváros graduating class caused a small scandal in town when they appeared in photos for their formal composite graduation placard with no clothing (i.e., the students appeared to be naked, but had posed in bathing suits), against the backdrop of a brick wall covered with graffiti including such expressions as "Sex & Drugs & Rock 'n Roll." Students customarily wear formal attire in these placard photos (white blouses or shirts, dark suits, ties) which are then proudly placed on display in fine shop windows in the city. This group's display was so controversial that it was returned to the school, where it appears on the wall in one dark corridor on the ground floor.

Many students were quite aware that the *felelés* is a local, cultural, pedagogical phenomenon normally practiced in Eastern European countries but not normally in English-speaking countries or, at two of the schools, in their Hungarian-English DL programs. They also recognized that teachers from other countries might not be familiar with its conventions, purposes, advantages, and disadvantages. In spring 1991 DL students reflected:

We should have to do [*felelés*] but we don't. It's the Hungarian method. We have to learn speaking – you know that final exams we need it. History and biology and everything is orally there. We had it sometimes in first year, it's not a tradition here in this school and in America they don't do it at all. And when I told them that we have to do it at home here in Hungary, they were laughing and said that it would be terrible. (Nagyváros, English interview)

Well this was the problem of our British English teachers, that they didn't understand what this means, this giving a report or something. And ah, I think it must be (a) typical Hungarian system or something, when somebody – someone is called out, and he's asked to – to – to say something about the last week's material something. And uh – well I think they want to uh control us or they want us to – they want to make us learn from one lesson to another with this. . . . That is another thing – giving marks – which is quite strange ((laughs)) for many foreigners. . . . Because they couldn't understand uh how . . . I make someone stand up and then . . . how can I tell him to – to – or force him to say something. I dunno. (Vidékiváros, English interview)

Despite their overall displeasure with the stressful recitation process, students remained very aware of and motivated by the short-term goals of revision and the daunting longer-range requirements (e.g., for success at university) that they be skillful at *felelés*.

The history lessons, I think this *felelés* is good because uh we have to uh prepare for every lesson, and it's also good because you have a continuous work on that subject. (Vidékiváros, English interview)

It's necessary for us I think. Because we are forced to learn. (Vidékiváros, English interview)

Well I think you should get used to give your knowledge in speaking because the last exam of the school is made up of two parts, writing and speaking. (Nagyváros, English interview)

Beyond the *felelés*

How was oral assessment achieved in the absence of *felelés*; and what opportunities were there for students to develop and display their discourse competence?

In Nagyváros DL lessons, which were conducted by Hungarian nationals almost entirely in English, assessment took place through normal question-answer exchanges, through pair and small group work, and through class discussions. The speech event most comparable to the *felelés* was a prepared, scripted presentation called a student *lecture*, done by volunteers who were likely to get a mark of five for this activity. The Nagyváros teacher and her students were found to intervene frequently during lectures for a number of reasons, but provided very little post-lecture discussion of the presentation itself (Duff 1995). In Kisváros, student lectures were also encouraged (and English also used), but the teacher and his students intervened little if at all during lectures, providing much lengthier post-lecture commentary instead. Furthermore, because of his background as an EFL teacher and his fascination and familiarity with other languages, the second teacher made far more metalinguistic comments than his Nagyváros counterpart, whose comments tended to be directed at content and at a manner of presenting that would facilitate audience comprehension and note taking.

At the time lectures were delivered, DL teachers seated themselves among students while the class-fronted lectures were about to begin. One teacher (at Nagyváros) would watch the lecturer and intervene when appropriate, sometimes looking for pictures in books she had brought along that might illustrate the lecturer's point. The other (at Kisváros) was more inclined to take notes, looking up from time to time, and commenting later. During the post-lecture phase, he changed his stance, turning toward others in the class to ask them questions or provide other information related to the lecture.

In every solo (as opposed to group-based) student lecture I observed, the speaker stood at the blackboard, notes in hand. In Kisváros, one student also used an overhead projector, apparently at the teacher's suggestion, although it caused delays because of a shortage of power outlets. Whereas in the *felelés*, in which the student was oriented more toward the teacher than toward his or her classmates, in the lecture, with the teacher seated among the students, the lecturer addressed the whole class.

In the *felelés*, students were instructed to close their textbooks and notes, but were often allowed to keep their atlases open. However, in lectures, students in the audience took notes and lecturers were entitled to consult their notes or other visual aids, such as illustrations in books or drawn on the blackboard.

Although the lecture resembled a *felelés* in so far as it contained a list of facts or a narrative linked to a key historical figure or event and was presented to the class and teacher by a student up at the front of the room, the two genres were distinguished by the sequential and participation organization as well and the use of reference materials (see Duff 1993). However, in the Kisváros lectures, during which speakers presented material from six to eleven minutes in length with virtually no teacher or student interventions, differences from *felelés* were less apparent, although the two required distinct sets of skills. Student lecturers could consult their written texts, as was previously mentioned, and in two observed cases read their prepared lectures from beginning to end, seldom pausing or looking up from their notes. The texts they referred to sounded as though they came from published sources, but this information was not revealed. In the other two cases with the same teacher, students had either memorized and rehearsed their texts very well, or presented their material hesitantly but without relying too heavily on their notes. In short, except for their dependence on present materials, these four lectures were rather similar to the *felelés* done at Vidékiváros in a DL class (where the teacher also intervened very little).

In the quickly read or recited lectures at Kisváros, which were conducted in English, the speed and sophistication of the language of the texts made comprehension very difficult for even a native speaker at times, and note taking would have been all the more demanding. The student (S1), in Example 5, read so softly and with such accented English in a room with terrible acoustics that it was extremely difficult to follow at the time or later to transcribe her lecture. The second reader (S2), whose turn came shortly after S1's, had been advised to speak more loudly, and was therefore audible, but read the academic prose at such a pace and with such rare eye contact as to seriously impede comprehension and audience involvement. Her behavior even suggested a stance of opposition (Canagarajah 1993), for reasons that will be discussed presently. Yet, what is noteworthy is that the teacher, who later identified these points as weaknesses, did not intervene until the post-lecture phase: namely, 10.5 minutes after S1's and 5 minutes after S2's lecture began. He then praised the students, sometimes profusely, for other aspects of their lectures and posed questions to them or other members of the class to check their comprehension.

Example 5 (Regarding S1, Kisváros, English in original)

T: But otherwise, I appreciate it and let me tell you I enjoyed the legend, the tale, the map, and the drawing and everything else. So I liked it a lot. Thank you very much. Good. So one thing I'd like to ask ((continues, asking other Ss three questions concerning what the lecturer said about the village, and then asks about differences between some Latin and Greek terms))

In the case of S2, perhaps suspecting that she had simply copied the text of her lecture from an encyclopedia without understanding it (which certainly appeared to be the case), the teacher then asked her for the main point: "*Why* do you think he was a great ruler?" to which the student was unable to give a satisfactory answer. Nevertheless, the teacher went on (following some critical remarks) to say that it was "excellent," that he "enjoyed it," that it was a "brilliant summary," and so on.

There appeared to be a striking mismatch, then, between students' performance and the teacher's softened but critical comments, on the one hand, and the quantity and types of praises he offered them, on the other hand, for the *same* problematic lectures.

Example 6 contains the beginning and end of one of the most impressive lectures I witnessed at Kisváros, on Cicero. Well rehearsed and delivered with animation, if a little too rapidly, the text was a six-minute oral rendition of a written passage from the *Encyclopedia Britannica* – the newly acquired and much coveted source of instructional reference material at Kisváros.

Ironically, although the teacher at that school claimed to have rejected practices associated with the *feleLés*, the following presentation was performed by P very much like a *feleLés*, with the possible exception that P, and not the teacher, framed the text with opening and concluding remarks.

Example 6 (Kisváros, English in original)

P: So. I would like to talk about th' person that played a very important role – in Roman history, – and this person is Cicero. You can see – his picture – here. ((holds up picture in book)) (1.0) Cicero was a statesman lawyer scholar writer, – and he (x tried) to afford republican principles – in the final civil war that destroyed the republic of Rome. (1.5) His writings include books of rhetoric – orations, philosophical and political treatises – and letters. He is remembered in modern times – as the greatest Roman orator, and the innovator – what became known – as the Ciceronean rhetoric. (1.5) Well. Cicero was born. . . . ((A continues to speak eloquently for several minutes))

. . . Cicero in his work brought ((/brut/)) us-gives his own ((/aun/)) description of his uh-equivalent as an orator. And this is as follows. A grounding in philosophy, a thorough knowledge of literature, and a storehouse of history. (1.0) The capacity to <u>tie</u> up an opponent, and induce the jury to laughter. . . . Cicero's importance in the history of philosophy – is a transmitter o-of Greek thought – and uh he gave Rome and therefore Europe – its- philosophical vocabulary. So. ((very quickly)). That's all I wanted to say about Cicero, I hope you enjoyed it. Thank you very much.=

Ss: =((laughter)) ((applause for about 5 seconds))

T: ((speaking VERY quickly during the last second of the applause, while still sitting at back looking at the group)) Well. A. Congratulations it was marvelous.

It is quite unusual that the student concluded his lecture by thanking the audience and hoping that they enjoyed it (expecting, evidently, that they should). In many respects, the speaker (P) appeared to model himself after both Cicero and the teacher in his method of addressing the class; and in his own (borrowed) text, P even presented criteria by which to judge a good orator, and perhaps a lecturer as well: "A grounding in philosophy, a thorough knowledge of literature, and a storehouse of history. (1.0) The capacity to <u>tie</u> up an opponent, and induce the jury to laughter."

Indeed, P's own jury was moved to laughter, praise, and admiration (if not a genuine understanding of the content). In his assessment of the lecture, the teacher did not comment initially on the content or the plagiarism so much as the form: that it was marvelous, grammatically sophisticated, wonderfully delivered, and so on. That P's text may have been difficult for other students to comprehend (because of the processing demands of academic vocabulary, syntax, an essentially memorized written text, with little visual support) is suggested when the teacher later observes that P has not written enough key information on the board.

The topic, manner of delivery, and response to this presentation are significant because, while perhaps not typical of most lessons taught by DL teachers, and none that I had observed in previous years at Kisváros, these data were collected during a period of great turmoil at this school, in which the teacher himself was embroiled. The grievance that form

427

(e.g., rhetoric) was taking precedence over content, and appearances (beautiful school facilities) over substance (education and truth), united the majority of teachers and students in their opposition to what they considered the politically chameleonlike administration of the dysfunctional "showcase" school. My analyses of lesson transcripts, summarized very briefly earlier, gave me a better understanding of certain tensions and contradictions that members of the school community had been wrestling with for some time. Another such indicator was a letter submitted to a Hungarian national newspaper (but possibly never printed) by two or three teachers at the school; an excerpt from this follows.

[The headmaster's] contributions to the school are mostly control measures, which he concocts in secret and imposes on the school community without forethought or consideration. . . . He is more concerned with the school's – and his – image, no matter how untruthful it may be, than with the actual functioning of the school. . . . His style of management is that which prevailed in our country in the past forty years. The issue is not one of support or opposition; nor is it one of personalities. The issue is effectiveness. Most East Europeans can bear witness to the failures of this style of management.

Like so many institutions established under the previous regime, the Kisváros DL school and the preceding teacher's excerpt (as well as numerous comments from other teachers and students not presented here) invoke the metaphor of "new wine in old wineskins": the DL model of education was new, as was the (Western) language of instruction, the communicative methodology, much of the teaching staff, and the technical equipment and school facilities. However, the infrastructure, discourse, and leadership apparatus (with which this history teacher was closely aligned) were decidedly "old" (or old under the guise of being "new") – conditions conducive to explosion and ruin (both in the cases of wineskins and social institutions). The rigid rhetorical approach conflicted with other more pragmatic modes of communicating inside and outside of classrooms espoused by expatriate teachers at the school (from various English-speaking countries) and by some of the Hungarians affiliated with the "liberal" group as well, who ended up leaving the school in dismay. (Note that parallel criticisms on the political level have also been leveled in the post-communist era).

By fall 1991, major staffing changes had taken place at Kisváros, including the resignation of eighteen teachers who had been unhappy with the situation the previous year. In their place a large number of new teachers were hired. The new Hungarian teachers (several of whom I observed and spoke with in November 1991) embraced a much more traditional, conservative approach to teaching than their predecessors had, whether in EFL or other subjects. Hence, the pendulum seemed to be swinging back to (a) a more structural EFL curriculum (e.g., more focus on grammar, translation, drills); (b) the practice of *felelés* in some courses where previously it had been absent (e.g., history); and (c) a more disciplinarian attitude among teachers toward students with an emphasis on moral education.

Of the three schools, Nagyváros was the most calm and optimistic during the period of fieldwork. In contrast to Kisváros classrooms, in the average student lecture at Nagyváros there were far fewer extended stretches of talk by the lecturer, and instead, much more interaction. The number and kinds of questions posed by classmates – not just by the teacher – and requests for the student to slow down, to repeat information, and so on, contrasted sharply with the traditional *felelés*. In the latter, students were expected to speak quickly, not to be repetitious, and not to worry about the rest of the class. Students were really only licensed to comment or quiz the reciter when invited by the teacher, formally or informally, at relevant points in the event (e.g., the map quiz) or during post-*felelés* invitations to comment. Then, during the post-lecture phase, the Nagyváros teacher generally just asked whether students had any questions. There was frequently little uptake of this solicit because queries were generally addressed earlier in the lecture.

Summary and conclusion

As a genre of discourse development and assessment, the *felelés* has attracted criticism from those who associate it with some of the problems of past authoritarian political structures (or the hardships of primary school, for younger critics). In DL classrooms, therefore, which have already departed from traditional Hungarian education by conducting lessons through a foreign (and notably Western) language, and which seek to create a more liberal and democratic atmosphere with opportunities for language practice, the *felelés* has been subject to scrutiny, reform, negotiation, and sometimes outright rejection. However, as in non-DL lessons, each class of teachers and students comes to terms with the *felelés* in its own way, exhibiting a plurality of options in variation and change. In Vidékiváros, for example, although the *felelés* was retained in DL history lessons, some of its properties were being challenged, questioned, and recast at the same time as dual-language education at that school was being challenged and questioned because of fundamental uncertainties and perceived mismanagement.

In 1991 Kisváros was a school struggling to find a balance between the use of two languages in the curriculum and school on the one hand, and a balance between discipline and democracy on the other. There, a genre called the "lecture" had supplanted the *felelés*, the latter event likened by one teacher at the school to an inquisition. However, at the same school, where criticism was mounting about double standards and "double-speak," the lecture proved strangely traditional after all; it embodied many properties of the *felelés* – perhaps even omitting some of the best – and yet was implemented in the name of a new genre or a new approach to educational discourse. Evaluation of lectures was also contradictory in some respects when enthusiastic words of praise and highly problematic performances did not correspond, and when the lecture became no more than a read-aloud exercise, a charade. In the face of such discrepancies, changes were called for but to no avail; after much restructuring, the *felelés* was reintroduced (in name, form, and substance, and in Hungarian) by a new non-English-speaking history teacher with apparent success.

Nagyváros, the most stable DL school during the course of this study, also supported a reduced emphasis on *felelés*, replacing it with student lectures fostering greater learner input in the selection of students and topics, and in negotiations of meaning during the presentations themselves. Moreover, alternative participation organization was used in some cases, backgrounding the role of the teacher and foregrounding the role of student, as both expert and novice, or something in between. Assessment was managed in less formalized and planned ways as well – for example, through lively discussions of homework assignments or questions concerning a teacher's lectures.

As this chapter has shown, even in the relatively progressive DL classroom there was still a slipping and sliding along a continuum from highly controlled to more democratically distributed leadership and discourse. Whereas many of the DL history classes had (rightly or wrongly) rejected the *felelés* as a legitimate or productive model of classroom discourse and assessment practices, it still cropped up in classes under certain conditions or under different labels (such as the student lecture). The voluntary student lectures were used in place of *felelés*, but they were typically not graded (i.e., publicly, or even critically evaluated when graded, since fives were expected) and students had much more flexibility in their use of materials, aids, and contributions from their classmates. In doing these lectures, however, with competing emphases on authoritative source and accuracy, on the one hand, and relaxed requirements regarding manner of presentation, on the other, students had a tendency to rely heavily on the written word. For this reason, and probably because it reduced preparation time, students were often found to *read* rather than to recite or informally discuss issues when it was their turn to lecture.

Aside from formal speeches of one sort or another, everyday oral assessment in DL lessons took the form of Initiation-Reply-Evaluation (see, e.g., Mehan 1979) interaction and discussions involving other students as well as the teacher. The Nagyváros DL history, in particular, often tried to reconfigure the social organization of lessons so that students would be more responsible for tutoring one another or for coming to shared understandings through task-based discussion and the negotiation of meanings in small groups.

Students in the DL classrooms were found to be more spontaneously active than non-DL students in asking questions, disagreeing with one another, or evaluating a teacher. The smaller number of students in a class, their motivation for studying, confidence levels, and quick intellect fostered lively exchanges in DL lessons. However, students were ultimately still held accountable for the same basic curricular material as in non-DL lessons, a situation which has given rise to a number of political, pedagogical, and sociolinguistic tensions in DL schools (c.f., Daoud 1991; Duff in press). Hence, different models of discourse socialization prevail and evolve in ways that may be in greater or lesser harmony with existing cultural and government-mandated assesment practices.

Appendix: Transcription conventions

1. *Participants*:   T = teacher; S = student; Ss = two students; SSS = many students.] Initials are used for students identifiable by name (e.g., M, SZ, J) rather than S.
2. *Left bracket* [:   Indicates the beginning of overlapping speech, shown for both speakers; second speaker's bracket occurs at the beginning of the line of the next turn rather than in alignment with previous speaker's bracket.
3. *Equal sign* =:   Indicates speech which comes immediately after another person's, shown for both speakers (i.e., latched utterances).
4. (#):   Marks the length of a pause in seconds.
5. (Words):   The words in parenthesis ( ) were not clearly heard; (x) = unclear word; (xx) = two unclear words; (xxx) = three or more unclear words.
6. Underlined words: Words spoken with emphasis.
7. CAPITAL LETTERS: Loud speech.
8. ((Double parenthesis)):   Comments and relevant details pertaining to interaction
9. *Colon*: Sound or syllable is unusually lengthened (e.g., rea::lly lo:ng)
10. *Period*: Terminal falling intonation.
11. *Comma*: Rising, continuing intonation.
12. *Question mark*: High rising intonation, not necessarily at the end of a sentence.
13. *Unattached dash*:   A short, untimed pause.

14. *One-sided attached dash-* : A cutoff often accompanied by a glottal stop (e.g., a self-correction); a dash attached on both sides reflects spelling conventions.
15. *Italics*: Used to distinguish L1 and L2 utterances.

References

Alexander, T. 1918. *The Prussian Elementary Schools.* New York: Macmillan.
Aronowitz, S., and H. A. Giroux. 1991. *Postmodern Education: Politics, Culture, and Social Criticism.* Minneapolis: University of Minnesota Press.
Bakhtin, M. M. 1981. *The Dialogic Imagination.* Austin: University of Texas Press.
Banac, I. (ed.). 1992. *Eastern Europe in Revolution.* Ithaca, NY: Cornell University Press.
Bourdieu, P. 1977. *Outline of a Theory of Practice.* [Translated by Richard Nice.] Cambridge: Cambridge University Press.
Brown, J. F. 1991. *Surge to Freedom.* Durham: Duke University Press.
Bruszt, L., and D. Stark. 1992. Remaking the political field in Hungary: From the politics of confrontation to the politics of competition. In J. Banacs (ed.), *Eastern Europe in Revolution.* Ithaca, NY: Cornell University Press.
Canagarajah, A. S. 1993. Critical ethnography of a Sri Lankan classroom: Ambiguities in student opposition to reproduction through ESOL. *TESOL Quarterly,* 27, 4, 601–626.
Daoud, M. 1991. Arabization in Tunisia: The tug of war. *Issues in Applied Linguistics,* 2, 7–29.
Duff, P. A. 1991a. Innovations in foreign language education: An evaluation of three Hungarian-English dual-language programs. *Journal of Multilingual and Multicultural Development,* 12, 459–476.
1991b. The efficacy of dual-language education in Hungary: An investigation of three Hungarian-English programs. Final Report for Year-Two (1990–91) of the project. The Language Resource Program, University of California, Los Angeles.
1993. Changing Times, Changing Minds: Language Socialization in Hungarian-English Schools. Unpublished doctoral dissertation. University of California, Los Angeles.
1995. Ethnography in an immersion context: Language socialization through EFL and history. *TESOL Quarterly,* 29, 3, 505–537.
(forthcoming). Immersion in an Eastern European context: Case study of a Hungarian EFL experiment. In R. K. Johnson and M. Swain (eds.), *Immersion Education: International Perspectives.* New York: Cambridge University Press.
Duranti, A. 1985. Sociocultural dimensions of discourse. In T. A. van Dijk (ed.), *Handbook of Discourse Analysis.* vol. 1. London: Academic Press.
Echikson, W. 1990. *Lighting the Night: Revolution in Eastern Europe.* New York: William Morrow.
Garton Ash, T. 1989. *The Uses of Adversity.* New York: Random House.
1990. *We the People.* London: Granta.
Giddens, A. 1984. *The Construction of Society.* Berkeley: University of California Press.

Hammersley, M., and P. Atkinson. 1983. *Ethnography: Principles and Practice.* New York: Routledge.

Herbart, J. F. 1898. *Letters and Lectures on Education.* [Translated by H. M. Felkin and E. Felkin.] London: Swan Sonnenschein and Company.

Jacoby, S., and P. Gonzales. 1991. The constitution of expert-novice in scientific discourse. *Issues in Applied Linguistics,* 2, 148–181.

Kuran, T. 1992. Now out of never: The element of surprise in the East European revolution of 1989. In N. Bermeo (ed.), *Liberalization and Democratization: Change in the Soviet Union and Eastern Europe.* Baltimore: The Johns Hopkins University Press.

Mehan, H. 1979. *Learning Lessons.* Cambridge, MA: Harvard University Press.

Newman, D., P. Griffin, and M. Cole. 1989. *The Construction Zone: Working for Cognitive Change in School.* Cambridge: Cambridge University Press.

Ochs, E. 1988. *Culture and Language Development.* Cambridge: Cambridge University Press.

1990. Indexicality and socialization. In J. W. Stigler, R. A. Shweder, and G. Herdt (eds.), *Cultural Psychology.* Cambridge: Cambridge University Press.

Ochs, E., and B. B. Schieffelin. 1984. Language acquisition and socialization: Three developmental stories and their implications. In R. A. Shweder and R. A. LeVine (eds.), *Culture Theory: Essays on Mind, Self and Emotion.* New York: Cambridge University Press.

Ortner, S. B. 1984. Theory in anthropology since the sixties. *Comparative Studies in Society and History,* 26, 126–166.

Poole, D. 1992. Language socialization in the second language classroom. *Language Learning,* 42, 593–616.

Ramet, S. P. 1991. *Social Currents in Eastern Europe.* Durham: Duke University Press.

Schieffelin, B. B. 1990. *The Give and Take of Everyday Life: Language Socialization of Kaluli Children.* Cambridge: Cambridge University Press.

Schieffelin, B. B., and E. Ochs. 1986a. Language socialization. *Annual Review of Anthropology,* 15, 163–191.

1986b. *Language Socialization Across Cultures.* Cambridge: Cambridge University Press.

19 The tapestry of diversity in our classrooms

Denise E. Murray

> I am here   you are there.
> We are so different   so far apart.
> Through knowledge   we can bridge the gap.
> Through love, we can fill the emptiness.
> (Student's poem, Anonymous)

This chapter, unlike others in this book, does not focus on one ethnographic study; rather, it draws from many different studies to demonstrate the diversity of our students. The 1980s in the United States was a decade in which "celebrating diversity" was a major theme. This chapter will illustrate what that diversity is like and how we as teachers can go *beyond* celebrating diversity to capitalizing on what our students bring to the classroom – that is, how we can treat diversity as a resource, not a problem. I will draw on the lives of many English learners – children, young people, and adults – and, mostly let them talk in their *own* voices. I have chosen the metaphor of a tapestry to weave these stories together because I want us to think of our classrooms as multiple threads, patterns, and colors which together make an intricate design.

Diversity is obvious

That the United States and many other nations have linguistically and culturally diverse populations is clear from the statistics (see, for example, Ward and Anthony 1992: 142). California portends many of the growth patterns in the entire nation. Between 1980 and 1990, the white population (as a percentage) fell, the Hispanic population grew, the Asian and Pacific Islander population doubled, and the African American and Native American populations grew slightly. California in 1993 classified one million students in kindergarten to grade 12 schools (approximately twenty percent of the public school population) as limited English proficient (LEP). One-third of Californians use languages other

An expanded version of this chapter was given as a plenary address at the 1993 CATESOL Conference (California Teachers to Speakers of Other Languages).

than English in their homes. A survey of a large California campus (Murray, Nichols, and Heisch 1992) showed that almost one-third of the college students were born outside the United States. This diversity surprises our immigrant students:

Before I came to America I had dreams of life here. I thought about tall Anglos, big buildings, and houses with lawns. I was surprised when I arrived to see so many kinds of people – Black people, Asians. I found people from Korea and Cambodia and Mexico. In California I found not just America, I found the world. (Olsen 1988: 10)

Most reports about the changing demographics and school dropout rates are pessimistic, seeing these changes as inevitable problems, seeing the tapestry as essentially flawed. Our difficulty is the general perception about our linguistically and culturally diverse friends, neighbors, and students – the perception that a person who speaks three languages is trilingual, a person who speaks two languages is bilingual, and a person who speaks one language is – American.

The challenges

Linguistic diversity does present challenges, some that threaten to un-ravel the whole cloth, and we do our students a disservice if we pretend they do not exist. The California Tomorrow Project (Olsen 1988) clearly demonstrated the difficulties faced by children who are immi-grants or refugees, who do not know English or American culture, or the culture of school.

Some young people have already experienced war and violence. A tenth-grade Cambodian girl who emigrated at age ten recalls:

The first camp was terrible. Soldiers were mean and would push us down. There was little food and water and the children cried all the time. I was very sick but I had to go stand in line for a long time to try to get water. I was there for four months. (ibid.: 24)

A ninth-grade Mexican boy who immigrated at age seven remembers:

It was very scary for me. We went separate across. I was caught the first time and sent back to my aunt's house. This time she paid a lot of money to a *coyote* to get me across. He put me in a sack in the back of a truck with potatoes and told me to be totally quiet until he came to get me. I was hot and I couldn't breathe and so scared. I cried with no sound. After hours I think he came to get me. I had gotten across, but where was my mother? (ibid.: 26)

Not only do these children bring adult experiences with them, they often find a society and school climate that not only fails to accept them, but outright rejects them. Members of the California Tomorrow Project found that almost every immigrant child they spoke with had been

435

called names, pushed, kicked, teased, and laughed at because of race, language difficulties, or clothing. As one tenth-grade Cambodian boy says:

The Americans tell us to go back to our own country. I say we don't have a country to go back to. I wish I was born here and nobody would fight me and beat me up. They don't understand. I want to tell them if they had tried to cross the river and were afraid of being caught and killed and lost their sisters, they would feel like me, they might look like me, and they, too, might find themselves in a new country. (ibid.: 35)

As ESL and bilingual teachers, we are on the front line – we hear these stories, try to comfort, try to understand. But so often our efforts highlight what these students do *not* know, rather than what they *do* know – highlight the flaws in the tapestry rather than the joyful patterns and vibrantly different colors.

One colleague, using *The Cat in the Hat*, asked all the children to bring a hat to school. The day for the story came – no hats! What she thought was a very simple request that did not require major resources was impossible for these students. When she'd used this story with white mainstream children, they had brought a father's golf hat, fur hats from when a family lived in the midwest, wedding veils, a variety of hats about which students could recount tales. But the children in her linguistically and culturally diverse class either had no hats in the family or the only ones they had were in use, on father's head while he worked as a gardener or in the fields picking lettuce. The next time, she was prepared, taking along the hats herself. In many cases, our students' life experiences have been so different from ours, their teachers, that we cannot assume that they bring the same background knowledge to the classroom as white, middle-class children.

Diversity as resource

So what can we as teachers do? Here I want to turn the problem into a resource to show how the threads and the colors of the tapestry together make the whole – all different, but all contributing to the entire cloth. Our students bring with them many riches, not outwardly perhaps, but riches in their heads and hearts. When their riches and those of the school clash, however, children experience problems, such as when we assign children to classes based on their age. Some have missed schooling but they are placed in a class that assumes they have done fifth-grade math when in fact they may have only had math for two years. And the reverse is also true, as a twelfth-grade Filipino student who immigrated at age seventeen complained: "They put me in the 10th grade because of my English. . . . The work was too easy for me. For my first two years here I did all the work I did back in the Philippines all over again" (ibid.: 50).

To illustrate even more vividly that teachers can make a difference, that diversity can be a strength in our classrooms, I will relate the stories of two young people who are adding a new literacy to their repertoire (adapted from Murray and Nichols 1992: 180–181). The first story is Trung's; the other is Virginia's.

Trung's story

Trung is a twenty-year-old Vietnamese who entered the United States at age fourteen, having studied English for two years in Vietnam. He went to high school and then to a community college before entering the university. In high school he made Vietnamese friends and did not speak much English. He keeps in touch with these friends and continues to speak Vietnamese with them, although he uses English for school work and for expressing intimate feelings not usually articulated in Vietnamese. He uses English because "[it] is very easy to express feelings, you know, when I get mad with my mom, when I want to say intimate things, I tend to speak English. . . . I can't tell my mom 'I love you' in Vietnamese, you know, I can tell her in English easily . . . Because, you know, Vietnamese people tend to not to express their feelings." He resists his girlfriend's pressure to tell her that he loves her in Vietnamese "because it's so damn hard . . . it's more committed."

Trung also sees himself as "a poet and a writer." He began writing as a child in Vietnam and was much praised for his work. As a child, his favorite books were about geniuses, who in Vietnamese culture all knew a lot of poetry. He feels that his writing in Vietnamese "really got good recently." He belonged to a Vietnamese club at a community college, which exchanged its newspaper with other clubs; through these exchanges his poems have gotten wide circulation: "girls love them, they fall over me for that."

After the tenth grade Trung went without schooling for two years before he arrived in the United States. His reading now consists of English and Vietnamese newspapers, but his writing is extensive: poems, short stories, political essays, and correspondence with his many readers. He writes in English for school work, but in Vietnamese for his published work and correspondence. He made As in his two English composition classes at the community college and says that his teacher frequently read his work to the class. He used writing to express himself in that context more than speaking, observing "I was shy in that class, you know, 'cause I'm the only Vietnamese." A stand-up comedian in his native language, he chooses humor as a vehicle for reaching his American readers, telling his interviewer "I joke at everything. I write as probably the teacher love, like humor" (adapted from Murray and Nichols 1992: 180–181).

Trung was successful in college, achieving good grades and passing the university's upper division writing test. The essay he wrote for this test, "Social Rituals Represent Social Values," is humorous and shows a flair for language. The essay is well organized but has surface-level errors and does not explore the topic thoroughly. It is personal – the only time when the language becomes more academic and abstract is when he takes language directly from the prompt. Yet, he weaves this language skillfully into his whole argument. The instructors who read his paper and graded it holistically saw the positive characteristics, not the negative.

Now is probably the worst time of the year. Christmas and New Year have just gone by; I'm flatly broke, ten pounds overweight (from eating so many *bûche de Noël*) and have a thick stack of bills to pay. Oh, how I hate Christmas and New Year, the stupid holidays that drive everybody nut. First, one must carry a stupid christmas tree home, stand it in the middle of the living room, decorate it with stupid little ornaments. Then, one has to fight stupid slow traffic to get to a stupid crowded mall to buy a whole bunch of stupid expensive gift and wrap them up in stupid red-and-green papers. One also has to send out stupid greeting cards, drink stupid eggnog, eat stupid cakes, wear stupid Santa Claus clothes, listen to stupid holiday songs and watch stupid parades, etc.

Why the heck do we have to celebrate Christmas and New Year, anyway? Probably we do it to feel that we belong, that we are part of a long tradition, that we share common beliefs, and most importantly, that we are loved. I guess it's true that social rituals represent social values. Our society values peace, love and caring highly. That is why we go through lots of troubles every year to celebrate Christmas and New Year, to show family, friends and relatives that we love them and care for them. Giving gifts to a person is a way of telling that person that you care for him (or her, of course!) The monitary value of the gift is not significant; but the amount of trouble one must go through to get the gift, and the thought, are.

Social rituals should be enjoyable if one understand the meanings of them. Celebrated correctly, Christmas and New Year should be joyful. So, I think I better stop complaining about these holidays.

Virginia's story

Virginia is a twenty-two-year-old from a New York Puerto Rican family. (See Casanave [1992] for more details on Virginia's adaptation to the academic community.) She finished her B.A. in sociology from a good East Coast university near her home in the Bronx. She entered a Ph.D. program in sociology on the West Coast. In her first year, she took the core theory courses, which lay the foundation for and socialize students into the field of sociology. She experienced varying degrees of discomfort, resistance, and alienation as the year proceeded. Like many other students, she was trying to learn sociology as a second language – the specialized language of the theory courses, which suggested a scientific sociology, with the values of science embedded in the terms themselves.

In her first written assignments, she struggled to internalize this new language: "I think the exercises helped reinforce the definitions in my head. So that now I can tell you what a lawlike statement is supposed to look like. And now I can tell you what an empirical generalization is supposed to be. Whereas before, I was very much confused about the differences." But she also began to express her misgivings about the way language was used in her courses, stating that the directions could have been stated more simply, that the courses could be more applicable to everyday things. Her own gauge of whether she was using language clearly was whether she could explain her ideas to her mother. But, more and more, she found she could not translate her new knowledge into language her mother could understand. She was torn between the two worlds: If she used her professor's language, she felt she was aligning herself with scientists, not with the populations with whom she wished to communicate at home and in her future work.

In addition to her discomfort with the literacy practices of this discipline, she became frustrated with the ways of knowing promoted by the particular paradigm at this university. This paradigm pushed students to distance themselves from their objects of study. Virginia missed the engagement with issues involving real people. She felt particularly committed to the plights of women and minorities and wished to find ways to better understand and alleviate their difficulties. Added to this difficulty was the fact that the very people she wanted to study were grossly underrepresented in the sociology she was learning. In her literature review assignment on collective violence, she found no mention of Latin America in the bibliography provided. So she thought this might be a fruitful area of research for her next writing assignment, yet received unproductive feedback on her paper – an "incomplete" because she had not completed the formal logical analysis of her hypothesis correctly. She began to believe that the world of sociological theory was elitist, run by white, middle-class European and American males. Ultimately, Virginia decided this was not a world in which she could participate, and she left the doctoral program. She has since been working on her master's in social work at an East Coast university.

These two stories tell about different literacies and their effects on the people who acquire them. Trung took control of even the academic genre, drawing on the strengths he had built up in his Vietnamese poetry and his work as a stand-up comic. His humor and flair for interesting juxtapositions in language helped him overcome his limited English surface grammar. Virginia, finding no way to use her own preferred literacy style – that of more human, down-to-earth reporting of research and theory – chose not to join the theoretical literacy club, finding her voice through a different degree program. Trung's story tells us that students with open-minded teachers who view their students' literacies as resources, can have literacy practices that are not those of the mainstream or the particular task at hand and still succeed, adding new literacies to their repertoire. Virginia's story tells us that institutions which impose their form of literacy from the outside, without acknowledging their students' literacy, allow students no option but to seek another place to find their voice.

Teachers capitalizing on diversity

Let me provide some very practical suggestions that teachers have used to capitalize on the diversity in their classrooms, ones that empower both students and teachers as we learn from each other. These tasks and techniques all share a common approach to curriculum, best summarized by the California Tomorrow Project "Embracing Diversity" (Olsen and Mullen 1990: 19):

1. A curriculum which teaches to and from the specific experiences of the students.
2. A climate of high expectations and positive affirmation.
3. A curriculum which validates and builds learners' self-esteem and a sense of their own culture and national background and, at the same time, broadens the students' perspective to incorporate new worlds.
4. A physical and social environment which reflects an acknowledgment and excitement about the diversity of its human inhabitants.
5. A human relations climate which deliberately and clearly sets norms of acceptable behavior with regard to mutual respect, emotional safety, and diversity appreciation.
6. A pedagogy which emphasizes classroom processes in which students learn from each other through group work and sharing.
7. An emphasis upon concept development, verbal and written expression and communication.
8. An emphasis upon developing complex intellectual skills, critical thinking, and analytical tools.

These criteria for curricula are clearly demonstrated in the classroom stories that follow.

A garden project

At one school (Mitchell Senior) in California's Central Valley, the ESL instructor, Lucinda Smith, involves her multi-grade class in a garden project. She has developed an integrated curriculum around making a garden. These students, whose English language skills are very limited, have built the raised garden beds, installed an irrigation system, bought the seeds, transplanted them, nurtured them, and then savored their produce. As they work on this project, the students use math, science, language arts, and geography, and develop a sense of community. This project develops their intellectual skills, critical thinking, and analytical tools. It also contributes to their self-esteem because other students in the school see the products of their handiwork.

A cross-age class

At Yerba Buena High School in San José, each year one teacher from the high school and one from San José State University teach a high school and college class together. Jonathan Lovell's college class is an advanced writing course for teacher candidates, mostly native English speakers. The college and high school students (most of whom are language minority students) meet together on the school campus, where they all follow the same reading and writing assignments, including ethnic American literature. In peer writing sessions, high school students are paired with university students. In this way, the high school students get help and feedback from an advanced writer and see models of good writing. The teacher candidates learn to be mentors and learn about the cultures of the students they will be teaching in the future. For example, when discussing Rudolf Anaya's *Bless Me, Ultima*, the Mexican and Mexican American students serve as informants, providing the college student with information about Mexican value systems and beliefs.

Tapping into the community

Another resource for our students is their community. Heath (1983) first suggested that students be mini-ethnographers, gathering literacy and other data about their own lives and the lives of people in their community. In this way, they investigate their own speech communities. I often begin ESL and other classes by having students keep a journal of their language practices over one or two weeks at the beginning of the semester. Students whose English is advanced keep the journal in English; others may keep in it their primary language. They may even use magazine pictures to illustrate if their literacy skills are not yet adequate. When I suggest this approach, I'm always asked, "What about beginning students? They just couldn't do that." Nancy Rubio, who was teaching a beginning adult education class, tried it out, asking students to keep a student profile sheet, on which they responded to two main questions: (1) When and where did you use English? (2) To whom did you speak? Where? What happened? These beginning students *were* able to relate incredible uses of language, such as the following conversation from Cam (Murray 1992: 265–266).

Cam: Good morning. How are you?
Neighbor: Fine, thanks.
Cam: Your dog came into my backyard. Please keep him at your
               house. Please repair the fence. Your dog came into my back-
               yard two time.
Neighbor: Yes, I will.
Cam: Thank you.

Another student, a grandmother, proudly told the following story:

I always help them to made homework. . . . Jamie want learned 11–20. I
took some number card what she pronounce. Of 16 she say sixty. I say sixty
is 60 isn't 16. A little while she can say sixteen. (ibid.)

By analyzing these students' real-world dialogues, we can determine our syllabus – to help Cam with the language needed to make a polite complaint to her neighbor or to help the grandmother learn the functions used for U.S. schoolwork.

An ethnographic study of students' speech communities might include interviews with community leaders. McLaughlin (1992) includes this task in Mesa Valley's Bilingual Program on the Navajo reservation. McLaughlin recognized that the GATE (Gifted and Talented Education) students were drawing on their experiences *and* being required to think critically and develop complex intellectual skills. The mainstream, regular students, in contrast, did workbooks. So McLaughlin developed the research program for *all* students. Students first articulate research questions, interview at least two experts, and finally write an article for the bilingual community newspaper. They may videotape part of an interview for broadcast on the Navajo television station. The Navajo literacy projects are successful because students are able to work from their own experiences, ones that are affirmed by their teachers, but they are also required to think critically and communicate their ideas to a real audience.

I have used this technique often in my classes by having students choosing a variety of people to interview. One class, Academic English, includes ESL, EFL, second dialect, and mainstream students. In one such class, one of my Mexican American students (José), whose language skills in English are quite limited, chose to interview his mother. I choose his paper to illustrate since it was his favorite piece of writing because he now felt he knew his mother better and understood her experiences. Consequently, while his writing is still flawed, his essay is well developed, drawing on the information he had gathered from his interview. His paper illustrates how engaged he was with writing his mother's story. He was even aware of his audience, translating *burro* as "donkey" for his non-Spanish-speaking readers. In his earlier writing, José had never written more than one or two paragraphs because he said, "I don't have any ideas about this topic. I don't know what to write." Given a topic that engaged him (his mother's life story) and access to information on that topic (his mother as informant), he blossomed. Here is José's essay, in his own words.

I always wanted to know something from my mothers past experiences. I decided to interview my mom. I learn that my mother childhood was great. She grew up with a wealthy family from Michoacan Mexico. My grandfather used to own a couple of lands, cows and horses. They used to earn their living by renting their land and sell cows. My grandmother Maria was a very religeous person. She always used to get up early in the morning to go to church after church she would have a cup of hot chocolate. My mother had two brothers and three sisters. My mother was the youngest of the whole family. My mother had only one school year because she used to lived far away from where the school was. "I really missed out in having all the fun with friends and to learn a lot of new subjects."

My parents meet each other during a cold night in December in the counties fairgrounds in Mexico. We dated for one whole year my mom said. My parents were married one year later in 1954. My mother was sixteen and my dad was nineteen years old. My mom says that "back in the 50's it was proper for a young woman like me to get marry a young men from the village like your father." The first year of my mothers merriage she went to live with her in-laws. Living with my in-laws was worst time in our merriage because we didn't have any privacy, and top of that I had to cook for all the people that was living with us, I also had to clean all the house. "I felt like I was their maid". during the time we were living with my inlaws, one of my aunts past away trying to give birth to you're causin, she also left behind four children. The only ones to take care of them was me while you're father worked." My mother felt like she was being abuse, because she had to do most of the house work plus she had to raise othr children who were not her own. My mom says during that time she thought of many things such as leaving my dad or going back to her parents house and leave all tose poor kids behind unfortunately she didn't. "These were the worst years of my life with you're dad."

My mom was nineteen when she gave birth to her first child. We named him Miguel but one year later he past away due to a terrible cold. My parents did'nt have money at that time and did'nt take him intime to the hospital and died. One year later my mom gave birth to my sister Marina, but my dad wanted a boy and they kept trying but all they had was girls before I was born. My parents had already six girls. My mom says that after she had us she didn't want to have anymore babies because she said "I had to deliver you guys by myself I didn't have any medicine or a doctor to help me when I was in labor."

My parents have been marry for thirty nine years. I asked my mom, what life do you prefer now the one you have here in the U.S. or the one you had back in Mexico?

". . . well I think I prefer the life I have now because now I don't have to work as hard as I use to in back in Mexico, and now I have everything I ever wanted. I wouldn't go back to Mexico because there are no jobs, and I wouldn't want to have another life like the one I used to have. I wouldn't want to work like a burro (donkey) again. I used to worked for someone all day that gave me a little money, and you're dad used to work out in the sun for the whole day". My mom said, we work our little but off to put food on the table. Thats why I prefer the life I have here. The last thing I asked my mom was. What is that you love more in your life? she said most I love in my life is you guys because you have given me reason to live. I love all of you and I also love your father who has been there when ever I neded him the most.

It's not enough to have students merely relate their experiences. As the California Tomorrow Project states in its curriculum proposal, tasks and projects need to help students develop complex intellectual skills, critical thinking, and analysis. José, as he began asking higher-level questions of his mother (e.g., Which do you like better – your life in Mexico or your life in California?), was beginning to analyze his mother's experience in this essay. His piece is an early draft, one that had peer input for content and organization and self-input for editing. Indeed, this essay is quite impressive for this student. It has some surface level errors, but many are because he has never typed a paper before and so included typographical errors (e.g., *did'nt* for *didn't*). It is well organized, but more important, it is rich with detail and voice, as none of his previous writings had been.

I have used a variation on show-and-tell with my writing classes such as José's. The classes are extremely diverse, with immigrant students from Mexico, Greece, Vietnam, China, and the Philippines; with native-English-speaking students of Chicano, African American, and white heritage.

I ask each student to bring a cultural artifact and tell the class why it represents their culture. This activity differs from a show-and-tell because it helps students examine their cultural values. As an Australian, I begin with my own cultural artifact, a boomerang, telling students it represents my culture on several levels. It is an artifact of the indigenous people. It is a returning boomerang, representing the fact that, although many Australians travel and live abroad, most return because they have very strong ties to their culture. The returning boomerangs are used for play, representing an important aspect of Australian culture – Australians value sports and other leisure activities.

Having given students a model of how to tie their artifact to their cultural values, I then have each student share his or her artifact and state how it represents the culture. A student born in China brought a hair paint brush used for calligraphy. For him, calligraphy represents Chinese culture because calligraphy is an art form, it is ancient, and each ideograph represents aspects of the culture. Students gathered around as he showed them how to do calligraphy; they were fascinated by this different writing system. A student from Cambodia brought a photograph of Ankgor Wat, the ancient Cambodian temple. For him, the temple represents the previous glorious civilization of Cambodia; but, because it is in ruins, it also represents the chaos and disintegration of Cambodia under the Khmer Rouge. This gave him the opportunity to tell his classmates that he could only bring a picture to represent his culture because he left Cambodia with nothing – all his immediate and most of his extended family members were exterminated in the holocaust. For many students this was a revelation. One African American student said she thought such dreadful things only happened to blacks when they were slaves and that was centuries ago! A student from Vietnam brought her national dress, saying that here in America she only wears it for very special Vietnamese occasions because she wants to be American, like other students her age.

For the class, the most important aspect is the learning of personally relevant information about the cultures from which other students come, and the revelation that stereotypes are inadequate for defining the lives of individuals. The sharing of such important information leads to a cohesiveness that does not always exist in such diverse classes.

Writing to an audience

We know the importance of writing to a real audience, of learning how to adjust our language not just for the here and now of conversation, but for a removed and perhaps remote audience. My colleague, Pat Nichols, and I did this with our writing students by having them write to each other as pen pals. We found more than an awareness of audience. One remarkable incident was the conversation between two African American women. One student became pregnant and was considering dropping out of school. Her partner was able to scold her, plead with her, advise her, and finally convince her that she should stay in school. This anecdote demonstrates tellingly how students can be resources.

In many classes, teachers prepare books that are a collection of their students' writing. San José State University conducts a summer bridge program that brings to campus students who do not meet the requirements for admission, but who demonstrate exceptional drive and desire for college education. For six weeks they study together from dawn to dusk, they learn time management skills, they become acquainted with the university community, and they take several college classes. In one Academic English class, the instructor had the students write on the theme "Who Am I?" Some of the pieces were poems, others were paragraphs. The pieces were published for all students and faculty in the program. I have chosen two pieces that reflect the sophisticated language such at-risk students are capable of. (The second also appears as the opener to this chapter.)

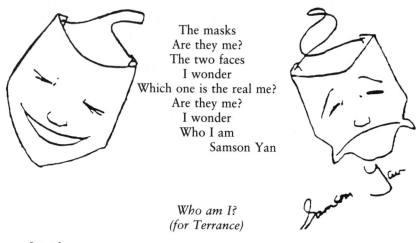

The masks
Are they me?
The two faces
I wonder
Which one is the real me?
Are they me?
I wonder
Who I am
Samson Yan

Who am I?
(for Terrance)

I am here   you are there.
We are so different   so far apart.
Through knowledge   we can bridge the gap.
Through love, we can fill the emptiness.

Another project that capitalizes on students' experiences, but also guides students' literacy to audience awareness is the "Poets in the Schools Project" in California. Living poets work with students in a workshop setting, which makes the students feel important. Also, poetry frees them from many of the conventions of English with which they are not yet familiar. Each year, the project produces a book of selected poetry for sale. Galileo High School in San Francisco has a similar project, and one student's poem is chosen to be read during the football team's half-time show. These students are not usually considered ready for creative writing classes because their basic skills are so poor. They are usually consigned to fill-in-the-blank workbooks, an activity that neither draws on their funds of knowledge nor gives them the opportunities to extend their knowledge and critical thinking.

Let me conclude with poems students wrote during this project. These poems show that our students are not empty vessels to be filled by some omnipotent and omniscient teacher; rather, they are creative and thoughtful beings whose understandings and experiences can be resources in our classrooms.

The black and white box

Once there was a black
and white box. It had Jamaica inside
    also little purple
    men that sang, come
    to Jamaica, and had dreadlocks
    on their feet and arms.

When I woke up I
    saw a black and white
    box but, of course, that's
a different story.

> Kaseem Sills
> Grade 4, Booskin Elementary School
> (Cumpiano 1988: 66)

I could remember the immense ocean
The day pirates attacked our boat.
I could remember the pirates' ship.
They are big, huge, and large.
I could remember my mom screaming.
The pirates were all over our boat.
I could remember the pirates' faces.
They are round like an orange.
I could remember the day I got hit.
It hurt like a bullet went through my heart.

> Huu Tran
> Grade 9, Pioneer High School
> (Cumpiano 1988: 40)

President[1]

I will be 33 in 2010
I will be the first non-American President of the United States

---

1 The author and editors are grateful to Ranjit Skiralkar for permission to reprint this poem, which originally appeared in *Bigger Than the Earth*, by A. Soldofsky and C. Tasaki (San José Unified School District, 1985: 5).

447

I will play tennis with Gorbachev
I will win, since he will be in his 80's
I will ride my bicycle through every room in the White House

I will ban all nuclear weapons in the world
I will build giant houses for the homeless
I will decide when children should go to school

I will change the voting age to 13
I will be Ranjit Shiralkar, President of the United States

Please vote for me!

> Ranjit Shiralkar
> Grade 7, Bret Harte Middle School

References

Anaya, R. 1972. *Bless me, Ultima.* Berkeley, CA: Quinto Sol Publications.

Casanave, C. P. 1992. Cultural diversity and socialization: A case study of a Hispanic woman in a doctoral program in sociology. In D. E. Murray (ed.), *Diversity as Resource: Redefining Cultural Literacy.* Alexandria, VA: TESOL Publications.

Cumpiano, I. 1988. *Language Is My Zoo.* San José, CA: San José Unified School District.

Heath, S. B. 1983. *Ways With Words: Language, Life and Work in Communities and Classrooms.* Cambridge: Cambridge University Press.

McLaughlin, D. 1992. Power and politics of knowledge: transformative schooling for minority language learners. In D. E. Murray (ed.), *Diversity as Resource: Redefining Cultural Literacy.* Alexandria, VA: TESOL Publications.

Murray, D. E. 1992. Unlimited resources: Tapping into learners' language, culture, and thought. In D. E. Murray (ed.), *Diversity as Resource: Redefining Cultural Literacy.* Alexandria, VA: TESOL Publications.

Murray, D. E., and P. C. Nichols. 1992. Literacy practices and their effect on academic writing. In F. Dubin and N. Kuhlman (eds.), *Cross-cultural Literacy: Global Perspectives on Reading and Writing.* Englewood Cliffs, NJ: Regents/Prentice Hall.

Murray, D. E., P. C. Nichols, and A. Heisch. 1992. Identifying the language culture of our students. In D. E. Murray, (ed.), *Diversity as Resource: Redefining Cultural Literacy.* Alexandria, VA: TESOL Publications.

Olsen, L. 1988. *Crossing the Schoolhouse Border.* San Francisco, CA: California Tomorrow.

Olsen, L., and N. Mullen. 1990. *Embracing Diversity.* San Francisco, CA: California Tomorrow.

Soldofsky, A., and C. Tasaki. 1989. *Bigger Than the Earth.* San José, CA: San José Unified School District.

Ward, J. G., and P. Anthony. 1992. *Who Pays for Student Diversity?* Newbury Park, CA: Corwin Press.

Section V Questions and tasks

1. Each of the chapters in this section deals with the intersection of sociopolitical concerns and classroom issues. Have you ever taught or studied in a context where social and/or political issues had a clear impact on classroom practices? If so, describe the situation. What are the similarities and differences between your situation and those described in these four chapters?

2. In Chapter 16 by van Lier, we learn of an attempt to introduce bilingual schooling (Spanish and Quechua) in the *altiplano* of Peru. The author describes, in some detail, the physical environment in which the teachers and pupils worked. Have you ever taught or studied in a similar situation? If so, what was the influence of the physical context on the teaching and learning that occurred?

3. Adendorff in Chapter 17 gives us numerous examples of code switching in Zulu and English and makes a case for the social functions of code switching. The next time you are in a verbal discourse context with bilingual people, listen (unobtrusively) for the code switches that occur. What purposes does the code-switching serve in that social setting? How do your observations compare to Adendorff's?

4. Duff's study (Chapter 18) portrays changes in an education system influenced by massive social changes outside the classroom. If you were an experienced Hungarian teacher in one of the DL schools, what changes would be most notable to you? Would you continue with the traditional *felelés* or introduce some other activities? If the latter, which activities would you introduce? Why?

5. In Chapter 19, Murray makes a case for viewing cultural diversity as a resource rather than as a problem. The voices she quotes are largely those of students, particularly ESL learners writing in English. How do these students' voices compare with those of learners you have known?

6. Murray cites examples of teachers utilizing cultural differences to good ends. What examples from your own experience, either as a teacher or a language learner, can you add? What is the attitude where you live, in society at large, toward cultural diversity?

7. In the chapters by van Lier, Adendorff, and Duff, the teachers' and students' voices are conveyed through the researchers' transcripts and fieldnotes, rather than through their own introspections (as in the first three sections of this volume). How convincing are these three researchers' depictions of the teachers and learners? What makes a research description convincing?

8. If you could choose a year-long teaching job in any of these four settings, which place would you choose? Why? What language

teaching materials and/or cultural artifacts would you take along with you? Why?

9. Imagine yourself in the role of a language learner in each of these four settings. Where do you think you would learn the most? Why?

10. Imagine yourself in the role of a language teacher in each of these four settings. What would be your attitude toward van Lier, Adendorff, Duff, and Murray collecting data in your classroom? What would you want them to do and to refrain from doing? What feedback, if any, would you want from each of them? Do your answers differ from one author to another?

11. Imagine yourself in the role of researcher. Identify an environment where you would like to conduct an investigation along the lines of those reported in these chapters. What sorts of data would you want to gather? How would you collect those data?

12. If you could talk with Adendorff, van Lier, Duff and Murray, what questions would you like to ask them?

Index